CAMERA HUNTER

GEORGE SHIRAS III AND THE BIRTH OF WILDLIFE PHOTOGRAPHY

JAMES H. MCCOMMONS

UNIVERSITY OF NEW MEXICO PRESS | ALBUQUERQUE

Library of Congress Cataloging-in-Publication Data
Names: McCommons, James, 1957– author.
Title: Camera hunter: George Shiras III and the birth of wildlife photography /
James H. McCommons.
Description: Albuquerque: University of New Mexico Press, 2019. |
Includes bibliographical references and index. |
Identifiers: LCCN 2019013027 (print) | LCCN 2019015936 (e-book) |
ISBN 9780826354273 (e-book) | ISBN 9780826354266 (jacketed cloth : alk. paper)
Subjects: LCSH: Shiras, George, 1859–1942. | United States. Congress. House—
Biography. | Legislators—United States—Biography. | Wildlife photographers—
United States—Biography. | Wildlife conservationists—United States—Biography.
Classification: LCC E748.S455 (e-book) | LCC E748.S455 M33 2019 (print) |
DDC 328.73/092 [B]—dc23
LC record available at https://lccn.loc.gov/2019013027

Cover photographs: (*top*) courtesy of the John Hammer family;
(*bottom*) courtesy of National Geographic Creative.
Back cover photograph: courtesy of the John Hammer family.
Auhtor photograph: courtesy of the author.
Frontispiece: courtesy of National Geographic Creative.
Designed by Felicia Cedillos
Composed in ITC New Baskerville 9.75/14.15

CONTENTS

PREFACE   vii

1 | Whitefish Lake   1

2 | Pittsburgh Roots   6

3 | Boyhood Days in Michigan   17

4 | School Days for Blue Bloods   34

5 | Camera Hunting   43

6 | Pennsylvania Politics   64

7 | The Great Bird Mystery   76

8 | Camp Life and Camera Traps   83

9 | A Progressive Goes to Washington   99

10 | The National Geographic Society   119

11 | Ormond Beach   131

12 | Bahamas, Mexico   140

13 | Newfoundland and Nature Fakers   147

14 | Eminent Personalities   166

15 | Yellowstone and the Shiras Moose   177

16 | The Kenai Peninsula   189

17 | Roosevelt-Newett Libel Trial   198

18 | The Crusade to Save Birds   221

19 | The Shiras Bear   236

20 | Gatun Lake and Panama   246

21 | The Bullet Is on the Way   255

22 | The Bird Treaty   269

23 | Yellowstone Dam Fight   279

24 | Kaibab Plateau   284

25 | Final Bird Battles   296

26 | The Big Book   303

27 | Last Days   319

Epilogue   330

ACKNOWLEDGMENTS   335

NOTES AND REFERENCES   339

INDEX   383

PREFACE

One night just before Thanksgiving, I drove deep into the woods of Michigan's Upper Peninsula and turned off the highway onto a county gravel road, then a seasonal dirt road, and finally a rutted two-track. Hemlock, cedar, and aspen pressed close, their branches raking the sides of the truck.

The headlights illuminated a crude sign nailed to a tree: Camp–30–. To most visitors, it's nonsensical nomenclature, but I'm a journalist, and "dash three zero dash" typed at the end of a news story is the traditional way to tell typesetters there's no more copy coming. The end. Appropriately, the two-track terminated at Camp–30–.

Built in the 1960s by printers at my old newspaper, the camp consisted of a six-bed bunkhouse and a large common room with a linoleum floor, a wood cook stove, and a kitchen area with sink and hand pump. A two-seater privy stood a respectable distance out back.

Chairs and couches ringed the edges of the room, and a penny-ante game of euchre was underway at a wooden table. Crammed into the room were more than twenty men and boys attired in wool pants and camouflage shirts, felt-pac boots, and vests of hunter's orange. Rifles leaned in the corners, and head-and-shoulder mounts of glassy-eyed deer stared down from the walls. The air hung heavy with humidity and the odor of cooking meat. Steam opaqued the windows. Someone had propped open the back door with a boot to let in a cold breeze.

On the stove, a blue enameled roaster held a haunch of venison ringed by fixings of onions, potatoes, carrots, and rutabaga. The men, unshaven and unwashed, ate from paper plates, wiped the juices with slices of white bread, and drank from cups filled from a quarter-barrel of beer.

It's a deer feed. It's hunting camp. Tomorrow morning after they sleep off the beer, most of these guys will drive to town for Thanksgiving dinner with family and then head back to the woods for the final week of deer season.

I've been coming here since the early 1980s when I was a young reporter at the *Daily Press* in Escanaba, but I don't know many of these guys. The printers are retired, now in their seventies and eighties. A few can no longer hunt, and the camp has gone over to the next generation.

Neither am I a deer hunter, and that too makes me the odd man out. However, I once edited the outdoor page at the newspaper and later got a degree in environmental science and wrote about nature as a freelance magazine writer. I can talk deer, the politics of baiting, and the decline of the whitetail herd in Michigan. In recent years, however, I discovered another conversation starter.

"Who's got a trail cam?"

Out came pictures processed at the drugstore or run off on home printers. The younger guys pulled out smartphones and finger-swiped through images.

Trail, or scout, cameras became widespread a decade or so ago. Hunters strap them to trees along a game trail or on a fence post at the edge of a field—places where a buck rubs his antlers, scent-marks territory, or feeds on piles of bait—corn, apples, beets, and carrots.

The images I saw that night weren't only of deer but porcupines, coyotes, ravens, rabbits, skunks, and turkeys—any critter that came into camera range, tripped a motion detector, and opened the shutter.

From the front pocket of his bib overalls, an unshaven hunter handed me a well-thumbed photograph.

"That's the SOB I'm looking for," he said.

The photograph—time stamped 11-16, 2:32 a.m.—showed a ten- or eleven-point buck standing next to a bait pile. The deer, its head back, eyes glossy and wet nose sniffing, appeared wary, perhaps sensing danger an instant before a flash of light—the camera strobe—took the night away. Had the hunter used an infrared trail camera, there would have been no flash at all.

In the 1890s on Whitefish Lake some sixty miles northeast of Camp–30–, George Shiras 3d invented what he called the camera trap—a box camera holding a glass negative rigged to a chemical flare of magnesium and potassium chlorate powder. When a deer stumbled into a trigger wire, the shutter released and the chemicals exploded with the force of a mortar, flooding the woods with a sizzling, brilliant light.

Bewildered and blinded, deer reared back in alarm and sometimes charged into trees, knocking themselves senseless. Pictures revealed wide-eyed, startled animals, muscles tensed for flight. It was a crude setup, but one that yielded extraordinary images.

Shiras was the first to take nighttime pictures of wildlife and the first photographer to publish wildlife images in *National Geographic* magazine. He, too, worked out of a deer camp, where he spent his evenings with woolen-clad men eating venison cooked over a wood fire and debating the quality of the hunting, the predation of gray wolves, and the effectiveness of new game laws to halt the decline of the herd.

It was not idle talk. At the turn of the twentieth century, the future of many wildlife species—including whitetail deer—appeared bleak.

After denuding and taming much of the East, loggers and settlers attacked the ancient forests of the Great Lakes. Much of the Upper Peninsula was cutover country, a landscape of stumps and leftover slash that occasionally ignited into huge firestorms in the summer months. Market hunters riding the new railroads killed tens of thousands of deer and millions of passenger pigeons. They packed the meat into barrels and shipped the bounty to the big cities. Refrigerated rail cars, chokebore and breech-loading shotguns, and communication by telegraph enabled "pothunters" to target, kill, and ship animals as never before.

Ducks were slaughtered on Chesapeake Bay for table fare. Shorebirds in Florida died by the tens of thousands so their feathers could decorate women's hats. Herring, whitefish, lake trout, and blue pike on the Great Lakes were no longer abundant. On the Great Plains, only the bones of the bison remained—and even these remnants were gathered into mountainous piles, shipped to factories, and ground into fertilizer.

It was not until the coming of the Progressive movement in the early 1900s that a new ethic of conservation and the strong hand of the federal government—wielded largely by Theodore Roosevelt—brought any hope of conserving resources for future generations. George Shiras 3d watched the wilderness of the Upper Peninsula nearly vanish in his lifetime and, along with it, many animals and fishes too. The loss informed his advocacy of conservation.

That night at Camp–30– I stepped outside with Bob, who had left the printing trade years earlier to take a job at the paper mill. We crunched through the snow over to the buck pole where two gutted animals hung by their feet, their bodies frozen, the meat curing.

The bare trees cracked with the cold. Stars blinked between the branches. There was no moon. Just as it was in Shiras's day, the Upper Peninsula is rural country with vast tracts of state and federal forest and a sky largely unpolluted by artificial light. I pointed out Orion and Cassiopeia, and we silently pondered the great sweep of the Milky Way.

From the woods came the howl of a gray wolf.

"That's no coyote," Bob said.

Wolves had been extirpated from Michigan but made their way back in the 1990s, naturally migrating from Minnesota and Ontario. This time they were protected by the Endangered Species Act and by residents—including hunters—who appreciated the wildness the presence of wolves added to the region.

Still some folks in Camp–30– aren't fond of wolves, believing the animals were planted by the Michigan Department of Natural Resources in a conspiratorial plot hatched with environmentalists. George Shiras didn't like wolves either. They were bad animals to be dispatched in order to improve the prospects for deer—the good animals. That theory of game management—of eliminating predators—was disproved long ago, but some hunters today would not condemn anyone who shot a wolf, shoveled it into the ground, and kept quiet.

Back inside, I didn't mention the wolf. Neither did Bob, but for a different reason. Hearing a wolf howling out of the blackness of the night is no longer a remarkable occurrence in the Upper Peninsula of Michigan.

One of the hunters called out, "Where have you guys been?"

Bob answered, "I was showing Jim that six-pointer, and then we were out looking at the stars."

He took a sip of beer and clapped me on the shoulder.

"We're astrologers, you know."

Close enough. I smiled and nodded.

George Shiras was a native of Pittsburgh, Pennsylvania, raised in a moneyed family of lawyers and industrialists who could afford private schools and a gentrified life of multiple homes and summers spent in the cool climes of the Great Lakes. The young scion from Pittsburgh courted and married the daughter of one of the richest men in the Upper Peninsula. Though the couple relocated to Pittsburgh and Washington, DC, where George was a lawyer and a congressman, they summered each year in the town of Marquette, visiting family and enjoying the big woods and waters. George was a gentleman sportsman who roughed it out-of-doors but also employed guides to row and sail the boats, set up camp, and prepare the meals. At his father-in-law's "game preserve" on Whitefish Lake, he put down the gun to shoot with the camera and adopted a new career of wildlife photographer and faunal naturalist.

I, too, grew up in western Pennsylvania, graduated from the University of Pittsburgh, and like Shiras sought out wild country. After college, I wrote for small dailies in Wyoming and spent weekends camping in the mountains and on the sagebrush plains.

Eventually, I felt the need to be closer to home, a day's drive from family and aging parents. One afternoon at the library, I opened an atlas to the Midwest and examined the cartographic features of the Upper Peninsula, a three-hundred-mile-long sliver of land reaching into the blue of Lakes Superior, Huron, and Michigan. I had never been there, but I visualized deciduous trees, canoes and kayaks, rivers and inland lakes. The map showed lots of blue water and green national forests. It looked like a good place.

Weeks later, I was in the newsroom at the *Daily Press* in Escanaba. I stayed three years, wrote, photographed, and camped all over the Upper Peninsula—often in the company of a young woman who sold classified ads. We married and moved to the East Coast to pursue more schooling, careers, and eventually a family. Like the Shirases, our summer vacations were spent in the Upper Peninsula.

On one of those trips in the mid-1990s, I peeled away from the kids and in-laws and drove north to Lake Superior for a day of mountain biking on Grand Island, recently purchased from a mining company by the US Forest Service. As I waited for a friend to meet me, I killed time in a used bookstore. In the nature section, I found a heavy, rather plain-covered book: *Hunting Wild Life with Camera and Flashlight.*

How strange . . . I imagined the author traipsing through the forest waving a battery-powered incandescent lantern. When I examined the book—published in the 1930s by the National Geographic Society—I saw that the monochromatic images were old, and that flashlight referred to a chemical technology prior to flashbulbs and electric strobes.

As I paged through the book, the deer-in-flight photos made me chuckle, but other images displayed an artist's eye for composition and aesthetic renderings of songbirds, tree leaves, fungi, and Michigan's north woods. I recognized iconic locations in the Upper Peninsula—waterfalls, rocky shorelines, and sites now protected as national parks and recreation areas.

That day as we pedaled our bikes along the trails and cliffs of Grand Island with the transparent blue of Lake Superior below us, I told my friend all about this Shiras fellow and his nineteenth-century ambush photographs of deer.

A few years later my wife and I—now with three young sons—returned to the Upper Peninsula, this time so I could teach journalism and nature writing at Northern Michigan University.

In our new home of Marquette, the name Shiras was inescapable. In summer, my boys swam in the Shiras municipal pool. We went to sky shows on Monday evenings at the Shiras Planetarium. When the aurora borealis appeared over Lake Superior, we loaded up the minivan and gawked at the lights from Shiras Park. A colleague from school had a home in the Shiras Hills. On its second floor in the Shiras Room, the public library preserves his collection of nature books and displays his images of deer.

Over the years, I came to understand that George Shiras 3d (he preferred the lawyerly 3d to III) was a seminal player in the early conservation movement, a naturalist of national reputation, a pioneer in wildlife photography, a friend of Theodore Roosevelt, and one of the Progressives in the early twentieth century who saved several species of wildlife.

As a congressional representative, Shiras introduced and established the legal foundations for the bill that became the Migratory Bird Treaty Act, the most important environmental law for the preservation of wildlife prior to the passage of the Endangered Species Act in 1973. He traveled and photographed for the National Geographic Society and served on its board of managers for thirty years, when the society grew from a few hundred members to one of the world's most respected science institutions. He discovered a subspecies of moose in the Rocky Mountains, which today is known as the Shiras moose.

But it was the Upper Peninsula and especially the camp at Whitefish Lake that served as his touchstone, the place where he formed his love for wildlife and expressed his passion for photography and wild country. He came home to Marquette to die and is buried in the city cemetery just a block from my house. As compared to his Victorian contemporaries—wealthy mine owners, ship captains, and timber barons—Shiras has a modest marker on his grave. His father-in-law lies beneath a towering obelisk.

One spring, a yearling moose wandered into town. It trotted up the street, scattered my oldest son and friends waiting for the school bus, and set up residence for a few days in Park Cemetery. Each morning, it strode through the gravestones crossing Shiras's grave to reach an ornamental pond where it breakfasted on lily pads. Townspeople crowded the cemetery holding up cell phones and digital cameras.

Shiras would have enjoyed the spectacle and celebrated the fact that moose—like wolves, peregrine falcons, trumpeter swans, sandhill cranes, fishers, mountain lions, bald eagles, and several more species—have returned after being nearly wiped out a century ago. The best monument to Shiras is the restored wildness of the Upper Peninsula of Michigan—the second-growth forests that cover the muscular shoreline around Marquette, the chevrons of Canada geese passing over each fall, and warblers migrating through the cemetery in spring. When I paddle a canoe through the woods, hear loons calling as I lay in my tent at night, or sit with hunters at a deer feed on a cold November day, I consider myself to be living in Shiras country.

1 | WHITEFISH LAKE

THE TWO BOYS trudged through the woods most of the day, following behind Jack La Pete. They were just eleven and ten years old, but George Shiras and his brother Winfield hefted canvas packs, shotguns, bedrolls, and fishing poles.

They had breakfasted on fresh trout caught at the mouth of a river where it emptied into Lake Superior. From there, La Pete led them south and inland along drainages and through valleys where they left behind the surf sounds of the big lake and gained the hush of the forest.

It was an ancient woods of five-hundred-year-old hemlock and white pine interspersed with giant hardwood specimens of beech and maple. The lowest branches of the white pine hung fifty to seventy-five feet overhead. Beneath their feet, the bed of needles packed down nearly five feet thick.

In 1870, the Upper Peninsula of Michigan was still largely untouched by wagon roads and railroad rights-of-way. Professional hunters killing game for city markets and loggers leveling the forests had yet to reach this far north. The tributary streams and near-shore waters of the Great Lakes teemed with spawning fish. Clouds of passenger pigeons darkened the skies spring and fall. Game trails five feet wide and rutted by hundreds of years of deer movement cut across the peninsula as the animals migrated from the heavy snow country around Lake Superior to wintering grounds near Lake Michigan.

To the Shiras boys who lived in the booming and foul-smelling industrial city of Pittsburgh, the Upper Peninsula was uncontaminated, exotic country and Jack La Pete, a French-Indian man, was colorful and enigmatic— the kind of character they'd only read about in their adventure books.

A man of indeterminate years (he was not sure himself), La Pete spent most days in the woods. His face was wrinkled, desiccated from wind and weather. He had a deeply scarred and shriveled arm after being mauled by a black bear that he surprised as it slept between two logs.

He served as a guide and a packer for the boys' father and grandfather who came north each summer to fish, hunt, and practice the sporting life of gentlemen. La Pete was an affable man and so trusted a guide and friend that he was given charge of the two young boys.

He had come by the hotel where the Shirases were staying in Marquette— then a rough-hewn village on the south shore of Lake Superior—saying he had discovered a lake twenty miles to the southeast where there were many deer. Two years earlier, he guided surveyors laying out a railroad route between Marquette and Lake Michigan—a distance of sixty miles—but they abandoned the route when they encountered a gorge too difficult to bridge. Jack followed the gorge to the south and came to a lake. He hewed a dugout canoe, put up a small cabin, and wintered there trapping beaver, muskrat, and wolves. For meat, he killed whitetail deer coming down to the shore. The boys could kill deer there both day and night, he said.

George and Winfield were keen to go, and they set off with Jack on a buckboard to an "Indian cabin" where the road ended a few miles south of the village. They slept on the attic floor and in the morning shouldered guns and provisions and worked their way east along the shore of the big lake. They overnighted at the Sand River where Jack had built a lean-to as a halfway point to the lake. The boys were glad for it—tired and amazed, as George recalled, at "how heavy an object becomes when it had to be carried for hours." The boys spent the early evening fishing and, to Jack's surprise, caught a dozen trout on fishing poles and line. La Pete was more inclined to a net in Lake Superior. The near-shore waters were so filled with Mackinac and brook trout and whitefish that the curious white-man habit of using a fishing pole never occurred to most Indians, according to

George. Jack cleaned and prepared the fish and brewed tea. He lifted a heavy, flat rock and took from a hole a can of pulverized maple sugar he had concealed from a bear that had been tearing through the lean-to in his absence. That night, they heard bawling and whimpering downstream. Jack informed the boys that it was the sow and her cubs. George gripped his gun, ready to rush out and slay the bear. Jack dramatically rolled up his sleeve and displayed his scarred arm. Best settle down, he said. There would be no bear hunting.

The next morning, they were off early. The guide was untiring on the trail, exceptionally strong and quick on his feet. As they struck inland, they hiked a ridge between swamps and timber falls, following game trails that coalesced into wide "deer runways" that pointed the way toward the lake. The trails were packed down, impressed with hoof prints.

Early afternoon, they reached a crude log-and-bark cabin on a hillside overlooking the lake. The side walls were made of cedar logs about four feet high. The pitched roof consisted of black ash bark—inches thick and six feet long—cut from giant trees and lashed down by cedar strips. A hole near the top vented the smoke from a fire. The camp was pure woodcraft, constructed by a man skilled in using materials at hand.

After gathering downed wood for a fire and cutting pine boughs for a bed, they went down the hill to see the lake. Years later, George recalled it this way:

> About a mile long, heavily forested along the shore with pine and hemlocks, except at the end where rows of reeds backed by cedars and black ash indicated an outlet stream. To the south a beautiful bay, or slough, lay between high hills with reeds, water lilies and sandy beaches at the end through which an inlet stream issued from a gorge filled as far as vision reached with stately elms.

Eventually, he would give the lake its name, Whitefish, and it would become a nature retreat for his family, a place of solace and escape, and a setting to hunt animals and watch birds. Most importantly, Whitefish Lake would be the touchstone for his life's work as a photographer and conservationist. But all of this was yet to be.

The boys had come to hunt big game. George was the oldest so he went first. From the brush, Jack dragged out his dugout canoe. He positioned the boy in the bow, and they paddled to the opposite end of the lake and into a shallow bay. Jack soon whispered, "Put up your paddle. There is a deer ahead."

As the canoe flattened and parted the reeds near the shore, a little buck jerked its head up. For a moment, the deer didn't move and the boy aimed at the shoulder and let go with load of buckshot. The deer leaped backward and was gone.

After the report echoed from the hills and the smoke cleared, Jack let loose an amused chuckle. Buck fever; the boy had shot wide. George wanted to beach the canoe and search for a blood trail. In the split second after buckshot left the gun, the boy, sighting along the barrel, was certain the deer had jerked and caught some buckshot. Jack shook his head and paddled on. There would be other deer, but they saw no more that day.

As evening fell, it was Winfield's turn. First, they cooked more trout packed in from Sand River. Again, Jack lifted a rock and took out a can of maple syrup boiled the year before. The elixir looked blackened and a bit unsavory, but it tasted sweet and the boys poured it on their fish and slices of bread. In another tin can, Jack brewed tea.

He stirred the fire and filled a cast-iron skillet with glowing coals. He peeled strips from a white birch tree, wound the resinous bark around a stick of wood, tied it with bark cordage, and then lit the torches so they could see their way to the lake. Winfield got into the front of the dugout and Jack placed the pan of coals on the bow. At Jack's command, the boy would toss in birch bark, dried pinesap, and hunks of fatwood—the resinous heartwood of a downed pine tree.

They were going fire hunting.

They glided into the lake and arced toward the slough. The black shapes of the hills scalloped the horizon. Stars shined above. George followed the glow in the bow until it faded into the blackness and then he climbed the trail to Jack's lean-to, tossed more wood onto the fire, and waited. In time, he heard the blast of the shotgun.

When Jack and Winfield came into camp, the guide carried a string of pickerel, or northern pike, which he had taken from a net set up in the slough. Winfield wielded bloodier trophies—the heart and liver of a deer impaled on a stick.

The gutted deer hung from a tree at the lakeshore, a place the boys would come to call Old Jack's Landing. While the guide roasted the heart and liver over the fire, the boys took a torch and went down to see the deer.

Winfield described how they had heard movement on the water and in the low light saw the shape of a doe grazing on succulent plants in the shallows. As Jack swung the canoe to face the deer, Winfield built up the fire in the skillet. The birch bark curled and ignited. The pinesap and heartwood sizzled and popped. The animal froze, mesmerized by the approaching fiery light. Winfield rose up in the bow, aimed at its chest, and fired. The deer took a step and collapsed on shore.

George was envious. He remembered the deer flinching after his own shot, and he was convinced he had hit it. At daybreak the next morning, he snuck out of camp, trotted down the path, and got into Jack's dugout canoe. With difficulty, he rowed to the other end the lake. It was a bold act for an eleven-year-old and indicative of his pluckiness.

He entered the bay. When the canoe grounded out, he crawled to the bow and reached out to grab a branch and pull himself ashore. What he grabbed was not a stick but the stiff leg of a deer jutting into the air. So he had killed a deer and done so hours before his brother. He examined the carcass and saw where several big pellets of buckshot had torn into the body. It wasn't exactly a clean kill—the kind he would learn to accomplish much later—but he had, despite Jack's derision, slain a deer and done so before his brother.

Nearly fifty years later he wrote, "I sank down trembling with emotion and eyed the crumpled body of the little buck. Had a humanitarian witnessed the scene, my action might have appeared to him like evidence of contrition over the destruction of a beautiful and innocent creature."

Actually, he felt only joy and relief. He wrestled the body on board, smearing himself and the dead animal with mud. He rowed back to Jack's Landing, hollered out, and brought the other two running.

Butchering the deer, they found twelve pellets, one piercing the heart. The deer may have taken a big leap, but it must have died quickly. The next few nights, they fire hunted—Jack in the stern and a boy seated in the bow behind a sizzling skillet with his shotgun in his lap.

Eventually, the practice of fire hunting or jacking a deer—shining a light into its eyes to freeze motion long enough to take a shot—would become illegal and unethical, but in the 1870s, there were no game laws, no limits, no season. George would abandon these old ways, but he never forgot the method; it would make him famous as a camera hunter.

2 | PITTSBURGH ROOTS

THAT FIRST VISIT to Whitefish Lake occurred during the Gilded Age, a satirical appellation coined by Mark Twain to describe the years from the 1870s to early 1900s. It was a time in America characterized by industrial expansion, mass immigration from Europe, the exploitation of natural resources, and the accumulation of great personal wealth. Nowhere was the promise and the dark side of the era more in evidence than in Pittsburgh.

The city was known as "Hell with the lid off," and it was no exaggeration. With the development of the Bessemer converter and the age of blast furnaces, massive steel works were erected in and around the city. The skyline glowed at night. Smoke and smog filled the skies, and soot filtered down so thick that at times it turned the rain gray. Industrial waste and sewage fouled the rivers. Tens of thousands of workers toiled in the factories and mills, typically working twelve-hour shifts, seven days a week. They lived in slums or company towns set up by the new czars of steel.

Of his childhood, George 3d recalled, "I lived most of my early years beneath a sun often obscured by clouds of smoke. At night that part of the Ohio Valley resembled an inferno from the glare of the blast furnaces, coke ovens, and many standpipes shooting lurid flames far overhead in a wasteful consumption of the natural gas from adjoining oil fields."

Many of the workers were immigrants: Scotch-Irish, Germans, Italians, and later Slovaks, Hungarians, Russians, and Jews. The companies advertised for workers in Europe. As much as they melted pig iron, the furnaces melded cultures and fired passions about labor and unions and robber barons and private armies. Pittsburgh was volatile, a brawling city of strikers, capitalists, anarchists, company thugs, crooked cops and politicians, and the scrum of the proletariat.

The Shirases, however, were atop the social pyramid and, like many wealthy city dwellers, they spent summer—or at least a few weeks—in the cooler, cleaner climes of the Great Lakes.

The family's relationship with the Pittsburgh region went back a couple of generations when Fort Pitt was an outpost of the United States. The family's original fortune was earned from brewing beer and doing commerce along the three rivers—the Allegheny, the Monongahela and the Ohio.

The Shirases were Scots. Peter Shiras, great-great-grandfather of George 3d, immigrated to America in 1765 and ran a store in Mount Holly, New Jersey. After the American Revolution, his son George joined the militia to help put down the Whiskey Rebellion led by farmers and distillers in western Pennsylvania. Living on the edge of the wilderness and accustomed to making their own spirits, these settlers refused to pay excise taxes to the new government.

After negotiations between the groups failed, Henry "Light Horse" Lee, a Revolutionary War hero and father of Robert E. Lee, led a thirteen-thousand-member militia into the region. Resistance melted away at its approach.

Young George liked the region and convinced his parents and other family members to join him there in 1795. Although there were just a thousand residents in the village, the area was no longer a frontier outpost and relatively safe from warfare between the whites and Native Americans. The Indian wars had moved into Ohio, Indiana, and other parts of the Midwest.

At the confluence of the three rivers, Pittsburgh was a natural crossroads for river traffic and settlers moving overland across the Allegheny Mountains. There was opportunity.

Peter Shiras, who was in his sixties, had capital to invest. With a partner, he purchased from the government the remains of the old Fort Pitt military installation, which was abandoned on the point of land where the Monongahela and Allegheny Rivers met to form the Ohio. Today, the area is Point State Park at the tip of the city's Golden Triangle.

He set up a brewery to supply porter, ale, and beer to the growing number of taverns in the town and to the emigrants heading west to take up new land. Son George became manager and master brewer. In 1804, Peter Shiras returned to New Jersey and sold his interest in the brewery to his partner, who sold it again. Through each sale, George remained the manager. That year, George had a son, also named George. This was the grandfather of George Shiras 3d.

Eventually the Shirases took over the entire operation of what became known as the Pittsburgh Point Brewery. They shipped casks as far south as Natchez, Mississippi, and New Orleans, where their porter beer was especially valued because it did not spoil in the heat.

Pittsburgh thrived and hummed during the summer months with river traffic and settlers. The valleys around the city were rich with coal, iron ore, and timber. Glassworks, flour mills, gun and powder manufacturing, boatyards, and other commerce grew in importance. Raw materials and finished goods moved easily on the river. When Meriwether Lewis outfitted the Corps of Discovery to cross the continent to the Pacific Ocean, his journey began in Pittsburgh, where he bought provisions and the expedition's keelboat.

In those days, manufacturing beer and liquor or keeping a tavern was a respectable and highly profitable business. The sons and grandsons of Peter Shiras stayed in the brewing business for the next forty years. In 1837, when the brewery relocated from the point to Penn Street on the Allegheny River, it produced six thousand barrels of porter, ale, and beer. Brewing made the family rich and influential in civic affairs. Shirases served on the common council and helped raise money to build piers and other structures to protect the city from flooding.

They were leaders in the Presbyterian Church. George Sr., the 3d's grandfather, married Elizabeth Herron, the daughter of the foremost minister in the city. They had three sons: George Jr., Oliver, and Frank.

George Sr. was able to retire at age thirty-six and for the rest of his life lived off a share of the brewery profits and his other investments, which included banking and real estate.

Preferring the country life where he could raise his sons, farm, fish, and hunt, George Sr. in 1840 moved the family twenty miles north to the east bank of the Ohio River near what is now the town of Baden. He purchased a hundred-acre farm with fine springs of clear water and called it Crow Bottom. George Sr. grew apples, pears, and peaches in orchards bordered on one side by the Ohio River and on the other by wooded hills.

His oldest son, George Jr., born in 1832, loved the farm as a boy. There were Indian arrowheads and artifacts along the river. Deer and bear prowled the nearby wooded valleys. Each spring and fall, tens of thousands of red and gray squirrels swam across the river. Sometimes a steamboat paddled past, creating a wake that wet the squirrels' tails and impeded their passage. Dozens would drown at a time. Farmers cleared the land of mast trees—beech, hickory, and walnut—and mercilessly shot the squirrels to protect the grain in their fields.

Settlers also destroyed the flocks of passenger pigeons that swept through the valley in prodigious migration flights. Wherever the birds roosted, they were set upon with guns, clubs, stones, poles, traps, and nets. People ate pigeons, particularly the young squabs, but the birds also provided feed for hogs.

George Shiras Sr. and his boys fished the Ohio River for black bass, suckers, perch, pickerel, carp, and crappies. In the cooler feeder streams, they found speckled or brook trout. Channel catfish and "blue cats" were prized for their sweet flesh and sold in markets from Pittsburgh to New Orleans. Although his father preferred trout, George Jr. was content as a boy to take any fish as long as it put up a fight.

In the 1840s, the river was busy with boats: mail packets, freight haulers, and swift passenger boats outfitted with salons, barrooms, chandeliers, and carpets. Steam propulsion was still primitive. Boiler explosions were not uncommon as riverboat captains pushed for speed.

George Sr. commissioned construction of his own sternwheeler, a small pleasure craft for fishing the Ohio River and ferrying him and his family between Crow Bottom and Pittsburgh. He christened the boat the *Izaak Walton* after the English writer, sportsman, and early proselytizer of fishing with artificial flies. The Shiras boys loved the boat and learned to navigate the river and fish from its decks. They took along fowling pieces to shoot at ducks, geese, and other game birds.

George Sr. had settled into a life as a gentleman farmer and sportsman. In the summer of 1849, he left the family for several weeks and made his first trip to the wilds of the Upper Peninsula of Michigan, lured there by Pittsburgh friends who reported that speckled trout (eastern brook trout) weighing up to five pounds were caught easily on flies along the Lake Superior shoreline.

George Sr. took a stagecoach to Cleveland and boarded a steamer to Detroit and then another to Sault Ste. Marie at the northeast end of the Upper Peninsula. Known by its nickname—the Soo—it is the third-oldest city in the United States, founded by the French in 1668. Native Americans, however, had been there at least five hundred years earlier to take advantage of the good fishing on the St. Mary's River, which carries the outflow from Lake Superior into Lake Huron.

At the Soo, Shiras found a village of about five hundred residents, mostly French but Ojibwa, too. Many were of mixed race. Some Ojibwa fished with dip nets in the rapids and dried whitefish over smoky fires. Others were employed to portage boats around the rapids by pulling vessels with horses and cable and wood rollers across a mile-wide strip of land. The place was full of saloons and, as Louis Agassiz Fuertes, the naturalist, had observed during a visit, "Nobody is busy who was there and no one seems to know what he is going to do next."

The St. Mary's runs about seventy-four river miles between the two big lakes with a fall of twenty-three feet. Its rapids—now bypassed by the Soo Locks—were a destination for sportsmen who needed guides and boats. In 1865, Robert Roosevelt, uncle of the future president and a noted expert on fish, called the Soo Rapids the finest brook trout fishing in the world.

The speckled trout sought by George Sr. was the coaster brook trout, a potamodromous fish that migrates wholly within freshwater. The fish spawned in rivers and on shoals and then spent much of their life in the near-shore waters of the big lake. They could get enormous, partly because of their open-water habits but also because, prior to the European introduction of brown and rainbow trout, the fish had no competition. Today, naturally occurring coaster brook trout in the Great Lakes are rare. Much of their spawning habitat—the rocky cobbles of tributary streams to Lake Superior—was buried under sand and soil in the late nineteenth century when timbermen leveled the forests, drove the logs down to the big lakes, and damaged the river systems.

But in 1849, the tributaries and lakes were unspoiled. Shiras Sr. stayed a few days in the Soo and then took a sailing ship west along the south shore of Lake Superior. It was wild, picturesque country. He was impressed with the Grand Sable sand dunes and tens of miles of three-hundred-foot high cliffs that today are protected as Pictured Rocks National Lakeshore. About one hundred miles west of the Soo, the boat entered the protected waters of Munising Bay and berthed at Grand Island, where the American Fur Company had a trading outpost. Between what are now the towns of Munising and Marquette—a stretch of forty miles—Shiras beheld a mature forest of mixed hardwoods with climax species of sugar and hardwood maple as well as yellow birch and oak. It was a forest more advantageous to moose and woodland caribou—which were the top ungulates—than white-tail deer. Black bears, wolves, beaver, and grouse were common. Shiras also noted enormous flocks of passenger pigeons.

Tributary streams ran copper brown, a hue reminiscent of tea or beer, because they carried in solution tannins, or decayed organic matter leached from cedar swamps and the detritus of the great forests. At river mouths and over rocky reefs, Shiras caught scores of speckled trout on artificial flies often no more intricate than a piece of red ribbon knotted onto a hook.

He traveled two hundred miles to the tip of the Keweenaw Peninsula, where the village of Copper Harbor and Fort Wilkins, a military outpost, had been established to accommodate miners and settlers moving into the region to extract its copper. Native Americans had been finding chunks—even boulders of nearly pure metal—in the region for thousands of years and had hammered the copper into amulets, axes, knives, and other tools. Fortunes lay in these hills for the whites, and the mining rush to the Keweenaw had been underway for nearly five years. However, when Shiras arrived at Fort Wilkins, gold had just been discovered at Sutter's Mill, and many miners were leaving for California.

He stayed a few days and then made his way back to the Soo, stopping and fishing several good trout streams near a settlement called Worcester that was being hacked out of the wilderness around a quiet bay ringed by hills heavy with white pine. The settlers were building a forge and dock—not for copper but for iron ore.

Five years earlier, William Burt, a surveyor for the federal government, was running a section line thirteen miles inland from Worcester when his compass began spinning wildly. The variation in the magnetic field led the team to outcroppings of iron ore.

When word got out, entrepreneurs organized mining companies, including two investors from Worcester, Massachusetts. An eighteen-year-old boy named Peter White came to the site with the first settlers to help build a town. Legend has it that White came ashore and cut down the first tree in the new settlement. In the coming decades, White's fortunes would grow with the town, and he would become the richest, most influential man in the Upper Peninsula. Eventually his family would become linked with the Shirases from Pittsburgh.

George Sr. didn't meet White on that first trip, but he liked the rawness of the town, the determination of the settlers, and the superb fishing. He determined to come back.

That fall, the Shiras boys—George Jr. and Oliver—went off to college at Ohio University in Athens. Brother Frank moved to Pittsburgh to work. George Sr. sold the farm at Crow Bottom. He and Elizabeth moved into a hotel run by the Harmony Society in the town of Economy.

The Harmonites had come from Germany in 1804, led by their spiritual founder Johan George Rapp, who had run into trouble with Lutheran authorities when he and his followers refused to accept communion and would not attend church. They began to separate themselves from society and many immigrated to the New World.

In America, they built three different communities, the last being Economy, Pennsylvania, on a thousand-acre tract along the Ohio River. The Harmony Society was run as a cooperative, along socialistic and religious tenets. The group anticipated the second coming of Jesus Christ at any moment and adopted celibacy to purify themselves. This, of course, limited recruitment of new members and gradually—much like the celibate Shakers—the Harmonites aged, waned, and died out by the turn of the twentieth century.

George Sr. never joined up. He did not share their religious views, but he was charmed by their industriousness and the tidiness of their community. They lived among the Harmonites for nearly twenty years.

The Shiras boys were well educated for the period, learning from tutors brought to the farm at Crow Bottom and attending private school in

Pittsburgh during the winter months. They were well read at home, inheriting their father's love of books. After graduating from Ohio University, George Jr. and then Oliver transferred to Yale University in New Haven, Connecticut, in 1851. Both boys studied law.

Yale was still a new university in a country largely rural and yet to be knitted together by the railroads. A trip between their parents' home in Economy and New Haven required the use of a steamboat, a stagecoach, and finally a train. When the Pennsylvania Railroad connected Pittsburgh and Philadelphia in 1851, Pittsburgh became the most important city west of the Alleghenies.

While at Yale, George Jr. met Lillie Kennedy, the daughter of one of Pittsburgh's pioneer flour manufacturers. Attending a boarding school in New Haven, Lillie was intensely shy, small and dainty, but had a good sense of humor.

Junior returned to Pittsburgh in 1853 and set up a law practice in the area known today as the Golden Triangle. He and Lillie married in 1857. Their first child, George Shiras 3d, was born in Pittsburgh in 1859 and was joined by a brother, Winfield, the following year.

In the summer before the outbreak of the Civil War, George Jr. left Lillie and the babies and made his first trip to Lake Superior with his father, mother, and brother Frank. They put up in a new hotel in the town that was no longer Worcester but renamed Marquette after Pere Marquette, the daring French priest who first explored the Upper Great Lakes.

By this time, George Sr. had made several trips to the region and touted the fishing to friends back in Pittsburgh. In July 1856, he wrote a letter from Michigan to a sportsman in Pennsylvania, saying he had bought a rowboat in Detroit and brought it to Marquette for an extra two dollars in freight: "In our first attack on trout, we caught twelve trout in the harbor weighing a total of twenty and half pounds. Our next fishing was at the mouth of the Chocolate and in two and half hours we caught ninety-five, some of them over two-and-a-half pounds."

The Shirases became fast friends with Peter White, who had become the indispensable man in the village. White ran a store and the post office, delivering mail by dogsled. He spoke French, Ojibwa, and English. He helped organize the railroad to bring the iron ore down from the hills. He started the bank in town, organized the school board, and was elected to the state legislature. He studied law and opened a practice. He speculated in land and accumulated dozens of building lots in town and large tracts of forestland, including all the land surrounding Whitefish Lake twenty miles to the west.

White went fishing and hunting with the Pittsburgh men and introduced them to guides in the town, including the Indian Jack La Pete, who was to become a favorite of the family.

When the Shirases returned from Michigan in 1860, Pittsburgh was in a war frenzy. Frank and Oliver joined the Union Army. George Jr. joined the Pittsburgh militia and helped build earthworks and rifle pits for home defense. His brothers-in-law, the Kennedy boys, joined as well, leaving Junior to take on financial responsibility for some of his wife's sisters—she was from a family of eleven. He decided to stay in Pittsburgh to earn money.

Both Pittsburgh and Marquette boomed during the war years. Pittsburgh was an arsenal for the North, forging cannon, ammunition, and artillery capable of hurling thousand-pound projectiles. It made gunboats and ironclad ships. By the war's end, one-half of the nation's steel and one-third of its glass was manufactured in Pittsburgh.

The iron deposits of the upper Great Lakes were a critical resource for the Union. In the decade prior to the war, the deposits in the hills west of Marquette were being fought over by a number of entrepreneurs—mainly the Jackson Iron Company and the Cleveland Iron Company. The Cleveland Iron Company was operated by the Mather family descended from Cotton and Increase Mather, famous Puritan ministers who helped rule the Boston Colony. The Mathers put local dynamo Peter White in charge of its acreage in Marquette and sent Dr. Morgan L. Hewitt to run the mines. In 1857, Peter White married Ellen Sophia Hewitt, the daughter of the president of the Cleveland company.

In 1852, Marquette shipped just six barrels of iron ore to New Castle, Pennsylvania. In 1861, the Marquette range shipped 120,000 tons of ore; by 1868 500,000 tons; and in the 1870s and 1880s, with the expansion of railroads and the building of bridges and cities, the flow of iron ore and ingots of refined iron—known as pig iron—became a steady stream from the docks in Marquette.

At first, the ore came out of the hills in raw chunks of reddish stone hauled down to the lakeshore on a wagon road and dumped into the holds of sailing vessels. That proved inefficient, and furnaces were built to make pig iron on site and concentrate the product for shipping. At the end of the war, White anticipated the industry would need even more iron to build the railroads. He went on a buying spree, purchasing all the pig iron warehoused in towns like Detroit, even pig iron he had sold earlier out of Marquette. He resold the iron in Cleveland, often for double the price.

White and his wife, Sophia, built a mansion on Ridge Street overlooking the town's harbor. It soon became a street of beautiful, even pretentious homes lived in by mine supervisors, businessmen, lumber barons, and entrepreneurs to display their wealth. George Shiras Jr., after deciding that he and the family would make Marquette their headquarters each summer, bought a house nearby. Already, two of his wife's sisters—the Kennedy girls—had summered with the family in the Upper Peninsula, been courted by local businessmen, and married. Now there was a familial connection to Marquette.

Back in Pittsburgh, Junior was doing quite well in the law, supporting his little family and the extended Kennedy clan. The Shirases lived in a large brick house in the city of Allegheny, which was on the north side of the Ohio River. (Allegheny was later annexed by the city of Pittsburgh.) They employed a cook, a houseman, and two other servants. Junior liked to play cards (mostly euchre), read Dickens, and entertain friends. Lillie was known as a gourmet cook and a fine hostess. Being from old moneyed families in Pittsburgh, they hobnobbed with the city's other elites, which included the nouveau riche of the manufacturing class.

George Jr. was a leading counsel for the Baltimore and Ohio and the Junction Valley Railroads and frequently litigated transportation cases over rights-of-way of both railroads and canals. Twice, he argued cases reaching the US Supreme Court. The first case involved a demand by a member of the Harmony Society to discover the financial condition of the commune. The man—a member for thirty years—had left the group and demanded a share of the assets. The Harmony Society refused to give him either, and the case was upheld. However, Shiras won his second case involving a patent infringement.

He had the reputation of being "an able debater, forcible and logically reasoned and quick and ready in the progress of an argument." George 3d described his father as "tall, self-possessed with a philosophical mind but one, by reason of his sense of humor, free from pedantry."

In the 1870s, at a time when there was no income tax, his annual earnings averaged $75,000, or about $1.5 million in early twenty-first-century dollars.

Junior was a charter member of the Duquesne Club begun by Henry Clay Frick, who ran the steel works in Homestead for Andrew Carnegie. Frick, known as the most ruthless of the city's robber barons, organized the private club to cater to the industrialists and the business elites. As one historian wrote, "Ever since the Duquesne Club opened its doors in 1873, the captains of industry have swaggered through them."

He joined the club's Number 6 Group—men who met for lunch nearly every day and became close friends. The group included Henry Oliver, who helped open the Mesabi Iron Range in Minnesota; Tom Carnegie, brother of Andy Carnegie and cofounder of the Edgar Thomson Steel Works; and B. F. Jones, known as the ablest man in the steel industry, whose works of Jones and Laughlin Steel dominated the skyline of Pittsburgh for nearly a century.

The power and prestige of the club was on display at its first formal dinner. The guest speaker was Ulysses S. Grant, then president of the United States. Also attending were Generals Phil Sheridan and William Tecumseh Sherman. The men were in town for a reunion of the Army of the Cumberland.

After the members feasted on wild game—terrapin consommé, salmon-decorated grouse, boned quail, duck, saddle of venison, and pheasant—Grant gave his address and assured the audience that he understood the importance of the protective tariff for the city of Pittsburgh and, of course, the business interests of his hosts. By this time, Pittsburgh supplied the nation with 60 percent of its steel, and its financial center rivaled Wall Street in New York.

George Sr. and George Jr. invested in banks, bonds, stocks, railroads and, of course, steel. They had interests in iron ore production up in Michigan. Consequently, the Gilded Age was a profitable period for both the Shiras and White families.

3 | BOYHOOD DAYS IN MICHIGAN

ALTHOUGH THE SHIRASES were city gentlemen of means, they weren't prissy men. They relished fishing, hunting, and camping and enjoyed the company of their rough-hewn guides.

George 3d and Winfield learned outdoor skills from their father and grandfather in the country near Economy, where there was land and woods away from the city. In 1869, when George was ten and Winfield nine, they were given their first shotguns to hunt squirrels, rabbits, and quail along the banks of the Ohio River. The guns were in anticipation of a trip to the Upper Peninsula the following summer.

George 3d had heard stories of Lake Superior, speckled trout, the big woods, and the raw frontier town of Marquette. Years later, he wrote in *National Geographic* magazine, "How I wanted to see with my own eyes this wonderful body of water and tributary streams, the great forests of pine and hardwood, the picturesque Ojibwa Indians in their birch bark canoes."

In early summer of 1870, the Shiras men and their boys arrived in Marquette and then took a small steamer to the west, which deposited them five miles off shore near what is now the Huron Islands National Wildlife Refuge. Lake Superior was cold, deeply blue, and transparent. They could look over the bow of the steamer and see the bottom forty feet below. The big lake was nothing like the murky Ohio River.

The campers transferred to yawls—two-mast boats with paddles and canoes in tow—and set off for the mouth of the Huron River. It was wild country, a remote shoreline. There were no settlements between the Huron and Marquette—a distance of sixty miles. The group spent ten days at the river mouth, fishing for trout and shooting grouse, deer, and passenger pigeons.

Exactly who was on the trip has been lost to time, but it was Jack La Pete who most impressed the Shiras boys. La Pete had spent time with white men in the Soo and Marquette and had even passed a year in Washington, DC, acting as interpreter for the Ojibwa in treaty negotiations. La Pete had a "greater knowledge of worldly affairs," recalled George 3d, than the other guides, who were parochial and rather ignorant.

The boys asked the Indian endless questions. Around the campfire, La Pete made toy birchbark canoes initialed with porcupine quills. He gave them the tail of a grouse to use as a fan against the heat and flies. He made a pouch for shot from the skin of a muskrat. In the evening, he told ghost stories of the manitou who had floated down his chimney and restored his sight. It was exotic stuff for boys, and Shiras recalled "being much impressed with the experiences of first camp."

Prior to buying the house on Ridge Street, the Shiras family put up in a Marquette hotel for several weeks each summer. George and Winfield befriended the Ely brothers who lived in a mansion alongside the hotel. Their father, Sam P. Ely, ran the First National Bank for Peter White. The friendship between the boys lasted into manhood.

Their first adventure together occurred close to home when George was twelve. A group of boys—the youngest being just nine—asked to go camping without guides or adults and were given permission to overnight at the mouth of the Dead River just north of town.

Back then, George recalled, "Marquette had no suburbs. The wilderness started right out the backyard."

A one-horse wagon driven by a guide hauled the boys and equipment along the lakeshore on the hard-packed beach and deposited them next to the river at a set of rocks in the shape of a pyramid. There was driftwood for a fire.

The boys were forbidden both axes and guns and given strict orders and warnings by the parents. George recalled, "No one was to risk quick sands by wading in the shallow river or venture into the pathless swamps and dense forests beyond. These were to be occupied by beasts having a particular preference for boys."

The boys tossed lines in the river and cooked fish and flapjacks for dinner. Having forgotten lard and butter, they scorched the fish. Flapjacks had to be pried off the pan with a knife. However, there was jam and bread and cookies and, for breakfast, a big beefsteak, which they planned to roast on a spit.

Despite a bonfire, their courage faltered as it grew dark. When the wind shifted seaward, they heard a roaring noise coming from upriver. They were certain a forest fire was about to pass over.

As the oldest, George took the front of the tent next to the opening. As he eyed the fire, he reassured himself that the light and smoke would keep away wild beasts. Wrapped in a blanket, he soon fell asleep.

"Suddenly I heard a snuffing sound beyond the tent. Heavy feet pressed down on the blanket. Followed the noise of some animal seizing the meat and dragging it away."

Shiras scrambled over his companions to the back of the tent yelling, "Bear! Bear!"

Everyone jockeyed for position and howled in confusion, until one of the Ely boys pulled a pistol—he had been certain they would be set upon by wild beasts no matter what the parents had said—and fired several shots through the open flap.

They rebuilt the fire and stayed up the rest of the night. In the morning, they retreated to town and learned to their chagrin that the breakfast meat had been stolen by a stray Indian dog and the roar of the forest fire was actually a waterfall on the river.

Normally the boys were accompanied by a guide, someone the parents trusted, a man who knew the woods, could row a boat, cook a meal, and act as a sort of wilderness nanny. Samson Noll, a black man who worked for the Ely family, accompanied one of the Ely boys that summer to a salt lick not far from town on the Carp River. The boy shot a deer from a scaffold built as a blind and shooting stand.

The kill created quite a stir among the young boys in town, and Ely agreed to bring George on his next visit—this time without the guide. The boys walked down the shoreline and mounted the scaffolding overlooking a giant downed tree. The tree had been augured full of holes and packed with salt. They soon heard the breaking of branches, trained their guns, and waited. Instead of a deer, a man emerged from the brush. He checked the salt in the holes—apparently to see if they needed refilling—and then moved on, never looking up at the scaffold where two young boys stood armed and aiming.

Shortly afterward, a deer came by. They fired but missed.

It was the only hunting opportunity George had that summer. His first buck waited until the following year when La Pete took him fire hunting at Whitefish Lake.

George Sr. called La Pete the "Jack of Spades" because he resembled the figure on the playing card. His Ojibwa name was Bakakadoose, but his mother told him he was Sioux, revealing that she had been kidnapped from Manitoba many years earlier by the Ojibwa. Jack kept this secret from his Indian and white friends until late in life.

The other popular guide for the family was Jake Brown, a rugged market hunter in his twenties who killed whitetail deer year-round to supply the hotel in Marquette with venison, which it labeled on the menu as mutton.

Brown, born in New York's Finger Lakes region in 1857, worked as a boy on the Erie Canal, driving a mule along the towpath. When he was just thirteen, he joined his brother in southern Michigan, where they made a living as market hunters until the game played out. They followed the timber camps north. For several years, Brown shot most of his deer near the mouth of the Laughing Whitefish River a few miles from the lake discovered by La Pete.

George 3d first encountered Brown in the rear quarters of the hotel where Jake had just delivered his mutton. The guide was telling stories surrounded by the waitresses, who apparently found him quite appealing. Brown was handsome and had an effusive personality and quick wit, but when he came to Marquette, he hit the taverns, raised hell, and drank hard for days at a time.

George once quipped, "He seemed to regard the time in town lost if his wages were not put into immediate circulation."

Once the binge was over and he was broke, Jake retreated to the woods.

In camp, he forswore liquor and utilized the wilderness as a sobriety check. Among the trees and on the water, he was dependable, skilled, and a lot of fun. The Shirases and Peter White overlooked the drinking, employed him whenever possible, and trusted both Brown and La Pete with the boys.

When Shiras was in his early teens, La Pete and Brown rowed the boys and their friends along the lakeshore to Shot Point, the first rocky outcrop east of the town. After about three miles on the water, the guides realized they had forgotten to pack cooking gear. George wanted to row back, but La Pete insisted it was bad luck to return once they had made a start. He could manufacture whatever they needed, he said.

While the others fished for brook trout, La Pete erected the canvas tent, kindled a fire, and whittled knives from hardwood branches. He made forks from sticks. He laid potatoes in the coals and steamed a can of tomatoes by perforating the lid. They cleaned the trout, wrapped them in wet brown paper, and laid the fish on the coals. Slabs of birch bark functioned as plates. The tomatoes went into a birchbark bowl, and then Jack made a bail and used the tin can to cook tea over the fire. Later, he flattened another can into a makeshift frying pan for flapjacks and bacon.

Shiras noted, "Such was my first lesson in the ease with which supposed essentials might be left behind. The knowledge proved useful when I was forced to travel light, or when a capsize of the canoe sent the outfit to the bottom."

The preferred camp cook was Samson Noll. He was born a slave in 1819 and held in bondage on a Virginia plantation. In 1858, he apparently got into a fight with the overseer and clubbed the man on the head with a stick. Noll fled into the swamps, evaded the dogs and searchers, and miraculously made it to Detroit. He crossed the river into Windsor, Canada, where he married. After the Civil War and emancipation, he reentered the states and came north to Marquette. His wife cooked in a restaurant in town, and Noll worked for the Ely family. Although he was illiterate, he was smart and apparently quite fierce when roused.

In the 1870s, Noll accompanied George and one of the Ely boys on a fall deer hunt along the newly laid railroad tracks west of Marquette. Hunters had built scaffolds and tree stands along the tracks to ambush the deer as they migrated south away from the heavy snow regions along Lake Superior.

Such seasonal migrations had occurred for centuries; the game trails were deeply rutted and well known to the Ojibwa. However, patterns were shifting. Livestock fencing and rail rights-of-way impeded the deer, who concentrated in isolated yards or wintering grounds—usually swamps where there was thermal protection and cedar trees to browse. In the yards, the deer were easily picked off by hunters and predators—typically gray wolves.

Market hunters—also known as pothunters, for they killed and sold meat for the cooking pot—took an enormous toll on the herds. In southern Michigan, deer were extirpated by the 1870s, but in the north, which had been elk, caribou, and moose country, logging created more openings, brush, and second-growth forest. The deer populations exploded in the 1880s and '90s, but so did the killing by market hunters and settlers hunting for subsistence. In 1880, seventy thousand deer were taken in Michigan, but only an estimated four thousand were killed by sport hunters.

As it was with the bison on the Great Plains or passenger pigeons in the hardwood forests, the game was there for the taking and the attitude at the time was to take all you wanted. The market hunters went about the annihilation in a methodical manner, using telegraphy to communicate the animals' location and riding the rails to reach the hunting grounds and transport their kills.

A typical market hunter working along the railroad might kill one to two hundred deer each fall, selling the venison to lumber camps, restaurants and saloons in towns, or cooks working the trains. Often, the hunters took only the hindquarters and saddles—the prized meat on the animal's back and hips—and left the rest to rot in the woods.

Noll and his young charges rode the train out of Marquette and dropped off in the woods. They put up their tent next to a rough-hewn cabin occupied by market hunters led by a burly man from Chicago known as the Captain.

George and his companion rose early the next morning and set up in two of the empty scaffolds strategically placed between a swamp and patch of the woods. The etiquette of the scaffolds was first come, first served. The Captain arose well after daylight and found the Ely boy in what he claimed was his scaffold. He cursed the boy, but the teenager did not budge. The Captain stomped off.

Within hours, Ely shot a big buck and George helped his friend rope up the carcass and drag it several hundred yards to the railroad cut. They left the deer there and crossed the tracks to have breakfast that Noll had waiting.

When they returned to dress out the animal, it was gone. The Captain sauntered by a few minutes later and told the boys a passing iron ore train had stopped. Perhaps a brakeman or engineer had stolen the buck, he said. Obviously, the boys were tenderfeet and it was unfortunate they were so careless with their kill. He assumed the boys and "their negro" would move on to another spot since there were already so many hunters here.

Noll heard the exchange and wandered over. He glared at the Captain and said, "I bet you I can find that deer within three hundred yards."

The boys were alarmed. Clearly, Noll was calling the Captain a liar. Wishing to avoid a confrontation, they immediately agreed that yes, yes, they had been very careless. The Captain interrupted with an unrelated story about "a darky" who had been punished for breaking into a warehouse in Chicago. It was a not-so-veiled threat, but Noll was undeterred.

"I'm going to look for that deer."

He marched a short distance and within a few minutes hauled the deer out of the brush where it had been hidden. The Captain stomped off. The boys quickly dressed out the animal.

Shiras recalled, "It took only a few minutes to decide that we should break camp. On the return of the Captain and his fellow hunters, there was apt to be quite a big row in which it was more than likely that Noll would be seriously injured."

In retaliation, however, the boys went into the hunters' cabin and pulled out the bedding and left the mattresses in the rain before they boarded the next train for another part of the county. Three days later at a stop called Little Lake, they got onto a train with another dead deer and encountered the Captain in the baggage car.

Noll looked at the Captain and then at the dead deer and said, "Here is an old friend of yours."

Pointing at the buck and giving it a kick, Noll warned the baggage master to keep his eye on the deer because it had the habit of disappearing at the first opportunity.

"The Captain can tell you about it," he said.

The Captain replied, "Shut up. I have heard enough of this."

Noll answered, "Never open a ball unless you can dance."

They reached Marquette without incident, with Shiras noting that Noll "never backed down when aroused."

George and his family were never as profligate as the pothunters, but they typically killed several deer each year and likely wounded as many. In the early days of the 1870s and '80s, hunting was not limited to fall. In his journals, Peter White wrote of a trip taken in July 1880 to the Au Train River about thirty miles east of Marquette. White, the Shiras and Ely men, and their boys killed fourteen deer in three days. White boastfully recorded, "Slaughter!"

In summer, their hunting and fishing expeditions ranged up and down the shore, from the Salmon Trout River to the northwest and east to what is now Pictured Rocks National Lakeshore—a width of eighty miles. They shot whatever showed itself: mostly deer, occasionally a black bear, ruffed grouse (known as partridge), ducks, teal, geese, and rabbits. Wolves, foxes, hawks, and other "varmints" were killed as a matter of course. Peter White kept score, noting the bag of game and the size and number of fish. What wasn't eaten in the field was brought back to Marquette.

Eventually, the deer hunting centered on the lake that La Pete had discovered years earlier. According to Shiras family lore, it was young George 3d who gave the lake the name Whitefish after the river that served as both the inlet and outlet. Peter White, an exceptional land speculator, had gotten control of four by ten miles of forest surrounding the lake to create what he deemed a "game preserve."

The Shirases, White, and important men in the region's emerging iron industry—some of whom had married into the two families—went to Whitefish Lake for several weeks each fall. They dried the meat and brought in extra packers to take it home. Jake Brown and Jack La Pete, who still maintained his lean-to at the south end of the lake, guided the hunters. Samson Noll served as camp cook.

In the first years, the hunters came by wagon from Marquette or took a boat to the mouth of the Laughing Whitefish River where it emptied into Lake Superior and then walked into the interior, a distance of about eight miles. The railroad came through in 1879 when venture capitalists from Detroit built a standard-gauge track across the 160 miles between Marquette

Hunting guide Jake Brown and the first cabin erected at Whitefish Lake, 1882.
Courtesy of Northern Michigan University.

and the Straits of Mackinac. Where the tracks crossed the Laughing Whitefish River, a stop was established and given the apt name of Deerton.

The hunt in those days was all about getting meat, not trophies. Jacking
deer at night was practiced by all the pothunters and sportsmen too. Hunters stalked the railroad right-of-way at night with a kerosene lamp outfitted
with a parabolic mirror to concentrate and project a beam. The hunters
shined the light fifty or so yards ahead looking for a pair of gleaming eyes.
Shiras recalled that "trying to put a ball between the few inches separating
these brilliant orbs required an accuracy of aim, a knowledge of the woods,
and a skill in still hunting quite up to the standard of daylight shooting."

Of course, the hunter—no matter how skilled a marksman—never knew
exactly what he was shooting at in the dark and killed owls and beavers and
other nocturnal animals. Hunters sometimes fired into distant cabins and
campsites, mistaking lamplight or even the glow of a cigar for eyes.

In the early 1880s, the Shirases and their guides were camping and trout fishing about thirty miles east of Marquette near Grand Island. The older folks had bedded down in the tents for the night while George, Winfield, and a teenage companion sat around the campfire on the lakeshore.

In the flickering light, George spied a large animal passing through the bushes. Certain it was a deer, the boys rigged up a jacklight and stalked the shoreline where a game trail terminated at the beach. George carried a rifle, another boy a shotgun. They shined the torch and illuminated a glowing pair of eyes on a stretch of sand frequently visited by deer.

George aimed below the eyes and fired. The other boy let fly with the shotgun. Immediately, they heard a loud, plaintive and weird wailing coming from the thicket where the animal had fled. It was a cry no wounded deer had ever made.

They crept up and saw a long, yellowish body lying on the ground, bleeding into the sand, its head concealed by a drooping branch. The animal was dead. They dragged it out and were astonished to discover an enormous dog, a cross between a mastiff and some kind of hound. It must have weighed 150 pounds and stood nearly three feet at the shoulder.

They were in trouble and decided to do what has been termed today as "shoot, shovel, and shut up" when killing an animal that might be protected. They dragged the dog to shore, tied on a large rock, rowed a boat into deep water, and tossed it overboard.

They snuck back into camp, sure that the older men—despite the gunshots—had slept through the affair.

The next week in Marquette, Jake Brown was confronted at the dock by a French-Canadian who accused the party of making off with his dog, which he used to pull a sleigh and haul cordwood in winter. In the summer, the dog mostly ran loose, but it had not been seen for several days.

The men nearly came to blows, but Jake's defense of knowing nothing about the dog convinced the owner he was telling the truth.

Later on, the boys anonymously sent the man compensation for the dog and, when the adults got wind of this monetary payout, they put two and two together.

For Christmas that year back in Pittsburgh, George and Winfield received a plaque of three armed hunters with a jacklight approaching a fierce-looking beast. The inscription below the carving read, "Who saw him die? I said the fly with my little eye. I saw him die."

Shiras wrote, "Apparently some of the older campmates had been more awake than we gave them credit for."

Buck fever and an itchy trigger finger were dangerous, too.

In 1883, George nearly killed his friend Prescott Ely when he misidentified him as a deer while they hunted on the Laughing Whitefish River. Prescott dropped George at a tree stand and then paddled their canoe downriver. He was to wait until dusk and then come back, spooking any deer toward George. It was still late afternoon when Shiras saw a deer enter the brush along the river. He braced himself against the tree, fired a long shot, and noticed an odd "smoke-line appear to come from near the deer's head."

There was a deer, but what he had aimed at was Prescott's head—covered in a gray hat and havelock, a cloth extending down his neck and back.

Prescott had been so harassed by mosquitoes, he had come upriver early. As he approached the tree stand, he, too, saw the deer, reached for his rifle and fired—apparently at the exact instant as Shiras. The gun reports were simultaneous. Neither knew the other had taken a shot, but the deer fell dead.

When George ran up to his friend, he wasn't certain what had happened, but as they gutted the animal, he noticed that Prescott's hat appeared to have been sliced open.

"I took the garment and examining the inside found several small tufts of his hair adhering to it, that it had been clipped by the bullet. These were quickly removed and in my humiliation, I determined that the occurrence should be concealed indefinitely. Noticing my gloominess, Ely attributed it to my failure to get the deer and tried to comfort me by assuring that I would certainly get one with the jacklight at night. Later pleading a severe headache, I refused to go out for the night hunt."

It was many years later before Shiras confessed his errant shot to Prescott.

In the early '80s, George Jr., his brother-in-law Colonel William M. Kennedy of Pittsburgh, and young Winfield went fishing off the mouth of the Sand River. They invited George along to make a four-person party around the fire for a game of whist, a fashionable trick-taking card game in the nineteenth century. It was a favorite of Junior's.

George declined. He was going bear hunting with Prescott. The anglers, with Jake Brown as guide and cook, had not been gone an hour when there was a rumor in town that bears had been sighted near Sand River. The next day George and Prescott jumped on a train and walked from the tracks over to the mouth where the family was camped. Peering through binoculars, George spotted the boats a few hundred yards offshore, the men dropping anchor and catching speckled trout. They would be out there for a long time, but George and Prescott were hungry and they wanted Jake Brown to cook lunch.

"I think I can bring them back in fifteen minutes," said George.

He went into a tent and came back with a large, black rubber coat. He wrapped a dark shirt about his head, donned the coat and dropped to his hands and knees on the white sand and stalked around like a bear for several minutes.

Prescott hid back in the woods, snickering, and remarked, "you look so much like the animal that I have to refrain myself from shooting you."

The ruse worked. Ely saw the fishermen pulling hard toward shore. George shuffled over to a pine tree, reared up and raked the bark like a bear sharpening its claws. Then he and Ely retreated to the woods.

They watched the men land the boat down shore, rush into the tent, load rifles and go off in search of the bear—arguing about who would take the first shot. George and Ely circled about, came back to the camp, and seated themselves at the fire. When Jake returned and saw George, smoking a pipe, still wearing the black coat, he knew they had been hoaxed.

Jake snorted and said, "The bear hunt is off and it is time for me to get dinner."

Afterward Winfield, Junior, and Jake rowed back out to the reef to fish. A great blue heron passed over the boat. Winfield pointed the bird out to his father.

"I wouldn't pay any attention to it," said Junior. "It's probably George."

Outdoor adventures were mostly for men, but every summer the Shiras family, Lillie and her sisters, White and his children, and friends from Marquette camped in canvas tents at Saux Head, a small cape or peninsula jutting into Lake Superior. Consisting mainly of rock and a few pine trees, Saux Head offered fine offshore fishing for coaster brook trout. In his journals, Peter White routinely referred to brook trout in the range of sixteen pounds and the occasional Mackinac, or lake trout, up to forty pounds.

Colonies of passenger pigeons nested in nearby trees. Hunters also brought in deer and grouse for the table, usually prepared by Samson Noll in the cook tent. In an 1880 trip, White noted that he and George Jr. killed five deer for the camp. Driftwood along the shore fueled a large nightly fire where everyone gathered under the big dome of sky. On moonless nights the stars were multitudinous, and sometimes waves of the green and red light of the aurora borealis undulated across the star field. In July and August, the sun did not set until nearly ten p.m., and twilight lasted another hour. In the often chilly and cloudy north country, these were the warm, halcyon days of summer.

George recalled, "There was an absence of insect life in this place free from brush and subject to the lake breezes, so that in daylight or darkness, it afforded the tented occupants a pleasant haven "

It was at Saux Head in 1886 that George brought his new landscape camera and captured what he called his first fishing picture. It shows a woman, probably his young wife, in an ankle-length skirt, button shoes, and a white blouse with puffed sleeves. The fashion is Victorian but she wears a man's hat. She stands erect on a sloping boulder as large as a boxcar. Her arms are up, pulling on the line, the cane pole bent dramatically. Jake Brown kneels at the edge of the rock, reaching down to net a splashing fish—a four-pound speckled trout, according to George.

The Shirases were fly fishermen, but they weren't so pure as to not thread a worm on a hook. George explained, "In those days, the use of live bait, especially angleworms was regarded as sportsmanlike and was apparently justifiable for fish habitually lying deep below the surface on the rocky bottom. To hook these big fellows was only an incident in the long, hard contest with a slender rod."

The men brought earthworms from Pittsburgh because there were no *Lumbricus terrestris* in the Upper Peninsula. Natural colonization of terrestrial worms occurs at a rate of just a half a mile every century, and in the thousands of years since the ice sheets covered much of North America, native worms from the south had yet to reach the north woods. It's believed the English who settled at Jamestown in Virginia and the Puritans in Boston were the first to bring worms to the New World in the rocks and barrels of soil used to ballast their ships.

When they were boys, George and Winfield were employed to dig through the leaf litter in Pennsylvania and fill a two-gallon can with worms for the annual excursion to the north. In Marquette, the worms were held in a wooden box under lock and key to prevent theft. At the end of their trips, the Shiras men gave whatever crawlers were left to friends.

In 1878, young George buried a large remnant in the Ely yard near the

Fishing at Saux Head, Michigan, 1886. Courtesy of Northern Michigan University.

hotel in Marquette. In three years, the worms became so abundant in the lot there was no need to bring any north. He also placed worms in the soil next to Jack La Pete's cabin on Whitefish Lake where, he noted, they "grew to extraordinary size and far exceeded in lustiness their Pennsylvania progenytors [sic]."

When George Shiras Jr. died in 1924, the *Marquette Mining Journal* in his obituary claimed, "Recent reports have shown that these Pennsylvania worms have circled the lake extent for a distance of about 150 miles on the north shore."

Where they established themselves, earthworms changed the ecosystem by consuming the leaf litter and eliminating some plants—tree seedlings, ferns, and flowers—that obtained their nutrients from the forest detritus.

Earthworms were only one element in the ecological alteration of the Upper Peninsula.

The coming of the railroads along with logging opened the country to exploitation. The state of Michigan granted James McMillan, a Detroit businessman, and his partners a windfall of 1.3 million acres to build the Detroit, Marquette and Mackinac Railroad from Marquette to the east to the Straits of Mackinac. The investors began logging the land on either side of the right-of-way and selling it to timbermen.

In 1879 when crews reached the Laughing Whitefish River, George Shiras, who was just twenty-one, and Jake Brown took a construction train to the new Deerton stop. They camped there along with Shiras's uncle, Colonel William Howe, a Civil War veteran and an executive of a steel works in Pittsburgh. He came to Marquette every September to escape the hay fever that plagued him in Pennsylvania.

Howe was middle-aged and of a rather corpulent build. The plan was for the younger men to strike cross-country, blaze a trail directly from Deerton to Whitefish Lake, and create a shorter route to Old Jack's lean-to. Shiras figured the lake was perhaps three to four miles south of the new tracks. Howe was to follow the next day.

George led off with a compass while Jake came behind and hacked notches into trees. Shiras worked to maintain a straight line but kept the meandering river in sight. At one point, they stopped and observed six pileated woodpeckers, which Shiras called the cock of the woods.

"Apparently this party consisted of a pair with their four young, which was engaged in a family celebration. Their loud calls and repeated drumming on a dead pine tree furnished both vocal and instrumental music for the occasion. Usually these fine birds were seen singly or in pairs and I never again saw such a gathering."

By noon, they had hiked six miles and had yet to reach the lake. Frustrated, they halted for lunch, but when Jake unbuckled his pack, he realized he'd left the salt meat and sandwiches back at the railroad crossing. They drained their canteens and kept moving. Near the north end of the lake, they eased past snares set by La Pete to catch bears or any other critter that might stumble into the traps. They abandoned the trailblazing, scrambled over downed timber, and slogged through wetlands to reach La Pete's camp at the south end. Trailblazing could wait. They were hungry.

La Pete, to their surprise, was not in residence. They searched the lean-to for canned goods but found only a tin of pork grease wired to the ridgepole. Jake dropped his pack, took a long drink from a spring, and then went back to get the supplies and bring along Colonel Howe. He promised to return by ten a.m. the next day, the trip made quicker by the newly blazed trail.

The next morning, Shiras considered eating the grease. Instead, he took his .44 carbine down to the slough near Old Jack's Landing with the notion of picking off a deer, muskrat, or beaver, which he could cut up and fry in the grease. He saw nothing all day and, while walking back to camp in the darkness, nearly fell over a porcupine. He considered cooking it too, but "this fat animal I classed in the same category as Jack's can of grease."

Instead, he built a large fire and lay down with a blanket, concerned that Jake had been hurt in the woods. But around midnight, he heard the men approaching, stumbling through the woods. Howe, "the doughty war veteran," entered the firelight limping and leaning on an improvised crutch to support a turned ankle.

It was the last time they camped at Jack's lean-to. In 1881, George, Jake, Peter White, and the Ely boys built their own hunting camp on the Laughing Whitefish River just a few hundred yards north of the lake. There, they could easily put in a canoe and descend through the marshy wetlands into the open lake.

The new camp was primitive, just hip walls of logs crowned by a peaked roof of birch bark, weighed down with half-logs. There were rough-hewn bunks and tables indoors and benches and logs for sitting outside. Cooking was done over a grate and open fire. They stored pots and pans in a hollow log. Once after making coffee—which everyone said had been excellent but had a unique taste—they discovered a dead toad in the pot. For years after, the joke around camp was, "Do you want coffee a la mode or coffee a la toad?"

Some of George's first photographs were set pieces of the camp and hunters—men in wool jackets, puttees, and high-laced boots posed with pipes and cigars clenched in their teeth and guns across their shoulders or in the crook of arms. Gutted deer hang from a pole, and bunches of passenger pigeons and grouse tied by the feet dangle from the rafters. They were wealthy men with Marquette connections—the White and Shiras men and relatives, owners of mines, iron forges, and ships, even an English lord who was in the country looking over his land holdings in the upper Midwest. Samson Noll, Jack La Pete, and Jake Brown remain in the background, gaping at the camera. All the men—rich or poor—look rough, even dirty.

Hunting party at Whitefish Lake, 1884. *From left*: Guides Fred Bawgum, Samson Noll, and Jack La Pete; English lord Henry Brassey (with shotgun), who had Upper Peninsula iron mine holdings; Douglas "Ducker" McLean, champion rower at Oxford, England; and Peter White, a town founder of Marquette, Michigan. Courtesy of Northern Michigan University.

Whitefish Lake provided excellent hunting. At a time when deer were being decimated by settlers and market hunters, whitetails remained numerous about the lake, especially in the slough.

George explained, "This was the center of deer country. Several natural salt licks were located beneath each bank, forming the central points of century-old gathering places of all the deer within a radius of ten or fifteen miles. Here, at any time, between spring and early winter, they could be seen almost continuously."

Such a magnet for game was good for hunting with a gun and, later, good for hunting with a camera.

4 | SCHOOL DAYS FOR BLUE BLOODS

ALTHOUGH THE FOREST, waters, and characters of the thinly populated Upper Peninsula colored his boyhood and adolescent summers, George spent most of his formative years in dignified and privileged life in Pittsburgh and the East. He was a city boy, educated by tutors, prep schools, and elite colleges in the company of other blue bloods.

George and Winfield entered prep school in 1876 at Phillips Academy in Andover, Massachusetts. Founded in 1778, the school was a well-established destination for American boys of privilege.

George Jr. took his sons to Andover and secured them rooms in a boarding house managed by a woman and her husband—a Mr. Blunt, who told the boys that he was "Blunt by name and blunt by nature." They were assigned a room on the first floor where years earlier Harriett Beecher Stowe, author of *Uncle Tom's Cabin*, wrote and lived while her husband taught at the Andover Theological Seminary.

George settled in well at school, but Winfield paced the floor the first few weeks and finally wrote to his parents begging to come home, vowing to "take up solid reading such as Dickens and Thackeray."

It amused those back home. Both authors were considered light reading in the Shiras household, but the homesickness was genuine. The sympathetic parents allowed Winfield to return to Pennsylvania. He finished prep school in Allegheny.

The academics of Andover may have been daunting for Winfield. The boys had been home tutored in Pittsburgh, and George soon learned that their "easy, good-natured tutor had not satisfactorily prepared us for the thorough and exacting curriculum."

Many classmates were offspring of the American elite. Friends included Edwin Pierrepont, the son of Edwards Pierrepont, then ambassador to the Court of St. James of the United Kingdom and an enlightened reformer in President Grant's administration. Another classmate was Cyrus McCormick Jr., son of the president of the Harvester Company in Chicago.

Shiras remembered McCormick as a "happy-go-lucky fellow who too often spent his time in social pursuits." The three boys became friends and one spring morning, they went hiking. The plan was to circle through the countryside and return by evening. They did not have a permit to be absent overnight.

They walked straight to Lowell, assuming they could catch the evening train home, but once in town, they discovered there was no evening train on Saturday. They passed the night at the home of a classmate and then came back to Andover on the Boston Express, which would get them back in time for morning chapel.

On the train, they discussed how to handle their absence with the school authorities, mainly the principal, Cecil F. P. Bancroft—a diminutive but feisty man the students called "Banty."

Pierrepont thought it best to go directly to Bancroft, explain themselves, and ask for forgiveness. However, McCormick, who had many demerits already, wanted to take his chances. Perhaps they had not been missed. He refused to go along to the principal's office and asked Pierrepont not to mention his name during any confession.

Edwin, whom Shiras derisively described as the "saintly scion of the Ambassador," replied that he would not lie in any way because it might create a scandal for his father.

Shiras and Pierrepont were lightly rebuked, but it was the end for McCormick. He was expelled and his parents notified by wire to come fetch their boy.

That night, McCormick exacted his revenge by tearing shutters off an unoccupied dormitory and using them to build a fire in the middle of campus. As the fire bells rang, Shiras and other students watched him dance about the flames and taunt Banty, who confronted the boy.

The next day, McCormick told Shiras it was better to be punished for a "proven wrong than unjustly disgraced for an innocent act."

Later in life, he became president of International Harvester and in 1886 locked out the workers during a strike, which helped foment the Haymarket Riots in Chicago.

In 1877 Shiras entered Cornell University in Ithaca, New York, largely because his father was friends with its president and he wanted to avoid studying Greek, which was a requirement at Yale. He majored in history and political science, but his political passion was tepid until the 1880 presidential contest between James Garfield and Winfield Scott Hancock, both Civil War generals.

He became fast friends with a fellow fraternity brother, Edward M. House, the son of the mayor of Houston, Texas, who had gotten rich by running guns to the Confederacy. The young men were on opposite sides. House was a Southern Democrat supporting Hancock and Shiras an affirmed Republican but, each evening after classes, they walked together to the newsstand to buy copies of the *New York Tribune* and the *New York World*.

Shiras made speeches for Garfield in country schoolhouses, while House used his family's money to support local Democratic organizations. Garfield won in one of the closest elections in history but was assassinated only one hundred days into his term.

Shiras and House both pledged the Alpha Delta Phi fraternity and lived in its house with a living room, lodge room, library and bedrooms. At elite universities, it was an era of clubs, secret societies, and fraternities—the type of social organizations in which a young man made connections that would pay benefits later in life.

Looking back on his school days Shiras wrote, "While I believe it is quite true that the social life within the chapter detracted somewhat from the quality of work within the classroom, yet all learning is not to be found within the textbooks."

House went on to a stellar career, becoming head of the Democratic

Party in Texas and later a confidant of President Woodrow Wilson. He championed the League of Nations and acted as the chief US negotiator at Versailles at the end of the Great War.

The fraternity also brought about Shiras's first meeting with Theodore Roosevelt in 1879, when both attended a general convention of the Alpha Delta Phi fraternity in Rochester. Shiras didn't recall the event until reminded of it years later by a fraternity brother.

William S. Edwards, who later became speaker of the West Virginia state house, and Shiras were the two delegates from Cornell. Roosevelt represented Harvard, whose chapter had a reputation—at least in previous years—of being too exclusive and not showing "the proper fraternal spirit towards the members of smaller colleges." In other words, the Harvard boys were stuck up.

There was a motion on the floor to withdraw the Harvard chapter. The two Cornell delegates had been instructed by fellow fraternity members back home to support it. During the debate, Roosevelt declared that current members were being punished for the offenses of previous classes. "It was not a square deal," TR said, using a phrase that emerged later during his presidency when he promised Americans "a square deal" in regard to control of corporations and the promotion of labor rights.

Shiras asked permission to interrogate Roosevelt to assure himself as to the Harvard chapter's good intentions going forward. After hearing Roosevelt's responses, Shiras indicated that he would not vote for expulsion. This apparently swayed the others in the room to change their own votes.

Afterward, Roosevelt thanked Shiras for his sense of justice.

At Cornell, Shiras was a good but not great student, partly because he had discovered duck hunting. Although he had shot many deer and wild pigeons in Michigan, there were not that many ducks in the central Upper Peninsula because the birds avoided the widest part of Lake Superior in their migrations and went across the narrower western and eastern arms of the lake.

Cayuga Lake (one of New York's Finger Lakes), however, was excellent habitat for lesser scaup, canvasbacks, goldeneye, redhead, and black ducks. Typical of the country at that time, there was no closed season in New York and shooting extended well into the winter months.

One weekend, Shiras and friends planned to shoot ducks from the edge of the ice.

The friends arrived early at a cabin at the southern end of the lake near the town of Dryden. After nightfall, Shiras left town by himself with gear, food, and gun, walked up the railroad tracks on the eastern shore, and then looked across the lake to where his friends had set out a signal lantern.

He started across the ice. In this narrow spot, it should have extended to the other side. "The night was dark, and I could not even see the hills against the sky. When I had gone about halfway across, a great flapping of wings and loud quacking of ducks startled me. Less than ten yards in front of me was open water. Had this water not contained some black ducks, I should have plunged in and loaded down with ammunition gone to the bottom."

It was a perilous moment, and it did not end immediately. He tried to retrace his steps to the eastern shore, but there was no lantern for a guide. Fortunately, it started to snow and the dusting on the bare, black ice showed up in the dark and allowed him to differentiate between ice and open water. He took the land route to the cabin instead. The next day, he refused to shoot any black ducks because they might be the birds that warned him of what likely would have been certain death.

At Cayuga Lake, Shiras got a close look at market hunting of ducks. In Ithaca, he often encountered an "old trapper peddling a basketful of dressed ducks whose plumpness would appeal to most housewives."

The ducks were goldeneye, which tend to be solitary, wary birds. Yet each week the man had a large number for sale. Shiras inquired how he did it. The market hunter explained he would carefully row around the edge of the lake, finding a single goldeneye feeding in the shallows on crayfish. When the duck dove, the trapper beached the boat, ran along the shore perhaps for fifty yards, and waited for it to surface. He would kill it on the water or when it took wing. Shiras followed along and saw the man take several birds this way. When other species were numerous—typically during fall and spring migrations—the hunter simply blasted into flocks and brought down dozens.

What Shiras then thought of such slaughter and the lack of state and federal game laws isn't known. A paper he wrote his senior year is revealing, considering his later work on the Migratory Bird Treaty Act, which called for the national government to take jurisdiction over animals moving between state borders.

His professor politely panned the paper "The Origins and Objects of the United States Constitution." Years later, Shiras the attorney agreed with the assessment, but he saw a couple of prescient paragraphs. The Constitution, he wrote, "is not an iron band upon the body corporate and constrictive of future growth, but like the bark of the tree, it expands to meet new and unforeseen necessities. . . . It is not always necessary to amend the Constitution when some additional powers are needed, but can come by judicial interpretation or by acts of Congress."

Even as a young man, Shiras was not a strict constitutionalist and was willing to interpret the document to pursue matters not strictly spelled out.

He graduated in 1881 and might have garnered cum laude honors had he devoted more time to study. Yet he had no regrets about his hunting trips on Cayuga Lake. "I have always felt that these outings contributed greatly to my good health and they gave me an impetus to take that interest in wild life which was to be so intensified in future years."

Determined to be a more serious student, Shiras entered Yale that fall to study law, but "the Long Island Sound with its winter duck shooting proved a temptation to which I frequently yielded."

He rented a room at a boarding house near the mouth of the East Haven River where he was the only tenant in the winter months. He purchased a Barnegat sneak boat. Made for waterfowl hunters and trappers working the marshes, the cedar boat sat low in the water and could be rowed or poled in as little as four inches of water. The low railing stuffed with tree branches, reeds, and other natural camouflage turned the boat into a floating blind—thus the designation "sneak."

Shiras's landlord took one look and named it *Certain Death*. However, the boat was quite seaworthy with a sail, centerboard, and cockpit. One night during a violent storm, when Shiras had to land ten miles down the shore and take a buckboard back to New Haven, he found the landlord hitching up his horse, about to ride up to the college and break the news that the young man from Pennsylvania had drowned in the sound.

The only real danger came one bright winter afternoon. He rowed out to large exposed boulders known as the cow and calf, dropped his wooden duck decoys, and concealed the sneak boat behind the rocks. Some time later, he heard a ping next to one of the decoys and almost immediately the crack of a rifle on shore. Obviously, someone with a "repeater" rifle was on shore firing at his decoys. Amused, Shiras felt safe behind the rocks but changed his mind when a bullet ricocheted off a decoy and landed at his feet. When the shooter paused to reload, he stood up, waved his hat, and fired both barrels of his shotgun. The shooter, realizing his mistake, fled into the woods.

After college, he shipped the boat by rail to Michigan and hauled it out to Whitefish Lake where, after many years of use on the water, it ended up in the middle of the camp garden filled with soil and flowers.

At Yale, his most intellectually stimulating activity was not the classroom but mock trials put on by the Kent Club, where he practiced debating and legal argument. The exercises focused on questions of national interest and issues of the day.

In the run-up to the 1884 presidential election in which Democrat Grover Cleveland narrowly defeated James Blaine, the issue was protective tariffs. In this period before income tax, tariffs on imported goods provided for the national treasury. While tariffs kept prices on domestic goods artificially high, they also protected domestic agriculture and industry against foreign competition. Democrats saw tariffs as a tax on consumers, while Republicans considered tariffs a necessary protective measure for business.

Shiras, a Republican, found himself in the minority of the Kent Club. At least two-thirds were "free traders," which Shiras believed was due to the influence of a popular and emphatic economics professor on campus. Because Shiras came from Pittsburgh, his support of tariffs was seen as "a selfish local interest to subject the entire country to a policy that particularly benefited the industrial centers."

He argued, however, that small manufacturers—such as New England textile mills—required tariffs to stay in business. To sway his detractors, he arranged for club members to tour the nearby Willimantic Thread Mills. The wealthy young students interacted with laborers and townspeople and a few came away with a different attitude. Shiras wrote his final thesis on "The Legality and Benefits of the Protective Tariff." It was a subject that interested him for the rest of his life.

In his senior year, he was unanimously nominated and elected president of the Kent Club but astonished his classmates by declining the office. He explained he would rather debate than become an administrator whose main charge was to introduce faculty and distinguished jurists addressing the club.

Shiras finished sixth in a class of forty but missed cum laude again because every Saturday he skipped the recitation in criminal law and went duck hunting or hiking. When other students found Saturday diversions, too, the professor took roll and factored attendance into grading.

A classmate chided him for missing the honor, but Shiras reasoned, "The result for me was not a happy one, but I told my protesting friend that he should not overlook the pleasure and exercise I had on my hunting trips or how grateful some of the men on the honor roll should be because I cut Saturday classes."

Thirty-five years later, he and Theodore Roosevelt received honorary degrees from nearby Trinity College for their work as conservationists. Shiras reflected, "While I perhaps lost a possible honor as a student by reason of my devotion to the study of game, the loss was more than compensated for by the gain of a later degree in recognition of the persistence with which I had pursued it."

In June 1883, he took the examination and was admitted to the Bar of Allegheny County and then, after spending the summer in Marquette, he went into the practice with George Jr. and Charles C. Dickey, his father's partner. Shiras and Dickey was a well-established and busy firm in downtown Pittsburgh, handling both corporate and private clients. Brother Winfield joined the firm a year later.

During the latter part of his school years and those summers in Michigan, George had taken notice of Frances or "Fanny" White, the daughter of Peter White. Fanny was two years younger than George and the two had known one another since childhood.

They married October 31, 1885, in St. Paul's Cathedral in Marquette. The well-heeled, good-looking young man from Pittsburgh marrying the daughter of the richest man in town—it seemed fitting, within one's social class. Apparently, it was a good match, too, for the pair remained married for nearly fifty years.

The *Marquette Mining Journal* covered the wedding as a news event: "There is no name more conspicuously and honorably associated with the history of the iron region than the bride's father and George Shiras Jr., the father of the bride groom is the most prominent member of the Pittsburg bar. The high standing of the parents and the popularity of the contracting parties made this the most notable social event which has occurred here for several years."

The *Milwaukee Sentinel Journal,* under the headline "Brilliant Nuptials," gave details of the reception held at Peter White's mansion on Ridge Street, "which was crowded with the elite of the county." More than two hundred presents filled the billiard and adjoining rooms.

The *Detroit Journal* said the presents were "handsome and very costly." White presented the couple with $10,000 in bonds and round-trip tickets to Europe and a winter's sojourn in the south of France. George Shiras Sr. gave a check for $1,000, and the bride's mother presented Fanny with a diamond necklace. The groom received a matching diamond brooch. Best man Winfield gave a gold loving cup from which the young couple drank and pledged their love.

The young couple boarded the train to Chicago and then on to New York. On November 7, they set sail for Liverpool. They crossed in just eight days, wintered in southern France, and came home to Pittsburgh, where George was an up-and-coming young lawyer and a new face in the Republican Party in the steel region.

5 | CAMERA HUNTING

MANY YEARS AFTER he gave up jacklighting deer, Shiras recalled those night hunts with fondness and detail:

> There was a keen enjoyment derived from paddling on the winding streams and along the well wooded shore and bays of some inland lakes where in the quietness of the night every sound was audible and one might recognize the different animals before they came into the circle of light . . . the crooning of the porcupine, the chirping of the cricket, the croaking of the frog, or the soft flutter of an owl circling on wings of velvet. When a muskrat jumped off a log or a pickerel in the shallow water darted against the side of the boat, one gave an involuntary start at sounds magnified by the high tension of the watcher.

He longed for Whitefish Lake when he was living in the city of Allegheny—what is now the north side of Pittsburgh (at the time it was spelled "Pittsburg"). Each day, he took a streetcar or cab livery into the downtown offices of Shiras and Dickey. Some mornings, factory smoke, coal soot from home heating, and dust and smog hung so low in the streets that the miasma engulfed the telegraph lines. Horses and streetcars a block away disappeared into a mist of nitrous oxide, particulates, zinc, and hydrocarbons. Summer heat formed temperature inversions over the city and capped pollution in place for days until relief arrived with fresh winds. George typically brought an extra white shirt to work and changed midafternoon, when the soot settling through his downtown office windows turned collars gray.

George was a busy attorney, a married man, and a father.

The times he could make it out to the woods or water were rare. As he remembered it, "The call of the wild became intensified by the confinement and exactions of city life."

Two years after his marriage, he was approached by William S. Edwards, his fraternity pal from Cornell and then a politician in Charleston, West Virginia, to form a hunting and fishing club near Cheat Mountain, one of the highest and most remote territories in West Virginia. Shaver's Fork, a tributary of the Cheat River, ran through the property and had an outstanding native brook trout fishery. It still does today. About one hundred sportsmen—mainly wealthy men from the business and political communities in Pittsburgh—joined as founding members of the Cheat Mountain Sportsmen Association. The club took out a fifty-year lease on sixty-four thousand acres, much of it still in virgin timber and containing trenches and fortifications dug by soldiers during the Civil War.

In breathless hyperbole, the *Pittsburg Press* called it "The Largest Hunting Grounds in the World." It was not, but there were good numbers of deer, bear, and turkey in the woods, which today are part of the Monongahela National Forest.

The reporter added, "It seems to have been preserved as a happy hunting ground where all the cares of life can be forgotten and the only disagreeable thought be the pity for the unfortunate beings left behind in the shuffle of business."

The association immediately erected a clubhouse and built a fish hatchery. Colonel William M. Kennedy, Shiras's uncle and his mother's brother, served as its first president. George was on the board of directors along with Stephen B. Elkins, an industrialist in coal and a US senator from the state.

In 1888, according to *Sporting Life* magazine, "The Cheat Mountain Association is flourishing and in good shape financially."

A few hours by train, the club offered a getaway, but his time in Northern Michigan was limited to summer vacations and perhaps a brief hunt in the fall. Fanny typically extended her stays, living for weeks with her father and mother, especially when awaiting the birth of their children. Both a daughter and a son were delivered in Marquette.

At Whitefish Lake, deer hunting in the off-season and fire hunting were no longer acceptable, falling to evolving game laws and new ethics of sportsmanship.

During his visits, George always saw deer at the slough.

"On seeing the wild animals in the woods and about the waters, I missed the thrill of my shooting days. To paddle within range or cautiously approach some clearing and then see an animal slink away became monotonous for I was accustomed to keener and more exciting sport."

He had, however, a new hobby—photography, which would not become popular with the masses for a few more years until George Eastman invented roll film and the convenient, handheld Kodak camera: "You press the button, we do the rest."

In 1886, his first child, Ellen Kennedy Shiras, was born in Marquette. That same year, he took to Whitefish Lake a five-by-seven landscape camera with a single lens and a slow film plate, so slow that to make a proper exposure—to let in enough light to make an image—he had to remove the lens cap for a few seconds. There was no shutter.

Like many photographers of the period, he had captured images of family and friends in which people posed stiffly to keep still during the exposure. The camera required a tripod or secure station to eliminate camera shake. Focusing obliged the photographer to peer through ground glass at the back of the camera and then remove the glass in order to insert a film plate for the exposure. It was a simple but clumsy mechanism.

Still, the small aperture of the diaphragm in the lens allowed for deep depth of field. A landscape, a person or anything else motionless long enough to be photographed came out well defined and sharply focused.

In early July, Shiras and Jake Brown mounted the camera on the front of a hunting skiff, a craft akin to the sneak boat. They placed green boughs in the front to shield the camera. Shiras sat in the bow. In the stern, Brown paddled and aimed the boat and the camera by swinging the bow from side to side.

That first morning on the lake, they snuck up on a young buck whose snout was deep in shallow water ripping away fresh shoots of duckweed. The deer didn't see the camouflaged boat approaching.

The men got within forty feet before bottoming out on a sunken log. Shiras removed and replaced the cap. The deer ran a short distance, stopped, and then looked back in a classic over-the-shoulder pose. Shiras had time for another exposure, but when he pulled out the plate holder and reversed it, he failed to cover the exposed plate. Then just as he made the next exposure, the deer leaped and bounded out of the frame. As a result, he failed to take the second exposure and ruined the first. This first attempt at "camera hunting" was a self-described case of buck fever.

Later, they spied a doe in the slough. They got close enough for an exposure, but as Shiras removed the lens cap, the deer ran away. When he developed the plate, the image showed a faint outline of the doe and then a blurred streak.

Many years later, Shiras wryly noted, "It seems odd now that in the beginning I had selected as an object for the first camera hunts, the most cunning and elusive of the deer family instead of trying an easier subject like a porcupine or a squirrel or some of the many semi-tame birds nesting in the clearing about my camp. Of course, the explanation lay in the fact that I simply wanted to hunt deer and the camera gave me the means of gratifying this desire."

There were no deer images that season, and Shiras realized he needed another "outfit." A landscape camera just wouldn't do.

Back in Pittsburgh, Shiras spoke to a friend who owned a Schmid Detective Camera, the first commercially produced handheld camera. Patented in 1883 by William Schmid of Brooklyn, the camera had a reflex viewfinder. Users held it at the waist and looked down into the glass to center the image. It was a box camera—wooden, of course—but it enclosed the plate holders, shutter, and lens in a rugged, water-resistant box.

The shutter could fire at 1/25 of a second—fast enough to image a person standing at attention but slow enough to absorb the low light of early morning and late evening when the deer came to the lake to drink and feed.

"Had I not possessed a good lens and one of the first hand cameras made in this country, it is likely the pastime would have lost an ardent advocate," Shiras recalled.

The following season in Michigan, in 1887, using his Schmid camera, he and Jake Brown captured his first pictures of deer, but the animals usually were distant in the image. The lens had a short focal length, and Shiras had to get within twenty-five feet to fill the frame with his subject. More often than not when he got close, the deer ran away before he could trip the shutter.

In summer of 1891, he took a fine picture of a buck from the skiff and then shot it with a rifle as it ran away, badly wounding the animal with an ill-placed bullet. It took half a day to follow the blood trail and find the deer—still alive.

After they put it out of its misery, Jake remarked sardonically that from then on it would be better to dispatch the deer with a rifle and then photograph it.

Shiras added, "In those days the idea of using a camera instead of a gun did not take very well with most guides, who naturally thought in hunting big game there should be something [more] substantial to show than an image of what, in the flesh, represented a fine stew or roast."

Shiras, too, was chagrined about so badly wounding the deer. Later when he was writing in sporting publications and advocating the use of the camera rather than the gun, he quipped, "an awkwardly handled camera leaves no wounded animal."

Deer were hard to approach by boat in daytime, so Shiras built a blind of branches and boughs near a game trail on the Laughing Whitefish River. For hours, he sat with his camera waiting for an animal to pass by. But the deer often caught his scent and kept their distance. They came close enough, he noted, to be shot by a gun but too far away for a camera.

A camera hunter had to get close. The solution, he decided, was to put distance between the operator and the camera. The shutter release could be triggered by the pull of a string. After some experimentation, he attached a fine thread and then a strong string. He mounted the camera on a platform in the slough just a few yards from the shore and then ran the thread and string across the narrow neck of the lake through eyehooks screwed into trees and tall stakes driven into the lake bottom. The distance was nearly eighty yards, and it took trial and error to get it right, but eventually he was able to gather up the slack and give a sharp tug to snap the shutter.

Multiple camera traps for daylight shooting. Courtesy of the John Hammer family.

Brown and Shiras camouflaged the camera and platform with boughs of pine and then built a tight little blind for George where he sat observing, pestered by daytime mosquitoes and buzzing gnats. It took hours, even days, of patience to get a single shot and, each time the shutter released, the plate would have to be changed.

As he described it, the process was tedious but ultimately successful: "Whenever a deer passed in front of the camera, a sharp whistle by the operator would cause it to stop; then a steady pull on the cord released the shutter. The sport proved most interesting and exciting for the deer could not see, hear or scent the photographer. The approach of the deer to the focus point of the camera gave all the tenseness of feeling provided by hunting with a rifle, but the cord was pulled instead of the trigger."

He was camera hunting.

By the 1890s when the camp had been remodeled into a cabin of several rooms, George was regularly emerging from the new darkroom—he called it a laboratory—with images of deer on his photographic plates. Because of the wide-angle nature of the lens, the animals were still small in the frame, sometimes a bit hard to pick out against the background foliage, but they were in their element—feeding, looking about, and moving naturally.

Deer weren't his only subjects. In July 1892 while he was in his blind, he noticed a flock of cedar waxwing swooping back and forth over the slough, evidently in pursuit of insects. He waded out and set the camera on a tripod in about two feet of water. He drove a sapling with bare branches into the lake bottom, hoping the birds would use it as a perch. Minutes after he retreated to the blind, the birds lighted on the sapling and camera itself. He had preset the focus, opened the aperture to blur the background and captured a remarkable image he called "Three Sitters."

The photography required technical expertise, but just as important was understanding the habits of the animals and setting the camera in a place where they would pass by or linger. He was a good observer, curious about

Cedar waxwings at Whitefish Lake, 1892.
Courtesy of Northern Michigan University.

all types of wildlife, and noted their movements and inclinations for particular locations and food sources. Back home in Pittsburgh, he had accumulated a large private library of hunting and game books and works of
natural history.

A game trail was a natural thoroughfare, but George had gotten his best
pictures in early summer when whitetails came to the lake's edge to eat
aquatic plants or escape the blackflies in the woods. Out on the shoreline,
deer were strongly illuminated by direct sunlight.

In the following seasons, he purchased more equipment and set up a
bank of cameras along the slough, each with its own string running back
to the blind. As the deer passed along, he fired the various shutters.

Those hours in the blind, however, could be monotonous.

In June 1891, Shiras came up with what he called the "camera set" or
"camera trap," one of his most important, original inventions in game photography. He may have gotten the idea from a device known as a set gun,
which shot a small-caliber bullet into the head of a beaver or mink after it
pulled on a baited string.

He fashioned a trip wire, running a black silk thread between a camera
and a stake, tree, log, or rock—whatever presented itself to the situation. A
passing animal could take its own picture. There was much experimentation about where to place the camera and trip wires. Natural objects—a
mud hole, rocks, a narrow opening on a trail, or a pile of driftwood—could
lure or detour an animal into the trap.

When he set the trip thread high, the deer felt it against their breasts
and forelegs and retreated from the pressure. When he ran the thread just
a few inches above the ground, they literally walked into it. Sometimes, he
threw down a handful of salt on the beach and ran a thread just above. The
deer licked and pawed at the pile, eventually tripping the string.

He also captured images of other animals.

He baited the traps and found that raccoons, opossums, skunks, muskrats, woodchucks, rabbits, and squirrels would all come to smelly hunks of
fish, carrots, or other bait, regardless of human scent or the presence of a
poorly concealed camera. Bear, foxes, wolves, and deer were more wary
and required, in Shiras's words, "the cautious methods of a trapper who
erects a deadfall or sets a steel trap."

Natural light photography had its limits. Deer were not very active in daylight hours, and unless the sun was bright, the negative might under-expose—due to a passing cloud, shifting light, or the broken shadows from foliage.

"After an unsuccessful day either because of cloudy weather or an inability to locate any deer, I often felt how unfortunate it was that I could not go out after dark and take pictures of deer with the aid of a jacklight with the same ease I formerly got their carcasses."

In the summer of 1892, he arrived at camp from Pittsburgh and told Jake Brown that he wanted to go out that night with a camera and jacklight to see if they could sneak up on deer. Although the jacklight—a kerosene lantern with a parabolic reflector—was an improvement over a skillet of flaming wood chips and pine pitch, it did not throw enough light for a photographic exposure.

Shiras had to ignite flash powder, a mixture of magnesium and potassium chlorate set off with a match or a spark from a flint. Held in a pan or a tray, the dry chemicals produced a brief brilliant light, white smoke, and a bit of ash.

Such pyrotechnics involving magnesium powder or thin ribbons of the metal had been in use by photographers since the mid-nineteenth century. Vacuum flashbulbs sparked with electric current wouldn't be perfected until the 1930s. Flash powder was an inexact technology and dangerous—especially indoors. The explosions and intense light frightened people sitting for photographs. Rooms filled with smoke. Furnishings and ceilings sometimes caught fire. Photographers had been burned, even killed.

Eventually, George Shiras 3d became a master at using flashlights, but this first time in the woods, he knew little and had to improvise. He took a tin plate from camp, punched a hole in the middle, and threaded in a strip of oily paper to serve as a fuse. He poured a layer of magnesium powder into the tin. If the Schmid Detective Camera could be considered a precision machine, the flashlight was a crude affair.

In July 1892 on a night of the new moon, they mounted the camera on the skiff and pushed off. Being back on the lake in the blackness seeking prey brought on the old anticipation, which he described in an article for the *New York Independent* newspaper.

The canoe pushes out in the silent waters of the lake or river. The paddle sends the slight boat ahead so easily that no sound is heard except a gentle ripple, not noticeable a boat's length away. The wooded banks are wrapped in deepest shadow, only the sky line along the cresting showing their course. . . . At the bow of the boat, the bright eye of the jacklight is turning from side to side, cutting a tunnel of light through the mass of darkness, showing as it sweeps the banks, the trunks of trees and tracery of foliage with wonderful distinctiveness.

In the bright beam of the jacklight, Jake and George soon located a deer and snuck toward shore. They got within photographic range, but just as the fuse began burning, the deer snorted, bolted, and was gone. The powder went up in a blast, but George never tripped the shutter.

While Jake guffawed, Shiras prepared another charge. Within the hour, they came upon a doe. George lit the fuse and pulled the shutter: "A white wave of light breaks out from the bow of the boat—deer, hills, trees—everything stands out for an instant in the white glare of noon day. A dull report and then a veil of inky darkness descends."

When he developed the plate back at the cabin, he experienced a fusion of excitement and disappointment. The deer appeared decapitated. Its body was clear but the head blurred because it moved during the exposure.

Images made in the following weeks were blurred, underexposed, and muddy. The shutter speed was too slow, the shutter and flash not in synchronization (one went off before the other), and the powder inadequate to light such a big space. He experimented with different amounts of powder and noted that in just two days, he shot fourteen flashlights—all to poor effect.

The answer again lay back in Pittsburgh. That winter Shiras learned of a flashlight apparatus designed for lighting up large interiors: ballrooms, theaters and, in his mind, the open woods. It consisted of a candelabra of alcohol lamps in which the operator squeezed a pneumatic rubber ball or blew through a tube to send a stream of magnesium powder over the open flames of the alcohol lamps to create instant, complete ignition.

At Whitefish Lake, George opened the jars of alcohol and sealed tins of magnesium powder and assembled his flashlight. Jake readied the boat and they set off. Coming along the shore of the lake, the boat grounded on a half-submerged rock. They stepped out into the water and portaged over the obstruction.

As they approached a deer, George dimmed the jacklight, lit his alcohol lamps, and got ready to fire the camera and spray the powder. The deer, however, moved to one side. When George turned his head to whisper instructions to Jake, his elbow caught on the rubber tubing for the lamps and toppled the apparatus into the skiff. The magnesium powder scattered and alcohol splashed over the bow and onto Shiras's boots and pants. The open flames ignited the whole mess and the flash powder went up in a "tremendous explosion." The skiff and George were on fire, and he tumbled into the lake to extinguish himself and then bailed with his hat to slosh water into the boat and put out the fire.

Fortunately, his boots were damp from the portage and he had his face turned away when the powder exploded. Once Brown determined the boss was unharmed, the guide "gave vent to unrestrained mirth. Standing waist deep in the slowly moving current, my hands smarting from the touch of the flames and the little camera floating about in the murky water. I was in no mood to appreciate the humor of the situation."

Shiras found the jacklight still lit and focused it on Jake. When Brown kept up his laughing, even slamming the boat oar on the water in emphasis, Shiras seized the front of the boat, lifted the bow and dumped his assistant into Whitefish Lake.

They both had a good laugh and Jake remarked how surprised the deer must have been "when the moon blew up." They found the camera soaked and beached on a nearby sand bar.

Shiras noted in his "Camera-Game Diary" that the "new flashlight blew up tonight and caused quite the amusement."

No one got hurt, but it was clear Shiras needed to be careful with such volatile mixtures and equipment. Other photographers found the alcohol-and-magnesium contraption a danger as well, and it soon went out of favor.

During the succeeding months back in Pittsburgh, George experimented with Blitz Pulver, a powder combination of magnesium and potassium chlorate manufactured in Germany. Blitz Pulver generated strong light but little smoke and was somewhat less volatile than pure magnesium.

To fire Blitz Pulver instantly and safely, he fashioned a "pistol flashlight" out of a tin pillbox—one inch deep, seven inches long, and four inches wide. He put a bedplate of iron under the box and added a trigger device with a spring. Pulling the trigger released the spring that set off a blank pistol cartridge, which in turn ignited a half-ounce of powder poured into the tin. "This contrivance when tested showed it could be fired with the quickness and certainty of a pistol, the strong metal bedplate protecting the hand when the mechanism was aloft."

Later, he made other improvements, including a lid that sprung up upon explosion, functioning as "both a reflector for the flash and as a shield for the operator when fired in the hand."

He took out a patent on the device with some idea to produce it commercially. According to the patent, the portable flashlight could be whipped from the pocket, held aloft, and fired in a few seconds "in alleys, interiors, cellars, garrets, warehouses, and vehicles—anywhere for the most difficult and dangerous detective work." It could also work as a camera trap. A flashlight and camera mounted on a support with a trip thread "could be exploded involuntarily by any person passing within a given distance of the apparatus, thus making possible important photographic results without either fatigue or danger of detection to the photographer."

Shiras never produced the device commercially, nor did anyone else. It's not likely any detectives adopted his camera trap, but the patent proves he had created a portable flashlight mechanism when many photographers were still blowing magnesium powder into the flames of alcohol lamps.

In 1893, when Jake Brown was unavailable as a guide, Shiras hired John Hammer, a Norwegian immigrant living in Marquette. Hammer had been a machinist at an optical works in the old country. He sometimes served as a guide and carpenter for Peter White. He was especially good at handling boats, rowing, and mechanical tinkering.

Shiras told Hammer he was to be a "flashlight guide," and thus began a partnership that lasted for the rest of George's life. Over the following forty years, Hammer aided Shiras in his photography, took field trips to different parts of North America, and became caretaker at Whitefish Lake and Shiras's winter home in Florida. To a degree, the men collaborated in innovations in game photography. Hammer, the machinist and inventor, improved upon the early flashlight and triggering mechanisms. With Shiras's help, Hammer took out patents on his inventions, but like the early pistol

Pistol flashlight patented in 1892 by George Shiras 3d.
Courtesy of the John Hammer family.

flashlight, the apparatuses were largely impractical for the general photographer. They were clever but complicated—and always dangerous because of exploding flash powder. Nor was there a market for such inventions. Until the development and convenience of the flashbulb, few people were interested in night photography.

The men became friends and companions in the field, but the class distinctions between them remained strong. Always Hammer was in the employment of the Shiras and the White families. In a 1903 entry from the camp journal at Whitefish Lake when Shiras was serving in the US House of Representatives, Peter White referred to John Hammer as "the congressman's 'Man Friday'"—a literary reference to the faithful and competent servant in *Robinson Crusoe*. In his own writings, Shiras always referred to Hammer as "my guide" or "my assistant."

Success for Shiras the nighttime game photographer came that summer not far from Old Jack's Landing, where the Shiras boys had first shot deer while fire hunting. The coincidence was not lost on the photographer. Hammer navigated the boat up on a yearling buck standing in the water, and Shiras leaned forward in the bow and fired the camera and flashlight pistol in synchronicity.

He had not learned to close one eye before setting off the explosion of light; several seconds passed before the men could see. They heard the buck bolting away through the woods. Back at camp developing the plate, Shiras watched the image of the deer emerge in the center of the plate, standing in a raft of floating duckweed. Against a deep, black background, the animal stood out sharply focused, beautifully illuminated.

He had his first flashlight image.

Through the 1890s, he and Hammer refined their techniques. Shiras designed a table to swivel the cameras left or right if the deer moved at the last minute. Determining exposures remained tricky. Photoelectric light meters were decades away. For daylight shooting, tables and calculators provided rules of thumb—a set shutter speed and diaphragm opening (F-stop). But night shooting required hit-and-miss testing. There's evidence of flashlight experiments, placing objects or himself and Hammer at different distances to determine focus and proper exposure. In his camera traps, he also employed redundancy, placing several cameras side by side and varying the settings of each instrument.

A well-composed, properly exposed image was the result of days or even weeks of work. Exposures were made on dry plates—four-by-five-inch pieces of glass coated at the factory with gelatin emulsion. The cameras were primitive yet elegantly simple, constructed of hardwood, brass fittings, and leather. Shiras owned a number of Poco Folding cameras made by the Rochester Camera Manufacturing Company in Upstate New York. The pleated bellows and lens tucked neatly away, convenient for traveling and storing on the boat. He owned a rare Ascot view camera manufactured in 1899 and 1900 by E. H. & T. Anthony, also of Rochester. The view cameras on the front of the skiff were mounted inside handmade wooden boxes, the lenses recessed a few inches to protect the optics from weather.

For some night shots, George employed a stereoscopic camera, probably a Verascope, which had two lenses about three inches apart. When processed in the darkroom, the plate preserved nearly identical but slightly offset side-by-side images. Stereoscopic photography was popular at the turn of the century. The printed images, when viewed through a stereoscope, simulated a three-dimensional effect.

Deer image from the *Midnight Series*. Courtesy of Northern Michigan University.

Shiras (front) and John Hammer running exposure tests at Whitefish Lake.
Courtesy of the John Hammer family.

Folding cameras used on bow of skiff at Whitefish Lake. Courtesy of the John Hammer family.

When he was running out of glass plates in the field, Shiras could cap one lens of the stereoscopic camera and expose just half the plate. Then he could reverse the process to expose the other half—thus getting two different images.

All his cameras got hard use. They fell overboard, were scorched by flashlights, and were ripped from pedestals by fleeing animals. The boxes, bellows, and film holders replaced easily. The real value and precision of the instruments resided in the lenses that contained built-in diaphragm (leaf) shutters. Focal-plane shutters—the shutter mechanism was placed at the point of focus just in front of the plate or film—came into use much later.

Poco Folding cameras typically contained a Bausch & Lomb lens equipped with the company's patented Unicum shutter. Introduced in 1897, the Unicum leaf shutter could shoot from 1/2 to 1/100 of second with a B (bulb) setting for a time exposure. Connected to a squeeze bulb, a piston activated a spring to open the leaves. Another piston served as a governor, releasing air to produce the various speed settings. Accuracy of leaf shutters varied with temperature, humidity, altitude, and wear. However, in these early days of photography, dry plates were not especially light

Bausch & Lomb Unicum leaf shutter, 1897. Courtesy of the John Hammer family.

sensitive, and a slight under- or overexposure could be compensated for in the developing laboratory.

Shiras also owned a Goerz Dagor lens that in bright light stopped down to F-128, a very small diaphragm opening that delivered extreme depth of field or deep focus. Although lenses were uncoated during that period—and susceptible to reflections and flares of light—the images could be extraordinarily sharp and detailed. The large size of the glass plate, too, allowed for high-resolution enlargements. The images of animals coming from Shiras's laboratory in the woods were remarkably beautiful, detailed, and uncommon. No one else was doing this type of work.

In the early 1890s, Shiras began writing about camera hunting, hoping other sportsmen would find photography as thrilling as shooting.

His first article and recognition as a camera hunter came in *Forest and Stream* magazine in September 1892, when he entered several daytime pictures in the magazine's amateur photography competition.

Forest and Stream was a highly influential magazine with a mission to "studiously promote a healthful interest in outdoor recreation, and to cultivate a refined taste for natural objects."

George Bird Grinnell, a historian, anthropologist, and naturalist, edited the magazine from 1876 until 1911. He lived an extraordinary life and played an important role in the early conservation movement. After graduating from Yale, Grinnell accompanied General George Custer on his military incursion into the Black Hills. Fortunately, he declined a later opportunity to go on the expedition that resulted in Custer's death at the Little Big Horn. Grinnell experienced wild country and indigenous people before whites penetrated the remaining wilderness. He worked to save the American bison from extinction and pushed for the creation of Yellowstone National Park. He organized the first Audubon Society to protect birds.

Prior to peer-reviewed scientific journals, *Forest and Stream* acted as conduit of communication between naturalists and conservationists, making them aware of one another's work in the field. Frank Chapman, an ornithologist who eventually headed up what was then known as the Department of Birds at the American Museum of Natural History in New York, read it from cover to cover every month. Both Chapman and Grinnell, who later became close friends with Shiras, first learned of his game photography from *Forest and Stream*.

The contest offered prizes for images of game and fish (dead or alive), camp life, shooting, and fishing. The three judges were illustrator Thomas Wilmot; Edward Bierstadt, a well-known sportsman; and Theodore Roosevelt. At the time, TR was the US Civil Service commissioner, living in Washington and making a name for himself by fighting the corruption of the spoils system.

Just four years earlier, Roosevelt and Grinnell had founded the Boone and Crockett Club, an organization to "encourage manly sport with a rifle, to promote the study of wild animals and assist in encouraging enforcing of existing laws."

Grinnell, Roosevelt, and other sportsmen worried about the decline in game animals. In editorials, Grinnell urged hunters to take up the camera as a way to interact with nature without using a gun, to bring home a trophy without the kill. Shiras, a close reader of *Forest and Stream*, advocated the same.

It was an approach in line with the Boone and Crockett ethic of "fair chase" in which the number of kills was not so important as the skill in which the killing was done. A camera hunter, Shiras understood, had to get closer to the prey than any man armed with a rifle did.

By the time of the contest, he possessed thirty-two images of deer captured at distances from fifteen to one hundred feet. Another one hundred exposed and developed plates proved failures.

The judges chose an image taken on July 1 of that year of a female deer crossing the outlet stream of Whitefish Lake. It was simply titled "Doe" and showed the deer with its head up, looking directly at the camera. Grinnell framed the image in a circle mimicking a gunsight. This image and other Shiras deer pictures were, he wrote, "capital specimens of work done with the camera."

A letter from Shiras served as the accompanying article. In it, he praised Grinnell's efforts to promote camera hunting, and then clearly put himself into a leadership position—"As one of the pioneers of this new sport, it is a pleasure to welcome all the newcomers."

He noted his frustration and many failed attempts and cautioned that "the instantaneous pictures of large game must necessarily be confined to a limited number of very patient sportsmen."

Others, however, could use the camera to take pictures of their kills and catches with the gun and rod for souvenirs after "the flesh pot has been put away and recollections and reminiscences must recall and recount the days gone by."

The publishing of his pictures in *Forest and Stream* capped a successful summer season. One night, George and Hammer pushed the boat into the lake and witnessed a spectacular display of the aurora borealis, which Shiras claimed was as bright as a full moon. Simultaneously a cloud moved overhead flickering with lightning—heat lightning, apparently, for there were no thunderclaps, no possibility of rain. The night being warm and quiet—and momentarily so bright that taking pictures would be impossible—the men floated about mesmerized until the dark returned.

That night, Shiras came across a fine-looking buck with a set of developing antlers: "Although intent on getting the picture, I was at the same time impressed with the beauty of the scene. Between the canoe and animal were hundreds of little white flowers and in the circle of light stood the big stag quartering and looking away. The black background obscured the distant alders and made more distinct and impressive this monarch of the forest."

He captured other images that year: a mother with twin fawns, a whitetail slinking head down as it hears the howl of a nearby wolf, and a doe drinking along the shoreline with its image reflected in the water. Other critters revealed themselves when he developed plates in the laboratory. To his surprise, he photographed a kingfisher perched in a tree and a porcupine walking a log just a few feet from a whitetail.

These black-and-white photographs, high in contrast and awash in deep blacks, were not mere snapshots but elegant images of animals in nature. They were art. Later, he grouped these and other flashlight images into an exhibition and a limited-edition portfolio known as the *Midnight Series*.

In the 1890s, exactly what Shiras was doing out there on Whitefish Lake was largely unknown to the local people. Loggers and settlers in Deerton, many of them Finnish farmers, reported detonations in the woods and otherworldly flashes of light. Market hunters complained that it was difficult to jacklight deer in the region of the Laughing Whitefish River. The animals there were extremely wary.

One summer night—when the last of twilight faded away—Fanny Shiras and her relatives on Ridge Street in Marquette went outside, gathered on

"Hark," from the *Midnight Series*. George Shiras 3d;
Courtesy of National Geographic Creative.

a bluff along the shore, and looked to the southeast across the waters of
Lake Superior and in the direction of Whitefish Lake. At the time, there
were no highways, streetlights, homes, or homesteads with electric lights.
When the day was over, it was dark.

Out on his skiff on Whitefish Lake, George looked at his watch and at
the appointed time fired a flashlight. Twenty miles away in Marquette,
Fanny saw the flash—like a meteor exploding, light rippling into a starry
sky and then fading to blackness.

6 | PENNSYLVANIA POLITICS

IN 1892 PRESIDENT Benjamin Harrison nominated George Shiras Jr. to the US Supreme Court in defiance of the Pennsylvania Republican political machine known as "the Ring." Junior was Republican but had no connection to the Ring. His appointment was the result of strong backing from Pittsburgh industrialists and financiers, including Andrew Carnegie, a member of the Duquesne Club.

Newspapers generally approved of Shiras. The *Muncie Morning News* in Indiana said George Shiras Jr. was "a man of literary attainment and he is a bright and interesting conversationalist and among those who know him, he is considered to be more than ordinarily fitted for the duties which he is soon to assume."

Junior was camping in the Upper Peninsula when he received the telegram that the Senate had confirmed his appointment. He and Lillie moved to Washington, DC, that fall, and he ended his law partnership with Charles C. Dickey. The firm's name remained unchanged because George 3d and Winfield still practiced law.

Despite being appointed a Supreme Court justice by politicians, Junior was not one for politics. His son, however, had a taste for it and soon joined the reformers trying to rid Allegheny County of the Ring.

The late nineteenth century was a period of municipal corruption, machine politics, and strong-arm tactics in city government. Patronage in big cities ensured that office holders, police officials, and city workers were beholden to the machine for their jobs.

The Tweed Organization of New York City was the poster child, but there were problems in many cities. Lincoln Steffens, the muckraking journalist, wrote an influential series of magazine articles published in book form as *The Shame of Cities*. Corruption had an ethnic component—Germans controlled St. Louis, Scandinavians dominated Minneapolis, and the Irish held power in Pittsburgh. The Republican machine of Christopher Magee and William Flinn dominated politics in Allegheny County for twenty-five years.

George 3d, whose feelings about politics came from his father and grandfather, held professional politicians in contempt: "I was thoroughly impressed with the feeling that the average state legislature was an assembly of politicians or men of mediocre ability and that collectively they represented a rather low stratum in public life."

Later, when he came to serve himself, he modified these views. He met legislators from rural towns and counties in Pennsylvania who were farmers, bankers, merchants, and men of standing in their communities. They entered politics not to line their pockets but to benefit constituents and reform a corrupt system.

Shiras was high minded, too, but oddly his foray into politics took the form of a dirty trick. He authored an unsigned pamphlet that "bitterly assailed the reputation and statesmanship" of Matthew S. Quay, the state treasurer.

Until 1913 state legislatures, not the general electorate, chose US senators. In 1887 the Republican Party nominated Quay, who was the state's most powerful political boss with the nickname "the Kingmaker." Reformers such as Shiras were livid. When the legislature assembled in joint session in Harrisburg for the election, an eight-page pamphlet entitled *A Pig Iron State and Pygmy Statesmen* appeared on the desk of every legislator, surreptitiously distributed by Quay's enemies.

The anonymous author called Quay a product of the "ring smitten cities of Philadelphia and Pittsburgh" and accused him of shenanigans using state monies in stock investments. Quay was a "boodle-scarred feline" and "the political Tomcat in our back alleys except when on one unfortunate occasion, he stealthily crept out into Wall Street and lost some of his hair playing with ill-mannered bears." The tone was caustic.

Aside from name-calling, the pamphlet leveled serious charges and created deep resentment among Quay's friends and associates. Legislators pounded their desks and demanded the author be revealed.

Shiras later wrote, "I had as much dislike for anonymous attacks as the most meticulous observer of propriety. . . . It [the pamphlet] was written with no idea that it would affect the election but as a protest against a candidate whom I thought unfit for the position."

Quay went to the Senate anyway, and Shiras eventually admitted authorship to a state senator who was a friend of Quay's. Shiras offered a deal: he would go public and admit authorship when Quay brought against him a libel suit that would allow Shiras and his cohorts to put Quay on the stand for cross-examination. Shiras offered to put up $10,000 in escrow to cover Quay's legal costs. Quay never responded, and Shiras was never revealed as the author.

The affair whetted Shiras's appetite for reform, if not for politics. The *Pig Iron* pamphlet clearly demonstrated he possessed killer instincts for the rough and tumble.

In 1888, after practicing law for four years, Shiras ran as a Republican for the state legislature representing the First District in the city of Allegheny. He was sanguine about what was possible for a young man of smarts, breeding, and family pedigree: "I came to the conclusion, after careful consideration, that it would prove to be an agreeable and instructive experience to serve as a member of the legislature for a term."

He wanted to do serious work on public problems but admitted that familiarity with the legislative process and the personal network he might weave with political and industrial luminaries would benefit his law practice.

Although he was not part of the Ring, Shiras generally was supported by Republicans. He won the election by seventeen hundred votes in a largely Democratic district and served two sessions from 1889 to 1890.

One Democrat complained that Shiras and his friends went to the German wards and pointed out that his great-grandfather had built the first brewery in Pittsburgh. "Then the same campaigners went into the Presbyterian ward at the other end of the district and told how another great-grandfather in 1810 founded the first Presbyterian Church, serving as its pastor for fifty consecutive years. . . . It made it possible to carry a beer bottle one day and a Bible the next."

A few days before he was to leave for Harrisburg, the general passenger agent for the Pennsylvania Railroad in Pittsburgh sent a note: his company was pleased to issue an annual railroad pass for his use. Would he please call and receive it?

In both Harrisburg and Washington, DC, the railroad cast a weighty influence in legislative matters. Issuing free passes to politicians and their families was only one component of the railroad's graft. The president of the Pennsylvania Railroad, Tom Scott, held veto power over important legislation in the state. Indeed, the local expression "Scott free" described legislation that passed through the Pennsylvania legislature without objection from Scott.

All of this, Shiras well knew. He ignored the note and failed to call at the railroad station. On the day of his departure to Harrisburg, however, a registered letter came to his home, addressed to the Hon. George Shiras 3d. Unwittingly, he signed and found the pass inside. He showed the pass to his father, and watched as he "took a pencil and ran a line through the prefix Hon., saying that if I were going to use it, the adjective was inconsistent with my attitude toward my public duties. I returned the pass and soon had the occasion to be glad that I had."

Republican leaders embraced the young man from Pittsburgh, awarding key appointments on the Judiciary Committee and the Banking Committee. Had they been aware of his authorship of the *Pig Iron* pamphlet, he certainly would not have gotten such a welcome.

He proved to be a maverick. In the first session, he went up against the railroads over what appeared to be an innocuous grade-crossing bill subtitled, "A bill to insure public safety by regulating grade crossings in cities of the first and second class." This classification affected only the cities of Pittsburgh and Philadelphia, so it did not interest most legislators. The bill was in its second reading before Shiras examined it closely.

His district was likely to be annexed by Pittsburgh in coming years, and the bill would certainly affect the city of Allegheny, for it would require new railroads seeking entry into these cities to elevate their tracks at municipal boundaries for a distance of ten to fifteen miles so as not to interfere with the existing railroads. The cost of the tracks would be shared between the railroads and the cities. The bill also barred new railroads from building terminals within the central business districts.

Opportunely, all existing railroads—the Pennsylvania, Baltimore and Ohio, and Reading Railroads—were exempt from these regulations.

Shiras wrote, "The measure should have been entitled, 'A bill to prevent the entry of new railroads into cities of the first and second class.' It effectively barred competitive lines in the future."

The lack of competition was likely to drive up shipping costs for producers of flour, feed, and other commodities.

The only member to speak against its passage, Shiras bitterly denounced the bill on the House floor. Other speeches and work behind the scenes by Shiras awakened the business exchanges and chambers of commerce in the cities to the "greatest corporation grab of the session." City councils in both Pittsburgh and Philadelphia came out against the bill and pressured their representatives to vote against it. The railroads fought back, but the bill failed.

John Hood, a member of the Feed and Flour Exchange in Pittsburgh, wrote, "Neither threats directed against his own bills nor specious pleas deterred him [Shiras] from doing his duty in the hour when the public slept and the enemy occupied every post."

Of course, politics and legislative victories are all about point of view. The grade-crossing bill had been written by the big railroads, but it was not unusual for lobbyists and business interests to write bills and put them in the hands of their legislators for passage. Shiras came to Harrisburg with two banking bills desired by the Bank of Pittsburg.

The bills permitted renewal of bank charters and allowed state banks to become national institutions without reorganizing. The bills sailed through his committee (Shiras was its cochair), passed the House, and were sent to the Senate. Shiras expected the bills to pass easily, and he left for a few days and traveled to Marquette for the birth of his son, George Peter Shiras, or George IV.

On his return, he received a bitter lesson in arm-twisting and horse-trading. He was called to the office of Senator John Newmyer, also of Allegheny County, who wondered what became of his own banking bill, which would punish bankers for accepting deposits after their institutions were known to be insolvent.

Shiras replied that his House committee had examined the Newmyer bill but determined it didn't properly define insolvency. In his opinion, the bill was unconstitutional, which is why it died in committee.

The following exchange Shiras recalled in detail:

"Well," remarked the senator gruffly. "I will tell you what is going to happen tomorrow."

"What is that?" I asked serenely.

"At the morning session, you will rise from your place and ask the speaker to refer this bill to the Committee on Banks for further consideration."

"I will do nothing of the kind."

"Oh yes, you will, and I have means of forcing this action. You have two bank bills before the Senate committee of which I am a member and there they will remain until you have my bill referred back to your committee and later reported out favorably."

Shiras tried to be conciliatory and pointed out that two banks would close unless his bills passed. The senator was unmoved.

Shiras had two choices. He could go to the floor and make a speech revealing this blackmail by a well-known senator, or he could silently acquiesce and help his constituents.

He did as he was told, although he found "it most irritating."

Shiras was not always so accommodating. Late in his term, he introduced a measure to impeach J. W. White, a prominent Republican judge in Allegheny County. White had taken bribes to reduce the number of liquor licenses in the county and concentrate the trade for his cronies.

Republican leaders and members of the Ring were aghast; it was bad politics and timing to draw attention to malfeasance when the party was in the midst of a gubernatorial campaign. Just as the impeachment issue came to the floor, Rep. James L. Graham used a parliamentary trick to adjourn the session and silence Shiras.

Shiras's term was over; he was not running for reelection. Except for complaints from the Democratic newspapers, the issue of the corrupt judge would likely fade away.

Shiras took a train to Marquette and spent a few weeks at camp, "glad of the opportunity to free my mind from the worry of the preceding weeks."

He suspected Judge White and Graham had colluded and likely had done so through written correspondence. When he returned to Allegheny, he went to Graham's home and demanded to see the letters. It was a gutsy bluff; he wasn't certain the missives existed. Graham acknowledged the letters but refused to turn them over. Shiras threatened to have Graham and the judge indicted for conspiracy.

"If the letters were surrendered to me, I assured him they would be returned with a promise on my part that this correspondence would not be published until after the Judge's death—if at all," recalled Shiras.

Graham relented. While Shiras made copies, he received a heartfelt letter from White, begging him to drop the matter. Shiras did, but he kept the copies until the end of his life.

Shiras had made a name for himself as a reformer. Young people in the party and politicians not beholden to the machine urged him to run for Congress in the Twenty-Ninth District.

He entered the contest just three weeks before the Republican primaries in 1890. The resulting fight for the nomination colored his attitude toward corruption the rest of his life.

His opponent was Colonel Thomas M. Bayne, who had served in the US House for twelve years. Another colonel, this one named William A. Stone, a US district attorney, also wanted the nomination. (In this period after the Civil War, there were many middle-aged men still using their military titles, including some of Shiras's own relatives. Theodore Roosevelt embraced his title from the Spanish-American War and preferred that his friends call him "the Colonel" even when he was president.)

Hundreds of young Republicans rallied to Shiras, surprising party insiders that he could line up delegates in so short a time. The press showed an interest in this newcomer, knowing that the real contest for any office under the Ring focused on the primary, not the general election.

Stone sent an emissary to Shiras, saying he would support him if Shiras agreed to serve only one term and then step aside for Stone. The latter had been waiting for Bayne to retire so he could take over the seat. Shiras was getting in the way.

Shiras refused, declaring that a backroom deal was unfair to his opponent and a betrayal of his own delegates. Stone went to Bayne with a similar deal, and the incumbent accepted, reasoning that he would lose unless Stone withdrew.

Shiras won the popular vote but was short of delegates. At the party convention, he instructed his people to support Bayne. However, a third of the delegates refused to attend the convention because they were elected to oppose Bayne at all costs.

Bayne was nominated but then surprised nearly everyone in the hall by refusing to accept. Instead, he threw his support to Colonel Stone seated on the stage. Stone was not even on the ballot.

There was an uproar in the hall, and in the midst of the shouting, someone quickly made a motion to nominate Stone by acclamation. A reporter observed, "As many apparently voted no as aye; there was no roll call to determine the number of votes cast. Protest was ignored and a secret plot openly consummated. Every rule regulating the party convention had been violated."

Even the Republican papers such as the *Pittsburg Commercial Gazette* were disgusted, calling it "a miserable game of deception."

"Bayne," an editorial proclaimed, "made fools of his friends who had labored day and night in his interest and when they had given him what he asked for, he flung it back in their face."

Washing its hands of "the whole disreputable business," the paper concluded, "Like two pickpockets in a crowd, they had agreed to raise a racket and in the excitement get away with the wallet they coveted. Bayne snatched the prize and in the twinkling of an eye, passed it over to his pal, Stone, who stowed it away."

Bayne admitted openly to the papers that the deceit was necessary to deny Shiras the nomination. Colonel Bayne, a veteran of the Battle of Fredericksburg, was humiliated by the whole affair. He returned to live in Washington. A year later, he committed suicide after he awoke one morning with blood on his pillow. Convinced he had tuberculosis, he shot himself in the head.

At a subsequent protest meeting, more than three thousand people crowded into Carnegie Hall in Allegheny and called for Shiras to be awarded the nomination. Stone, realizing popular resentment would hurt him in the general election, decided to make peace and suggested another primary and convention in the fall. This time Stone would put his name on the ballot.

It was a bizarre solution and Shiras was reluctant to participate, feeling the forces against him were too strong. He had manufacturers, merchants, mechanics, and young Republicans on his side, but Stone had corporations, contractors beholden to government patronage, and the Ring itself, which was moving to put down the young upstart.

In the second primary, Shiras again won the popular vote, but delegates mattered more. In some precincts, the Ring-controlled election boards threw out his majority and awarded delegates to Stone. Several Shiras delegates were disqualified. Others switched to Stone under pressure or after outright bribery.

The party convention was a sham orchestrated by the mayor of Allegheny, James G. Wyman. When Shiras's delegates threatened to walk out of the convention, the mayor called out Chief of Police John R. Murphy, who locked the doors of the hall and surrounded it with cops.

According to the *Pittsburg Dispatch*, the police chief "threatened to break any man's head who attempted to get out. The club was effective and the Shiras men were prisoners."

Finally, one of Shiras's delegates, a very large man, threatened to throw a cop out the window. A riot was about to break out until Winfield, George's brother, appealed for calm. The Shiras delegates were allowed to leave, and the Stone forces rushed through the nomination and announced their man the winner.

The Shiras delegates reassembled in a nearby hall and urged their man to run as an independent in the general election. He declined because it would split the vote and secure a Democratic victory. In his speech, George assured his followers that he would take steps to punish the perpetrators and wrest control of the primaries from the Ring.

Stone went off to Washington, where he served four terms before being elected Pennsylvania's governor in 1898. Shiras went back to his law practice. He had plenty of evidence of bribery, coercion, and fraud, but the primary system itself was within the rules and purview of the party—sort of like the rules of a club. As far as civil authorities were concerned, no criminal laws had been broken.

He was able, however, to secure the resignation of the assistant postmaster and orchestrate an official rebuke of the Allegheny tax collector who used his city office to help Stone. His target, however, was Mayor Wyman.

With Shiras in the background, a group of businessmen decided to build up a reform organization. They enrolled one hundred prominent Allegheny citizens to pressure the city council to audit the mayor. Behind the scenes, Shiras wrote pamphlets outlining the purpose of the organization. Months later, auditors determined that the mayor had received thousands of dollars illegally—mainly through extortion. He was raking it in from people arrested for running disorderly houses, a euphemism for houses of prostitution. The corruption required the cooperation of the police chief and the police department. Wyman asked to appear in front of the reform committee but then begged off, saying he needed time to gather evidence of his innocence.

The *Pittsburg Leader* wrote, "Mayor Wymany's [*sic*] action in failing to put in an appearance and offering a defense, after having requested such a privilege, is the subject of much unfavorable comment."

Shiras consulted with the Allegheny district attorney, who formed a grand jury. Shiras even hired a lawyer to assist the local prosecutor. The reform committee later reimbursed him, but it was clear that Shiras was out to get Wyman and was using his own money to do so.

When the case was heard, the jury came back with a guilty verdict.

The *Commercial Gazette* lauded the prosecution, "When men who ought to be doing time in the workhouse or jail aspire to fill important and honorable positions, let them be told in plain English that they will not be permitted to take the oath of office, even though they have succeeded in having themselves chosen."

Awaiting sentencing, Wyman was free on bail. A few days later, he showed up at Shiras and Dickey in downtown Pittsburgh looking disheveled, contrite, and desperate.

The mayor's physical appearance reminded Shiras of a huge gray wolf he had once caught in a trap near Whitefish Lake.

The wolf, he recalled, was "the slayer in its day of hundreds of deer. As I stood close by the trap, the animal with bloodshot eyes seemed to be appealing for mercy. The mercy came in the form of a bullet through its brain."

He had trapped the mayor but could not quite shoot him.

The bulky mayor, with tears in his eyes, said he "wanted help from the one whom I hurt." His downfall had shamed himself, his wife, and their

"The Four Georges," circa 1891. *From left*: George Shiras Sr., Justice George Shiras Jr., George 3d, George IV. Courtesy of the Marquette Regional History Center.

children. He asked Shiras to speak to the judge so he might be sent to the workhouse rather than the dreaded penitentiary.

Shiras demanded that Wyman confess the election shenanigans and resign his office. The mayor admitted to using $5,000 to pay off police and delegates. He had gotten $3,000 from the Ring for the first election and $15,000 for the second, he said.

Once Wyman put it all in writing, Shiras intervened with the judge. The mayor served his time in the workhouse.

A special election was held, and Colonel William M. Kennedy, Shiras's uncle and former campaign manager, was elected mayor of Allegheny. Stone and Bayne kept silent through all the revelations.

Stone went to Congress. Supporters urged Shiras to run against Stone the next election, and he might have done so had his father not been appointed to the US Supreme Court. When George Jr. went off to Washington, Shiras took over his father's duties at Shiras and Dickey. He remained in Pittsburgh for the next ten years, where he practiced law and stayed close to his grandparents and brother.

One evening in early 1891 when his father was home from Washington, DC, and all the Shiras men were in the city, he posed his grandfather and father in front of a library of books at his home. He took a chair next to his elders and held his baby son on his lap with his right hand. With his left, he pulled a thread to trip the shutter of a view camera mounted on a tripod—an action he said "accounted for my alert expression when facing the camera."

The flash powder exploded, and the plate recorded a self-portrait of four generations titled "The Four Georges. Sportsmen All."

7 | THE GREAT BIRD MYSTERY

IN AUGUST 1885, just two months before his marriage to Fanny White, Shiras and an unnamed companion made a trip northwest of Marquette to the Yellow Dog Plains—cutover lands where the removal of the pine forest promoted the growth of brush and huckleberries.

They were hunting passenger pigeons.

Typically, pigeons arrived in the Lake Superior region in May and flew up and down the lakeshore in great flocks before establishing nesting colonies in the hardwood forests. Residents of Marquette took down their guns and from shore and small boats fired into the dense flocks as they passed overhead. Pigeons were good eating and a popular game animal. Many of George's early images from the camp at Whitefish showed dead pigeons strung up outside the cooking area. When returning to town, George always brought back birds for relatives and neighbors on Ridge Street.

Once the pigeons established breeding colonies, the hunters—particularly the pothunters filling orders for markets in Milwaukee, Chicago, and Detroit—moved into the woods and began the slaughter. Hunters went out at night and built smoky fires beneath a tree holding hundreds of birds. As the parents flew about disoriented, they were shot. Young birds, or squabs, were knocked out of the nests with long poles.

George called these night hunts "holocausts at the breeding sites."

Baited traps, decoys, nets, whatever the method, it did not matter how the birds were taken or how many were killed. There were no limits or regulations. Market hunters packed them up by the barrelful and sent them south to the cities. Some settlers fed the birds to livestock.

By July, the survivors moved into the "burnt-over" districts of the Upper Peninsula, areas where loggers leveled the virgin forests and left the slash (branches and other woody waste) on the ground. Lightning strikes, sparks from a passing train, crop burning, or other man-made causes often ignited the country.

There had been several spectacular and tragic fires, including a firestorm in 1871 that consumed Peshtigo, Wisconsin, and spread north into the Upper Peninsula. The Great Peshtigo Fire was the deadliest in US history, killing some two thousand people and burning more than a million acres.

Forest fires typically burned and smoldered all summer and were only extinguished by the snows of winter. The fires created perfect conditions for berries in the burnt-over districts. Passenger pigeons fed on huckleberries, blueberries, elderberries, wild cherry, and serviceberries.

Shiras was on the Yellow Dog Plains in the middle of berry patches that afternoon to kill a mass of birds: "It was my custom to kill, once a year, a large number of pigeons for distribution among friends. Such an expedition differs from the ones where shooting was limited to a few for camp use. Selecting the young, so readily told by their immature plumage, it would take only a few hours to accomplish my quest. At the time the birds were in their usual numbers and I returned under the belief the wild pigeon would continue for many more years in this region."

After shooting several birds, the men rested on a logging trail to eat lunch. Shiras looked up and spied a pigeon flying along the road. He grabbed his shotgun and fired just as his friend turned to look. The bird fell from the sky and smacked his friend right in the face. The companion "clapped his hand over his face and on withdrawing it saw his palm covered in blood."

Shiras recalled, "He shouted in terror, 'I am shot.' When I directed his attention to the feathers sticking to his hand, he became reassured and said 'it is almost as surprising for you to kill a bird on the wing as for me to be shot.'"

It was the last passenger pigeon Shiras ever killed. When he returned from his honeymoon in France the following year, he saw just one bird and, like other folks in the Upper Peninsula, he assumed the flocks had gone elsewhere—perhaps to Canada—and would return the following year. There were other theories: "People speculated it had to be some kind of epidemic, some convolution of the elements, an offshore gale with clouds raining down heavy hailstones."

It was "the Great Bird Mystery."

Northern Michigan and western Ontario were the final stands of the passenger pigeon, which had once been the most abundant bird on the planet, perhaps numbering two billion at the time of European settlement. When the flocks migrated spring and summer, they could take hours to pass and block out the sun. The sound of wings was akin to a thunderstorm.

One of the last big colonies was near Petoskey in Michigan's northern Lower Peninsula. In 1896, market hunters and residents wiped out this final flock of 250,000, even though they were aware it was the last roost in the region. Old habits were hard to change, and people did not believe a bird once so abundant could disappear. The Michigan legislature finally passed weak laws that limited netting and even established a season on the birds, but it was too late.

Shiras later wrote, "It was doomed because it was a migrant. The rule in each state was to have an open season when these migrants were present and a closed season if any, after they had gone. Such regulations resulted, of course, in the birds being subjected to continuous shooting throughout the year."

It wasn't only hunting that sealed the bird's fate but deforestation, too. Wild pigeons were colony nesters and required intact tracts of woodland and mast trees for survival. Their decline in the eastern United States after 1870 was precipitous, and their abrupt disappearance in the Upper Peninsula was characteristic. Suddenly nearly everywhere they had once been abundant one year, passenger pigeons were gone the next.

It was a terrible, emblematic loss—a lesson George Shiras and many American sportsmen and conservationists never forgot. The country at the end of the nineteenth century was learning hard lessons. Natural resources were finite—whether it be passenger pigeons, white pine trees in the northern Great Lakes, ducks on the Chesapeake Bay, or wading birds along the

Gulf Coast. Whitetail deer were no longer common in eastern states. The species was probably at its lowest level in thousands of years.

In the West, pronghorn antelope numbered just twenty thousand from the estimated 35 million that existed in the early 1800s. Many scientists expected antelope to go extinct in twenty years. Elk, once abundant on the Great Plains, were pushed back to mountain refuges. The American bison was gone from the plains entirely—only a handful of wild buffalo survived in Yellowstone National Park.

There were many causes: market hunting, lack of game laws or enforcement, a mentality of killing for killing's sake, and the impression there would always be more game to kill. Americans in the Gilded Age, a period of laissez-faire economics and unbridled growth and exploitation, simply did not recognize limits.

In the 1890s as he took up photography, Shiras became less interested in hunting. Although he was never to give up the gun completely, he no longer had the urge to simply kill and bag trophies. His sojourns in the woods and on the water made him a keen observer of all animals, not just game. He read books on biology, zoology, ornithology, fisheries, and forestry and other works of science and natural history. He interacted with naturalists and sportsmen who were seeing a bigger picture of the natural world. He was becoming a conservationist.

Part of his education was the massacre of all types of birds along Virginia's Atlantic Coast, which he saw firsthand and, to some degree, participated in himself.

In 1894, after his father moved to Washington, DC, the Shirases became charter members of the Revel Island Shooting Club, whose lands and waters encompassed barrier islands, saltwater marshes, and lagoons located on the bay of Paramore Island. The club existed until 1941. Today the area is part of the Nature Conservancy's Virginia Coast Reserve, the longest expanse of coastal wilderness on the Atlantic Coast. The conservancy calls it "one of the most critical migratory bird habitats on Earth."

In the 1890s the area was a shooting gallery for waterfowlers, primarily men of means. Although lawyering in Pennsylvania, George made frequent trips to the nation's capital to visit family and observe his father at the Supreme Court. There was always leisure time and money enough to take trips to the eastern shore.

Shooting clubs were common in the days before national wildlife refuges, state game lands, national forests, and other domains open for public hunting. Sport hunting then was a rich man's pursuit. Belonging to a club gave members access to shooting grounds, blinds, and guides. At one time, there were more than three thousand waterfowl hunting clubs and privately owned marshes on the Atlantic Coast between Maritime Canada and the Florida Everglades. Revel Island was fairly typical. Members put up a clubhouse with a common dining area and rooms. Small cottages could be rented by members. The Shirases, however, erected their own cottage, a two-story clapboard with a large porch and an open fireplace for oyster roasts. When George 3d became a member of Congress and moved to the District of Columbia, Revel Island was a favorite haunt to get away from the city, shoot ducks, and take photographs of birds.

Local guides—even whole families—carved decoys, plucked feathers, built blinds, rowed boats, cooked, and did laundry. At Revel Island, a "colored cook" with the patronizing name of "Auntie Caroline" prepared oysters, ducks, shorebirds, and terrapins. She made snipe pot pie and packed tin pails of pastries for members to snack on in the shooting blinds.

Locals made extra money as "eggers," collecting the newly laid eggs of many types of birds, including ducks, gulls, and clapper rails. Back then, people didn't only eat chicken eggs. One day Shiras made the mistake of telling Jonah, "the colored chore boy at the clubhouse," about a nesting colony of laughing gulls he'd discovered on one his photography excursions. A week later, he found that Jonah had collected more than four hundred eggs from the gull nests, which were closely grouped over several acres. Shiras castigated the young man but also made a photograph of the egg pile.

All along the Atlantic Coast, market hunters used sneak boats and punt guns to navigate the marshes and lay waste to flocks of ducks. The homemade punt guns, some eight feet long with bores up to two inches in diameter, could fire a pound of buckshot. One well-placed blast might bring down fifty birds. Like the passenger pigeons, ducks went to the city markets. In a New York restaurant in the 1890s, a diner could order a canvasback duck for $3, a redhead duck for $2.50, and a mallard for a $1.50.

The so-called sportsmen of the day were nearly as profligate as the market hunters.

During spring and fall migrations at Revel Island, it was not unusual for a club member secreted in a blind with a gun, dog, and local guide to kill one hundred ducks a day. And the kill was not only ducks but also geese and brants and a number of shorebirds that today would not be considered gamebirds, including greater and lesser yellowlegs, sandpipers and plovers, turnstones, curlews, willets, dowitchers, oystercatchers, and avocets. Bald eagles, hawks, fish crows, and osprey were considered varmints and shot on sight in order to "protect the game birds."

Shooters adored being out in the wilderness, dressing in canvas, wool, and puttees and then changing to evening clothes and spending hours in the clubhouse in the company of men, food, liquor, and cigars. President Grover Cleveland especially loved "gunning" and frequently hunted in the vicinity of Revel Island.

As George 3d remembered it, every clubhouse from Virginia to New Jersey was filled with sportsmen intent on slaughter. He himself had shooting days during spring migration in which he brought down dozens of birds headed to the breeding grounds in the North.

In those days, the wastefulness and cruelty of the shooting of birds that were already mating or those that were actually in the midst of their nesting activities among the shells and the tussocks of grass was not appreciated until several species were close to extinction. . . .

Day after day, I have seen otherwise reputable sportsmen bring in two hundred birds and when the weather was warm, it was practically impossible to keep such birds from spoiling. In later years, convinced of its wastefulness, I gave up spring shooting.

At Revel Island, George learned significant lessons not only about conservation but about himself. Gradually his lens for interacting with nature converted from a magnified gun sight to a square of ground glass in the viewfinder of a camera.

Shiras equipped the cottage with a darkroom/laboratory and over the years captured some of his most remarkable bird images on the club property. In spring 1899—apparently uninterested in duck hunting—he carefully combed a mile-long stretch of beach, searching the sand and hummocks for nesting birds. He saw an oystercatcher alight and located a pair of its eggs surrounded by broken shells in a little hollow in the sand.

A short time later, he found three dark-colored eggs in another depression and photographed the nest of a common tern while it stood nearby, protesting the invasion. His ear trained for birdsong, he heard the notes of a Wilson's plover and located the nest. He set up a camera with a thread running seventy-five yards to some sheltering bushes and spent entire days waiting to take a picture of the parents. In all, he obtained images of eighteen species, including a willet in flight and a northern flicker entering a tree cavity. His still-life photos of eggs laid in the sand, carefully camouflaged by grasses and stones, are elegant as well as instructive. His work was that of a naturalist, not just a camera hunter.

Perhaps the best indication of his greater appreciation occurred three years earlier, in 1896, when he was hunting alone in a floating blind on Revel Island Bay. It was a chilly November day and George looked out from his sneak boat, covered with green cedar boughs and other natural camouflage, and spied what appeared to be an approaching cloud. As it came nearer, the cloud revealed itself to be an immense flock of lesser scaups that came overhead, turning in spirals, their multitudinous wing flaps resonating like a strong wind. Three times they circled the blind, cautiously examining his decoys, and then in a rush dropped from the sky, splashing all around. Some birds slammed into the blind.

The scaup were obviously exhausted and hungry. Shiras stifled the urge to rise up and start firing and instead remained concealed, watching them feed, dip and pull in their heads, loaf, and rest. Shooting would have changed them and the day forever, he concluded.

"It was a delightful experience to sit concealed in their midst . . . as the wind and the tide forced the flock toward the opposite shore, I quietly withdrew, content in not having collected any toll from these newly arrived wanderers."

8 | CAMP LIFE AND CAMERA TRAPS

DURING HIS EARLY married life, George and family spent a few weeks a year in Marquette. His father and mother owned a summer home on Ridge Street where Lillie could be close to her sisters. George Shiras Sr. was no longer able to come to the north and died in Pittsburgh in 1893 at age eighty-eight. George and Fanny had two small children, as did Fanny's only surviving sibling, Mary, who had married A. O. Jopling, a civil engineer for the railroad and a partner in a wholesale hardware business in Marquette.

The primitive camp of logs at Whitefish Lake where only men went to rough it with their hunting guides had by the 1890s been transformed by Peter White into a comfortable log cabin with a stable, garden, chicken coop, icehouse, root cellar, and other amenities to make camp life pleasant for families and children. The guides were still there, but they had taken on the added chores of caretaking, building structures, and maintaining the place for the arrival of the Shiras and White clans.

The evolution logically followed the settling of the region. Marquette had turned into a prosperous town. Lumber companies were razing the forests and opening the land to small farmers. The railroad made access to Deerton—a twenty-four-mile train ride from Marquette—an easy, comfortable trip. The camp was still isolated, however, and visitors walked the

Family portrait at camp, Whitefish Lake, late 1890s. *Back row:* Ellen "Sophia"
White reading book. *Front row adults (from left):* Francis "Fanny" Shiras, Justice
George Shiras Jr., George Shiras 3d. *Front row children (from left):* Ellen Shiras, Mary
Jopling, Fanny Jopling, Morgan Jopling, George Shiras IV.
Courtesy of the Marquette Regional History Center.

four-mile trail—originally blazed by Shiras and Jake Brown—from the railhead to the cabin.

A description of the camp from a biography of Peter White reads:

> The camp is eight hundred acres in extent and consists of virgin forest
> with river, swamp, and lake and a little clearing in the center. The
> clearing is at the side of a maple grove and in it stands the dwelling,
> constructed most picturesquely of logs. The clearing is devoted to a
> garden where all fruits and vegetables that the peninsula will raise are
> cultivated. The river called Whitefish—probably because there are no
> whitefish in it—flows past the door. The whitefish is a dainty feeder
> and loves clear and sparkling water. The water of the Whitefish River
> like many of the little rivers in the peninsula is stained by the roots
> of the trees and shrubs through which it passes. But if there are no

whitefish in the river, there are far greater attractions in the camp. Free, wild and unfenced, it is the natural haunt of the deer.

Camp life was carefully recorded in a logbook kept by Peter White, family members, and visitors nominated to play "camp historian" during their holidays. The journal recorded seasonal activities, improvements to the property, wildlife sighted, the number of deer killed and fish caught, and always the weather. Entries chronicled the mundane—what was served for dinner—but occasionally soared to verse and prose rhapsodizing nature.

In a 1901 entry, White boasted, "We've had bishops, deacons, priests, doctors, sawyers and lawyers, and women of note, among which are the descendants of the Great Mather family of colonial days and celebrated authors and physicians from his Majesty's Dominion."

Some wealthy visitors rode to Deerton in private rail cars, which were shunted onto sidings before everyone detrained to walk to camp.

Peter White wrote, "We soon made up our pack and prepared for the trail. We left at three p.m. and found the trail wet. Two hours and ten minutes to camp."

Canned goods and other supplies came down the trail on a mule led by a member of the Rasmus Nelson family, which had settled in Deerton to farm the cutover lands. When snow fell during fall and winter visits, the mule pulled a sleigh. Nelson sometimes brought fresh butter and milk, newspapers, and even telegrams. He would wait while White and company wrote out replies to be transmitted back on the telegraph lines running along the railroad right-of-way.

Jake Brown and John Hammer typically opened camp in late March and early April, when patches of snow remained in the nearby cedar swamp. The "sapheads," as White called his party, arrived shortly afterward to tap trees and make maple syrup and sugar.

Gardening commenced in May with much labor and seriousness, because the camp garden provided fresh produce in summer and root crops well into early winter. They grew cucumbers, potatoes, sunflowers, cauliflower, tomatoes, potatoes, beets, beans, currants, apples, and twenty other varieties of fruits and vegetables. When Jack La Pete could no longer help with heavy camp work, he weeded the gardens and killed potato bugs.

In 1895, White, his wife, Ellen, and their butler, Charles, put in 162 hills of potatoes in one day while two carpenters nailed wooden siding onto a brand-new cottage. Teamsters hauled in lumber, bricks, and new "wire mattresses" from the railroad.

After that, there was the old cabin and the "new cabin." Workers built a root cellar of limestone to keep potatoes, carrots, beets, turnips, and rutabaga. A wooden bridge with a "handsome arch planted with clematis vines for a green bower" crossed the river.

Peter and Ellen spent a good deal of time at camp by themselves and with daughters Fanny and Mary and grandchildren, too. Mary unfortunately died in 1896 when she was in her late thirties, leaving Fanny as the only survivor of the six White children. Three of her siblings died within days during a diphtheria epidemic in 1878. Consequently, the time Peter and Ellen spent with grandchildren was especially precious.

In summer 1897, the Shiras children—Ellie and "Little George"—walked all the way to camp in the rain wearing their new "rubber capes." They fished from a houseboat, read books, and played cribbage and desperation, a popular card game at the time. They swam in the swimming hole, maintained in the river by a small dam and occasional dredging.

One August, the heaviest thunderstorm "ever known struck our camp" during the night. Ellen and Peter got up to light the lanterns. Ellen was sure lightning hit the cottage.

White wrote, "Our lady thought she smelled the sulfurous odor that the house was struck—the historian insisted it was matches she smelled. Our lady was so excited and frightened, we had to sit up for hours."

It did not quit raining for several days. *Certain Death*, Shiras's old sneak boat, broke loose from its mooring on the lake and careened down the river like "Noah's Ark." Jake Brown rowed out and fetched it. The trail to Deerton was inundated and railroad traffic halted, too.

John Hammer's occasional journal entries tended toward the utilitarian. He described preparing camp for winter: bringing in the cookware from the outside kitchen, rolling up and storing mattresses in the rafters, and winching *Certain Death* from the lake and covering the boat with brush.

On October 31, 1893, Hammer and boat builder A. J. Freeman boarded the train in Marquette with supplies to build a houseboat. They spent ten days at camp assembling components Freeman had manufactured in town. The following spring they built the internal fittings and then Hammer, A. O. Jopling, and Nelson cut skids and launched the boat, which proved to be "hard and heavy work."

The houseboat was moored at a landing on the lake, some distance from the actual camp. Over the years, it was a platform for fishing and swimming, a floating picnic area, and a place for Shiras to store his photography gear and prepare his plates. When baiting camera traps for muskrat, raccoon, porcupine, rabbit, and fox, George and Hammer moved the boat along the shore, anchored, set cameras, and then waited inside to hear the flashlight explosions.

When the women wrote in the journal, they talked of card games, the antics of the children, and the huckleberry or rhubarb pies and the dinners made with fresh ingredients from the garden. On September 15, 1897, the families dined on "delicious tender peas, beets, new potatoes, celery, cabbage, black beans, cucumbers, and a fresh chicken."

Forest critters were all about and often infiltrated the camp. Deer raided the garden. Weasels got into the coop and killed chickens. Skunks made a home under the developing laboratory. Porcupines chewed on ax handles, empty brine barrels, anything with salt. One spring when *Certain Death* was uncovered for launching, three porcupines were found living in the hull, where they had chewed up most of the ribs, apparently because of the residual salt from its former use in the ocean.

In May 1894, White wrote, "We saw Mr. Porcupine walking away from 'Certain Death' as satisfied as if he owned the land and the boat, too. I poured six loads of carbine into him before certain death came to him." That same night, White brained a porcupine with an iron bar on the porch after it had kept him awake with its gnawing.

Eventually the camp was endowed with the nickname, the Camp of the Fiddling Cat. Opposite the cabins on the far riverbank, an immense white pine tree when silhouetted against the sky resembled a cat on two legs sawing on a fiddle. Over the years, locations in the woods and along the shore also received appellations: the Devil's Fire Place, Snake Rock, Gull Rock, the Hermit Camp, the Meadows, Old Jack's Landing, the River Scaffolds and, of course, the slough.

Among Shiras's friends in Pittsburgh, the Camp of the Fiddling Cat had taken on mythic status. In 1894, a group of barristers came north, riding a train to Lake Erie in Ohio and then boarding a steamer to Marquette.

Passenger ships out of Cleveland or nearby Ashtabula were quite comfortable, but sometimes when Shiras and other Pittsburghers were in a hurry, they caught freighters loaded with goods or livestock. Alternatively, they came north by the land route, catching the Pittsburgh, Fort Wayne and Chicago Railroad to Chicago and then boarding a Chicago and Northwestern train to the Upper Peninsula.

Edwin W. Smith, a member of the Duquesne Club, recorded the 1894 visit in the camp logbook. After a night in Marquette, they took the afternoon train to Deerton, accompanied by Jake Brown who, Smith noted, was "already famous from the stories told us by Shiras."

"We had hoped to learn the truth from him, but Jake is ever faithful and when he catches the 'tip' he corroborates everything Shiras has said and goes on better." The men were astounded at the supplies unloaded from the railcars. They were relieved to see Nelson's mule waiting and a jumper, or two-wheeled cart, to haul all the goods: milk, melons, bacon, corn, coffee, butter, cream, and flour in tin cans and glass bottles.

It took the men about an hour to walk to the camp, where they were met by Samson Noll and John Hammer. It was camping, but it was comfortable. Noll cleaned fresh fish for breakfast each day to accompany his "famous eggs." Hammer made corn dodgers.

Jack La Pete lived in his cabin near the slough and passed much of his time there, boiling maple syrup in spring, killing deer, and occasionally netting fish in Lake Superior. The guests rowed over to Old Jack's Landing to purchase syrup to pour over brook trout and Noll's flapjacks.

Smith wrote, tongue in cheek: "we had some doubt about the cleanliness of the sweet stuff but Jake [Brown] assured us that it was all right since he'd seen Jack strain it through an old blanket."

Another day while walking the path to the houseboat landing, they spied a deer. Smith noted, "Some of us had never seen a wild deer in the woods." The men were obviously city dwellers, but game was scarce in Pennsylvania. Only five thousand whitetail deer then existed in the state because of overhunting and deforestation.

One afternoon, Smith caught a mess of perch in Whitefish Lake and wanted to keep them for dinner, but another Pittsburgher declared they were too small. When Smith found out that small perch were quite suitable for the frying pan, he swore never to go fishing without Jake or Shiras, "who might have proper knowledge of game or fish."

On July 15, Smith landed what Shiras proclaimed was the "largest pickerel which has ever been taken out of Whitefish Lake." George thought it might be a muskellunge planted in the lake by Hammer. They rowed over to the houseboat, where Hammer declared it a naturally occurring grass pike.

The catch was entered into the journal next to other notable events: the number of times fog engulfed the lake, the deepest snowfall, the hardest rain, rare sightings of birds, and the latest anyone ever slept in and was still served breakfast. A Pittsburgher on the trip wryly noted, "Shiras has a record for everything."

A. O. Jopling, Shiras's brother-in-law, arrived with newspapers full of reports of the great railroad strike of 1894. Also known as the Pullman Strike, it fomented violence and the arrest of the strike leader, Eugene Debs, and caused severe disruption of traffic. Some of the Pittsburgh men had difficulty returning home.

At camp, the men sailed *Certain Death* and bestowed nicknames on one another: Pickerel Sam and Natty Bumppo from *The Last of the Mohicans*. They went for swims, hiked a few miles to Whitefish Falls (now a Michigan scenic site), and drank from springs in the woods and admired how John Hammer cooked brook trout by wrapping the fish in wet paper and laying them on coals. During a hike, some men fell into the river while walking across a log. Hammer cut poles for balancing sticks.

Once they all got lost.

Smith commented, "Shiras goes by blazes, John by compass. They always know where they are but what is the use of knowing when you are in the 'solemn woods' if you can't go where you want to?"

Shiras made a photographic record of the visit: "Shiras has photographed us in every way, in havelock and on the roof of the cabin, together and separately, but we are always ready to humor him; it doesn't hurt us. He put three of us into a picture below the falls, each with a dead fish at the end of the line, straight and still."

Smith returned to the Camp of the Fiddling Cat in 1899 and 1903 and described the difficulty of making "flashlight pictures." In a rowboat, he and a companion followed Shiras and Hammer in the skiff across the lake to the slough.

We paddled up softly and by a misunderstanding of timeliness the second boat was behind. The first boat got within a few feet of a big buck and four does. But still the second boat was behind. Shiras made a few incidental remarks and then prepared to take the picture. At this point, we should have looked for a brilliant flash that would have lighted up the whole lake. But there was no illumination only a spark and a fizzle. Then came the words of Shiras over the water. "What ungodly luck. That buck had rocking chairs on his head!"

On July 17, 1899, they had success.

This time Smith sat in the skiff between Shiras and Hammer: "John paddled us cautiously up the river. It was a glorious moonlit night and the beauty of the scene was impressive. We got close to four deer. Shiras flashed the light, and we could see how it was done. Did not get to bed until 1 a.m."

Summer was for family, friends, and fishing. In the fall, hunting partridge (ruffed grouse), small game, and deer took precedent. The camp was dominated then by the guides and Marquette men. When he could get away from the law firm, George 3d came north for a couple of weeks of deer hunting. In 1895, Michigan first required a license to hunt deer. The season ran from November 1 to 25. The bag limit was five animals per hunter.

The men hunted from scaffolds, or homemade tree stands along the river. Blinds placed on game trails around the lake allowed the men to sit and wait for a passing animal. That year, Peter White recorded several chilly hours of "hopeless staring and hearing deer blow" but no opportunity for shooting. He concluded the day back at the cabin with several cigars, venison stew, and "a digestive snooze."

Although an 1887 law made it illegal to use dogs or lights for taking deer, the men in the 1890s were still night hunting under the illumination of the full moon and perhaps a jacklight, too. Apparently, old habits died hard, and game wardens were scarce anyway.

Typically, Jake Brown or John Hammer rowed the hunters toward Old Jack's Landing and the slough. They stalked the shore, stayed out for hours, and returned near dawn to "go back to camp to smoke the pipe of peace and sleep—beautiful sleep," recalled White.

The nights were quiet, star-filled, sublime, and even spooky, with loons calling across the water and wolves howling from the woods. Whenever the hunting was dismal or the weather too warm or wet, they walked back to the train tracks and returned to town, leaving "John Hammer alone in his glory."

R. H. Craig, a medical doctor from Montreal, wrote in the camp journal on November 16, 1901. Newspapers brought down to camp by Nelson reported harsh weather hammering the Midwest and eastern North America: "Our own Great Lakes are being tempest swept and many wrecks are reported. Snow fell last night and trees and bushes are completely wrapped in snowflakes which gives Mr. Shiras the opportunity of transferring to his camera some suggestions of the great white silence of the world." Across the top of the page he wrote, "The snow. The beautiful snow has come."

Snow and cold helped the hunters track deer, follow blood trails, and hang the carcasses to cure and preserve the meat.

Always, White kept score in the camp journal. "George 3d, Sept. 25 1893 shot doe, left sand beach in slough—by moonlight 90 yds. Next night, killed another doe at same spot by moonlight, 70 yards. Oct. 1 killed another doe, left for Marquette, in route for Pitts."

One hunting season, A. O. Jopling wrote in the journal, "Wolves Galore! With the result that only two (deer) have been killed and these very close to camp. . . . We as humble citizens of the neighboring republic recommend an active war upon the animal."

They did just that—setting out poison, traps, and snares.

And they were doing what men typically do in the close quarters of deer camp—drinking alcohol, eating big meals, devising practical jokes, and making fellowship. Journal entries noted that George 3d always wore socks when sleeping because his feet stuck out beyond the end of the mattress. The master of camp concocted "Peter White Punch" consisting of two types of rum, champagne, brandy, liqueurs, sugar, oranges, and lemons. One hunter, apparently after imbibing too much punch, "made a peculiar shot—aimed for breast, hit leg."

One evening, a party ate dinner on the houseboat, then anchored in a cove where they built a bonfire and sat talking, drinking and keeping off the chill. Shoving his hands into his canvas coat, Shiras found that a box of flashlight powder had spilled in one of the pockets. For fun, he took a pinch of powder and dramatically waved his arms and dropped the particles into the embers, turning the flames green, blue, and yellow—much to everyone's delight. Then he took off his jacket and began shaking the powder into the fire when abruptly there was a "heavy explosion."

A witness wrote, "There was a flare and the coat flew out of his hand and was recovered with a hole in the pocket and a horrible smell upon it. We sat around the fire, smoking, singing, playing on the mouth organ and then home by river at eleven o'clock."

Shiras remarked, "My first use of powder was thought to be a good joke, but the second performance was thought a far better one by the other members of the party."

Flash powder was a volatile substance.

During the early years of his work with *National Geographic*, he received dozens of letters from sportsmen wanting to know how he obtained his night pictures. In 1912, he wrote to the Eastman Kodak Company, suggesting it publish a pamphlet on "methods in taking flashlight pictures of wild game." In the letter, he described the detailed process, the requisite knowledge of animal habits, and the hazard of flash powders. "The method is a dangerous one for the inexperienced and should not be advised except where the methods are carefully set forth."

Not surprisingly, due to the limited audience, Kodak never published such a pamphlet.

By the late 1890s, Jack La Pete could no longer do the hard work of a camp man. He couldn't see well, had difficulty killing deer for meat, and depended on handouts from Peter White and other Marquette sportsmen. One day, he paddled the old dugout canoe over to the camp and told George he wanted to move to the Red River country in Manitoba so when he died, he would be buried there.

When he declared he was Sioux and not Ojibwa, he surprised everyone. His mother, he explained, had been abducted from the Red River and brought to Sault Ste. Marie, where she married Jack's father, a French trapper. He wanted to go and live among his own people, he said.

The Shirases, Peter White, Sam P. Ely, Jopling, and other well-off men in Marquette agreed to finance his trip to Canada and provide him with a yearly stipend until his death. They made pledges and signed the document. Ely, the banker, collected the money and sent it to Jack in care of the Catholic mission on the reservation.

No one thought La Pete had many years left, but he lived to be about one hundred—dying in 1911—and surviving all but three of his fifteen benefactors. George 3d sent the stipend each year until notified of Jack's death by a priest at the mission.

Jake Brown left Michigan in 1894. His drinking binges became more frequent, and the only way to stay sober was to keep to the woods. In late fall, he used his wages to buy pork, flour, and other supplies to get through the winter. He lived at the cabin on Whitefish Lake, shot deer, and stored the fresh meat under the snow. He formed a close friendship with La Pete and cut wood for the old man, checked his traps, and pulled nets set in the lake and on Lake Superior.

Jake was surprisingly witty. Shiras related how "Jake once had charge of a Pittsburgh visitor on a deer hunt near camp. This would-be deer slayer had hardly ever been off a paved street and clung closely to Jake's heels as they traversed the unbroken forest. At one point, they stood on a bank overlooking a dense and tangled cedar swamp, a favorite hiding place for deer during the greater part of the day.

After a glance at the scene below, Jake's companion exclaimed, "My, what an evil looking place."

"Yes," said Jake. "Primeval."

When Jake declared he wanted to leave Michigan, Colonel William Howe, the steel executive and George's uncle from Pittsburgh, offered Brown a job in Idaho to serve as caretaker of a new hunt club he was organizing there. At Henry's Lake, the club lay in isolated country just west of Yellowstone National Park and well away from saloons.

When he quit the Camp of the Fiddling Cat, Brown posted a note on the door. "Farewell old log cabin, to you I bid adieu; I may emigrate to hell someday, But never back to you."

He was missed by everyone.

Henry's Lake proved a deliverance for Jake until a saloon opened in the woods and he began drinking again. Warned by his employers that he needed to straighten up, he declared, "Either that saloon has to go or I have to go." He soon joined up with a partner to take a pack train overland to Alaska. That fall, however, the two men got into an altercation in the Canadian Rockies. Jake shouldered his pack and rifle and defiantly marched into the wilderness just as winter came on. The partner made it back to Idaho, cursing Jake for leaving the pack train and surmising that he perished in the mountains.

Samson Noll died in 1898 in a cabin near Whitefish Lake. The year of his birth on a Virginia plantation was unclear. He was about eighty years old. He was interred in a friend's plot in the section of the Marquette city cemetery set aside for "coloreds." Later, Shiras had the body moved to its own plot, where he erected a marker.

When the new century arrived, John Hammer became the main caretaker and guide at Whitefish Lake—and a person increasingly important to Shiras's work as a photographer.

When they weren't shooting from the skiff, Shiras's other method at night had been to set out camera traps on the shore, open the lens in the dark, and then retreat to the houseboat or a place in the woods to wait for the flashlight explosion. Then he would return, close the lens, and collect the plate. Waiting could be interminable and, in the summer, uncomfortable in the insect-infested forest.

He looked for ways to automate the process so he could position the cameras during the day—when it was impossible to leave the shutter open—and then collect the plates the following morning. To do that, the shutter and flashlight needed to fire in synchronization.

First, he tried a taut rubber band that tripped the shutter when the flashlight exploded, but rubber bands were unreliable. There were other technical problems as well. Flashlight powder could be formulated to fire a brief bright light or mixed for a longer, more intense illumination—a term he called "powder speed"—which was best for fast shutter speeds because it was difficult to synchronize the flash with the shutter using the rubber band. The longer the period of illumination, the more likely the shutter would open when there was enough light for an exposure.

Hammer, the machinist, came up with the idea to replace the rubber band and make the reaction more precise with an air pump connected to a rubber tube that would set off the shutter. When they used slow powder speed and the air pump, the shutter released during maximum illumination. It was a delicate ballet. The animal tripped the wire and set off a blank cartridge, which in turn ignited the powder. The explosion triggered the air pump that released the shutter.

Eventually, they got it to work so well and faithfully that they were setting and baiting camera traps all over the lake—often hearing one go off while busy setting another or relaxing back at camp.

Typically, Shiras placed one-half to three-quarters of an ounce of flash powder into a small, round paper box previously soaked with paraffin to keep out moisture. When the charge ignited, the report could be heard three miles away.

George wrote, "Lying beside a blazing camp fire that accentuates the darkness of the night, the sportsman may suddenly see a dazzling column of light on a distant hillside or above the gloomy valley of some watercourse. The deep, dull boom of the exploding powder a few seconds later raises a mental vision of an animal fleeing in needless terror from a bullet-less weapon and leaving a record of its visit that will give pleasure to one who means him no harm."

More than once over the years, he set camera traps only to have one of his companions or a passerby stumble into the trip wire and explode the device, much to their terror. Sheep, hogs, cats—and once, a bull belonging to a Finnish settler near Deerton fired off a flashlight and singed its tail in the flames and fumes. Frank Chapman, the ornithologist, and Louis Agassiz Fuertes, a painter of bird life, went on collecting and photography expeditions with Shiras and always cautiously approached camp at dusk due to what Chapman called "those infernal machines secreted anywhere and everywhere."

Hammer, with Shiras's encouragement, took out patents on the air pump mechanism, but like Shiras's flashlight pistol, it was never produced commercially. Later Shiras bought the patents for about three hundred dollars so he could make them available to anyone interested in flashlight photography. According to Hammer's descendants, the guide did not get full credit for all he contributed to Shiras's work and innovations. Undoubtedly, his skills and invention were important. Some devices may have been produced in combination by Hammer and other craftsmen in machine shops in Marquette. A. O. Jopling, Shiras's brother-in-law, was an engineer and partner in the hardware business. And Shiras clearly had some abilities of his own, if only as a designer and experimenter.

He was a published author and a photographer of growing reputation. In 1895, he wrote an article entitled "Hunting with a Camera" in the *New York Sun* in which he encouraged fellow sportsmen to consider taking up the camera and employing it much like a gun. The following year, he produced the ten photographs of what he called the *Midnight Series*, which were his best nighttime shots of deer from Whitefish Lake.

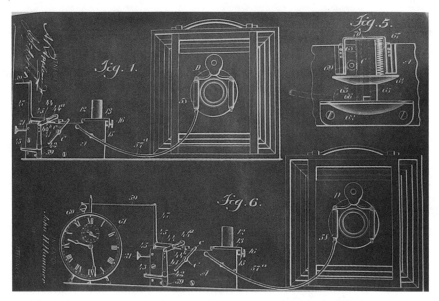

Schematic for a shutter-release mechanism on a camera trap, patented by John Hammer, 1904. Courtesy of the John Hammer family.

Much like paintings, each image carried a title: "Innocents Abroad" of two fawns following their mother, "Hark" of a buck staring at trees lit up by the flashlight, and "Midnight Reflection," a sharp image of a deer reflected in the shallows of the lake.

It was not quite wildlife photography of animals moving naturally in their environment. They are on edge, cognizant of the photographer. Yet the pictures were entirely novel. No one had ever produced such images of nocturnal wildlife.

He published sets of bromide enlargements in limited editions, shown in galleries and at sportsman exhibitions in several cities.

The editor of *Recreation* magazine wrote, "These pictures attracted a great deal of attention at the Boston show. I noticed hundreds of people, who after looking at them once, would go away and bring their friends to see them. Some of them would spend half an hour each time pointing out the beauties of them and in discussing the various features."

The standard edition cost $3.50 per seven-by-twelve-inch print, limited to one thousand in the set. A miniature edition (seven by ten inches) limited to twenty-five hundred sold for $1.50 per print. The salon edition offered "Hark" and "Innocents Abroad" in big enlargements of thirty-six by forty inches for $25 each. Shiras estimated he earned more than $20,000 from the *Midnight Series*, which one hundred years later would be the equivalent of nearly $500,000.

In 1900, the US Forestry Division, part of the Department of Agriculture, asked to borrow some prints to display at the World's Fair in Paris.

The Paris Exposition Universelle celebrated the turning of the new century. Open from April to November 1900, the exposition attracted fifty million visitors. Several countries funded pavilions showcasing the wonders of their homelands.

The four wildlife images in the American Pavilion attracted the attention of European sportsmen and photographers fascinated by the use of the flashlight to take pictures after dark. Judges from the photography exhibit heard about the pictures, went over to view them, and then sought permission from the exposition organizers to award a medal to Shiras, even though the images had not been entered in the photography exhibit.

In 1900, in *Outdoor Life*, Shiras warned readers that wild game photography was a difficult endeavor and suggested the editor print some of his "failures": "I have some amusing pictures, some deer with two heads, some with eight legs, some in the air with half the body missing, and some plunging into deep water with the spray more conspicuous than the deer."

All *Midnight Series* images were taken from the skiff. Camera traps had yet to yield such well-composed and properly exposed results: "The difficulty in taking such pictures partly arises from the fact that seldom is the deer properly centered on the plate and in sharp focus and partly because the deer is usually in motion when firing the flashlight—so that unless the flash is very rapid, some portion of the deer, usually the legs, are blurred, making a good enlargement impossible."

To the animals, the explosion and brilliance of the flashlight was akin to a modern-day stun grenade. The startled critters, blinded for a few seconds, crashed into trees and brush or, on occasions, splashed into the lake and ran toward the boat.

One night after they had just finished shooting a picture of a mother and two fawns, one of the youngsters—confused and bleating—swam by the boat, heading blindly for open water. Shiras seized it by the neck and turned it around. John Hammer wanted to pull it aboard because he had a standing order from someone in Marquette who would pay for a pet deer.

Shiras refused. "The thought of a capsize with the loss of a negative more valuable to me than the prize money in sight for the guide, and the reluctance also to separate forever these frolicsome twins, led me to turn the swimmer ashore."

On another night that season, he let Hammer pursue a fawn after the flashlight scared off the mother. Hammer stepped from the boat, circled behind the deer, and jumped on its flank. Man and beast struggled for several minutes, while Hammer tried to bind its feet with a belt. The deer got away and the guide ended up with a bloody nose and a torn shirt, much to the boss's amusement.

As time went on, Shiras gained more sympathy for the critters he was pursuing, and his attitudes hardened against what he saw as needless slaughter in shooting circles.

Late in 1900, he wrote in the *New York Independent* newspaper, "The camera substituted for the gun gives all the mental satisfaction of conquest with none of the ordinary ills to the victim. To every hunter there comes periods of disgust, almost of remorse, at the slaughter of game . . . the hunter brings war and destruction. The bird or animal which a moment ago was conscious of nothing but pleasure of its wild existences is now but a lump of bleeding flesh, knowing nothing but an intolerable pain and agony of fear."

9 | A PROGRESSIVE GOES
TO WASHINGTON

ALTHOUGH GEORGE SHIRAS 3d was gaining a national reputation as a camera hunter and a sportsman, he seemed destined to follow his father's path, settle into a lucrative corporate law career, socialize with the elites of Pittsburgh, and summer on Lake Superior with family.

But at the end of the Gilded Age, revolutionary changes swept across America, fueled by an educated middle class demanding reform, investigative journalists exposing the ills of society, and a young, dynamic president wielding federal power in unprecedented ways.

The Progressive Era—as it came to be known—was a volatile and hopeful time, and it swept up George Shiras 3d, who would move to Washington, DC, serve in Congress, and become a partner and friend of Theodore Roosevelt.

Progressivism started in the 1890s as a social movement by reformers who believed the problems society faced—poverty, violence, greed, unregulated capitalism, racism, economic inequality, class warfare, and alcoholism—were best addressed by government providing citizens with a good education, a safe and healthy environment, and an efficient and fair workplace. Unlike the socialists of the period who wanted to eliminate capitalism, the Progressives felt the system could be reformed and brought under control by regulation and the strong hand of federalism.

The conservationists of the Progressive Era were the first to organize a large-scale movement to combat environmental deterioration and exploitation—the disappearance of wildlife, denigration of public lands, pollution of the environment, and the unfettered harvesting of timber.

Muckraking journalists—Ida Tarbell, Lincoln Steffens, Nellie Bly, Ida Wells, and Frank Norris—writing in magazines such as *McClure's, Cosmopolitan, North American Review, The Outlook,* and the *Atlantic Monthly* provided plenty of evidence that despite all the advances and prosperity of the Gilded Age, there was a rottenness to the system. Millions of people read these magazines and demanded action.

The biggest target was elimination of corruption in government.

As Shiras well knew from his political experience in the Pennsylvania legislature, the cities of Pittsburgh and Allegheny were in the grip of political machines beholden only to themselves. In December 1901, the Citizen's Party was born when thirty-five hundred people met in Pittsburgh's Old City Hall to "defeat efforts to elect dishonest and incompetent men as public officers, prevent perpetuation of fraud upon the taxpayers, and secure and maintain economic and efficient government."

Across the river in the city of Allegheny, a group of seventy-five men met to organize their own Citizen's Party and draw up a platform, which included creating a civil service, giving labor unions representation, and making sure public monies were properly deposited and held. It wanted to revoke unlimited time franchises for businesses using public streets and property, which enabled corporations and their factories to control the waterfront and pollute the waterways.

The movement was a serious challenge to the Ring, but the machine fought back with its grassroots organization and patronage system. It had abettors in high places. William A. Stone, after besting Shiras for Congress, became the governor of Pennsylvania. The despised Matthew Quay held a seat in the US Senate.

To win offices, the Citizen's Party teamed up with the Democrats, who had largely been out of power for many years. A conference was arranged where party bosses literally divvied up who should run for what office and which districts would be given over to the Democrats and which to the Citizen's Party. This "fusion ticket" spelled trouble for the Ring.

In those meetings, George Shiras's name immediately came up for the Twenty-Ninth District seat in the US House of Representatives. He would go up against W. H. Graham, who had been handed the seat by Stone when he left to become governor.

Shiras was reluctant to reenter public life, but the reform movement was too exciting and important to stay on the sidelines. He accepted the nomination of the Citizen's Party, saying he did not want "to turn my back upon the principles which I have adhered to all my life and upon friends whose associations I value more highly than I can express."

His nephew later wrote about this decision: "This [nomination] came to him quite unsought and as something of a nuisance. By that time he had made up his mind to be a field naturalist, but the Ring was anathema and he accepted with the proviso that he would serve for one term only, at the end of which he would be free to resume his studies in natural history and biology."

George fit the profile of a Progressive. He was young, college educated, lived in a city, and believed that government could be a tool of positive change. He had high ideals. He was wary of corporate power and abhorred political corruption. Yet he was an elite himself, on the social registry in Pittsburgh, a man who employed "colored servants," moved in the rarified circles of men's clubs, and whose wealth was generated—or at least maintained—by his holdings in large companies.

He was a Republican, too, but he declared in a campaign brochure, "Any Republican voting for a Citizen's Party candidate was not a traitor. The real traitors were those in possession of the party organization and under them there was no hope of improving conditions."

The Citizen's Party was a movement to end "bossism," he wrote. It had a sense of mission and purity. "The candidate of such a movement is strong not because of any personal qualification but because he is representing the people in their efforts to secure for themselves the benefits of a full and equal government."

It was a hard-fought campaign with open-air mass meetings, bands, parades, and speeches. The *Pittsburg Dispatch* characterized a Citizen's Party rally at the Old City Hall as a "jollification meeting":

No one except those in the front rows could hear the speakers or, even their introductions. It didn't matter. The stage was crowded with candidates. There were bands and more than a thousand people in the streets who couldn't get in the hall.

Hats were in the air and no man could hear his neighbor, everyone seeming to give himself over to the wildest abandonment of enthusiasm . . . the scenes of the opening demonstration which lasted almost an hour, were repeated at frequent intervals. Time and time again the cheering would break out.

The Shiras-Graham fight was close all the way, the hardest contest in Allegheny County. George Shiras 3d, the *Pittsburg Dispatch* noted, was "a fighter of no mean ability."

There was mischief on both sides. Court papers objecting to the fusion ballot were allegedly "misplaced" for several days. Governor Stone wrote letters to state workers in Allegheny County instructing them to vote for Graham. The Ring dismissed police and firefighters not in sympathy with their candidates and even taxed city employees two percent of their wages in Allegheny to fund the campaign. Union leaders connected to the Ring accused the Citizen's Party of open bribery. The health department, controlled by the Ring, found an imaginary case of smallpox in the headquarters of the Negro Citizen's Committee.

The Citizen's Party distributed thousands of slick, twenty-page pamphlets that recounted the Bayne affair and how the Ring stole the nomination from Shiras a decade earlier.

As the campaign progressed, the Citizen's Party gained popular support. It held some four hundred meetings. Both parties gave free beer to everyone coming to their rallies. The *Dispatch* quipped, "It would be well for one or the other of the two political factions on the Northside to purchase a brewery outright."

On Election Day, turnout was heavy. There were fights and arrests at the polls. Voters were instructed to bring tax receipts to prove their residency, and there was talk of the Citizen's Party issuing fake receipts. Both parties posted guards to keep an eye on the metal safe holding the election returns.

The final vote, tabulated five days later, gave Shiras the edge by just 18 votes—14,553 to 14,535. Graham did not challenge the results. Shiras attributed his success to an "uprising of the people in the cause of good government."

Change was in the air. Congressman-elect Shiras arrived in Washington at the beginning of Theodore Roosevelt's second term, when the president aggressively began to move his conservation and Progressive agenda through—and often around—Congress.

Shiras met Roosevelt at a reception for new congressional representatives. Neither man remembered they had encountered one another while collegians, but Roosevelt was quite aware this young man was the son of a sitting justice of the US Supreme Court. As well, his uncle, Oliver P. Shiras, brother of Junior, was on the Iowa federal court. The president also remembered Shiras's game images from the *Forest and Stream* photography contest, and he had prints from the *Midnight Series* hanging in the White House. In 1902, Philander Knox, the US attorney general, sent several images to Roosevelt as a gift. Knox, a lawyer from Pittsburgh and a member of the Duquesne Club, received a written thank-you at the Justice Department via George Courtelyou, the president's private secretary: "The President directs me to say that the game pictures you so kindly sent him are splendid and that he is really obliged to you for them."

Knox passed the note on to George with the note, "The President has asked me personally to thank you."

The Fifty-Eighth Congress convened on November 9, 1903. As a new member, Shiras had no seniority and no great standing to participate in floor debates. As a reformer, he did not curry favor with Joe Cannon, the powerful Speaker of the House. Known as "Uncle Joe," Cannon was a conservative Republican from Illinois and the head of the Old Guard of the party who saw the reformers and the young president as dangerous upstarts.

Shiras applied for appointment to only one committee—the Committee on Public Lands, whose tasks included the creation of national parks and monuments. He was the only representative from the East; the rest of the members were from the Middle West and what were then the frontier states of the Rocky Mountains. It was an impressive group headed by the renowned John Lacey, a Republican from Iowa who was responsible for some of the first environmental laws in the country.

The Lacey Act of 1900 made it illegal to kill game in one state and

Deer image from the
Midnight Series, 1890s.
Courtesy of Northern
Michigan University.

transport it across state lines for sale. The law was designed to put market hunters out of business and help states protect their resident wildlife. Tied to the commerce clause of the US Constitution, the law was an important legal precedent because it conferred on the federal government and its courts a responsibility and jurisdiction for the preservation of game animals.

During Roosevelt's terms in office, Public Lands was a busy committee, with the president setting aside land for national parks and refuges. However, it was human health that first got Shiras's attention as a congressman and, oddly enough, the episode spurred his interest in federal jurisdiction over migratory birds.

Just as he took office, an outbreak of typhoid fever killed 111 people and sickened nearly 1,300 in Butler, Pennsylvania, a town of 18,000. Not untypical for that period, Butler's water was supplied by a private company that pumped from underground wells but also took water from a creek and ran it through a sand filter. In August 1903, a dam burst on the creek and, while making repairs, the company bypassed the filter and took water directly from the stream. It did not inform residents, even after the first deaths occurred, nor was it required to do so. Pennsylvania's public water supplies were unregulated until 1905.

In the nineteenth century, typhoid outbreaks plagued American cities and towns, and it was only in the 1890s that experts determined the etiology of typhoid fever and connected it to sewage-polluted waters. Typhoid is a bacterial infection caused by the pathogen *Salmonella typhi.* Once in the bloodstream, the bacterium multiplies and causes a high fever, which can last for weeks or even months. Prior to the introduction of antibiotics, there was no cure.

Victims were quarantined and kept comfortable until the fever ran its course. About 20 percent of those infected died, and anyone who carried the pathogen could pass it along by touch, food preparation, or fecal contamination.

Pittsburgh led the nation in cases of typhoid fever, with about five thousand people sickened annually. The three rivers abounded with dangerous chemicals and factory wastes; the sewage system emptied directly into the waterways from which the city took its water.

State and local authorities were ill prepared for the outbreak in Butler. Clara Barton, founder of the Red Cross, came to the town and issued an appeal to raise money for relief. The state Board of Health had no expertise to make its own sanitary inspections and hired an outside consultant to come from New York City to determine the cause, which was sewage running into the creek upstream. It was weeks before the state issued a boil-water advisory and told people to stop drinking the city water.

Like many Americans, Shiras was appalled at the Butler debacle and understood that the dangers knew no borders nor class. Rich people as well as poor died of contaminated drinking water.

He wrote, "If one case of infected sewage could imperil the lives of an entire town, what must be the situation in the Ohio River Valley, with the Pittsburgh sewers emptying into the headwaters of a system extending to the Gulf and through a dozen states?"

Partly what motivated Shiras was the Supreme Court decision in the 1901 *Missouri v. Illinois & Sanitary District of Chicago,* generally known at the time as the Chicago Drainage Canal Case. To prevent frequent outbreaks of typhoid fever, Illinois dredged the Chicago River, reversing its flow into Lake Michigan—where Chicago took its drinking water—so sewage would flow away from the city and flush downstream. His father had written the majority opinion concluding that no state could unreasonably pollute water flowing into another state. The arguments over the canal went on for many years, but the original ruling established federal control over contamination of interstate waters.

During the Butler outbreak, Shiras called upon Surgeon General Walter Wyman of the Marine Hospital Service to send an inspector to the town. The bureau could investigate the epidemic and make a report, but Wyman said it had no authority to supervise or manage the situation unless the contamination crossed an international border.

Wyman suggested Shiras prepare a legal brief on the matter, which was later published in the annual report of the Marine Hospital Service. In the brief, Shiras made a case for federal oversight of the nation's waterways to regulate pollution and harmful organisms moving across state borders. He also made a speech on the House floor in early 1905 supporting such a bill, but it languished in committee.

His conclusions would impact his thinking regarding migratory birds. If the federal government could take jurisdiction over an undesirable organism—a bacterium—then why not a beneficial organism such as a bird?

Being a member of the Public Lands Committee had its perquisites for a sportsman and game photographer. In summer 1904, Shiras went on a fact-finding mission to Yellowstone National Park to determine whether the park should be extended southward to encompass Jackson Lake and the Teton Mountains. He combined the mission with a visit to the hunting club his uncle had helped establish at Henry's Lake, Idaho.

Enlarging Yellowstone National Park was not a new idea. A report in 1898 by Charles D. Walcott, director of the US Geological Survey, recommended the park expand to include the upper portion of the Jackson Valley and most of the Thorofare region along the headwaters of the Yellowstone River.

When Yellowstone was created in 1872 as the world's first national park, its boundaries had been hastily drawn to encompass geysers, mud pots, and other thermal features—what were then called "freaks and curiosities of nature."

By the turn of the century, however, it was evident the Yellowstone eco-system extended beyond the park's physical boundaries to include the winter ranges of its big game herds. For thousands of years, elk had migrated into the Jackson Valley to escape the cold and deep snows of the Yellowstone Plateau. But as the Jackson area became more settled with ranches, barbed wire fences, and livestock, the grasslands and sagebrush flats were less available to wildlife.

In the year prior to Shiras's visit, elk starved and died by the thousands in the valley. Market hunters picked off and poached animals along their migration path. Sport hunters took the biggest and strongest members of the diminished herds. And then there were "tuskers," people who killed elk simply to remove their ivory canine teeth. A pair of ivories sold for as much as one hundred dollars. Members of the Benevolent and Protective Order of Elks (BPOE) wore elk ivory watch fobs as a symbol of prestige. In an era when fraternal organizations were very popular, the BPOE had hundreds of thousands of members.

Consequently, elk were in trouble. In May 1902, President Roosevelt added five million acres to the forest reserve in northwest Wyoming and southwest Montana, but that action could not create the protection offered by national park status. National parks could serve as game preserves to repopulate dwindling numbers in the forests and on the plains. Yellowstone was critical to the American bison's survival as a species.

Shiras and John Hammer arrived on the Northern Pacific Railway in Gardiner, Montana, in late summer and lodged at the National Hotel at Mammoth Hot Springs. There, Shiras met with Colonel S. B. M. Young, the military commander of the park.

The establishment of the National Park Service was still several years in the future (1916), and the US Army was in charge of the park and trying to protect the animals. However, soldiers were not present in enough numbers to prevent poaching, and the forest reserves and the winter ranges south of the park were outside their jurisdiction. Very little science was being done, and no one had a good handle on the numbers or health of the big game herds.

After they talked about elk, Shiras asked Young about moose and learned the large ungulates were largely unknown, rarely seen. Young believed there were no more than a dozen in the entire park. Shiras was intrigued. From his readings and discussions with other sportsmen, there seemed to be plenty of moose in the Rocky Mountains north of the US border. Why not in America? Could they have been extirpated during settlement much like the bison, which was then teetering on extinction? Certainly there was still plenty of habitat available. Perhaps predators were to blame?

The moose question stayed with him.

Exactly what other investigations he made on the trip are unclear. In his writings, Shiras glosses over his official task and recounts more about the several days he and Hammer spent at Henry's Lake, which sits at six thousand feet at the head of a long valley in an amphitheater of the Centennial Mountains. It was there that Shiras's uncle Colonel Howe and other easterners established a hunt club in 1888 at the ranch of Dick Rock and Vic Smith.

Smith had been a buffalo hunter and Rock his skinner. After the buffalo ran out, they established themselves as hunting guides. Dick Rock built corrals and brought some of the last remaining buffalo to the lake. He would ride them to entertain tourists, but shortly after the clubhouse was built, Rock was killed when an animal impaled him against one of its walls. Jake Brown, Shiras's former guide, had been caretaker for a few years, but he was gone and presumed dead.

Shiras and Hammer stayed at the clubhouse for several days: fishing for grayling in the Madison River, hunting grouse and sage hens in the foothills, and shooting ducks on the lake.

They spent several nights plying the lake in a skiff using their flashlights to take pictures of muskrat. During the day, Shiras photographed avocets, canvasbacks, blue-winged teal, and lesser scaups.

A row of foxgloves fronted the clubhouse, and Shiras knew that these had been planted by Jake Brown, who loved to garden and had a soft spot for flowers. Jake had brought vegetable and flower seeds from gardens he tended at Whitefish Lake. In Idaho, Shiras harvested ripening seed from the foxgloves and later replanted them back at Whitefish Lake—a sentimental gesture to his old friend.

When he returned to Washington, Shiras recommended the park's southern boundary be extended, but he immediately ran up against Congressman Frank W. Mondell of Wyoming, also a member of the Public Lands Committee.

Shiras wrote to William Loeb, Theodore Roosevelt's secretary, "Tell the president that I visited Yellowstone Park this summer with the view of preparing legislation extending the southern boundary of the park so as to cover the winter range of the Elk, and likewise include the beautiful Teton Mountains, but found unfavorable conditions in the State of Wyoming."

Mondell and a good many Wyoming citizens were not inclined to give the federal government any more jurisdiction over their state. Some were still displeased over the establishment of the park, and later Roosevelt's enlargement of the forest preserves, which included much of the land in the Tetons. They rightly suspected he wasn't through with Wyoming. In 1906, TR declared Devil's Tower a national monument and in 1908 set aside more forest as part of the creation of the new National Forest Service.

In a compromise, Mondell agreed to ask the Wyoming state legislature to establish a state game preserve just south of the park as a way of heading off federal control over wildlife within those preserves. That way, settlers and ranchers around Jackson could graze their livestock, cut firewood, and even hunt within the preserve. The Teton Game Reserve gave the elk some protection, but what ultimately saved the herd was a winter feeding program begun in 1910.

In 1912, the National Elk Refuge was established, and today it is a winter tourist attraction with sleigh rides through the herds. This artificial situation is kept under control by allowing hunters to cull the herd and keep the numbers to around five thousand elk and five hundred buffalo. As for creation of a national park to encompass the Jackson Valley and the Tetons, that had to wait several more decades.

In the second session of the Fifty-Eighth Congress, George wrote committee reports on several pending bills. One report recommended giving title to lands settled by people along the railroad right-of-way in The Dalles, Oregon. Apparently, these folks had helped build the military road through the area before the Northern Pacific Railway and felt that the land was theirs and not the railroad's property.

Another report recommended giving North Dakota 640 acres encompassing the Whitestone Hill Battlefield near Kulm. The so-called 1863 battle was part of an expedition to punish the Sioux, complete their banishment from Minnesota, and clear the eastern Dakotas of Indians. The soldiers attacked an encampment and killed some three hundred people, many of them women and children. An army scout called it a "perfect massacre."

More to his forte was a report supporting a bill to create Elk National Park in Washington State. The 393,000-acre park would be carved out of the Olympic Forest Reserve, where 1.4 million acres were already set aside to "preserve the elk, game, fish, birds, animals, timber and curiosities."

Shiras wrote, "The lands lying within the proposed boundaries of this park are in every way suited for the purpose. It is a wild, beautiful and an almost uninhabited region lying within the heart of the Olympic Mountains."

A large band of elk lived there. "This is one of the very few bands of elk yet remaining in the United States. These noble animals are now being ruthlessly slaughtered by pothunters for hides and horns and sometimes merely for teeth and the remainder of the carcass is left lying on the ground to rot."

The report contained supportive affidavits from game wardens, county commissioners, newspaper editors, and even the Elks Lodges of Port Angeles and Tacoma.

The timber interests in the Northwest fought against it. They were powerful and continually encroached on the forest reserve to harvest old growth. The 1904 bill never got anywhere, nor did another effort in 1908. Just when he was about to leave office, however, Theodore Roosevelt declared six thousand acres the Mount Olympus National Monument. The fight went on for many more years until the creation of Olympic National Park in 1938. In honor of TR, the elk in the herd—physically the largest of the four surviving subspecies—were named Roosevelt elk.

In his pursuit of conservation, Theodore Roosevelt frequently acted unilaterally, and Shiras had a front-row seat in Congress to the battles between the president and the Speaker of the House. Uncle Joe Cannon did much to slow down the conservation movement and was quoted as saying "not one cent for scenery." Of the president he said, "Teddy Roosevelt has no more use for the Constitution than a tomcat has for a marriage license."

Under executive order, Roosevelt set aside refuges specifically for wildlife in Florida, the Great Lakes, and Louisiana. However, there were no laws preventing hunters from entering federal property or killing birds.

Roosevelt wrote, "My Dear Mr. Shiras: What I am doing in the effort to protect our birds, I know has your most hearty sympathy. Will you look over the enclosed communication and see if you cannot get through the legislation suggested?"

The following year Congress passed An Act to Protect Birds and Their Eggs in Game and Bird Preserves. It gave the federal government ownership of the game animals in federal preserves, despite the fact that those preserves were inside a state's boundaries.

Protecting land under the jurisdiction of the federal government was not new. In 1891, the Forest Reserve Act authorized withdrawing 39 million acres from the public domain as forest reserves. The 1897 Forest Organic Act created thirteen more forest reserves totaling 21 million acres. It also established a Division of Forestry under the Interior Department to regulate the use of logging, mining and grazing on public land.

When he became president, Roosevelt named his friend Gifford Pinchot chief of forestry, to combat what they believed was a coming "timber famine." Pinchot, a Yale-trained forester, was not a preservationist but a utilitarian who believed in sustainable development for future generations. In 1905 while Shiras was in Congress, Roosevelt transferred the forest reserves from the Interior to the Agriculture Department and created the US Forest Service to give Pinchot more freedom to manage the forests and control grazing and mining on public lands. By the end of the decade, the two men set aside 150 million acres of new national forest, including 16 million acres just minutes before a congressional law—championed by Uncle Joe—would have stopped them.

Their aggressive actions were an inspiration to the young congressman, who felt that only federal action could halt the slaughter of wildlife.

On December 5, 1904, George introduced H.R. 15601, A Bill to Protect the Migratory Game Birds of the United States. In approximately six hundred words, Shiras laid out the framework and justification for the law: The states were inadequate to protect birds that migrated through their lands and waters. The absence of uniform regulations across the country had resulted in the wholesale destruction of many game birds, and unless protected by the federal government, many valuable species of game birds would go extinct.

The bill called for federal jurisdiction over "all wild geese, wild swans, brant, wild ducks, snipe, plover, woodcock, rail, wild pigeons and all migratory game birds which in their northern and southern migrations pass through and do not remain permanently the entire year within the borders of the state or territory." Throughout the range, the birds would be "within the custody and protection of the government of the United States and shall not be destroyed or taken contrary to regulations." The Department of Agriculture would adopt suitable regulations and hunting seasons that took into account migration and nesting patterns. Although the states would have leeway within the regulations, state law could not supersede or nullify federal law.

The bill limited itself to game birds. George's frame of reference—at the time, anyway—was hunting. The unnecessary killing he had witnessed at Revel Island weighed on his mind, as did the disappearance of the passenger pigeon. Unless there was action, other birds were on their way to extinction.

Forest and Stream offered support for the bill, saying, "If the sportsmen of this country want this law, they can have it if they say so and work for it."

Charles Bingham Reynolds, the editor, sent the bill to several state game commissioners and received many supportive letters in return. He passed the originals to Shiras, hoping they would be useful in lobbying lawmakers.

Reynolds wrote, "The tenor of these communications indicates that your plan will be received with much enthusiasm and it looks as though the amendment could go through if its adoption depends on the sentiment of the sportsmen of this country."

It was an uphill battle. Sale of game was lawful in thirty-five states. Fifteen states had no bag limits, and spring shooting was allowed in twenty-eight states. Thirteen states had no game wardens or any type of game commission.

On letterhead of the Committee on Public Lands, Shiras sent his bill to William Loeb, Roosevelt's secretary at the White House.

In the near future when you find the President's attention reverting again to matters relating to the protection of wild birds, animals, and as he has been for years been regarded by the sportsmen and naturalists of this country as the foremost champion of progressive legislation, he may be interested in the bill I recently framed and introduced into the House, extending Federal supervision over that class of game birds which are most threatened with extermination, and which, in my judgment, can be legally brought within the control of the general Government.

He gave a short version of his legal justification: "The time is rapidly approaching when National laws will replace State legislation on a number of important subjects requiring uniform treatment and control. Many distinguished lawyers and legislators have been gradually taking advanced ground on this subject, but the President's attitude in one year has done more in this direction than all the accumulative causes in the last decade."

He knew he had a champion in the president. In 1903 by executive order, Roosevelt designated Pelican Island in Florida as the first federal wildlife reserve (the beginning of today's National Wildlife Refuge System). Two years later, he set aside the Huron Islands just three miles off the south shore of Lake Superior in Marquette County—not far from where Shiras and his family camped and fished for speckled trout. The islands were (and still are) a breeding ground for migratory birds, most notably herring gulls, which had been decimated by plume hunters.

The Audubon Society, the American Ornithologists' Union, and other conservation organizations (many just forming) called for increased protection of birds, too.

Speaking for the Audubon Society, George Bird Grinnell praised Shiras as "the most prominent member of the club. "It is a good sign for this country when men, of whatever walk in life associate themselves together with the honest purpose of protecting those natural objects which since the settlement of America have been regarded as belonging to whoever should take them without regard to the time or method of taking."

Sportsmen who joined such organizations would find—as the Boone and Crockett Club had—that conservation would become their siren call, said Grinnell: "We may imagine that while these newest of associations is organized nominally for the purposes of sport, it will like its older brothers judge that the protection of the big game is more interesting, as it is a more important matter than its destruction."

The bird law was not produced in a vacuum. Many conservationists were discussing the concept of the federal government taking ownership of wildlife. Shiras as a congressional representative and lawyer was in a unique position to introduce it into the political arena. The Shiras bird bill, as it was to become known, did not have a chance of becoming law and George Shiras knew it. His intention was to start the debate.

Writing twenty-some years later, he recalled, "I made no effort to have action taken on the original Migratory Bird Bill for I recognized that its purpose, at first, should be educational.

"The ever increasing necessity for more efficient and uniform protection of migratory birds was known by everyone familiar with bird life throughout the northern continent but these compared with the public at large were then limited in number."

The Shiras bird bill was referred to the Committee on Agriculture and was well received by its members, but passage was impossible in both houses of Congress at that time. Federal jurisdiction over wildlife would be a contentious issue with some members and states. Some regions, mostly in the South and West, would see it as another grab of federal power by northern and eastern elites.

The Businessman's League of Rockport, a small Texas town on the Gulf Coast, was dead set against any attempt to regulate the hunting of ducks. Market hunting the waterfowl that wintered in great numbers along the Texas coast in its salt marshes was big business.

The editor of *American Field*, a magazine focused on hunting dogs, railed against the businessman's league, "It is a rather high sounding title for a little coterie of greedy warehousemen, store keepers, saloon keepers and resort keepers who have been supported by market hunters and game hogs that has done much to exterminate the supply of waterfowl and make Rockport a byword among true sportsman and an eyesore on the map of the United States."

The editor called for support of the Shiras bill:

It is gratifying to note that the public spirit is being aroused and while Texas sportsmen are fighting the enemy in their state, all other sportsmen should lend a helping hand to Hon. George Shiras in his efforts to have Congress pass the bill he had introduced in the House of Representatives as to the migratory birds of the United States by placing them under federal protection. Someday this will be done and it might as well be now while there is a fair supply left, as later when their scarcity will make the task disheartening.

Shiras's office in Washington received a letter from the Tolletson Gun Club of Chicago, which owned and leased large parts of the Calumet Swamp in Indiana. In addition to duck hunting, the club was known for high-stakes poker games in the clubhouse and a condescending attitude toward local citizens. Members and their club wardens had gotten into a firefight with farmers who tried to enter the swamp to hunt muskrats and ducks. Combatants had been shot on both sides.

Edwin F. Daniels, the president of the club and of a coal company, wrote, "The entire sixty-five members from the best citizens of Chicago is enthusiastically in favor of your bill."

U. J. Hindert, a farmer from Minonk, Illinois, wrote Shiras saying spring shooting should be halted completely. He had been a part-time game warden for Illinois for six years and said "the states don't know enough to stop the wholesale slaughter and sale of waterfowl. I think the federal government should step in and call a halt . . . I hope you will do all you can to protect what little game we have left."

On February 1, 1905, Roosevelt wrote to Shiras from the White House: "I am very much pleased with your bill and am glad that we have in Congress a man taking so great an interest in the preservation of our birds, and nature generally. I particularly wanted wild fowl protected."

Roosevelt, a birdwatcher, once wrote to Frank Chapman, "The destruction of The Wild Pidgeon and Carolina Paroquet [sic] has meant a loss as severe as if the Cascades and the Palisades were taken away. When I hear of destruction of a species, I feel just as if the works of some great writer had perished."

Moral indignation aside, there was a legal argument to be made for passage of the bird bill, and George Shiras 3d, the attorney, was in a good position to make it. He would devote the next several years to writing legal briefs and position papers as well as articles in sporting publications. He would give speeches to sporting organizations, submit to newspaper interviews, and lobby members of Congress, but by then he would no longer be in the US House of Representatives.

True to his word, Shiras declined to run for reelection. After doing an interview with Shiras, a reporter wrote, "He said he was not feeling badly because he did not secure a nomination for Congress on the Republican ticket and added that he would have time now to devote to his favorite work of taking photographs of big game."

His friend Stephen Porter, a leader in the Citizen's Party movement, won the nomination and held the seat for the next twenty-five years. Later, Shiras expressed pride in his friend's longevity in office, for it "indicates how the temporary reform movement in Allegheny County broke the political shackles of nearly fifty years and gave the voters the opportunity to select candidates standing high in popular esteem."

In 1903 George Junior retired from the Supreme Court after serving ten years. During his tenure, he was no firebrand, usually upholding the status quo and voting with the majority. He was part of the seven-to-one decision in *Plessy v. Ferguson* that upheld states' rights to enforce racial laws. The case defined the "separate but equal" doctrine and legitimized discrete water fountains, public toilets, and schools for blacks and whites. The decision was not repudiated until 1954 in the landmark case *Brown v. Board of Education.*

In 1895 Junior received unfavorable publicity—apparently unjustly so—for allegedly changing his vote in *Pollock v. Farmers' Loan and Trust Company*—an income tax case.

Junior never took to politics or Washington and spent the remaining twenty-one years of his life between his homes in Marquette and Florida and a hotel in Pittsburgh.

George 3d, Fanny, and the children, however, established a home in Wesley Heights in the northwest section of Washington and never again lived in Pittsburgh. Like Junior, they summered in the Upper Peninsula and spent winters in Florida. George gave up his law practice to concentrate on his nature studies. Winfield remained at Shiras and Dickey.

George earned money from his photography and writings. The Shiras and White fortunes and investments of their own allowed George and Fanny to live quite well. They joined the country club in Chevy Chase, Maryland, where it was possible to both birdwatch and golf on the grounds. They attended state dinners at the White House as a guest of the president. Their daughter Ellie went to debutante balls and affairs of the Pittsburg Club in DC. For George, there was shooting and birding at Revel Island and hunting at Cheat Mountain on weekends.

Beaver, Whitefish Lake. Courtesy of Northern Michigan University.

He joined the Cosmos Club, a private social club for men on Lafayette Square founded in 1878 by John Wesley Powell, the explorer, and other distinguished men of arts and sciences.

Frank Chapman, Shiras, E. W. Nelson of the Bureau of Biological Survey, and other "bird naturalists" frequently met there for lunch and conversation over cigars and drinks in the library.

In 1905, George was invited to show his "flashlight pictures" in the form of lantern slides to members of the Boone and Crockett Club at the Willard Hotel on Pennsylvania Avenue. Among those in attendance were Theodore Roosevelt, the president of the United States; George Bird Grinnell; Gifford Pinchot; C. Hart Merriam, the premier zoologist in the country; Madison Grant, a conservationist; Henry Fairfield Osborne, a paleontologist; William T. Hornaday, director of the New York Zoological Park and the Bison Society; Secretary of State Elihu Root; John Lacey of the Public

Lands Committee; Charles Sheldon, a big game hunter who lobbied for the establishment of Denali National Park; Owen Wister, author and a Roosevelt confidant; and Senator Henry Cabot Lodge.

On February 14, 1906, the club elected Shiras an associate member. It was a proud moment, for he held the organization and its ideals in high regard. Two years earlier, he had purchased *American Big Game in Its Haunts: The Book of the Boone and Crockett Club,* and wrote on the inside cover, "Presented to me by myself with the hope it will prove more accurate than most books of the present day."

The men of Boone and Crockett and the Cosmos Club held high positions in the government. They were leaders in the biological sciences and in the new Progressive conservation movement. They moved easily between public service and their work within conservation organizations. Discussions and ideas at the clubs or in private conversations often turned into public policy. And he had forged a working and personal relationship with the Colonel, as Theodore Roosevelt liked to be called by his friends.

As Shiras later wrote, "Here in scientific circles, I found many congenial friends and continued my connection with several national organizations concerned in conserving natural resources."

Clearly, Washington, DC, was where the action was and where a Progressive and a conservationist could do important work.

10 | THE NATIONAL GEOGRAPHIC SOCIETY

IN EARLY 1906, George Shiras 3d walked from his home near American University to the headquarters of the National Geographic Society. He brought along a box of flashlight prints to show Gilbert H. Grosvenor, who had become the editor of the society's magazine three years earlier.

The entire staff of the magazine then consisted of Grosvenor, assistant editor John Oliver La Gorce, and one secretary. The society had just a few hundred members. La Gorce recalled that a person could walk five minutes in a radius from the headquarters and leave behind most of the magazine's circulation.

Grosvenor was at the War Department trying to borrow some photographs he could use in the magazine. La Gorce met Shiras and eagerly arranged a later meeting. The two editors had heard Shiras lecture at the Cosmos Club and viewed some of his lantern slides from Whitefish Lake, but it wasn't until Grosvenor examined the dozens of images of deer, raccoons, muskrats, and birds that he realized the extent and uniqueness of Shiras's portfolio. Grosvenor told Shiras he wanted to print them all. It was a decision that would forever change the magazine.

Photojournalism was still in its infancy, but in Grosvenor's mind photography was clearly the future—a way to excite and educate the public about geography, increase readership, and fund scientific research.

The magazine had done little to grow the membership or bring money into what was still a small and young organization. The National Geographic Society had been founded in 1888 by a group of thirty-three explorers and scientists including such notables as John Wesley Powell, explorer of the Grand Canyon; Alexander Graham Bell, inventor of the telephone; and Gardiner Greene Hubbard, first president of the Bell Telephone Company. Meeting at the Cosmos Club, the founders determined the society's purpose was for the "increase and diffusion of geographic knowledge." They would do this through publication and scientific research and exploration projects. At its founding, it was not expected the organization would be more than a local institution.

Hubbard was elected president. The first issue of the magazine went out to two hundred charter members in October 1888. Through the 1890s, it was largely a text-oriented publication, akin to a scientific journal aimed at a narrow, erudite group of readers.

Meanwhile, consumer magazines of all types were booming. In the 1890s, magazines emerged as important literary and journalistic vehicles, reaching millions of people. *Cosmopolitan, North American Review,* the *Saturday Evening Post, Everybody's, Colliers Weekly,* and *Ladies' Home Journal* informed readers about science and politics, entertained with fiction and essays, set fashion trends, and raised social consciousness.

The technologies of photography and printing were going through a revolution, too. George Eastman's invention of the Kodak handheld camera made picture-taking a national hobby. The halftone process enabled printers to break an image into closely spaced dots and produce a metal plate for printing on a letterpress. Photographs rather than illustrations began appearing in newspapers and periodicals.

When Hubbard died in 1897, the membership of the National Geographic Society was less than one thousand. It was not financially self-supporting and mostly held together by the wealth and charity of some founding members.

Alexander Graham Bell reluctantly took over the presidency and looked for a new editor to breathe life into a magazine as "dry as dust to most people because of its technical papers for scientists." He chose Gilbert Hovey Grosvenor, the son of a friend and a professor of history who had raised his children in Turkey and then educated them at the best schools in the East. Grosvenor left his job as a prep school teacher in New Jersey and moved to Washington.

It was the first time the magazine had a full-time editor. Bell paid the young man's salary out of his own pocket. Gilbert Grosvenor was just twenty-four when he took the job. He served as editor-in-chief for the next fifty-one years and became president of the society in 1920. When he retired in 1954, the magazine's circulation was 4.5 million, and the National Geographic Society was the most important scientific organization in the world.

Grosvenor and Bell worked as a team, a partnership made familial when Grosvenor married Bell's daughter, Elsie. The two young people had met on Bell's estate in Nova Scotia during the editor's initial interview.

The men embraced photography as a way to popularize the magazine with the public. Grosvenor suggested selling society memberships instead of magazine subscriptions. Members would get the magazine free as a benefit. It was a subtle change in enrollment but an effective one.

In January 1905, Grosvenor published eleven pages of photography taken by a Russian explorer in Tibet. He thought he might be fired, understanding that such a change in format would upset some of the society's board of managers. Instead, he received congratulations. Encouraged, he followed up with the photographs from the War Department, a series showing landscapes of the Philippines, a recent acquisition from the Spanish-American War.

By 1906, Grosvenor said, "the word *photograph* had become as musical to my ear as the jingle of a cash register to a businessman."

Now he came into possession of these remarkable game photographs. He asked Shiras to write an article describing how he accomplished such feats. The prose also should give readers an appreciation of the location— Whitefish Lake and the wild country of the Upper Peninsula.

After the publicity of the World's Fair, Shiras had been selling sets of the *Midnight Series* and giving talks with lantern slides. In 1904 at the Universal Exposition in St. Louis to commemorate the centennial of the Louisiana Purchase, he received grand prize for his *Flashlight Photographs of Wild Game.*

However, the fame derived from the National Geographic Society and the relationship he forged with the magazine and Grosvenor, too, served him well the remainder of his life. It would make Shiras a seminal figure of the early conservation movement and give him the reputation—despite no formal biological training—of being a renowned faunal naturalist.

The entire July 1906 issue consisted of George's photographs and writings. The title on the yellow-framed cover read: "Photographing Wild Game with Flash Light and Camera: With a Series of 70 illustrations of Wild

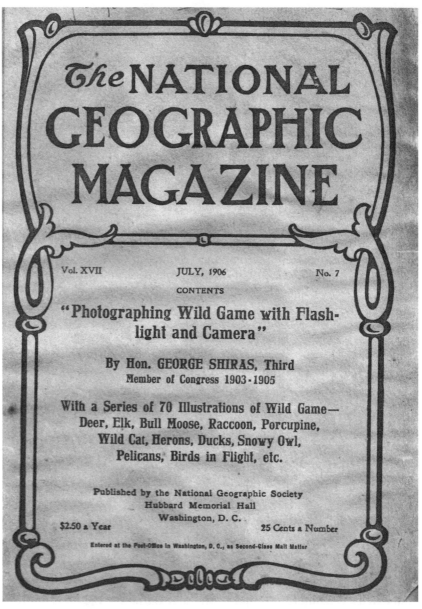

𝒯𝒽𝑒 NATIONAL
GEOGRAPHIC
MAGAZINE

Vol. XVII   JULY, 1906   No. 7

CONTENTS

"Photographing Wild Game with Flashlight and Camera"

By Hon. GEORGE SHIRAS, Third
Member of Congress 1903-1905

With a Series of 70 Illustrations of Wild Game—
Deer, Elk, Bull Moose, Raccoon, Porcupine,
Wild Cat, Herons, Ducks, Snowy Owl,
Pelicans, Birds in Flight, etc.

Published by the National Geographic Society
Hubbard Memorial Hall
Washington, D. C.

$2.50 a Year   25 Cents a Number

Entered at the Post-Office in Washington, D. C., as Second-Class Mail Matter

First wildlife images in *National Geographic* magazine, 1906.

Game—Deer, Elk, Bull Moose, Raccoon, Porcupine, Wild Cat, Herons, Ducks, Snowy Owls, Pelicans, Birds In Flight, Etc."

These were the first wildlife photos ever published in the magazine, and the pictorial content of the issue—and the uniqueness of the images themselves—captured public attention.

By this time, Shiras had accumulated nearly three thousand glass negatives of wildlife and woodland scenes. The breadth of the images showed all he had accomplished technically in terms of exposure, trip wires, flashlight setups, and camera traps. To illustrate his camera hunting technique on the water, the magazine ran a self-portrait of Shiras and John Hammer approaching the shore in the skiff. Taken in 1893 with a camera on shore to represent the point of view of the animal, the full-page picture shows Shiras in the bow wearing a black leather jacket, white shirt, and wool ascot cap. A wooden box anchored to the bow contains the Schmid Detective Camera. Atop the box sits the jacklight. Shiras extends one arm, pointing his pistol flashlight mechanism equipped with a metal shield to protect his face from the explosion. Hammer leans back in the stern, maneuvering the boat with his paddle dipped into the black water.

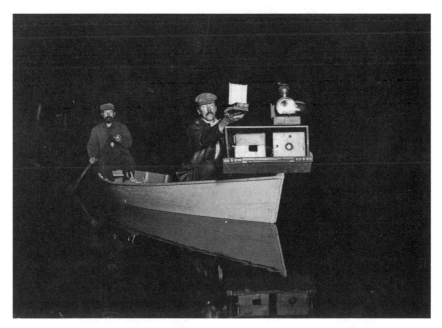

Self-portrait demonstrating camera and flashlight techniques from a skiff.
Shiras holding flashlight, John Hammer at oar, 1893.
Courtesy of Northern Michigan University.

Other images represented Shiras's wide interest in Animalia and his work at different locations: a northern flicker at a nesting cavity on Revel Island, a great white heron on Cumberland Island, Georgia, a lynx or wild-cat in Georgian Bay, Canada, pelicans on the Indian River in Florida, avo-cets flying at Henry's Lake, Idaho, and a moose stomping through a marsh on Lake Superior.

Some photographs were peculiar: a horde of butterflies lighting on a dead fish, a snowshoe hare chewing on a piece of salty paper bait, and a heron asleep in the reeds, head tucked under one wing.

This time Grosvenor got guff from the society's stodgy board of manag-ers. Alfred H. Brooks, a geologist, declared that Grosvenor and Bell were cheapening the magazine, turning it into a "picture book." Brooks, whose name was given to the Brooks Range in Alaska, resigned. Another board member quit in protest a few months later.

Grosvenor, however, remembered the July 1906 "number" (a term the editors used for an issue) as a "pioneering achievement of the *National Geographic*. . . . It was an extraordinarily educative series: Nobody had ever seen pictures like that of wild animals. I can't exaggerate the enthusiasm with which they were received by our members."

Theodore Roosevelt was so impressed that he wrote a congratulatory note to Grosvenor on July 14, 1906:

I thank you for your letter and the copy of your magazine. Those are wonderful pictures. Most of them Mr. Shiras has shown me himself, but some of them are new to me. I have been doing my best to persuade Mr. Shiras that he is derelict in his duty in not writing a book in which these wonderful pictures and his almost equally remarkable written observations should be recorded in more permanent form.

In the letter, Roosevelt asserts that pamphlets and photographs are ephemeral—only a book can serve as a permanent record. There is no record of what Grosvenor thought of the notion that his magazine was not on the same par with books.

That same day, Roosevelt dictated a letter to Shiras:

I have just been looking through your photographs in the *National*

Lynx image from the *Midnight Series*, Ontario, Canada, 1902.
Courtesy of Northern Michigan University.

Geographic magazine. Now my dear sir, no other work you can do (not even going to Congress; still less writing articles for pamphlets or magazines, utter evanescent in character) is as important as for you to write a big book—a book of bulk as well as worth, in which you shall embody these pictures and the results of your invaluable notes upon the habits not only of game but the numerous other wild creatures that you have observed.

I feel very strongly that this country stands much more in need of the work of a great out-door faunal naturalist than of the work of any number of closet specialists and microscopic tissue cutters. Do go ahead and do this work!"

Although he had been doing taxidermy since he was a child, Roosevelt was not enamored of scientists who spent their days in museums, analyzing skins and bones. Roosevelt was not formally trained; nor was Frank Chapman, a self-educated naturalist who never went beyond high school but eventually headed up the Department of Birds at the American Museum of Natural History in New York. The disciplines of forestry, wildlife biology, zoology, ornithology, and animal behavior were still in their infancy and schools, departments, and professional societies dedicated to these studies were rare or nonexistent.

As a sportsman, Shiras was of the same mold as Roosevelt. His love of the out-of-doors came by way of hunting and fishing. He was formally educated at fine schools, well read, spent a good deal of time in the woods, and was an excellent observer of wildlife and natural processes.

The letter was not the first occasion Roosevelt had urged Shiras to write a book. At a dinner of the Boone and Crockett Club held on April 7 of that year, Roosevelt had, according to newspaper accounts, made a "vigorous speech that was enthusiastically received. His theme was that the difference between the civilized man and the primitive man is the civilized man leaves behind a record of things done and with this statement as a text, he proceeded to urge an eminent naturalist present to publish the results of his investigation into the life histories of various North American mammals."

As an author, the president understood books, the writing life, and the market for hunting and nature literature. Just as boldly as he barged through life and politics, Roosevelt's strategy as a writer was to scribble away and work with what was at hand. He had made much of his ranching days in the Dakota Badlands and his hunting experiences in *Ranch Life and the Hunting Trail* (1888), *The Wilderness Hunter* (1893), and *The Deer Family* (1902).

Shiras had plenty of such raw material, and Roosevelt nagged him for years to write books. Shiras proved to be a perfectionist and wasn't anxious to undertake such a major project without more research, traveling, and observation. On several occasions, he told the president and others that he needed to make extended expeditions in order to get additional information on the fauna of North America. Writing up each trip and publishing in magazines, especially *National Geographic*, would lay the foundation of a book, he said.

When the July 1906 number appeared, Shiras was in Marquette on summer holiday. Roosevelt's letter was forwarded to Pittsburgh and then north to Michigan.

Shiras wrote back on July 28, 1906, noting it was the thirty-fifth year he had come north to camp at Whitefish Lake. With a sly reference to his migratory bird bill, he quipped to Roosevelt, "you can see I too am a regular migrant."

The magazine with so many photographs might strike the president as "firing in the air," he said, because camera hunting was a bloodless sport. Yet he took solace that the magazine was mostly targeting scientists and that few sportsman received it.

"Perhaps no harm has been done," he said.

The tone of the letter is oddly apologetic, as if he has to justify himself to Roosevelt, the big game hunter and someone renowned for hypermasculinity.

In the *National Geographic* article, Shiras admitted that his journey from gun to the camera required "a peculiar mental evolution" but said he came to his decision when he no longer felt joy from killing: "Every true sportsman will admit that the instant his noble quarry lies prone upon the earth, with the glaze of death upon the once lustrous eye, the graceful limbs stiff and rigid, and the tiny hole emitting the crimson thread of life, there comes the half definite feeling of repentance and sorrow . . . the time has come when it is not necessary to convert the wilderness into an untenanted and silent waste in order to enjoy the sport of successfully hunting birds and wild animals."

Yet he set himself apart from other proponents of the camera who did not approve of hunting: "Many such people come from the ranks of ultra-sentimentalists who decry the sportsmen as a set of ruthless butchers, blind alike to the beauty of wild life and to the ethics of ordinary decency."

Shiras defended true sportsmen who "constitute a high order of citizenship; generous, self-reliant and faithful; they have done much in keeping up the virility of the race, and in leavening those debasing influences of over civilization." He paraphrased the "fair chase" ethic of the Boone and Crocket Club and decried the killing of does and fawns, the taking of fish with a hand net versus an artificial fly, and the shooting of wild animals to sell in the marketplace. Game birds, he declared, should only be taken on the wing.

Camera hunting, because it was so difficult, he argued, was in the realm of the true sportsman. "Every camera hunter must see that a more immediate and lasting pleasure is afforded in raking a running deer from stem to stern with his 5 × 7 boor camera than driving an ounce ball through the heart at 100 yards."

As the article was being published, Shiras perfected his latest innovation—a trap with two cameras and two flashlights. The first flashlight recorded the animal unaware, in a rather static position—grazing, drinking from the lake, or pawing at a baited string. The second image, a split second later, was all-kinetic—recording the animal's alarmed reaction from the first explosion.

It worked best with deer, he wrote. "Some of the deer were caught bounding gracefully away, some bending or twisting their legs curiously in preparation for a leap and others crouching with their bellies almost touching the ground as if their legs had well nigh collapsed at the sudden alarm."

Frank Chapman, when he saw these pictures, felt the images were rather artificial and breached Shiras's earlier approach of visually eavesdropping on the deer's natural nighttime behavior.

"To yield to our curiosity to see 'what happens' is to destroy this feeling of seeing the unseen and at the same time to take unfair advantage of the animal," Chapman wrote.

George disagreed. Deer were constantly on guard and reacting to threats, he said. A picture in the *Midnight Series*, "Alert," showed a buck with its back to the skiff, turning toward a hillside where a wolf had howled a

Whitetail deer from the *Midnight Series*, Whitefish Lake; the motion is a result of using two flashlights. Courtesy of Northern Michigan University.

moment earlier. Recording an animal's attitudes of "fear and rage" were also a part of the story—as well as their agility, said Shiras. "I am impressed with the idea that the taking of these animated pictures will prove of value and I trust that others will follow this method."

Indeed, the most enduring of his images, the photograph most recognized and reproduced a hundred years later, shows three deer at Whitefish Lake reacting to the explosion of the first flashlight. They leapt away from a bait pile of cabbage leaves—muscles tensed, white bellies, muzzles, and tails flashing against dark trees and brush. The deer are airborne, birdlike, frozen as if in flight. No other means would have captured such an image.

Other action photos clearly have a different quality, and one can understand Chapman's point of view. The animals are obviously startled, scrambling to get away, bewildered and temporarily blinded.

The explosions were powerful. After some hard lessons, Shiras learned to close his eyes and turn his face away at the moment of ignition. Once he blasted some head hair off Jake Brown, and another time he singed his arm.

He and Hammer were on Grand Island one night in a canoe, paddling the shores of an inland lake, flashlighting any animals that came in for a drink. Grand Island was then a game preserve stocked with nonnative animals. Eventually, they spied a cow and calf elk. When Shiras raised up his arm and fired the flashlight, the powder exploded with such force that it blew the mechanism apart. The trigger guard bent around his fingers and his hand slammed against the side of the canoe, laming his wrist for several days. After that, he put the flashlight on an upright wooden support in the bow rather than holding it aloft in his hand.

By 1906 Shiras was not the only camera hunter working with nighttime photography. At the annual dinner of the Boone and Crockett Club that year, Hermann Speck von Sternburg, the ambassador from Germany, was the guest speaker. He focused his remarks on the accomplishments of Charles Schillings at the Berlin National Museum, who was about to publish a book entitled *Rifle and Flashlight.*

The ambassador said he was certain this august group of American sportsmen would be fascinated to hear about the pioneering photography being done in Germany. But as he made claims about Schillings's first use of the flashlight to record wild game, smiles were exchanged around the table. Noticing the amusement of the audience, von Sternburg stopped his speech and asked the source of the humor.

The president of the United States set him straight. Pointing to George Shiras, Roosevelt said, "The gentleman sitting opposite us developed his method many years ago and on two occasions has shown his flashlight pictures at our dinners."

Later in the evening, von Sternburg approached Shiras and apologized.

It turned out that Schillings had developed his methods with help from a member of the Berlin National Museum who had written to Shiras after seeing his pictures at the Paris Exposition Universelle. Shiras sent the man a schematic of his pistol flashlight.

Shiras recalled, "I had sent him a description and drawing of the apparatus with instructions for its use, expressing the hope that he would be successful in utilizing the information."

Some weeks later, Roosevelt had another discussion with the ambassador, who in turn spoke to his countryman. The second edition of Schillings's book included an acknowledgment of Shiras's expertise and his "firsts."
Ever the nationalist, Roosevelt was not going to have a foreigner take credit for an American invention. Schillings may not have been first with the flashlight, but he was first with a book and, as Roosevelt had been saying all along, a book established reputations.

11 | ORMOND BEACH

SEVERAL SHOREBIRD IMAGES that appeared in the 1906 *National Geographic* article were captured by Shiras near the Atlantic Coast town of Ormond Beach, Florida. Upon quitting Congress and abandoning his law practice in Pittsburgh, he built a winter home on the Halifax River. Ormond became as much a conservation touchstone to Shiras as Michigan's Upper Peninsula. At the turn of the century, wild game abounded in Florida, and its estuaries and wetlands were ground zero in the fight to save birds.

In 1903 Roosevelt signed an executive order establishing Pelican Island as a federal bird reservation. The three-acre island of mangroves located in the Indian River lagoon was the last breeding area for brown pelicans on the East Coast.

Frank Chapman and the Audubon Society urged Roosevelt to act because plume hunters who killed roseate spoonbills, pelicans, and snowy egrets for the millinery trade (the designing and making of women's hats) continually raided the island. Most women's hats featured elaborate and colorful feathers—even stuffed birds—as part of their ornamentation. Plume hunting was as devastating to shorebird populations as market and sport hunting was to waterfowl.

Pelican Island marked the first time the government set aside land solely for the sake of wildlife. Five weeks after Roosevelt declared the island protected, Shiras left Ormond Beach in Volusia County, where he was visiting his parents, and went to Pelican Island hoping to take flashlight pictures of the breeding birds. He rowed out to the island with a guide he had brought along from Revel Island.

After dark, they quietly drifted into the mangroves. Shiras stood up in the bow as he had done at Whitefish Lake, composed his shot, and fired his flashlight and alcohol lamp.

The entire colony took wing—perhaps some five hundred birds. Disoriented and frightened by the bright flash and the concussion of the explosion, the pelicans crashed into the men, fell into the boat, and knocked cameras off the bow. Shiras got a picture, but the tumult convinced him never to attempt such a feat again.

In 1905 he returned to the island with Frank Chapman, and they counted the carcasses of some eight hundred pelicans killed in a midnight raid by commercial fishermen, who considered the birds a menace to their livelihood. No doubt his commitment to protect birds was influenced by witnessing the slaughter up close and the relationships he forged in Florida with naturalists and game wardens. It could be a dangerous business. Two game wardens hired by the Audubon Society died in armed clashes with plume hunters.

Sometimes the problems stemmed more from ignorance and a penchant to hold on to the old ways. One year, he went to the Big Green Swamp near Mohawk to take pictures of sandhill cranes, which were fast disappearing from the area. He secured the services of a local trapper and guide. Deep in the swamp, they found nary a crane. All the nests were unoccupied. This was unfortunate, the guide remarked, for he had been collecting the eggs for many years and sending them north for a dollar apiece.

The coast north and south of Cape Canaveral was relatively pristine when the Shiras family began coming south in the 1880s. Railroads had yet to penetrate the coastal forests, and developers were just starting to turn the scrubby dunes and vast stretches of beach into towns and resorts.

George Junior, Lillie, and family would take rooms at the Ormond Beach Hotel on the east bank of the Halifax River. Built in 1887 by some of the town's pioneer families, the hotel was a sprawling, all-wooden structure with seventy-five rooms that rented for four dollars per night. Guests partook in parties and picnics, theatricals, horseback and carriage rides, and launch trips along the ocean and in the river. Guests could travel about the grounds on "Afromobiles": padded white wicker chairs on wheels—a kind of rickshaw—propelled by African Americans to get around the grounds. A bugle call summoned everyone to dinner.

Steeped in class and race divisions, the Ormond Hotel was a wholly white and privileged place populated by artists and poets, industrialists, rich debutantes and dowagers, and members of the New York and New England social sets.

Henry Flagler, one of the founders of Standard Oil and a railroad tycoon, bought the hotel in 1891, extended the rail lines into Ormond and Daytona, and built a wooden train bridge across the Halifax so guests could step directly from the train and walk up the steps of the hotel. He added a casino, swimming pool, and golf course. By the early part of the twentieth century, the hotel was grand and popular with northern elites—including J. D. Rockefeller, who would come for the winter and rent an entire floor.

In 1895 Ormond had just four hundred permanent residents, but the snowbirds and railroad brought money and business opportunities. Farmers established commercial citrus groves and vegetable fields and shipped their products north. The wide, hard-packed sand beach between Ormond and Daytona became a proving ground for the new automobile. Flagler built a brick-floored garage at the hotel where mechanics repaired and stored their racing machines.

In the early 1900s, the hotel's telegraph office frequently announced that "another speed record had been established at the Ormond-Daytona Beach course."

The location proved pleasant and the society of snowbirds so amiable that George and his father purchased building lots fronting the east bank of the Halifax River.

The *Daytona Gazette-News* announced on January 16, 1904, that "Ex Justice Shiras Jr., who was appointed to the Supreme Court bench by President Johnson has just purchased the Wicks Property at Ormond, one of the handsomest properties on the coast. Judge and Mrs. Shiras and servants will be at the Ormond (hotel) until the cottage has been prepared for their reception."

The cottages were sprawling, two-story clapboard homes with dormers, bay windows, an open front porch, and shaded, screened-in rear porches all surrounded by manicured lawns and immense live oaks draped with Spanish moss. The Shirases could walk to the hotel to dine, sit on the veranda, write and send telegrams, and interact with the guests.

Ormond became a gathering point for the family each winter. Josiah G. Reynolds, the manager of the Lake Superior Powder Company, which supplied explosives to the iron mines, bought an adjacent lot. Reynolds had married Jean Kennedy—Lillie's sister.

George 3d and Fanny were active in civic affairs. He became president of the homeowner's association. Fanny helped start the library and women's club. They attended and donated generously to the Episcopal Church, giving part of their property for the building of a new church.

In retirement, Junior spent many a happy winter in Florida. Most mornings he sat on the veranda, watching the birds and recording the wind direction and temperature. He fished in the river and on the ocean surf. He picked oranges from the grove behind the cottages and shipped boxes to friends and relatives in Pittsburgh and Marquette.

The cottages were located on a sandy peninsula between the Atlantic Ocean and the river. The Halifax is actually not a river but a tidal saltwater lagoon paralleling the Atlantic Coast. It begins seven miles north of Ormond in the Tomoka Basin, a large shallow body of fresh water fed by the Tomoka River. It ends eighteen miles south at Ponce de Leon Inlet, where it connects to the sea. The towns of Ormond, Daytona, and Sea Breeze lie on the land between the sea and river. There is usually a brisk breeze with a salty smell of the sea, and the river is often turbulent with the changing of the tides.

In those early days, the 1- to 1.5-mile wide peninsula was forested with yellow pine, palmetto, and live oaks thick with undergrowth. Near the ocean, the foliage morphed into low scrub palmetto and bushes and finally wide, white beaches. George 3d discovered a wealth of critters living behind his winter home. One winter, he set out camera traps on thirty-three consecutive nights and shot pictures of cottontail rabbits, nine different skunks (distinguished by markings), four raccoons, three opossum, one house cat, one dog, two swamp rats, and four wood rats.

He declared, "Few persons are aware of the abundance of night loving animals in the vicinity of country homes located near a dense thicket, a swamp, or rocky ravine."

The cameras and booming flashlights at first alarmed the neighbors and guests at the hotel. "The glare of light and the heavy report that followed astonished the people in the neighborhood but finally they became accustomed to it and would ask each morning what luck I had had the night before."

Few animals escaped his camera. One March, he found the burrow of a gopher tortoise in the beach grass and placed a trip thread across the opening, knowing the tortoise would soon emerge from hibernation. In a few days, it fired the flashlight and then hid for another week. When it came out again, it sprung another camera trap. Satisfied with the images, Shiras left the tortoise alone.

Out his front door, the Halifax River was rich with snook, black drum, sea trout, and redfish. There were middens, or mounds, of oyster shells and clamshells along the banks, discarded there for centuries by Native Americans. Manatees cruised the saltwater lagoon. Rafts of ducks floated on the river. Herons stalked the shallows. In winter, the oak forests were full of migrants from the north—flocks of robins, warblers, and neotropical species. More than three hundred species of birds live on or pass through Florida's Atlantic Coast.

He surrounded his cottage with feeding stations stocked with suet, bread, and scratch grain. He erected birdhouses—including a multicelled house for a colony of purple martins. He tossed out seed and lured Florida quail—a variation of the bobwhite—into the yard and took their pictures, along with squirrels, wood rats, or whatever took his fancy. It is clear from his field notes and copious observations that he spent much time on his porch watching and noting habits. Of the Florida scrub jay—a species now threatened by development along the beach—he remarked that he never saw it anywhere near his home. "In the bushes along the ocean front half of a mile to the east however, they are numerous and many cottagers living in the brushy sand dune belt had them as visitors."

He surmised correctly that it was a specialist. Today, the scrub jay is only found in the Canaveral National Seashore and a few isolated stretches of beach. And because central Florida was the last stronghold of the Carolina parakeet, George Shiras 3d saw these doomed birds before they went extinct. When he traveled inland, there were healthy populations of white-tailed deer, black bear, mountain lions, and gray wolves.

Close to Ormond, the Tomoka River became a favorite haunt. It was accessible, wild, and swarming with birds and alligators. A tributary of the Halifax, the Tomoka lay about six miles to the north and was navigable upstream for ten miles. Shiras first visited in the large, powered launches operated by the Ormond Beach Hotel, which took guests on waterway cruises to see alligators and hold picnics beneath the giant live oaks. The hotel's *Princess Issena* featured an open-air second deck. A small launch, the *Nemo,* came with awnings to protect women from the sun.

The marshy borders along the river were favorite places for sunning alligators and, for several years, people made sport of shooting the animals from the boats. A photograph of the era shows Annie Oakley taking aim from the bow of the *Nemo.* Eventually, there was a consensus that gators were good for tourism and were to be left alone. Once the alligators became accustomed to the big boats of people, they were largely apathetic to the shouts and rushes across the decks.

After taking his family on one of these picnic excursions in 1908, Shiras returned to shoot daylight pictures of the critters. By then, John Hammer was coming south from Marquette to act as a caretaker and guide. Shiras had a small cottage constructed. Later, he would build John a place at Whitefish Lake as well.

Packing a picnic lunch prepared by the "colored cook," he and Hammer mounted camera gear in a rowboat and headed north. Hammer apparently rowed the entire twenty-mile round trip which, Shiras said, "recalled our long hunting and fishing excursions along the shores of Lake Superior."

They reached the first marsh and immediately saw a half-dozen alligators on a muddy bank. As the men approached, the gators slid into the water and disappeared. Upriver, the result was the same. The gators may have been acclimated to the big excursion boats, but a small boat represented a hunter and clearly spelled danger.

Shiras also maintained a houseboat on the Halifax, and it was Hammer's charge to keep the craft ready for family cruises or photographic excursions. The boat had a draft of two feet and could travel nine miles per hour. Large windows ran the entire length of the cabin. There was a kitchen and "quarters for the guide."

Frequently they took the boat down the river and into the Ponce Inlet to observe colonies of nesting birds and further south along the coast into the marshes of what many years later became the space center at Cape Canaveral. The marshes were flat, grassy, and domed by a huge sky of puffy clouds.

Once they spent an afternoon photographing black skimmers. Shiras was especially fascinated by how the birds, when alarmed, took off in tight flocks and formations that filled his viewfinder. Wanting to take more pictures the next day, he and Hammer anchored the boat in the river about a half-mile from the ocean. The wind came up strong, and with a high tide running out, they worried they might drag the anchor.

About ten p.m., while listening "to the tumult outside there came a tremendous crash on the port side. The windows rattled, loose items fell to the floor, and the little craft shivered from stem to stern."

They'd been hit by a seventy-five-foot scow dragging anchor and swinging wildly. It came back again and missed the bow by just five feet. A square hit would have likely driven the houseboat underneath the barge.

There were many such adventures in Florida—photographic trips to the Everglades, the Keys, and Kissimmee Prairie north of Lake Okeechobee, which was open range in the early 1900s. Shiras and Frank Chapman spent many nights at Oak Lodge, a boarding house about nine miles up the Indian River from Pelican Island. "Ma" Latham, who ran the lodge, was described by Chapman as "a born naturalist." She collected, preserved, and catalogued turtle eggs, embryos, and birds. She also helped find the men who would take on the dangerous task of game warding and protecting Pelican Island against plume hunters. Her ten-room boarding house was a gathering place for naturalists and scientists including Chapman, Shiras, William T. Hornaday, E. W. Nelson, and Louis Agassiz Fuertes. They came to observe, paint, and sometimes collect birds for museums and research. There was an urgency to their tasks because natural Florida was already beginning to disappear, especially along the coast.

It was a good life for gentlemen and naturalists, and many of Shiras's colleagues who came to visit the birding hotspots would put up at his home in Ormond or at the hotel. E. W. Nelson of the Biological Survey would stay for a few days, even a few weeks. Norman McClintock, a fellow Pittsburgher and pioneer filmmaker of wild animals, often stayed several days to film birds on the beach and in nearby marshes. Over the years, Shiras helped finance some of McClintock's work and expeditions. Whenever he was in Ormond, McClintock would lecture at the hotel and show his "moving pictures" to the guests. Henry Fairfield Osborne, a paleontologist at the American Museum of Natural History and a fellow member of Boone and Crockett, also had a cottage not far from Shiras.

Frank Chapman chose Ormond Beach as a winter home from 1912 to 1922. He and his wife stayed on the beach side of the peninsula, renting rooms at the Coquina Inn where he could scan the beach with his binoculars, looking at shorebirds—pelicans, terns, plovers, turnstones, gannets— or swing round to another window looking landward and see white-eyed towhees and scrub jays in the palmettos.

Unlike Shiras, Frank Chapman loved to golf and often played rounds with J. D. Rockefeller on the course next to the Ormond Hotel. After renting whole floors for several years, the tycoon bought a house, the Casements, across the street from the hotel—not more than fifty yards from the Shiras homes.

According to local author Alice Strickland, who published *Ormond-on-the-Halifax*, a history of the town on its centennial in 1980, "The Shiras houses were a short distance from the Casements but their occupants did not have a friendly relationship with John D. Rockefeller. George Shiras Jr. was noted for his involvement in the income tax case of 1895, which, in general, provided for a tax of 2 percent on all annual incomes over $4,000. As only a small percentage of people received an income over that amount at that time, it was considered a piece of class legislation, and Shiras voted against it. As a result, he became a center of nationwide controversy."

Exactly why the income tax case would matter to Rockefeller is not clear, but there was never a mention of "Neighbor John" in any of the writings of Shiras, nor is there any mention of golf. It may be that Rockefeller and the Progressive Shiras family were on opposite sides of politics.

But Frank Chapman was quite friendly with Rockefeller. On the golf course and among the wealthy guests, Chapman found lots of "financial support for expeditions, new bird collections and the museum."

In the winter evenings, Chapman and George 3d were often seen strolling "the quiet unpaved streets around the little town."

In his book *Autobiography of a Bird-Lover*, Chapman remembered it this way:

> With undiminished pleasure I recall the walks through Ormond's moss-hung live-oaks, palms and pines. It was characteristic of these walks that wherever and whenever they began, they almost invariably ended at the side of George Shiras. Always I found this genial philosopher of outdoor life ready to discuss man's relations to nature from the observation of the moment to constitutional status of the latest move in conservation. With understanding of his fellow man deepened and mellowed with time; with sympathy toward all and malice toward none, he was an unfailing source of wise and generous comment who widened one's knowledge and put one in tune with the world.

12 | BAHAMAS, MEXICO

IN THE SPRING of 1907, Frank Chapman invited Shiras on an expedition to the Bahamas to visit breeding colonies of brown booby, *Sula leucogaster*, and frigate birds, *Fregata magnificens*—both birds of the open ocean.

Chapman was after specimens to complete *Habitat Groups*, a series of North American bird dioramas at the Museum of Natural History in New York. Once Shiras was out of Congress and done with corporate law, he was free to follow his muse and pursue outdoor adventure and photography.

He wrote to Roosevelt at the White House, "Chapman after finishing up his lecture course on February 28th is to join me here March 1st, in route to Florida and the Gulf of Mexico, where we hope to finish our study of sea-fowl upon which we have been working intermittently for the past ten years."

They met up in Miami and boarded the fifty-eight-foot yacht of the Marine Biological Laboratory of the Carnegie Institution, docked on the Dry Tortugas, a coral reef formation sixty miles west of Key West. The *Physalia*, named after a genus of jellyfish, transported scientists between the lab and mainland Florida. Alfred G. Mayer, the founder and director of the laboratory and an accomplished yachtsman, served as captain.

They left port on March 28, making Nassau in a couple of days. After obtaining collection permits from British authorities, they headed to Cay Verde 230 miles to the southeast. A cay is a low, sandy island atop a coral reef. Chapman planned to arrive at Cay Verde at the height of nesting season. His only information on the rookeries there were reports from 1857 and 1896. The birds might have gone elsewhere or been eliminated by hunters, but he hoped the cay's isolation might act as protection.

The first night they made forty miles and dropped anchor on the north side of a large cay that gave good cover from surf breaking on the windward side.

The calm did not last and the next several hours proved to be harrowing. A storm, which Shiras described as a "hurricane," moved in from the north. The barometer plummeted, thunderclouds gathered, and the sea foamed with white caps. Wind gusts hit eighty miles per hour. Waves threatened to cast the boat up on the reef.

They pulled anchor and headed toward open water but almost immediately struck a sandbar. Water swept the decks and flooded the engine room. They rushed to put up a sail until the engine could be restarted. Forced to run in the trough of heavy seas to avoid coral islands, the yacht with its tall masts was laid on its side several times. The lifeboats nearly ripped away.

As Shiras remembered, "It was perils of the shallows and of the reefs not of the deep."

All night, the yacht ran through darkness with a crew member clinging to the bow, throwing out a lead to measure the depth in the shallow water. Often there was no more than a foot between the keel and bottom. At midnight, the gasoline tank sprung a leak and contaminated the bilges. Fumes filled the boat. There was a real chance of an explosion. They rushed to extinguish all gas lanterns and steered using a small electric flashlight to see the compass. Finally, at 4:30 a.m., they found shelter in a bay ninety-one miles from their anchoring point the night before.

Chapman later wrote in a report to museum benefactors, "Had it not been for Dr. Mayer's skillful seamanship, it is probable that the expedition would not have returned at all." They laid up for two days, pumping out the bilges and cooking on shore because the boat smelled sickly of gasoline fumes. About the only items that didn't get wet with seawater or gas were the sensitive photographic plates that Shiras had carefully packed and secured in watertight containers. Fortunately, most of the food was canned goods.

Even after they cleaned up and refitted, they couldn't rid the yacht of gasoline fumes. Shiras and the other men who smoked had to climb into a repaired lifeboat, which was towed behind lest a spark ignite the whole works. They finally reached Cay Verde on April 8. Chapman feared the nesting birds might have returned to the sea, but they were there in abundance. The boobies nested on the rocky ground, and the frigate birds built their nests in cacti, wild grape, and brush.

There was no harbor. Shiras and Chapman rowed ashore in a small boat and set up a shade shelter using an old sail, tripod, and boat oar. A thermometer at ground level in the sun read 130 degrees. Mayer remained in the *Physalia* and moved the boat from one side of the cay to the other whenever the wind shifted. In case they might be marooned, Shiras and Chapman brought ashore a cask of water and a box of provisions.

The cay was about thirty acres populated by some three thousand boobies and three to five hundred frigate birds. It was a gorgeous tropical scene—billowing clouds and the waters rosy-colored at sunset. The two friends stood and looked out on thousands of nesting boobies, including one pair just ten feet from their shelter.

After the rough days at sea, Shiras noted, "We secretly rejoiced at having beneath our blankets solid ground, as hard at it was."

The boobies were amazingly tame. Chapman likened the rookeries to walking through a poultry yard. When the adult birds moved aside, the men examined the nests and the baby birds close up. Shiras set up his camera within inches of a nest and stopped the lens diaphragm down to F-32 or F-64 in the bright light, obtaining images of detail with great depth of field. The black-and-white boobies showed up well on the monochromatic plates. Several wider, more landscape-oriented pictures showed the *Physalia* anchored off shore at the edge of the surf. Eventually, Mayer came ashore and the three men did counts of the young and number of unhatched eggs. Chapman killed several birds and prepared the skins.

One day, Shiras waded into the brush and cacti to set up a camera beneath a frigate bird nest, capturing several stop-action photos of parents bringing food back to the young.

Frigates have extremely long wings and the ability to soar and stay airborne for days at a time. They are aggressive, known for stealing food from other birds. Repeatedly, Shiras marveled as the frigates overtook boobies

Frigatebird at Cay Verde, Bahamas, 1907. George Shiras 3d;
Courtesy of National Geographic Creative.

and gulls in midflight and forced them to disgorge their gullets of food—
typically squid and small fish. The frigates swooped down, caught the plun-
der in midair, and returned to their nests to feed their young. Some of his
most striking images revealed frigates in midair above the nest; wings
extended far forward of the body in a rowing motion, evidence of the camera's freeze-frame ability to reveal the mechanics of flying.

They stayed three days and departed for Nassau on April 16, trying to
run all night with a full moon and a strong wind. Chapman was eager to
get back to Florida to collect at another nesting ground there. However,
mishap befell again. At night, the boat ran aground on a sandbar, where it
held for three days. Cranking with a windlass did nothing to move the
yacht. Natives gathered in small boats at a distance, ready to scavenge if the
men abandoned ship. Finally, the scientists unloaded all the gear, anchors,
and provisions and the boat floated free at high tide. In Nassau, Shiras took
a steamer to New York and Chapman returned to Florida on the yacht.

Two years later, the men joined up for another adventure, this time to

Mexico on the Gulf Coast near Tampico. They were joined by Louis Agassiz Fuertes, a renowned illustrator of birds and the founder of the ornithology lab at Cornell. Fuertes was a native of Ithaca, where his father was a professor of engineering at Cornell. As a young man, he displayed a genius at portraying birds and their habitat on canvas. Fuertes and Chapman often collaborated on field research and other projects. The artist painted dioramas at the museum in New York. He illustrated the field guide *Citizen Bird* by Mabel Osgood Wright, which was an influential book in the early birding and Audubon movements. He sold illustrations to *National Geographic* magazine.

Shiras was in eminent company, and he appreciated being invited on the trip.

Shiras brought along John Hammer to handle the boats, serve as camp cook, and assist with the setting of camera traps. Their mission was to photograph and collect specimens of roseate spoonbills, a species nearly extirpated from Florida due to plume hunting.

A large colony thrived on the Tamiahua Lagoon. First, however, the men ascended the Tamesi River about seventy-five miles to the sugar plantation Paso del Haba at the invitation of its owner, Thomas H. Silsbee. An American, Silsbee promised they would see a wealth of bird life along the river. The country inland from the Gulf was arid and rather barren, but an intact riparian forest lined the riverbanks.

They pitched their tents in front of the ranch house some twenty feet above the river and were delighted to hear the loud calls of parrots, mainly the double yellow-headed Amazon, *Amazona oratrix*. Even then, the bird was sought after by trade hunters for its ability to mimic, sing, and vocalize. Today it is endangered in Mexico—largely because of the pet trade—and found mainly in Belize and Guatemala. But in 1908, the men saw scores of such parrots, lured to the river by Otaheite gooseberry trees that were bearing fruit. The river was just one to two hundred feet wide. Villages located up- and downriver supplied workers for the plantation.

They identified eighty-eight species of birds during their stay. Chapman, who wrote about the experience for *National Geographic* magazine, recalled that "Shiras hunted with camera by sunlight and flashlight, obtaining photographs of birds by day and of beasts at night, and left, no doubt, a more vivid and lasting impression on the minds of two natives who unwittingly sprang one of his flashlight camera traps."

After the explosion of the flash powder, the two girls fled from the river to their thatched huts, and Shiras went to the village to reassure them. He had been hoping for a picture of an ocelot or some other member of the cat family but succeeded in getting only surprised humans, a cow, and a couple of opossums. Shooting in the tropics over the coming years, he was to find there were too many small critters about who took the bait or tripped the string instead of his intended prey.

After descending the river to the Tamiahua Lagoon, the men picked up local guides and headed to the north end of the lagoon via a canal occupied by rafts of canvasback ducks, coots, gadwalls, and shovelers. Near dinnertime, two blue-winged teal passed overhead. The men reached for their guns.

"Fuertes, always alert to whatever was happening, deftly brought one of them almost into the frying pan," recalled Shiras.

Sunset found the men short of their goal and forced to camp on a mud bank of the recently excavated canal. The insects were terrific, Chapman recalled, and he was glad for his mosquito-proof tent with a floor.

"Shiras, a far more experienced camper, spurned such luxuries and set up a lean-to," Chapman wrote. "Doubtless, if alone, he would have not been caught in so undesirable a place; but there we were, there was the mud, and there were the mosquitoes in myriad. Life in his lean-to was impossible."

They headed to an island reported to be packed with spoonbills, but on their approach, they spied no birds. While the men set up camp, Chapman took a scouting walk and, to his delight, a hundred yards distant found dozens of nesting spoonbills, ibises, and wood storks.

While Chapman and Fuertes went to work—killing, painting, and preserving birds—Shiras photographed lizards, stilts, and a grackle—whatever struck his fancy. At night, he and Hammer set up camera traps but only managed to get images of opossums and wood rats.

In the evenings, Fuertes sketched the specimens or added detail to the studies he had made of live birds during the day. Fuertes also studied the freshly killed birds.

Shiras recalled, "After making a rough outline of one of his specimens showing its dimensions, he colored in only those parts of the drawing where the tints were perishable, such as the bill, eyes, iris, and the iridescence of the head and neck, if any, and the feet and legs if these parts were unfeathered."

Museum specimens faded. Feathers darkened over time, but paintings could be more lifelike and better studied by ornithologists.

John Hammer was wary of the chemicals Chapman used to prepare the skins. One night, he declined to eat his own corn dodgers, and Shiras asked, "Are you sick?"

Hammer said, "No, but I don't want to be."

He had observed Chapman taking scoops out of their cornmeal bag and mixing it with arsenic to preserve the skins. Hammer, who poisoned wolves in Michigan, suspected the remaining meal was tainted and in Shiras's words, "preferred being a live but hungry guide to becoming a well-preserved specimen." Hammer later fell ill not from poison but from typhoid fever. The symptoms plagued him for nearly a year.

The men had fun in camp. Shiras, known for his humor and practical jokes, was finally driven by mosquitoes from his lean-to. He had no netting and quietly entered the fortified tent occupied by Chapman and Fuertes. They had a cloth floor, netting, and two collapsible bunks. A pile of "insect powder" smoldered on a tin plate. After Shiras lay down on the floor between the two men, he shoved the tin under Fuertes's cot and waited.

He recalled, "Soon the sleeping artist became restless and finally sat up, calling to Chapman that he did not feel well and that he feared he had contracted some strange fever, his hips especially being affected. This was a new disease to Chapman. Telling them that I had a prompt and infallible remedy, I pulled the now blazing tin from under the cot."

13 | NEWFOUNDLAND AND NATURE FAKERS

WHEN SHIRAS QUIT politics, he was just thirty-eight years old, in good physical shape, and wealthy enough to fund his own expeditions and adventure travel.

"After studying the law of men, I wanted to study the law of nature," he quipped.

For the remainder of his life, he would hunt with camera and gun, promote conservation, and capitalize on his growing reputation as a faunal naturalist. In 1908 the Museum of Natural History in New York named Shiras chair of the section of mammals. He joined the Explorers Club on Sixty-Seventh Street in New York, where Frank Chapman was a charter member. He was asked to join the prestigious board of managers of the National Geographic Society, where he helped guide its research efforts and editorial stance on conservation. And in the latter part of Theodore Roosevelt's administration, he joined the president, scientists, and naturalists in a literary war of words against authors of so-called realistic animal stories and fiction.

Beginning in the 1890s, the authors, which included Jack London, made outlandish claims about the ability of animals to think, strategize, feel complex emotions, and in other ways act like humans. Such anthropomorphism was bunkum to naturalists who derided the writers with the label "nature fakers."

Two trips Shiras took to Newfoundland and New Brunswick between 1906 and 1908 provided him with ammunition to debunk and ridicule the claims of the nature fakers. The eventual victories over these sham naturalists were triumphs he relished for the rest of his life.

In September 1906 he went north to witness the migration of woodland caribou across Newfoundland—one of the last great migrations of ungulates outside of Alaska and Arctic Canada. The animals already were under pressure, being hunted from railroads penetrating the island's interior. A demand for meat during the coming Great War would nearly wipe out the herd.

Shiras went north by train and ferry with John Hammer, picked up local guides, and then rode a narrow-gauge railroad into the interior. They left the right-of-way at Sandy River and spent a few weeks exploring by canoes. For many days, they camped on Sandy Lake near a stony ridge bright with blueberries. They ate from the land, caught big brook trout, and shot small caribou to provide meat for the camp.

Unfortunately, they were early for the migration, which was keyed to cold weather. Days were mild and caribou scarce. He and Hammer went out with the camera at night but failed to flashlight any animals along the shore. Occasionally a few caribou swam across the lake, and the photographers were able to paddle over and get alongside in the canoes so Shiras could shoot with a hand-held Graflex. The earliest of the single-lens reflex cameras, the Graflex featured a cloth, focal-plane shutter and a mirror and prism so the photographer could look directly through the lens.

One day while shooting, they accidently separated a fawn from its mother. She ran into the woods and abandoned the baby. For several days, the fawn swam around the lake piteously lost.

Foxes were numerous even in daytime. Shiras hoped to photograph one, but they proved shy. They saw four silver-gray foxes feeding on blueberries. Three went back to the burrow before "we knocked over the fourth with a rifle ball as it started to leave and presented its handsome pelt to the Biological Survey in Washington."

What he did not see were wolves or any sign of them, which was an important fact during the upcoming nature faker fight. "A large bounty having been placed on them, the trappers soon reduced their numbers and at the date of my visit, there were supposed to be extinct. Our guide told us that no bounty had been paid on wolves they he knew of. He'd seen no tracks and believed the last one had been trapped or poisoned."

One day, a black bear sniffed at their canoes but fled before Shiras could focus the Graflex. He ruminated: "Every wild-life photographer sooner or later has such exasperating disappointments; but if success were always assured, the sport of hunting with a camera would lose much of the appeal of its uncertainty."

His most enduring images were of the landscapes and the men lounging in camp and canoeing the wild rivers. The Newfoundland guides were the best he had ever seen with a canoe, deftly able to switch from paddles to poles when negotiating a fast current or rapids.

He shot a wonderfully sublime image of Hammer seated in the stern of their canoe, paddle raised from the water as he looked toward low, forested hills. The flat lake presented as a perfect mirror. Because there were only six hours of daylight suitable for photography—and it was an overcast day—the light falls particularly soft and diffuse. The bow of the canoe is lifted from the water by the weight of the man and the absence in the bow of the other paddler. Shiras took the picture from the shore. His camera and swivel mount are clearly visible on the bow. Behind his empty seat sits a waterproof trunk holding his photographic plates. A line of water reeds in the foreground frames the composition. The picture became one of his most iconic images of the north woods.

Back in the States that winter, Shiras lectured in New York City at a meeting of the Canadian Camp Club, where he displayed his Newfoundland images as lantern slides. The club, organized the previous year, had a membership of around five hundred sportsmen. Members donated funds so that the club could buy land, build permanent camps, and promote hunting in an area north of Lake Huron. Shiras was on the board of directors along with a US senator, several judges and doctors, and other wealthy benefactors. However, when the club invited one of the infamous nature-faker authors to speak at its annual meeting the following year, he resigned.

He had missed the migration, so Shiras returned to Newfoundland the following fall without John Hammer. He hired guides from the previous year, set up camp on Little Sandy Lake, and awaited cold weather. He put

John Hammer in a canoe in Newfoundland with a camera in the bow, 1906.
George Shiras 3d; Courtesy of National Geographic Creative.

out camera traps around the lake and captured several daytime images of caribou moving along the game trails.

One evening, three college boys came into camp. "A set of manly fellows" from New England, they had killed three stags apiece—the number allowed by law—but when tasting the meat, they found caribou gamey and tough. They left the carcasses and removed the heads and hides. Shiras looked at their trophies and estimated the trio had left thirty-five hundred pounds of flesh rotting in the bush. Disgusted, he suggested they take up the camera rather than the gun.

A few nights later, a pair of French-speaking trappers arrived after tripping one of his camera traps. When the flash exploded, the terrified men were certain they had stumbled into a set gun, or trap gun. Shiras considered set guns "reprehensible devices" and after talking to the trappers, who stayed the night, he realized they were familiar with this method of taking animals.

That night, the wind came up and a heavy wet snow encased their canvas tents. When the front passed, caribou were on the move, crowding the shores of the lake and river. Hundreds of animals splashed into the water. Over the next few days, Shiras exposed all of his photographic plates. He wouldn't know the results until the plates were developed back in the States but felt certain he had some excellent images.

As they paddled back to the railroad, they saw a fire on the river and stopped at the camp to warm up. To Shiras's delight, he found an old friend, Major A. Radclyffe Dugmore, a fellow photographer and painter of wildlife who had come north, too, for the migration. Dugmore would later pursue flashlight photography in Africa and become known for spectacular game pictures taken at water holes.

At the railhead to catch the train back to Port-aux-Basques, Shiras ran into a sportsman from Boston about to embark on the hunt. The man inquired about their success and Shiras said yes, he had bagged caribou, but quickly explained that he had been hunting with the camera.

The hunter startled him by calling out, "You are George Shiras. You are the only darned cuss who could come so far for game pictures."

The man may have seen Shiras's photographs in *Forest and Stream* or *National Geographic*, but just as likely, he'd been reading newspaper and magazine accounts of the nature-faker controversy playing out in some of the country's most well-read magazines.

Rudyard Kipling had started the trend of animal fiction in 1894 with *The Jungle Book*, and Jack London had capitalized on it with *The Call of the Wild* (1903) and *White Fang* (1906).

Animals functioned as heroes and heroines in the novels, and the authors wrote from the animal's point of view, alluding to their emotions and interior thoughts.

Had such anthropomorphism been limited to fiction, it might have been passed off as whimsical romanticism, but other writers—Ernest Thompson Seton and Rev. William J. Long—were crafting nature essays with observations of remarkable animal behavior. Seton wrote about a fox who lured a pack of pursuing hounds onto a railroad trestle so a passing train could run down its pursuers. Other essays featured a crow who could count to thirty, frogs that preferred orchestral music to ragtime, and a porcupine able to curl into a ball and roll downhill to elude predators. Many scientists and naturalists, including Shiras, were appalled that the American public—particularly schoolchildren—was being fed such tripe.

When he arrived back in Washington and looked through his mail, he read that the Canadian Club had invited Rev. William J. Long to speak at its next meeting. The talk was entitled "The Wild Animal" and the invitation read, "In view of the recent controversy in relation to animal intelligence, his address promises to be of exceptional interest."

Not to Shiras.

He dashed off a letter to Robert T. Morris, a friend and doctor in New York who headed up the club's advisory committee. He copied the letter to George Bird Grinnell, another committee member.

Shiras poured out acid wit and disdain: "Were Long's toast 'Wild Fabrications by a Moral Pervert' then for the first time his veracity would go unquestioned. Beyond chipmunks, woodchucks and skunks, it is my opinion that Dr. Long never saw a real wild animal in its native habitat."

Long had been invited by L. F. Brown, the board member in charge of the arrangements. Earlier that year, Brown had dropped in on a dinner party Shiras was holding in Washington with Morris and other sportsmen. Shiras didn't know Brown but gave him a chair at the table and then reluctantly allowed him to look at letters that he and President Roosevelt had been exchanging about the nature fakers.

The letters, which had never been published, had been seen only by a few intimate friends. At the time, Shiras did not know that Brown was clearly in Long's camp.

When he returned from Newfoundland, he discovered that Brown had attacked him and Roosevelt in an article printed in the *Washington Post*. Brown called into question Shiras's wildlife expertise and referred to the Roosevelt correspondence.

Shiras told Morris he could handle criticism, but publicly mentioning the letters was an unforgiveable social breach. "Such a chap as this should never be accepted by strangers as a guest until he promises over his signature not to publish in the newspaper what occurs at a private dinner, and even then the companionship of such a character would be unpleasant."

He demanded that Morris "get me out of the club."

To understand the rancor of the nature-faker debate, it is necessary to examine how nature literature was viewed in the early twentieth century. Nature was in high demand with the public.

The population of the country doubled between 1860 and 1900. Mass urbanization of the Gilded Age, the expansion of railroads to all corners of the country, and the unbridled lust for making money, developing lands, harvesting timber, mining minerals, and penetrating the last remaining wild places had taken a toll on the American psyche. People felt divorced from nature and yearned for the pastoral, rural life of previous decades. Although that life often had been hardscrabble, it was romanticized as a simpler time.

A growing middle class had more leisure time to think about such things, engage in recreation, go camping, and travel the country. One could board a train in New York City and make a trip to Niagara Falls or north to Adirondack Park, which had been set aside to be "forever wild." Railroads promoted the establishment of national parks in the West and built tourist hotels near the Grand Canyon and Yellowstone.

Frederic Law Olmsted, the country's premier landscape architect, had put his mark on cities and towns, designing New York's Central Park, Chicago's Riverside Parks, Boston's Emerald Necklace, and even Presque Isle Park in Marquette. Peter White convinced the federal government to cede the three-hundred-acre peninsula just north of downtown to the city and then personally hired Olmsted to lay out a road, beaches, and walking trails.

People flocked to these parks—bicycling or taking trollies out to beaches, oceanfronts, and woods. Parklands were promoted as stress relievers for the working class, a way to escape the crowded conditions of the factory and tenement. Recreational camping grew in popularity along with organized camps of cottages and dorms where families could experience the countryside and summer in the wilds. In the White House, Theodore Roosevelt promoted the benefits of the strenuous life and led his children, staff, and even foreign ambassadors on hikes requiring the participants to go in a straight line and never go around an object, be it a river or a swamp.

The Roosevelt children kept lizards, snakes, and a badger as pets. For hobbies, people collected leaves, pressed flowers, bird eggs, nests, feathers, and animal skulls. Children had formalized nature study in public schools, and there was a demand for books to teach and entertain people about the outdoors.

The public was nature-crazy, and its guru was John Burroughs, a Santa Claus-like figure revered by schoolchildren. Roosevelt, expressing the national affection, called him "Oom John" or Uncle John. For decades Burroughs wrote from his farm in the Catskill Mountains, preaching spiritual pastoral pursuits as an antidote to making money and attaining status. He promoted a garden-style appreciation of nature. People need not travel to where wilderness still existed but only needed to walk through their neighborhoods, farms, parks, and yards. Appreciate what is there— especially bird life, he said.

His literary form was the nature essay, in which writers taught a bit of science, offered close observation of nature, and rhapsodized about the spiritual experience. Henry David Thoreau had pioneered the form during his short life, but his books had never been popular until the early twentieth century, when publishers looked to expand their booklists. Authors responded to the market, and as they did, they stepped onto the slippery slopes of anthropomorphism and Victorian sentimentalism.

An early practitioner was Ernest Thompson Seton, cofounder of the Boy Scouts, an illustrator, and a naturalist of some note. Born in Britain in 1860, he was raised in Canada and worked on the Manitoba prairies as a tracker and hunter. Like Shiras, he was a self-taught naturalist. He wrote the introduction to the booklet that advertised the limited edition of the *Midnight Series.*

He wrote nearly four hundred magazine articles and several books, the most popular being *Wild Animals I Have Known* (1898). It is still in print, and its success back then was primarily responsible for other writers supplying the demand for such literature.

In the prologue, he claims, "These stories are true. Although I have left the strict line of historical truth in some places, the animals in this book were all real characters. They lived the lives I have depicted and showed the stamp of heroism and personality more strongly than has been in the power of my pen to tell."

Seton's stories were often tragic, filled with pathos, and the animal meeting a sad end. "Lobo: The King of Currumpaw" is based on his experience of hunting wolves in the American Southwest. In the story, the hunters capture Lobo's mate, throw lassos about her neck and limbs and pull her apart. Lobo, lamenting the loss of his mate, seeks her out and is captured.

Seton showed sympathy for wolves, mountain lions, and other predators who were frequently reviled in literature. He wrote, "Animals are creatures with wants and feelings differing in degree only from our own, they surely have their rights. This fact, now beginning to be recognized by the Caucasian world was first proclaimed by Moses and was emphasized by the Buddhists over two thousand years ago."

William Long, pastor of the Congregationalist Church in Stamford, Connecticut, entered the genre in 1899, with the publishing of *Ways of Wood Folk*, a series of children's' stories. Long, the youngest of sixteen children, was born poor on a New England farm, where he watched birds and other wildlife. He worked his way through Harvard and several universities in Europe. He was smart, bold, and a free thinker who believed in the mercy of God, which occasionally got him into trouble with a faith that preached predestination and eternal damnation.

As a nature writer, Long positioned himself as a man who had intimate knowledge of the outdoors and had spent twenty-some years roughing it in the wild lands of eastern Canada, including Newfoundland. He often cited his intimate acquaintance with men of the woods, hunting guides and Indians, who supposedly knew better than anyone—certainly most urban white men—the nature of the beasts in the forests and on the plains.

George Shiras had spent many years in close proximity with woodsmen and guides such as Jake Brown and Samson Noll at Whitefish Lake, and though he admired their sagacity and skills, he knew them not as professors or philosophers of the woods but as rough-hewn characters, often quite ignorant, living in isolated places. He admired many of them as men but didn't exactly see them as sages.

Like Seton, Long opened his books with prefaces assuring readers that everything they were about to read was true, which might be paraphrased as: prepare to be amazed. The warning was for good reason. When *Wilderness Ways* came out in 1900, some of Long's assertions raised eyebrows.

He claimed to have watched a pair of kingfishers hold school for their young. The older birds went fishing and returned with minnows, which they dropped into a small pool. Then they brought the young birds to what Long called the kingfisher's garden and demonstrated how the little ones should dive into the water, retrieve a fish, and get a meal.

By summer 1903, John Burroughs had enough of this excess sentimentalizing of animals. Others had called the writing mawkish, without merit, and even supernatural, portraying the North American woods as a wonderland complete with fairies and wee folk.

But it was Burroughs's stature as the most eminent naturalist of the day and the public way he took on these writers—by writing an article in the March 1903 *Atlantic Monthly* entitled "Real and Sham Natural History"—that launched a bitter war of words in the nation's newspapers and magazines.

In the *Atlantic* article, he disparaged this "yellow journalism of the woods," an especially cutting insult considering the country had just witnessed the abuses and lies of William Randolph Hearst and Joseph Pulitzer. The newspaper magnates had been loose with the truth and utterly reckless when trying to sell papers during the Spanish-American War.

To Burroughs, these sham naturalists were equally shameless. Seton's book, he mused, should have been titled "Wild Animals I Alone Have Known." He wondered if the fox chased by the hounds possessed a pocket watch and railroad timetable so it would know precisely when to lure its pursuers onto the tracks. He was especially scornful of a Seton story about a fox leaping upon a sheep's back and riding it for some distance to throw the dogs off its scent.

Part of the quarrel came down to instinct versus animal intelligence. Burroughs believed animals did not think, reason, or change behavior. Actions were all instinctual.

In this post-Darwinian period when wildlife biology and the study of animal behavior were still emerging disciplines, the nature of animals was up for grabs. Who was there to say that animals did not think or talk to one another? Where was the proof? The data? Nature fakers justified their work by saying the stories enabled humans to see the natural world from the animal's point of view.

Society was rethinking its relationship to animals, which many people considered lowly forms of life put on earth by God to benefit humans. Animals were beasts of burden, there to do work or be hunted and slaughtered for food or, even, to provide feathers for women's hats. Some animals were good—farm creatures, deer, and turkeys—and others intrinsically bad—wolves, panthers, skunks, and crows. Even conservationists like Shiras who were eager to protect wildlife had their prejudices. Shooting an eagle, hawk, or owl—eliminating wolves from the woods—was a positive act that allowed more good animals to thrive.

Theodore Roosevelt read the *Atlantic* piece and cautioned Burroughs not to be so hard on young Seton, whom the president considered to be a budding naturalist. He wrote Seton, too, and advised him to stick with close observation and limit his musings about the inner life of animals. Not long afterward, Burroughs met Seton at a dinner put on by Andrew Carnegie and was charmed by the young man. Frank Chapman, who had used Seton's illustrations in one of his books, later brought the two men together, and Burroughs was impressed with Seton's sketches and field notes. Shiras, too, admired Seton and was dismayed that he had veered off course.

Seton was chastened by the criticism. Jack London chose not to respond, but Reverend Long, known to be impatient and volatile with critics within his parishes, lashed out in an article in the *North American Review*. Both Frank Chapman and Mabel Osgood Wright had become acquainted with Long at Audubon meetings in Connecticut and found him arrogant, even insufferable.

Animal behavior was so diverse, Long wrote, that Burroughs and other naturalists could not say that it wasn't so. He offered another example that he admitted would sound incredible. He once watched two orioles building a nest in a buttonwood tree. Because they could not find branches stiff or straight enough to support the nest, these clever birds flew to the ground, found three sticks, placed them into a triangle, and tied them together with a cord. Then, together they lifted this armature up to the tree and hung it below a limb securing it with reversed, double-hitch knots.

In September 1903, *The Outlook* ran a Long article, "Animal Surgery," in which he claimed animals practiced a crude type of surgery and medicine upon themselves. He once saw a woodcock with a fractured leg fly down to a muddy streamside and mix mud and grasses together to form a cast for the broken limb.

These wild claims were met with derision. Frank Chapman wrote in *Science* magazine that Long had "made more remarkable statements regarding the behavior of birds and mammals of New England than can be found in all the authoritative literature pertaining to the animals of this region."

That summer Roosevelt invited Burroughs to go on a camping trip to Yellowstone. At the park's Grand Canyon, the two men regarded a natural bridge of snow and ice spanning the top of Yellowstone Falls. As the men stood there, a pack of coyotes crossed over the bridge, and Roosevelt won-dered aloud "if Rev. Long had not seen the coyotes build the bridge."

Around the campfire and on their train trip west, the two men discussed the nature fakers. Roosevelt cautioned Burroughs not to be dogmatic when it came to animals and instinct.

TR endorsed a middle ground, believing animals experienced fear, anx-iety, perhaps pleasure—base emotions that allowed them to learn to avoid predators, find food, and deal with humans. Animals, he thought, certainly had some capacity for learning, even from their parents, but certainly not within some school of the woods.

The battle of words continued, with Burroughs and Long exchanging barbs in the nation's magazines and newspapers. The press enjoyed the fight, and the terms *nature faker* or *nature fakir* often appeared in print. At the Cosmos Club and in scientific circles, naturalists and scientists debated the best way to take on these lying outlanders.

Roosevelt publicly held his tongue until early 1907, when school author-ities in Washington, DC, tried to introduce Long's books into the curricu-lum. The president gave an interview to Edward B. Clark, a writer for the *Chicago Evening Post.* During a discussion about nature faking, Clark chal-lenged Roosevelt to go public with his criticisms, reportedly saying, "Why don't you go after them?" Clark then asked Roosevelt pointed questions on claims made by Long and wrote a piece for *Everybody's*, a general interest magazine with a large circulation of five hundred thousand.

Roosevelt was quoted, "If these stories were written as fables, published as fables and put into children's hands as fables, all would be well and good. As it is, they are read and believed because the writer not only says they are true but lays stress on his pledge. There is no more reason why the children of the country should be taught false natural history than why they should be taught a false physical geography."

He aimed his wrath at Long's story *Wayeeses the White Wolf,* in which the title character kills a caribou fawn in Newfoundland by running beneath the animal and administering a killing bite through the chest that pierces the heart.

Roosevelt cited the expertise of his friend the sportsman George Shi-ras 3d, who upon his return from Newfoundland had written Roosevelt a seven-page letter regarding the behavior of wolves and the population—or lack thereof—in that part of Canada. Shiras said he saw no sign of wolves and understood from guides and trappers that there had been no trace of the animals in recent years. And based on his experiences in Michigan's Upper Peninsula, the idea of a single, killing bite in the chest was ridiculous.

Roosevelt said, "Mr. George Shiras who's seen scores of such carcasses tells me that the death wounds or disability wounds were invariably in the throat or the flank, except when the animal was first hamstrung. . . . I don't believe the thing occurred."

The *New York Times* ran an interview with an angry Dr. Long ready to fight back. The animal stories were highly lucrative—his bread and butter—and he was determined to defend them. He produced an affidavit from a Sioux Indian in the Dakotas who said he had seen wolves kill deer, even horses, by biting into the heart.

"I have no desire for a controversy with the President of the United States. I have profound respect for that office, which is not modified or changed in the least by any man occupying that office. The point is that a man named Roosevelt has gone out of his way to make a violent attack on me and my books. Ordinarily I would ignore such an attack. If you read the article, even carelessly, you will see it is personal and venomous in spirit while its literary style makes it fit for the waste basket."

Long prepared an open letter to the president and sent it to newspapers throughout the nation. He cast himself as an honest, humble man being attacked by a giant: "You have deliberately gone out of your way to attack a man of whom you know nothing and who is honestly trying to do a man's work in the world. You have used the advantage of your high position to injure him and you have hidden behind another man in this alleged interview."

The latter was true. Roosevelt and Clark had worked together to cast this so-called interview as happenstance, but it was a result of planning and collaboration. Long also maintained that Roosevelt was doing this to help his friend John Burroughs.

The president told the press he would not respond directly to Long's attacks because Long was "too small a game to shoot at twice." The *New York Times*, in an editorial, thought it unseemly that a president would engage in such a dispute.

On May 29, 1907, Long again attacked Roosevelt, this time in a syndicated column that ran in the Sunday newspapers, which combined had a much wider circulation than *Everybody's.*

In Washington, Shiras read the papers with a mixture of alarm and amusement. He wrote to William Loeb, Roosevelt's private secretary, before he left for a weekend trip to Pittsburgh: "I read Dr. Long's splenetic attack upon the president and today I see it has appeared practically in every paper in the United States. . . . This morning's paper represents the Reverend gentleman, squatting on his haunches, watching for the president to drop, after his fatal onslaught—but I fear that like Dr. Long's deer, the president does not know that he has been gripped."

Still, Shiras worried Long was getting more press because his attacks had appeared in the daily newspapers rather than the more literary magazines. Readers who had never read Roosevelt's original comments were only getting one side of the argument. He wrote a long letter to Roosevelt, expressing his concern and refuting many of Long's claims based on his own experience and expertise as a faunal naturalist. He gave Roosevelt more evidence for future retorts.

Nevertheless, Long was good at dishing it out. In the articles, he poked fun at Roosevelt, the big game hunter: "Who is he to write, I don't believe for a minute that some of these nature writers know the heart of the wild things. As to that I find that after carefully reading two of his big books that every time Mr. Roosevelt gets near the heart of a wild thing, he inevitably puts a bullet through it."

It all made good copy and the press willingly gave column space to the combatants. When *The Outlook* ran another letter from Long, Roosevelt was appalled. On June 7, he wrote Shiras from the White House, "Just after you left yesterday, I glanced at *The Outlook* and saw that those eminently worthy people have swallowed the Reverend (or ex-Reverend) Mr. Long, bait, hook and sinker. Now these are honest people of more than average intelligence and while it is simply astounding and rather discouraging that they should be taken in by so shameless a faker, it shows to my mind the desirability of your writing such an article as you have in view. Above all, do go on preparing your great work."

Roosevelt had a soft spot for *The Outlook*, a weekly news magazine. While governor of New York, he had formed a friendship with its editor, Lyman

Abbott. The magazine was cerebral and influential, a leading periodical of the Progressive movement. *The Outlook* was for thinking people.

After he left the presidency, TR would take an office at the magazine in New York and become a contributing editor, frequently writing about matters of natural history.

Roosevelt gathered his forces, writing letters to and meeting with Shiras; E. W. Nelson of the Biological Survey; William T. Hornaday, director of the New York Zoological Park; Dr. J. A. Allen, curator and mammalogist at the American Museum of Natural History, and his old friend Dr. C. Hart Merriam. These were some of the best-known naturalists in America, and what he had in mind was a cowritten article, or a literary symposium, in which the group would take on Long and the other nature fakers, point by point.

On June 8 Shiras wrote the president that he was postponing a trip to Canada—the weather was nasty anyway—so he could begin work on his portion of the article.

On June 9 Roosevelt invited Shiras to lunch at the White House. "I am delighted you can postpone your trip long enough to write that piece. It is a fine thing to do. By the way, I have something of interest about passenger pigeons for you."

That last aside was a sighting Roosevelt had made of pigeons near Pine Knot, his retreat in Albemarle County, Virginia. Remarkably, it may have been the last time an accomplished ornithologist ever saw passenger pigeons in the wild. He wrote, "I saw a small party of a dozen or so passenger-pigeons, birds I had not seen for a quarter of a century and never expected to see again." The last known passenger pigeon died in captivity six years later in Cincinnati.

At lunch that day, Shiras and TR were joined by William Howard Taft, secretary of war, and Elihu Root, secretary of state. The men discussed the legality of taking federal action to protect migratory birds, but Taft and Root were not as sanguine as Shiras was about federal power.

But the more immediate issue for the president was nature faking. Throughout the summer, several newspapers criticized Roosevelt for wasting time on it and urged him to get back to the nation's business. The *New York Sun* ran a sympathetic piece on Long.

When Roosevelt wrote Shiras from Oyster Bay, Long Island, on July 22, he began his letter, "My dear Shiras: Long cannot write the shortest statement without some preposterous lie. . . . *The Sun,* which of course is bitter against me, recently printed an attack apropos of a visit of John Burroughs here. He could not resist a couple of fake statements in the article."

After inviting Shiras to spend a night at Sagamore Hill, his home on Oyster Bay, Roosevelt urged George to recast his letter regarding wolves in Newfoundland into the form of an article and send it to him and E. W. Nelson.

Things were moving fast. The next day, Roosevelt sent a telegram and a marked galley of his own article to Shiras in Marquette. The article was being sent off to John O'Hara Cosgrave, the publisher of *Everybody's* magazine, but Roosevelt wanted to make certain the three or four lines he inserted from Shiras's letter were accurate in context.

"I shall strike it out if you object, but your letter put the thing so neatly that I wanted to use your exact words."

Nelson wired Shiras from Washington on July 25, "Can you contribute about eight hundred words to symposium nature fakirs? Other contributions ready. Anxious to have you take part."

Hours later Clark cabled from Chicago, "President Roosevelt most anxious you should contribute to symposium in *Everybody's* September against nature-faking. . . . Time presses, other contributions from Hornaday, Allen and others will be in Saturday."

Shiras was at Whitefish Lake and did not see the letters and cables until he returned to Marquette on the weekend. He wrote Roosevelt on July 29 saying he was dictating an essay "on the mendacity of Dr. Long" but could not keep it under the word count.

"As you will see, it related wholly to the Newfoundland wolf. It likewise contains some levity—a thing I could not avoid dealing with this callous author . . . I hope my attempted jokes about Dr. Long will not impair my efforts in a matter of very grave importance to the entire country."

Shiras was not being facetious. The public might be ambivalent, the press amused by the controversy, but in his mind the fakers were harming science and the conservation movement.

William Loeb wrote on July 31 from Oyster Bay, "The President has received your letter of the 29th instant and thought the accompanying article an admirable one. He has sent it with your letter to Cosgrave, of *Everybody's,* telling him he most emphatically wanted it produced, no matter what else is left out."

"Real Naturalists on Nature Faking" appeared in the September 1907 issue in *Everybody's*. A teaser on page one proclaimed, "President Roosevelt and Seven of the Most Eminent American Naturalists Riddle the Pretensions of the Nature Fakers."

The symposium, Clark wrote in the introduction, "is made of the opinions of men who are the most eminent working naturalists in America and whose positions at the head of our leading scientific institutions, together with their practical work, give to their statements indubitable authority."

He prefaced Shiras's contribution with: "The following is a letter from George Shiras 3d, who has hunted and photographed animals in Michigan and Central Canada for thirty-six years and whose ingenuity in securing flashlight pictures of wild animals by night has been of great value to naturalists."

On his last trip through New Brunswick and Newfoundland, Shiras wrote, he had spoken with guides and associates of Long who were confused about the Reverend's assertions. Long wasn't just a liar in print, his own people up north were mystified by his tales, said Shiras.

He disputed Long's claim that he not only saw wolves in Newfoundland but sighted them as his boat eased into its harborage. "So here we have the keen eyed doctor pen in hand, sitting expectantly on the deck of the schooner and telling his readers just how a wolf looked and acted, half a mile away or more on the mountain top behind a fishing village. An owl with a telescope over each eye could not have done better."

Long said he had observed wolves rounding up plovers on the beaches. Wild ducks curious at the playful antics of the wolves came so close, they were seized "by these hungry gymnasts." The wolves supposedly caught wild ducks, geese, and trout and trotted back to the woods with the dead birds balanced on their shoulders

It was preposterous, said Shiras.

"All of this is frenzied fiction as rare as it is raw," he wrote.

He dismissed the stories of wolf raids on villages or how fishermen sit close to their stoves and behind barred doors in winter to keep out starving wolves. In fact, Shiras notes, wolves do their best killing in winter when caribou are rather helpless in the deep snow and on frozen lakes.

Shiras said he didn't believe Long even saw a wolf in Newfoundland, let alone tracked one across the island by hearing reports from frightened postal carriers, a silly notion in itself because the island had few letter carriers and certainly none in the interior.

Shiras concluded: "About five hundred American and English sportsmen hunt big game in the island of Newfoundland every year and none of these has killed a wolf, nor even seen one in recent years. They will unanimously vote that the doctor, having abandoned his degree of DD should have conferred upon him the new one of PP—Patron Prevaricator of the Ancient Order of Ananias."

George was harking back to the Bible and the unsettling story of Ananias and Sapphira, who wanted to be philanthropists to the apostles and the church of Christ in Jerusalem. They sold a piece of property, but instead of bringing all the money to Peter, they brought only a portion, yet they said it was the entire amount.

Peter asks Ananias, "Why has Satan filled your heart to lie?" and then he asked Sapphira, "Why have you agreed together to put the Lord to the test?" The lesson is that Ananias and Sapphira wanted to gain a reputation for being generous while minimizing the sacrifice necessary to gain that reputation. They tinkered with the truth to make themselves something they were not. God did not think it a trivial matter, and Ananias and Sapphira were struck dead on the spot.

In political rhetoric of the early twentieth century, a reference to Ananias—such as referring to a congressman as "a member of the Ananias Club" was a sly way of calling someone a liar. Obviously, the naturalists felt that Long had not been honest, had taken shortcuts and did so to gain a reputation as a great naturalist. One after another in the literary symposium, they refuted his reckless stories. Then it fell to Roosevelt to strike Long dead. After extolling the virtues and expertise of his fellow naturalists, Roosevelt wrote:

> The modern nature faker is of course an objection of derision to every scientist worthy of the name, to every real lover of the wilderness, to every faunal naturalist, to every true hunter or nature lover. But it is evident the complete deceit of many people who are wholly ignorant of wildlife. Sometimes, he draws on his own imagination for his fictions, sometimes he gets them second hand from irresponsible guides, or trappers or Indians.

. . . It would have taken a volume merely to catalogue the comic absurdities with which the books of these writers are filled. There is no need of discussing their theories; the point is that alleged facts are not facts at all but fancies. . . . I am not speaking of ordinary mistakes, of ordinary errors of observation, of differences of interpretation and opinion; I am dealing only with deliberate invention, deliberate perversion of fact.

The next day, the *New York Times* ran an article: "Roosevelt Whacks Dr. Long Once More."

Long never recovered from the onslaught—not as a nature writer anyway. He still traveled to Canada and Maine and spent time with his children in the woods. He wrote more essays with more careful and cautious descriptions of hikes in the forest, but in 1919, he published an article, "How Animals Talk," in which he postulated that animals were telepathic.

Seton recouped his reputation and went on to do serious work as a naturalist and bird illustrator. London, who said he preferred to "climb a tree and stay above the fight," wrote books from this home overlooking San Francisco Bay and came out mostly unscathed.

The bellicose Long never forgave Roosevelt and took another shot when the ex-president ran for office again in 1912 as an independent under the Progressive, or Bull Moose, ticket—so named because Roosevelt declared he was "fit as a bull moose" to run for president.

TR had once written that he saw a moose gallop, which Long considered to be nonsense. Long wrote, "I will not say that a moose never galloped. I only declare firmly that the man who saw him gallop was not sober."

That was a reference to the rumor being spread by the Old Guard Republicans that TR was a drunkard—that the reason he smiled so much, spoke rather strangely, and acted odd was that he was an intemperate man.

George Shiras would play a role in vanquishing that story, too.

14 | EMINENT PERSONALITIES

WHEN HIS FRIENDSHIP with the Colonel was in its early stages, Shiras was reluctant to write TR directly. Instead, he directed his missives to William Loeb, the White House secretary. Loeb knew that wild game, birds, and nature commanded the attention of the president as much as any subject. TR loved to dine with interesting people, and sportsmen and naturalists were welcome company.

Shiras began getting invitations to the White House.

When Cherry Kearton, the English photographer who published *With Nature and a Camera*, came to Washington, Loeb wrote to Shiras, "That Englishman Kearton who has taken such wonderful bird photographs, is coming here in March. If possible, the President wants to have you and Dr. Hart Merriam meet him at lunch."

Shiras answered, "I will try to be present—not only because I regard Mr. Kearton the most distinguished nature lover in all of England, but because the idea of meeting the President again and under such pleasant circumstances appeals to me more strongly."

Invitations to the White House were like command performances.

On another occasion, Loeb wrote: "The president *insists* you must come to lunch Monday next at 1:30 p.m."

Shiras never knew who might share the table. When he was still in Congress, TR greeted him at the door of the White House, mentioning he had invited two "young fellows" to stay after the cabinet meeting for lunch.

The youngsters turned out to be William Howard Taft and Elihu Root. While the men ate and swapped stories, Shiras told a tale about a friend from Pittsburgh who had visited Whitefish Lake, heard wolves howling in the night, and asked how he might shoot one.

A guide suggested the city slicker rub his clothes and soles of his boots with asafetida, a pungent, sulfurous-smelling spice used as a digestive aid. Then if he walked upwind from the swamp, the curious smell would bring out the wolves. It was a joke on the Pittsburgher, for wolves were especially scarce that year, having been relentlessly hunted and poisoned.

The man was only gone a few minutes when they heard several shots and saw the hunter dragging an immense gray wolf down the trail. Everyone was astonished. He had not only killed one, but saw another wolf approaching and killed it with two additional shots. There was a fifty-dollar bounty on each animal.

The president leaned over and whispered to Taft.

Taft announced, "The president would like to have Mr. Shiras's guide sent to the windward of the Senate."

Immediately everyone at the table laughed at the reference to the "gray wolves of the Senate," those conservative Republicans who were doing their best to thwart Roosevelt's trustbusting initiatives.

Over the years, there were many such social occasions, and eventually invitations came to visit TR and his wife, Edith, at Oyster Bay. Shiras sometimes shipped the Colonel haunches of venison harvested during hunting season at Whitefish Lake. He went to New York and tutored Kermit Roosevelt, TR's son, on how to use the camera in preparation for the safari Roosevelt undertook to Africa shortly after leaving office. Letters went back and forth (TR was a prolific letter writer) for several years after Roosevelt left office and began work at *The Outlook* magazine in New York.

As more of his work was published in national magazines and newspapers, Shiras felt free to follow his muse as a writer and wildlife photographer.

In 1907, *National Geographic* magazine published a rather odd story, "A Flashlight Story of an Albino Porcupine and of a Cunning but Unfortunate Coon."

Portrait of George
Shiras 3d, 1920.
Courtesy of Peter White
Public Library.

DABBS *PITTSBURGH.*

It tells the "biographies" of an albino porcupine on Whitefish Lake and a raccoon that raided the hen house. It was mostly a picture story told with images and legends—also known as the cutline or caption explaining the illustration. In the text, Shiras weaved in the natural history of the animals, their habits, morphology, diet, and distribution.

He first photographed the white porcupine in 1901 while he and Hammer were in the hunting skiff, stalking the northeast shore for deer with camera and jacklight. Hammer thought the porcupine looked like "a small white polar bear."

His biologist friends in Washington suggested he capture or kill the animal to collect it, but he wrote, "This I was unwilling to do, and as events proved, the wisdom of letting this freak of nature live and die natural death was duly rewarded for every year from 1901 to 1906, I succeeded in getting one to ten flashlight pictures of this animal and aside from its pictorial value, was able to learn much about the habits that were greatly modified through infirmities due to albinism."

The animal was both blind and deaf but able to navigate the seventy-five yards from its rocky den to the shore, always following the same path. It bred and one year he photographed the albino on a log with its naturally colored young. At the explosion of the flashlight, the black ones fled but the albino was unbothered by light and noise. Only when the smoke wafted past its nose did it scurry back into the bushes. If Shiras kept the boat downwind from the porcupine, he found he could take one picture after another.

He followed it for six summers, and then theorized, "Its cavernous home, later enshrouded in the immaculate snow of Lake Superior, became its tomb in the winter of 1907."

The mere presence of a raccoon at Whitefish Lake revealed just how much the forest and ecosystem in the Upper Peninsula had been altered by settlement. One day Jim, the hostler or "stable boy," came into the camp kitchen and announced that sixty young chickens had been killed during the night. Several were eviscerated and their livers consumed—the work, Jim declared, of a raccoon. Shiras recalled, "That statement excited some derision on my part, since this animal was utterly unknown in the region."

But with the advent of cutover lands and second-growth forests, raccoons had come into the country. Jim took Shiras outside and showed him where two large rocks had been removed to gain access to the pen. He pointed to a print in the mud next to the watering trough. Shiras said the "imprint in miniature resembled the track of a bear or that of a child; so this plantigrade track must have been made by a coon."

For the next two weeks, he set camera traps and baited what turned out to be one female raccoon and two young. Chicken parts, cheese, fish, and a dead duck lured in the animals. The images were rather contrived, showing the animals pulling on a clearly visible baited string.

However, one picture had an entirely different aesthetic, beautifully composed and lit. Usually the flashlight flattened the image, but apparently the foliage overhead bounced the light and produced a more subtle illumination. The female raccoon squats on a log where Shiras placed pieces of cheese. The bait is not visible and the animal looks natural, with its paws forward as if gnawing on a crayfish.

Raccoon taking bait and triggering a camera trap, 1901. George Shiras 3d; Courtesy of National Geographic Creative.

After taking the picture, Shiras went off on a Canada trip with John Hammer and, when he returned, found that Jim had set out steel traps and caught all the raccoons. The final image in the article shows the hides of the coons stretched and nailed to the wall of the woodshed.

In June 1908 *National Geographic* magazine ran seventy new wildlife photographs under the title "One Season's Game-Bag with the Camera by the Hon. George Shiras 3rd."

In the text, Shiras portrays himself as more of a camera hunter than wildlife photographer, and much of the opening prose calls for the sportsman to consider the camera as a substitute for the gun. "When the fagged, over civilized, not to say, overfed man seeks the solitude of the forest, he goes neither in search of food nor from a barbaric desire to see gaping wounds and a pitiful death struggle of some mighty beast. The exhilaration and delightful freedom of the wilderness, with an opportunity to pit man's dexterity and resourcefulness against the experience, strategy, and inherent cunning of the hunted, accounts in these later days for many unnecessary tragedy in the woods."

Men, he says, can get the same thrill from the camera, for "when the camp is abundantly supplied with wild food, the camera and the camera alone should be the means of further hunting; for skill, not kill, is the motive."

He does, however, make an exception for "the predaceous class, like the wolf, the cougar, or the crow" and then quotes Theodore Roosevelt who once wrote, "The older I grow the less I care to shoot anything but varmints."

The images in the article represent a productive year, covering from April 1907 to April 1908, when he used the camera for thirty field days in the Bahamas, New Brunswick, Newfoundland, Florida, and the Upper Peninsula. His previous photo essays in the magazine had been images resulting from many years of work. Back in the 1890s, he was experimenting and improvising. By 1908, he had perfected his techniques and worked with more precise equipment and faster plates.

Still there were mishaps and uncertainties. In the article, he tells how he flashed a "disreputable old cow moose" in Canada.

"It left the bank, bore down on the canoe, knocking both cameras overboard by striking the projecting table and passed out into the darkness of the lake to be seen no more." He fished the cameras out of the water and hurried back to camp to develop the dampened negatives.

On that trip, he discovered that if he flashed an animal directly—while it was looking at him, it often stood still—likely blinded. Or it fled away from the boat. But if the flash came from the side, the reflection of the flashlight on the nearby foliage frightened the animal to flee toward the boat.

He was nearly boarded more than once and often splashed.

The article included a few pictures from his "old camp on Whitefish Lake" where he had spent several weeks that summer. Most conspicuous was a photograph of a seventy-five-pound gray wolf trapped on a deer runway near the camp on July 29, 1907. The wolf, still alive, looked at the camera while one paw is firmly grasped in a steel leg-hold trap. The legend reads, "An animal that now threatens with extinction the deer in the Lake Superior region and Canada." He publishes the picture "with pleasure" but concedes "a feeling of momentary pity was felt" just before a "rifle bullet ended its cruel and cunning life."

It may be his most frank expression regarding his personal feeling toward predators and a telling anecdote about how sportsmen of his day—even educated ones like himself—could ignore all other factors causing the decline of game animals and zero in on predators.

He adds, "Every effort is being made to wipe out this most resourceful and destructive and elusive animal on the American continent. And to the Biological Bureau at Washington, much must be credited to the successful work now being done, both in the deer forests of the North and upon the cattle plains of the West."

There were other images from Whitefish: a sapsucker working on a tree, a mink taking its own picture by pulling on a string baited with a fish, and a porcupine Shiras did not see until developing the plate of a whitetail deer. The images demonstrated his broad interest in wildlife, his close observations of their habits, and his ability to place himself or the camera in the right locale.

National Geographic had evolved as well. The layout clearly emphasized pictures over text, and several horizontal images took up an entire page so the magazine had to be turned sideways for viewing. These images were suitable for display on a wall or in a frame, and it must have gratified Shiras to know that his images hung in deer hunting camps across the nation.

That year, *National Geographic* published its first "Scenes from Every Land," a special edition containing "two hundred of the best illustrations and photographs" from previous issues. It was the type of pictorial for which the magazine would become famous. Inside were pictures of exotic tribesmen from Africa and Papua New Guinea and cigar-smoking women in Peru—many of the natives half-clothed or naked. A map of the world highlighted all the places its photographers and writers had been traveling. In addition, advertising copy clearly promoted the importance of photography to the magazine, "Words, no matter how plain, often fail to convey complete understanding; more one frequently forgets what he reads and hears. Seeing is believing and to see is not to forget."

Prominent were *Midnight Series* images and other photographs achieved by the use of camera traps and baited strings. The legends beneath the pictures were elaborate and explanatory, often referring to the technique or camera settings. "Wing shooting with a camera 1/1000 of a second Robin snipe circling over a decoy." Another read, "New Brunswick, Caribou stag with symmetrical horns. Because of effective game laws, this noble animal is more widely distributed and is more abundant. Now no cows or calves can be legally killed."

There was a bit of humor, too, and an indication of what it was like for nocturnal wildlife to be confronted with the explosive and brilliant flash-light. Beneath a picture of a snowy owl perched on a dead branch against the black sky, the legend read, "White Fish River, Michigan. Author was looking for deer. Flash held in one hand and camera in the other. The owl fell 15 feet into the water, swore like a trooper and waded ashore."

The text claimed that all the pictures "are of wild game, not taken in parks and reservations."

In Shiras's case, that actually wasn't quite true. Several images were made on Grand Island, a fourteen-thousand-acre game refuge forty miles east of Marquette. Owned by the Cleveland Cliffs Iron Company, the heav-ily forested island in Lake Superior had been stocked with exotic animals by William Mather, the company's president, who was related by marriage to Peter and Ellen Sophia White. Mather had been a frequent visitor to the camp at Whitefish Lake.

For several years, George had an open invitation to come to the island and take photographs in what was essentially an open-air zoo. Mather's stated purpose on Grand Island was to create "a second Yellowstone." It was hyperbole but he had the money and freedom to try. Mather ran Cleveland Cliffs for fifty years and spent loads of company money on his pet projects.

Just a half mile offshore, Grand Island is the largest island on the south shore of Lake Superior. During European settlement, the island held a trading post for the fur trade and later a lighthouse to guide ships into Munising Bay. The company purchased the island in 1900 when it still contained untouched stands of birch and maple. Mather had met Gifford Pinchot, understood his ideas, and requested that the Bureau of Forestry (the predecessor of the Forest Service) survey the island and recommend a plan of sustainable forestry.

The island was exceptionally beautiful, with two-hundred-foot rocky cliffs dropping down to clear azure waters. There was a good-sized inland lake for fishing, a beach on the north shore, and to the east a flat peninsula, or tombolo, of sand dotted with stands of big white pine. Mather built a 150-room hotel for guests, cabins, and cottages for visiting executives of the company.

At the turn of the century before motor transportation, such wilderness hotels were popular, and Mather envisioned a resort akin to the Mammoth Hotel in Yellowstone or the El Tovar at the Grand Canyon.

Grand Island already had deer, but Mather augmented the herd with whitetails brought north from Pennsylvania. In 1902, he shipped in elk and mule deer from the Rockies, pronghorn antelope from the High Plains, woodland caribou from Newfoundland, and moose from Ontario. Belgian hare, jackrabbits, ptarmigan, and Scandinavian grouse were imported, too. He planted thousands of Scotch pine and apple trees for the ungulates and wild rice and celery for waterfowl. Hay, grain, and garden crops were brought over from the mainland for supplemental feed. Full-time game-keepers lived in cottages.

Mather invited luminaries to see his creation, including industrialists, wealthy friends from Cleveland, and William T. Hornaday, who had been so successful in raising bison and reintroducing them to the wild. Mather did not know what he was doing, but in terms of game management in that era, no one else did either. Little thought was given to the habitat and forage needs of such animals or their ability to weather the frigid winters of the Upper Peninsula.

They were foreign species isolated on a relatively small island.

The Grand Island Game Preserve experiment took years to conclude as a largely well-intentioned and expensive disaster. Wolves crossed the ice one winter and chased the first herd of caribou over a cliff, where they plummeted to their deaths. Mule deer were picked off one by one in the deep snow.

One wolf was hunted down and killed in a coordinated effort involving the gamekeepers and dozens of men. Shiras had "the beast" stuffed and displayed in a hotel in downtown Marquette. The antelope were unsuited to timbered country. A second herd of caribou, moose, and elk succumbed to brainworm, a parasite from which whitetail deer were mostly immune.

The lack of hunting and elimination of predators allowed the deer population to balloon to three thousand animals. The herd eventually stripped away all available browse. Supplemental feeding exacerbated the problem. Mather opened the island to buck hunting, but hunters coming from the mainland never killed enough deer to dent the population. Lastly, the company trapped deer and shipped them—oddly enough—back to Pennsylvania.

Animals by the hundreds starved to death.

Shiras wrote about the Grand Island Game Preserve in *Forest and Stream* and published flashlight photographs of the animals in *National Geographic*. The confinement of the deer and inbreeding led to a large number of albinos. Shiras had a special fascination with the genetics of albinism, and like the white porcupine of Whitefish Lake, he photographed the white deer extensively, both in daytime and during the night.

The island was wonderfully scenic and, being so close to shore, easily accessible. In summer, members of the Shiras and Peter White families came to the island to hunt and put up for several days in the hotel.

George Shiras Jr. and Lillie summered every year on Ridge Street in Marquette and wintered in Ormond Beach. In between, they set up residence at the Hotel Schenley in the Oakland section of Pittsburgh, where they could be near Winfield and available to old friends and members of the Duquesne Club who would stop by and play a game of whist. He and Lillie also spent time in DC with George 3d's family.

Peter White frequently visited Washington, DC, to see his Shiras grandchildren and lobby lawmakers on behalf of the Upper Peninsula. He dined with Theodore Roosevelt at the White House and advocated for public works projects, including the locks at Sault Ste. Marie that enabled freighters to bypass the St. Mary's Rapids between Lakes Superior and Huron. The Soo Locks opened the water route to ship iron ore from the Marquette range to the mills in Ohio, Detroit, and Pennsylvania.

For decades, White dealt in land, timber, and iron ore and converted the wealth from the land into businesses in town—banking, insurance, and real estate. He made quite a name for himself and was a generous philanthropist, bequeathing all types of civic gifts on the city of Marquette: parks, the library, the hospital, and the new normal school.

In June 1908 White was in Detroit on business and collapsed on a downtown street after complaining of indigestion. He apparently had a heart attack while walking back to the Pontchartrain Hotel to get medicine from his room. He was seventy-eight.

The headline in the *New York Times* bluntly reported,

Peter White Drops Dead
Had just left the City Hall at Detroit
Pioneer Mine Developer

White was a beloved figure in the town. On the day of his funeral, Episcopal bishop G. Motts Williams sermonized—as it was said of Christopher Wren, the great English architect: "If you want to see his monument, look around you."

Ellen Sophia White had died three years earlier. Despite all of their worldly wealth, the two had suffered great heartbreak in their private and married life. A son died in infancy. In 1878, three of their children died of diphtheria within just a few weeks. Their daughter Mary, who wed A. O. Jopling and bore two children, died in her late thirties in 1896.

At the time of Peter White's death, only Fanny Shiras of his six children survived. Consequently, the White fortune and the extensive holdings in the Upper Peninsula—including the Camp of the Fiddling Cat at Whitefish Lake—passed to Fanny and George Shiras, A. O. Jopling, and their children. Although Jopling took over the administration of White's estate, Shiras would in the future always describe Whitefish Lake as "my camp in Michigan."

15 | YELLOWSTONE AND
THE SHIRAS MOOSE

JUST TWO WEEKS after Peter White's funeral, Shiras and John Hammer left Marquette and took a train to Gardiner, Montana, to embark on an expedition to photograph moose in Yellowstone National Park.

Military authorities in Yellowstone Park informed him that moose had been sighted around Bridger Lake in the new Teton Game Reserve near the park's southeast boundary. Since his congressional fact-finding, Shiras had wondered why moose, the largest member of the deer family, were so rare in the Rocky Mountains. Certainly, habitat existed in Wyoming, Colorado, Idaho, and Montana, where there were large tracts of roadless and wild country. Perhaps the absence could be attributed to the wildlife declines of the nineteenth century when ungulates had been vastly reduced everywhere in the United States by killing and habitat destruction?

However, even from the period of the mountain men in the 1820s, moose had never been sighted in great numbers. In July 1872 the Hayden expedition to Yellowstone killed a cow and calf for meat while it camped in Jackson Hole, but over the next two decades, only limited observations were made. A few animals had been spotted in 1897, ironically enough by Ernest Thompson Seton, one of the nature fakers. Shiras had done his own research and found a mounted moose head at the New York Zoological

Park that was documented as coming from the region. In 1899 the state of Wyoming granted complete protection of moose by banning hunting.

Now there was this sighting in what was known as the Thorofare region, where hunting parties and park scouts occasionally took horses and pack animals along the eastern edge of Yellowstone Lake on the Scout Trail, which passes over Two Ocean Pass and descends into Jackson Hole. The Thorofare is about twenty miles above the lake where the Yellowstone River flows through a large, high valley (about eight thousand feet) and meanders back and forth among open meadows with willows, scrub brush, deadfalls, pools, and marshes. It was isolated country in 1908 and still is today—the nearest forest road being about twenty-five miles distant.

Shiras decided to go west and see for himself. Because he was more comfortable with boats than packhorses, he determined to reach the area by ascending the Yellowstone River where it empties into the southeast arm of Yellowstone Lake. He would ascend the river in a collapsible canvas canoe, which could carry a thousand pounds of equipment and three men.

In July he and Hammer put up at the Mammoth Hot Springs Hotel and then took a wagon of supplies over to Yellowstone Lake with George Farrell, a guide from Gardiner. Shiras hired Farrell because he reportedly knew the country north of the Teton Mountains better than anyone else. It was a two-day wagon trip. On the trail, they soon passed a smartly dressed man and an attractive woman riding on horseback at a swift gait. Shiras immediately recognized them and they him. They stopped to chat. The woman was Alice Roosevelt, TR's mercurial daughter from his first marriage, and her husband, Nicholas Longworth, who had served with Shiras in Congress. The couple was on vacation, newly married.

When the men arrived at the outlet of Yellowstone Lake, they were met by Billy Hofer. One of the park's early guides who ran an outfitters camp, Hofer was unwrapping a package of Roman candles to scare away a bear making raids on his storehouse. Shiras and Hammer were given bunks in the storehouse, and Shiras ruefully noted "a large ragged hole in the wall" where the raider had made entry. The evening was uneventful, however, and the next morning, one of Hofer's men took them on a launch across the lake and into the southeast arm of Yellowstone Lake. It was a rough, white-knuckle trip with sudden gusts of wind that kicked up big waves and "thoroughly tested the seaworthiness of the launch." According to the guide, they were the first men in fourteen years to boat into that portion of the lake.

Shiras wrote, "On the following days, I discovered that his description of a perfect wilderness was true. In our explorations along the shore, into the various lagoons, and up the smaller streams we saw no trace of camps or other evidences of man except a few signs of government survey camps occupied many years before."

They spent several days photographing nesting geese, white pelicans, and other waterfowl as well as "hundreds of elk, cows and calves" coming into the low country about the lake.

On July 26, they entered the Yellowstone River after a difficult search through bays and side channels to locate the river mouth. Once in the main stream, they found the going arduous; the water was high and much swifter than expected. George Farrell had no experience in poling a boat. The canvas boat itself was heavily loaded and cumbersome; the paddles and oars—connected by brass ferrules—proved rather flimsy. The men could not really bear down while stroking. As well, Shiras had forgotten a long towline and had only a twenty-foot rope to get around deadfalls.

A cedar canoe from Michigan's north woods would have had little trouble, he noted.

Around noontime, they paused on a sand bar where elk apparently crossed in great numbers. An "immense silver tip grizzly" broke from the brush and barreled toward them. Shiras fumbled in his gear and pulled out a .32 caliber revolver. He fired two shots over the bear's head but it kept coming. When it was just forty feet away, he fired at the grizzly's chest. A tuft of fur flew into the air, the bullet apparently creasing its hide. At the same time, Farrell let out a shout and waved his arms. The bear stopped and retreated. Shiras theorized it had been lying in wait for an elk. Because of its poor eyesight, the bear may have mistaken the canoe and men for prey. Greatly relieved, they shoved off into the water.

Shiras was not supposed to be carrying a working firearm. Banned since the military took over jurisdiction, weapons were to be "sealed" within the park as a way of preventing poaching. Days earlier when they had gone through a check by military authorities in Mammoth Springs, Shiras revealed he had packed a "little revolver." The officer asked him to produce it for sealing, but the gun was buried deep in their gear and he did not want to look for it. Instead, he appealed to Colonel S. B. M. Young, his friend and the military commander of the park, who let him go through with the gun.

A .32 revolver isn't much firepower against a grizzly bear, but Shiras was grateful for it.

When he wrote to Roosevelt about the trip, he quipped, "If Colonel Young had not kindly permitted me to carry a revolver we probably would have had a fourth passenger on board, comfortably larger than the next president."

The latter comment was a sardonic reference to Howard Taft's obesity, and it wouldn't be the only time in letters to Roosevelt that Shiras would joke about Taft's heft. It seems to have been an inside joke between the two men that would grow more acid when TR ran against Taft in 1912.

Shortly after the bear incident, they spooked a cow elk from the bushes. When they passed the spot, Shiras glanced at the bank and immediately saw moose tracks in the sand. Further up, hundreds of tracks crisscrossed the mud flats. Spying a pond back from the river where the water would be warmer and support aquatic vegetation, he left the canoe, cut through the bushes, and immediately saw a large bull moose standing knee-deep in the middle of the pond.

Over the next three days, making some sixteen river miles and eight miles as the crow flies, the party saw eleven more moose. Finally, the flimsy oars broke, despite efforts to strengthen and mend them by winding copper wire about the shafts.

The expedition failed to reach Bridger Lake, but Shiras had succeeded in finding moose, which didn't prove that difficult. He was certain many more would be found deeper into the Thorofare country and already had decided to come back the following year.

Shiras took no pictures of moose on this trip because he had a rule that he would only photograph animals in the wild, not in parks or zoos or game preserves.

He and Frank Chapman recently had established the League of Wild Life Photographers at the Museum of Natural History in New York with themselves as president and vice president. In *Bird-Lore*, the magazine of the Audubon Society, they announced, "The objects of the league are not alone to promote the interests of genuine wild life photography, but to expose the makers of spurious 'nature' photographs."

They were disgusted by so-called wildlife photographers who were then passing off their pictures as being the product of naturally occurring situations. Shiras considered such images as "mere picture taking" not camera hunting.

He expressed such to Roosevelt in a letter on June 23, 1908: "I hope to be successful, though still determined to take no bear pictures in the park, because of the persistent and unscrupulous use now being made of such pictures taken at the hotel garbage piles, and used, in very many cases by otherwise reputable publishers, under misleading or deceptive titles."

When he wrote about the trip in *Forest and Stream*, he said, "I had no idea of following any other ethics of sportsmanship than the hunting of wild life under conditions precisely similar to those pursued in hunting with firearms. To be sure, one might photograph game out of season or train his lenses upon rare birds and animals not ordinarily classed as game, but in most other respects the rules of the contest should be the same."

Shiras was being a bit of a purist because he certainly had no qualms back in Michigan of going to Grand Island or baiting his camera traps at Whitefish Lake so the animals could take their own pictures. Already, he had published images of raccoons, skunks, and weasels yanking on bits of smelly fish and scraps of meat. Bears feeding on garbage piles were not a great leap.

When Shiras told Colonel Young that he had not taken pictures of the moose, Young was surprised and disappointed. His scouts in both summer and winter had seen no abundance of moose in this area, and he wanted evidence.

Shiras did take one picture of a scavenging grizzly bear, which he recounted in the *Forest and Stream* article. It happened this way:

After the oars broke, the men drifted the canoe back down to the lake, passing along the way, dozens of elk. They camped on shore near the mouth of the river. That night a bear entered one of their tents and made off with a bag containing canned goods and salted meat. In the morning, they found a flattened can of raspberry jam about seventy-five yards away.

George Farrell blamed the incident on Shiras, who had been putting out camera traps and baiting each night to get flashlight pictures of coyotes or whatever else might come along. Throughout the trip, Farrell had been giving Shiras guff. He wasn't enamored of camera hunting or some of Shiras's observations and theories of wildlife management.

Shiras examined the ground and tracks and declared the marauder had been a grizzly. Farrell scoffed and said it was a black bear. He had never known a grizzly to enter an occupied tent.

Shiras wanted to get a flashlight picture of the bear. He sent the men north to Lookout Point, about ten miles up the eastern shore, where they were to build a large signal fire on an elevated point. This would alert Billy Hofer to send the launch over the next day.

After Hammer and Farrell left, Shiras set up two cameras on a bench fashioned from driftwood. He baited the trap with fresh-caught trout. That evening under a full moon, he watched from the tent. Hours went by and he eventually got into his bag and dropped off to sleep. Suddenly, he awoke, aware of having heard a mechanical sound. The shutter on a camera had apparently opened, but the flashlight did not go off. In the moonlight, Shiras saw a very large animal devouring the fish and then trotting away into the woods. He got up and began rerigging the apparatus when he heard heavy breathing behind him. He turned and saw just a few feet away an enormous grizzly rearing up on its hind legs. It stood perhaps eight feet tall and, he estimated, weighed eight hundred pounds.

Shiras let out a loud hiss, and the bear ran away.

Now he hurried to get ready, sure it would return. For good measure, he added more powder to the flashlight charge. An hour later, Shiras heard a noise and peered out of the tent flaps with his right eye just as the night exploded: "A dazzling burst of light such as I had never seen equaled by a bolt of lightning. It shot high into the air and extended on both sides for many feet. Several whirling missiles cut through the pine branches above the tent and a roar like that of a cannon added to the excitement."

His right eye blinded by the light, Shiras shoved his head out of the tent and was able to see the bear with his left. Blinded too, the frightened bear rolled down the bank to the lake and then came up at a run, nearly crashing into the tent and cameras. It veered away and plowed into a poplar tree with its shoulder. The tree broke off clean. Stunned, the bear lay on its back, all four feet in the air, and then righted itself and fled. Still blinded, it hit a rock, rolled into the water, and took off down the shore. Later, by the sound of falling rocks, Shiras could tell it was climbing the slope of a nearby hill.

The grizzly had likely been singed as well as blinded. The charge had been so great, it burned the leather off the camera boxes and blew apart the flashlight apparatus. Leaves thirty feet up in the trees and bushes for an equal radius on the ground were blackened.

Apparently, flashlights worked as well as Roman candles, because the bear never returned.

When Farrell and Hammer got back the next morning, Farrell asked if "old blackie" had returned. Shiras just pointed to the toppled tree, where Farrell found a tuft of hair among the splinters and said, "My God. It was a grizzly."

A week later Shiras developed the negative and found, to his surprise, he had gotten a blurred photograph showing the bear in motion among the whitish bark of poplar trees. It was not a good picture, but it plainly showed the humped shoulder profile of a grizzly bear.

Shiras wrote, "It is clear we have here a large tract of mountainous country in which generations of grizzlies have been born, lived and died without coming into contact with the hunter's rifle, the steel trap and the deadfall. It may be true, therefore, that at the present time, there are in this district, grizzly bears which still possess that boldness, that lack of fear of man, which made them so formidable to the pioneers."

The best photographs taken on the trip were of white pelicans on Molly Island, where Shiras counted nearly eight hundred breeding adults. It was the first time anyone established that the birds nested on Yellowstone Lake.

Shiras and Hammer returned the following year in late summer 1909 with a rowboat and a canvas canoe, hoping to make an estimate of the resident moose and see the rut and fall migration of elk from the valley.

Colonel Young had been replaced by Major Harry C. Benson and this time Shiras promised to bring back photographs of the moose. Over the winter, he had reconsidered his ethic and at Mammoth, the two men discussed the reasoning: "We both agreed that these particular animals, however numerous they might become in remote portions of the park, were beyond the range of tourists' Kodaks or that class of photographers who, taking pictures of semi-domesticated bears at the garbage piles, or elk, deer and antelope in the alfalfa fields, pass them off as pictures of wild animals taken in the remote portions of the country."

The rowboat made it a mile upriver where it was stashed for the return trip. They continued with the canvas canoe. Rather than the swift current of the year before, the party encountered low water and frequently had to pull the canoe with a long towing line. In several places, they unloaded the craft to get through the shallows and frequently scraped gravel bars and rocks, which required repairs to the canvas.

They soon saw moose. As the faunal naturalist, Shiras scrutinized these animals and observed that they were different from those in the north woods of the Midwest and eastern Canada. Smaller, with darker coats and even shorter legs, the moose seemed adapted to mountainous terrain. He wondered if isolation, interbreeding, and life at high altitude—the river valley averaged seventy-five hundred feet—had contributed to the differences.

They made a few more miles upriver before putting a two-foot-long rip into the canvas. They could not continue any further, but having brought along thread, needle, canvas, and pitch, Hammer repaired the canoe for the trip back down the river.

In the meantime, they made camp and Shiras spent several days hiking upriver, exploring the country, and photographing moose—getting within a hundred feet of a large bull and yearling. The moose broke into a trot and ran for nearly three miles across meadows and marsh before disappearing into the forest.

Lugging his equipment up several peaks, he photographed what appeared to be a moose paradise. The bottomlands on both sides of the river were dotted with small lakes, beaver ponds, streams, marshes, and willow groves. The nearby forest contained lodgepole pine and aspen. At one point, while glassing the country, Shiras counted seventeen moose, the most he ever saw at one time.

In the valley, moose had everything required: cover, food, and willows in winter. When snow came, they likely remained while the elk and mule deer moved down the slopes and migrated to winter ranges. Consequently, the moose of the Thorofare had been relatively hidden from observation, because the rarely used Scout Trail ran higher up on the forested slopes.

In the July 1910 issue of *Forest and Stream*, Shiras wrote an article illustrated with a picture of two moose near Trail Creek. "The trip verified my impressions of the preceding year that the country lying between the south end of the lake and the source of the Yellowstone River was the wildest area of its size in the United States, and that it probably contained the greatest abundance and number of the species of animal life wholly uninfluenced by man."

In ten days, he saw sixty-eight moose in daylight and knew that many more were active at night. He and the men collected ten shed antlers from the willow flats. The antlers were in remarkable condition. Typically, porcupines, mice, and squirrels gnaw on antlers for nourishment and minerals; however, annual spring floods and summer high water apparently kept these critters out of the bottoms. As soon as the men hauled the antlers up to camp, they had to chase away red squirrels that kept coming in to nibble at the points.

When Shiras and Hammer got back to Gardiner and loaded the massive antlers onto the train to take home, residents were astounded. None of them had ever seen a moose.

The remoteness of the valley and its excellent habitat allowed the animals to thrive. Still, Shiras was concerned. He had seen fewer yearlings and calves than the previous year, and he had detected evidence of elk and moose killed by mountain lions and wolves. He worried that those "cutthroat outlaws in nature's kingdom" might wreak havoc on these moose and contribute to their extirpation. The deep snow in the valley, the yarding habits of moose, and the distance of the military authorities from the region to "control" these animals might allow them to do their "predacious business."

It's not a surprising viewpoint. The idea of a national park protecting all wildlife and preserving intact ecosystems—including predators—had yet to emerge. When Theodore Roosevelt and John Burroughs visited Yellowstone, TR wanted to hunt mountain lions to protect the game animals. He only backed off when it seemed his public image could be damaged. The military also thought it might encourage poachers.

A letter in the Yellowstone Archives addressed to Theodore Roosevelt from F. E. Gorton of Colorado Springs is telling. Gorton had hunted in Indian Territory (Oklahoma) and Colorado for many years but was running a general store. He had taken to poor health, he wrote, due to "the confinement" and wanted to get out "roughing it" again. "I would like to know if you have secured all the help necessary in destroying the wild animals in Yellowstone Park, such as the mountain lion or of any other place in the US. If not, I would like very much the pleasure of assisting in destroying them as I do delight in the sport."

The ungulates in the Thorofare region of the park, away from visitors and open to predation for time immemorial, had managed to survive without the assistance of man or military authorities. In future years, conservationists would learn hard lessons about game management policies that eliminated predators and allowed ungulates to proliferate. Shiras would see the folly of such policies on the Kaibab Plateau in Arizona and at Grand Island and Isle Royale on Lake Superior.

In 1910 he and Hammer returned to Yellowstone Park for a final trip. This time they did not ascend the river and camped on Peale Island in the south arm of the lake. He photographed all sorts of animals—from phalaropes to Canada jays to ducks and, of course, moose. He captured fine flashlight pictures of elk in the midst of the bugling and rutting seasons. Bulls sparred with one another and even did battle with trees. The males were so oblivious that he camouflaged the boat with pine brush and snuck in close for daylight pictures.

One young bull was knocked into the mud. When he hadn't moved for several hours, they figured him dead and argued about the legality and ethics of butchering the critter for an elk roast over the fire. There was no decision and the next day the little bull apparently had recovered and left the scene. On September 20, a heavy wet snowfall hit the park. The men watched as nearly one hundred young pelicans died from exposure and high water on Molly Island opposite their camp.

It wasn't until July 1913 that Shiras wrote about his Yellowstone experiences in *National Geographic*. Gilbert Grosvenor, capitalizing on Shiras's reputation as a wildlife photographer, included a special pullout pictorial supplement.

In Washington, E. W. Nelson at the Bureau of Biological Survey was intrigued with Shiras's photographs and descriptions of these moose. Nelson, a man who loved to be in the field discovering new species, had more than one hundred plants, birds, and mammals named after him. Both he and Shiras were members of the American Society of Mammalogists.

Nelson asked the state of Wyoming for permission to collect two specimens. Shiras agreed to finance the hunt. On December 11, 1913, on the Snake River four miles south of Yellowstone Park's southern boundary, a bull and cow were shot by John "Jack" Shive, who had established a ranch near Jackson Hole on the Buffalo Fork River. In 1898, Shive was in the party of the first white men to climb Grand Teton.

The moose were shipped back to Washington and examined by scientists at the Biological Survey. The Rocky Mountain moose differed from the moose of eastern North America. It had a "pale, rusty yellowish-brown coloring." The hooves were shorter and smaller. At the time, the color of an animal's fur was perceived to be an important—even defining—difference between subspecies, but it wasn't as important as the animal's morphology. And clearly the bone structure of these moose was different.

The male served as the type for the new subspecies, which Nelson named *Alces americanus shirasi*, or the Shiras Moose. Nelson described the new subspecies at the Proceedings of the Biological Society of Washington on April 25, 1914, which met in the grand assembly room of the Cosmos Club. The society was founded in 1880 with the primary purpose of taxonomy and systematics.

Nelson said,

We are indebted to George Shiras 3d for nearly all we know concerning the life history of these animals. Mr. Shiras visited the head of Yellowstone Lake and ascended the Yellowstone River and to the surprise of everyone, discovered that moose were amazingly numerous there. Mr. Shiras gives an account of his observations of these moose, a map of their distribution in the park and a series of fine photographs of these animals taken by day and night in their haunts. This is a remarkably interesting and valuable contribution to the life history of one of our least known big game animals.

Although *Alces americanus shirasi* can reach eight hundred pounds, it proved to be the smallest of the four subspecies in North America. Shiras moose don't migrate far, typically spending winter at low elevations and then ascending in summer to the closed-canopy coniferous forest to keep cool.

The worry about predators cleaning out the Thorofare herd never panned out.

Eventually, wolves were extirpated from the Rockies for several decades. Mountain lions and grizzlies were hunted and squeezed out of much of their habitat. And this may have allowed for the expansion of the moose's range. Shiras moose—as they are still known today—increased in abundance and distribution in the park and moved into Utah, Idaho, and Montana along the spine of the Rockies. Certainly there were smaller numbers in other areas of the West, and not all the progeny resulted from the core group in the Thorofare region, but those animals were extremely important to the comeback of the subspecies.

By the early 1920s, Wyoming was issuing one hundred licenses annually to kill bull moose. Shiras supported the move because he felt the park was acting as a great game refuge. The population could sustain harvest and by allowing sportsmen to kill "surplus animals," it would help justify the aim of game refuges and national parks to be important sanctuaries for animals.

16 | THE KENAI PENINSULA

ON THURSDAY EVENING, July 20, 1911, the *Pittsburg Press* ran the headline: "Pittsburg Attorney Risks Life in Wilds of Alaska."

According to the writer,

The doughty Pittsburger was on an adventure outside the common experience . . .

With hardship such as few men have endured staring him in the face, George Shiras III, the Pittsburg attorney who is a great friend of Theodore Roosevelt is on his way to the heart of Alaska, accompanied by two guides for a two months trip in the interior to obtain pictures and photographs of wild animals which are practically unknown to civilized man.

He would receive fabulous sums, it is said, for the rights to reproduce eleven sets of pictures of Alaskan wild animals in their native haunts. One of the transcontinental railroads had contracted with Mr. Shiras for a picture of an Alaskan moose, which will be enlarged and placed in the depots of all the principal cities.

George's expedition to Alaska was consummation of a desire decades in the making. Alaska had loomed large in his imagination since boyhood, when he devoured his father's books on polar exploration and big game animals. In 1891, he believed President Benjamin Harrison might make him the next governor of the District of Alaska, which was then an unorganized US territory without a civil government. Prior to the Yukon Gold Rush in the late 1890s, Alaska contained just thirty thousand people.

It's not clear why Shiras had this conviction—perhaps there had been personal assurances made by the White House or Pennsylvania politicians working on his behalf. Also, A. P. Swineford—who had run a newspaper in Marquette, served as Michigan's lieutenant governor, and then became governor of Alaska—may have recommended that young George, with Marquette family connections, replace him. But it was not to be; Swineford stayed on as governor. President Harrison named George Jr. to the US Supreme Court, and George 3d stayed in Pittsburgh and took over his father's legal work.

During his years in Washington, amid the storytelling and lunches at the Cosmos Club and the meetings of the Boone and Crockett Club, Shiras befriended Charles Sheldon, who had earned a fortune in railroads and retired young to pursue big game hunting. Sheldon had become especially enchanted with Alaska and hunting Dall sheep. He eventually moved to Washington to lobby for game protection and the establishment of what is now Denali National Park.

Dall sheep, *Ovis dalli*, which inhabit mountains from British Columbia north into Alaska, were first described in 1884 by their mutual friend, E. W. Nelson. Specimens were many, but there were few good images of these animals in their native surroundings. Photographing the "white sheep" became Shiras's goal on his 1911 expedition to the Kenai Peninsula. The National Geographic Society shared the costs of the journey and commissioned Shiras to write an article and publish photographs. As mentioned in the newspaper article, he also made side deals to sell images.

John Hammer was still feeling poorly from contracting typhoid in Mexico. In his place, Shiras took Charlie Anderson, another outdoorsman from Marquette. Fanny and the children accompanied the two men to Vancouver, where they boarded a steamer, traveled up the Inside Passage, and landed in Resurrection Bay at Seward. The town, established just eight years earlier, was a rough-hewn place with feral dogs roaming the dirt streets and raising a chorus of howls when boats arrived at the dock.

Construction of a railroad into the interior had stalled at mile seventy after two private owners had gone bankrupt, and it was not until the 1920s that the federal government stepped in to finish the road to Fairbanks. They took a gasoline-powered rail car to mile twenty-four at the head of Kenai Lake accompanied by Tom Towle, an Alaskan guide and gold miner who had built a cabin in the wilderness there.

They transferred camping and photographic gear to a boat, crossed the lake and went up the Kenai River to set up a base camp at Skilak Lake. Like the Upper Yellowstone River in Wyoming, the Kenai Peninsula was a spectacular and roadless wilderness that, according to estimates of the period, supported as many as ten thousand moose.

From the canoes, Shiras spotted several bulls but was unable to get close enough for a decent image. Of one animal, he wrote, "all I could see on the focus mirror was his slowly retreating rear—an unattractive sight for the camera however vulnerable it might be to a ball projected by a modern rifle."

An unidentified "eastern sportsman," likely Sheldon, had told him of a mineral lick and, after some searching along the shore, they located a large, muddy hole surrounded by a bare area where grasses and soil had been trampled. The surface was lower than the surrounding marshy area because the animals, mostly moose, had eaten or scraped away the soil to get to the mineral- laden spring water.

As he had done on Whitefish Lake, Shiras erected a canvas blind and spent the next several days hunkered down waiting for moose. Blinds over licks were acceptable for camera hunters but not gunners, he wrote in *National Geographic.* "And here the game photographer should locate for a while without any fear of criticism that every true sportsman would voice at the destructive custom of killing visiting animals at a lick be it natural or artificial."

His most memorable encounter came on August 17, when the temperature hit a balmy seventy-four degrees. An old cow came down and drank a gallon or two of the muddy water. "So active was the effect upon her salivary glands that long strings of saliva drooled to the ground."

Determined to get a closer picture, he stepped out of the blind and approached with his Graflex, getting within fifteen yards. She allowed two pictures and then began to move away. Shiras fumbled with his plate holders and when he looked up again, the moose had turned and was coming toward him at a slow trot. He assumed that she was just trying to get his scent. As he explained the incident in his *National Geographic* article, he could not help but take a jab at the nature fakers: "To the uninitiated this would have meant a bold charge and to the nature faker sufficient grounds for an exciting story."

When the moose got within five feet, he moved ever so slightly to allow the breeze to blow across his body and toward the animal. "The effect was instantaneous as she realized man was near. She sank back on her haunches and I noticed her shoulders trembled violently, just as if a rifle ball had penetrated her through and through."

The cow left in a hurry.

Moose over a lick were easy prey for the camera. The bigger challenge came in the nearly ten days he spent in the mountains near Tom Towle's cabin. John Hammer arrived at camp, apparently urged by Shiras to come north on his own if he felt able to make the trip.

Four days were taken with hiking up and back and hauling gear three thousand feet above the lake. The guides hefted much of the gear, and it was clear from Shiras's own descriptions that they were in his employ. That first day was hot, his pack heavy, and the underbrush a nuisance: "Gradually I shed all extra clothing and then lightened my pack, the guides good naturedly picking up the discards as they fell by the wayside."

They set up a small tent above the tree line on a saddle between two peaks. Shiras spent the evening there alone while the guides descended to get more gear. He lay on a cushion of moss and glassed the country through binoculars. Easily visible one hundred miles distant was Mount Redoubt, a volcano in the Aleutians that erupted just a few years earlier. Denali, then known as Mount McKinley, made up the other horizon. From this distance, the Cook Inlet resembled the blue line of a river. He turned his gaze and camera on marmots whistling in the nearby rocks. A dozen porcupines grazed on green grasses just below a melting snowdrift. A fox spooked a covey of rock ptarmigan. One bird came within five feet of the tent, apparently mistaking the white canvas for a snowdrift.

That evening, just at sunset, he saw two large brown bears ambling up the slope. Although he had a rather disdainful attitude regarding the threat of bears, this pair gave him pause: "From my own experience and the carefully sifted experience of others, I had long ago concluded that there are no dangerous wild animals whatever in the northern hemisphere, except the grizzly, and this is dangerous only occasionally when molested."

These were grizzlies—wild and unmolested—and he admitted to having a bit of nerves while lying in his sleeping bag. Hearing no movement outside, however, he fell asleep and the bears apparently never approached the tent.

The next day when the guides returned, they moved higher to Tom's cabin on Benjamin Creek where he had explored for gold. It was a rough day of lugging cameras, plates, tripods, and heavy camp gear. After dinner, they fell asleep exhausted, especially Hammer, who was feeling ill.

They climbed higher the next morning and sighted Dall sheep on the ridges, although the animals were no more than white dots in distant rocks. Finally, they erected a tent near a pond on the tundra where two drainages met below large, melting snowfields. According to Towle, the sheep would come down during the day to drink. Working out of what Shiras christened Big Pond Camp, the men spent the next several days positioning themselves in hastily constructed blinds and waiting hours for the sheep to descend within camera range. As a hunter, Shiras understood that scent could betray their position as much as their visibility, so they were careful to always be downwind. Camera traps were out of the question. The sheep were scattered and the landscape too open, rocky, and rugged. The habits of the sheep and game trails were unknown to Shiras. It was impossible to know where to place the camera.

Tom was more accustomed to the animals coming within gun range—measured in hundreds of yards—and not the closeness required for telephoto lenses, which at that time did not exceed a magnification of 3×. That first day a band of sheep came within one thousand yards, and the men made a little blind out of brush at the edge of a thicket and waited for several hours. No sheep approached but, in their observations, they determined the animals were coming down to eat snow rather than drink from streams.

They moved to a ledge overlooking a meadow full of snow and constructed a wall of flat stones to serve as a blind. After sleeping back at Big

Pond Camp, they approached the blind during a thick fog at daybreak. Unfortunately, the fog lifted suddenly. They found themselves about two hundred yards below the blind looking up at two magnificent rams and perhaps thirty ewes and lambs. The animals immediately fled the valley, moving up and away. Shiras was certain the day's camera hunt was over, but he went into the blind anyway and spent several hours there.

Persistence paid off. Hours later, a big ram crossed into the valley. Hundreds of yards away, he nibbled gradually toward the snowfield and then was hidden from sight by a slope. Nearly an hour passed and the men needed to get out of their uncomfortable crouched positions. Shiras was up and nearly over the rock wall when Tom pulled him back, whispering "Good Lord, here he comes right at us."

The ram was just forty yards away, and he had not spied the men. He kept moving, grazing as he went, and when he was just fifty feet away, Shiras could wait no more. When the ram turned sideways and bent down for a sprig of grass, he stood and fixed his eyes on the focusing mirror rather than the animal: "In the ground glass I saw his head raise suddenly and turn my way. Quickly the milled head of the focus screw brought him into focus and the focal-plane shutter clanged harshly."

Towle and Hammer gazed up at Shiras with the unspoken question, "Did you get it?"

He thought so, but it was two days later in Tom's cabin, long after the sun went down and no light penetrated the walls, that he dropped the plate into the developer and saw the big ram, broadside, head up, gazing at the camera.

A few days later, after another stalk and hours lying behind a rock, Shiras was able to step out and shoot a ewe from perhaps one hundred feet away. But that was as close as he got in several days of excruciating work. To read the account of the men wading streams, enduring biting insects, turning ankles on uneven ground, building numerous blinds, and crouching for endless hours waiting for the right moment is to understand the difficulty of the photographic enterprise.

The remaining pictures were mainly of snowfields, rocky crags, dark meadows (the images were all black-and-white, of course), and small figures of sheep—white dots on the vast landscape.

Yet Shiras did come back from the mountains with sheep pictures, better than anyone had previously, and the results appeared in *National Geographic* magazine in the May issue: "The White Sheep, Giant Moose and Smaller Game of the Kenai Peninsula."

When Shiras and Hammer came out of the Alaskan bush in 1911, Hammer received the terrible news that his wife, Jenny, had died unexpectedly. He never married again and raised two children on his own.

By 1911, Theodore Roosevelt had left the presidency and become an associate editor at *The Outlook* magazine, albeit a rather special editor with his own suite of rooms and even a separate entrance so he could avoid people if necessary.

On December 11, *The Outlook* published an editorial, "The American Hunter Naturalist," which was ostensibly TR's review of Charles Sheldon's book on the wilderness of the Upper Yukon, but in it, the Colonel gave a few paragraphs over to George Shiras 3d. First, he praised Shiras's photographic work but then let him have it with both barrels for not taking TR's advice to write a book.

That fall, reports of Shiras's Alaskan expedition and quotes from the faunal naturalist had appeared in some newspapers and been disseminated by the wire services. In Roosevelt's opinion, newspapers were a lowly form of journalism.

TR wrote,

Mr. Shiras has done extraordinary work in the woods with a camera as well as a notebook. He is a great hunter but he finally almost abandoned hunting and became a great field naturalist and observer of wild life. His photographs are extraordinary, his notebooks are filled with matter of extraordinary interest; but he will not publish them!

He comes out of the wilds and gives his photographs to some daily paper and talks about his experiences to a reporter. He might exactly as well talk about them and show his photographs in a smoking car, so far as any real value in the way of recording what he has seen is concerned. If he could or would put into book form his experiences, thus preserving his written notes and his pictures, he would render a very real service to the cause of science; he would confer a boon upon lovers of nature; and unless he does so, his experiences will really amount to very little excepting in so far as they given him personal gratification.

Shiras was taken aback by Roosevelt's rebuke and, when he returned to Washington, DC, he sent a letter on December 18 to Oyster Bay.

It was long, single-spaced, and contained a bit of humor but some justification, too. He blamed the newspaper reports on a congressional friend from Washington who set "the whole Seattle press at my heels. . . . had I not been able to hide part of the time in Billy Hofer's little fur store down on the waterfront, I would have had all my Alaska material taken from me. On the other hand, an occasional article in *National Geographic* magazine does no harm and is rather expected of me now since I became one of the board of managers of the society."

As for his writings, he told Roosevelt he had been more engaged in his legal work, preparing a brief on the "Supervisory Powers of the Federal Government." In the letter, he reminds TR that the president's New Nationalism would require legal justification and expanded federal powers.

The previous year, in 1910, Roosevelt had set out New Nationalism in a speech delivered at the dedication of John Brown Memorial Park in Osawatomie, Kansas. New Nationalism called for greater regulation of the economy, a guarantee of social justice, a minimum wage law for women, an eight-hour work day for all workers, and social insurance for the elderly and unemployed. New Nationalism would be the platform of the Progressive Party in 1912.

Shiras continued, "While it is true that I began this analysis of Federal powers partly as the result of my interest in health legislation, and partly in the effort to sustain my position of a Federal jurisdiction over migratory birds and migratory fish, yet as I advanced in this field of research, it became very apparent that I was laying the legal foundation for many new national powers you had already advocated, and yet had hitherto lack a constitutional basis acceptable to a considerable portion of the legal profession."

Then he referred specifically to "your nice little *Outlook* jab."

"As to your prospect of your ever getting anything out of me in the way of sportsman's literature, I may say it is not entirely hopeless. I shall be greatly pleased to submit to you a summary of chapters completed and in progress, 'Hunting Wild Game with Camera and Flashlight, An account of forty years' experience as a sportsman and animal photographer in the American Wilderness.' A title that is purely tentative—since a year or more must elapse before the typesetting begins."

The main title did not change but the deck, or reading line, did. Rather than being forty years, it was sixty. Typesetting would not begin until the 1930s. And though the book would be dedicated to the Colonel, he would never live to see it.

Roosevelt responded with a letter from *The Outlook*'s offices: "Dear Shiras, If anything should make me pardon your not turning your attention to hunting and natural history, it would be such admirable work as you are doing in placing before people the proper conception of the supervisory powers of the national government. Now when are you coming on here? I want to see you and talk over both things. You must get out that 'Hunting Wild Game with Camera and Flashlight,' and, on the other hand, you must go on with your governmental work. More power to your elbow in every way!"

17 | ROOSEVELT-NEWETT
LIBEL TRIAL

GEORGE 3D WAS unabashedly a Progressive, but his father had his doubts about its dogmas and reforms, which the retired justice expressed to a reporter in Chicago in 1912 as he changed trains and made his way north to Marquette. Congress had just passed the proposed Seventeenth Amendment, which called for direct election of US senators. The amendment was then going through approval by state legislatures.

Direct election, which would become law in 1913, would mean a change in "the established order," said George Jr. "I don't believe ward politicians will be able to name as fine a body of men as now compose the Senate."

He was even less impressed with the muckraking journalists who had helped bring about such changes. "They are usually inexperienced young men writing for the profit of their publications rather than for the prosperity of their country, and I don't believe they can improve on work of the founders of this country."

Yet people were reading the muckrakers, and the country was undergoing a transformation, much to the mortification of Old Guard Republicans. Progressivism had made substantial inroads into the American psyche, spawned a crusade for conservation of national resources, and shunned the laissez-faire style of government characterizing the Gilded Age. Under

Roosevelt and through executive order, conservation was now government policy.

William H. Taft was Roosevelt's friend, vice president, and handpicked successor, but he was not a firebrand conservationist. Soon after he took office, a schism developed between Taft, Gifford Pinchot, and other Roosevelt disciples.

Taft forced out Secretary of the Interior James Garfield, son of the assassinated president, and replaced him with Richard Ballinger, a former mayor of Seattle who had served in the General Land Office. Within weeks, Ballinger reversed policies from the Roosevelt era, opening up three million acres in Wyoming, Alaska, and Montana for development. He approved the sale of land containing coal deposits to a group of Seattle businessmen, who then profited by selling to New York financiers.

It was a return to the old ways of resource exploitation and of politicians and bureaucrats being cozy with big business, ranching, and timber interests. Gifford Pinchot was openly critical of Ballinger and declared that he was trying to "stop the conservation movement." Pinchot fired off a letter to Roosevelt, then on safari in Africa, and told him that Taft was reneging on promises. A muckraking article in *Colliers* magazine outlined the whole suspicious affair—including the firing of a whistleblower in the Interior Department—leaving readers with the impression that Ballinger and Taft, too, had been compromised by special interests.

After talking to his attorney general, who assured him no laws had been broken, President Taft issued a public letter absolving Ballinger of any wrongdoing. He tried to reassure Pinchot and progressive conservationists that he had not abandoned their cause, but Pinchot was having none of it and wrote a fiery letter to Senator Jonathan Dolliver, a Progressive Republican from Iowa. Pinchot defended the Forest Service and criticized Taft. Dolliver read the letter aloud on the Senate floor and into the congressional record. Pinchot had overstepped the bounds of criticizing his new boss and, in 1909, Taft fired him for insubordination. Congressional hearings ensued, and the fight dragged on for months, but Pinchot was now on the outside of government after more than a decade of leading the charge. He took a boat to Italy to discuss the matter with Roosevelt, who was on a European tour after his African safari. Pinchot urged TR to run for president in 1912.

What became known as the Ballinger-Pinchot controversy divided the Republican Party between the Old Guard, which had ruled since the Civil War, and the new Progressive wing, which included Pinchot and Shiras. Ultimately, the fight cost Taft reelection and his friendship with Roosevelt.

When Roosevelt returned to America, he initially tried to bring the factions together, but he concluded that Taft was not able to forward a Progressive agenda. His New Nationalism speech alarmed the Old Guard. TR clearly had the White House in mind. He was restless. His trip to Africa and work as an editor at *The Outlook* had not sated his desire to be back on the national stage wielding power.

When Roosevelt agreed to challenge Taft for the nomination, Old Guard Republicans were beside themselves in anger and, in response, reinvigorated rumors that Roosevelt was a drunken, volatile, and unstable man—one unfit for office.

Rumors of intemperance had plagued Roosevelt for years. His strange way of talking, his excitability and animated behavior, led people to believe the man was prone to drink. His behavior could be bizarre. When he was president, he took reporters and diplomats on jaunts through Rock Creek Park in which everyone had to strip off their clothes and swim across the creek. He often carried a pistol while traveling. He would interrupt a conversation to comment on a bird flying by his office window. He boxed and fought with pugil sticks with members of his administration, including Pinchot and Leonard Wood, who had helped TR organize the Rough Riders brigade for the invasion of Cuba. The first time the president met Pinchot, he challenged him to a wrestling match. The president could be so bruised and sore from these manly jousts that he could hardly shake hands in receiving lines.

One day in 1907, Shiras was lunching with Roosevelt in the White House. The president asked a butler to retrieve some of Shiras's wildlife pictures, which were upstairs on a bureau. The waiter returned with stereoscopic images only.

Such prints had little value, said Shiras, except when viewed through a stereoscope. "Why should I used a stereoscope when I only have one eye?" TR asked.

"What?" replied Shiras.

Two years earlier, a young naval artilleryman hit the president so hard during a boxing match, the blow broke a blood vessel and blinded him in his left eye—a fact few people knew outside the family. Shiras and the other lunch guests—including cabinet members—were astounded at this revelation, and TR delighted in the fact that he kept it secret.

His odd behaviors had nothing to do with alcohol, which had consumed his brother Elliott, who began drinking at an early age and went through treatment several times. The father of the future First Lady Eleanor Roosevelt, Elliott killed himself by jumping out a window when he was just thirty-four. Alcoholism was a serious problem in America. Many states had passed dry laws, and there were calls for national prohibition. Politicians were forced to choose sides—were they wet or dry? Most politicians voted dry and, if they drank, did so privately.

In the fall of 1912 while Roosevelt was on a campaign swing in Atlanta, a local reporter asked him about the drunkard charges. Roosevelt answered politely that he was no drinker.

When the reporter left, TR looked at his staff and vowed that the next time a newspaper—one with enough assets to pay damages—published such a story, he would sue for libel.

A few days later the *Gazette* in Salinas, Kansas, did so, but Roosevelt learned it was owned by an ex-senator who had been put in the federal penitentiary for malfeasance. The *Gazette* could not pay damages, so he waited.

He swept all the primaries, but most delegates were chosen by state party organizations and the Republican National Committee, who were in no mood to deny Howard Taft, a sitting president, his party's nomination. Jay Hayden, the Washington correspondent for the *Detroit News*, covered the 1912 GOP convention in Chicago. In Toledo, he boarded the train carrying TR to the convention and found the ex-president alone in a compartment quietly reading a book. The two men had a nice chat for half an hour. The Colonel was quite sober, noted Hayden. But when the train arrived in Chicago, "Rumors had been set loose on Roosevelt. . . . I scarcely had stepped from the train in Chicago, before I began hearing that Roosevelt had been roaring drunk on the trip and had smashed dishes in the dining car."

It was a harbinger of the animus toward Roosevelt. The convention nominated Taft on the first ballot. Roosevelt walked out and formed the Progressive, or Bull Moose, Party.

Shiras served as a delegate at large from Michigan to the Progressive convention also held in Chicago. He also served on the Committee of Resolutions and Platforms. Shortly after Roosevelt accepted the nomination of the Progressives at the convention, a man stood on a chair and demanded, "Where do you stand on prohibition?"

Roosevelt gritted his teeth and windmilled his arms, but no one heard what he said in the roar of the disapproving crowd—who simply did not want the matter raised. The man was hustled from the building.

When Roosevelt began his third-party campaign, the Old Guard understood that the Colonel would take votes from Taft and likely throw the election to Woodrow Wilson and the Democrats—which is exactly what happened.

The coming campaign was fierce, especially in Michigan where, as one reporter noted, "the name Roosevelt is as much as a red rag to a bull." Marquette, however, was a Bull Moose town. Frank Russell, the publisher of the local paper, the *Mining Journal,* was a forthright Progressive. In 1912, Russell was a prominent figure in the town and a confidant of the Shiras family. In 1925, he would become George 3d's son-in-law when he married daughter Ellen, also known as Ellie. At the time of the marriage, Russell was forty-five and Ellie thirty-nine. It was his second marriage and her first.

In early October, Roosevelt went on a campaign swing through Michigan, covering small cities and villages in the Upper Peninsula. It might seem an odd, empty region to seek votes, but a century ago when steel was king and the riches of the country were bound up in iron ore, copper, and timber, the region was flush with working people and votes. Taft himself visited Marquette in 1911.

George Shiras 3d was in the Upper Peninsula that fall, taking photographs and keeping a sharp eye on the elections. He had exchanged letters with Roosevelt on the prospects of the Progressive Party both in Michigan and Florida.

Shiras spent several days camera trapping in the western part of Marquette County, where a large beaver dam was discovered over the summer. Figuring that trappers would take all the animals that winter, he and a guide set up a tent and camped for two days in a grove of poplars. Trees had been gnawed and toppled as the animals laid in a supply of winter food. Shiras first tried to set a trip wire to get a picture as the beavers emerged from their lodge but had no success. Then the men removed part of the dam, creating a hole that within a few hours lowered the pool by six inches.

That got the attention of the colony.

Shiras tied a string between a camera trap and birch branch that he placed in the dam breech. He figured the beavers would have to pull this branch aside to start repairs.

After midnight as he lay in the tent, he saw "a faint flutter of light on the white canvas roof. Almost immediately, I heard the boom of the flashlight."

He had no time to rig up for another picture because Theodore Roosevelt was due into Marquette. The next morning, he headed back to town.

Roosevelt began October 9, 1912, with two speeches before breakfast in Cheboygan, a town in the northern Lower Peninsula. He crossed the Mackinac Straits on a ferry and then boarded a westbound train. Throughout the day, the train stopped at towns, stations, and rural junctions— sometimes for just two or three minutes—where he came out to wave or speechify. In total, he was seen by forty thousand people.

Much like the present day, when candidates go on television or issue statements throughout the day to sling mud and respond to charges, Roosevelt kept two secretaries busy, picking up telegrams with news of the other campaigns, sending out responses, and issuing press releases, often to the reporters traveling on the train.

By midafternoon when he reached Marquette, about six thousand people awaited. As the train backed into the station and halted so he could step directly onto a special stage, TR scanned the crowd for Shiras. He was well aware that his friend had been in the woods the previous night and on a mission to get a photograph.

Standing on the back rear platform with thousands of people on either side trying to get a look at him, Roosevelt found Shiras, waved and yelled, "Did you get a beaver picture last night?"

Shiras cupped his hands, and hollered back that he wasn't certain. The plate had yet to be developed. He would let him know.

Roosevelt spoke to the crowd for twenty-five minutes, delivering a decidedly populist message well suited for a district of workers, many of them immigrants, toiling for the big trusts of copper, iron, and steel.

The Progressive campaign, TR declared, was a great moral crusade for human rights that would answer one dominant question—"Shall the people rule rather than the money interests and the big corporations?"

He reminded his listeners of the party's platform supporting labor unions, worker's compensation, safety and health standards, and more rights for women and child laborers. New Nationalism also called for steep graduated income and inheritance taxes: "We have come with you Progressives to champion the right of the people themselves to rule. And it is not an empty phrase . . . let us bring nearer to the day when every man and every woman in this country shall have social and industrial justice."

He called for direct primaries and an end to party bosses: "Remember my friends, nominally they stole the nomination from me; really they stole it from you. The bosses and the trusts should have but one vote, and not be in control of parties, governors and legislatures."

A man stood up in his car and called the president a liar. The two got into a shouting match. Philip Roosevelt, who had accompanied his famous cousin on the trip, recalled that as soon as TR discovered the man was an Old Guard Republican, "He tore the hide off the man's words."

The speeches, however, were not amplified. Reporters estimated that three-fourths of the crowd never heard the president and will "have to depend on published reports to gain an idea of his remarks."

Also he was hoarse with a sore throat. A paper noted that an hour later, when speaking in Ishpeming to a crowd of eight thousand that included iron miners who came directly from the shafts carrying their dinner buckets, "The Colonel Roosevelt, tired with his previous speaking, was heard but briefly and for all but those in the immediate vicinity of the car his remarks were no more than pantomime."

He recovered somewhat by the time he reached the Keweenaw Peninsula, where tens of thousands of workers toiled in the mines and smelters of the copper industry. Reporters on the train marveled at the size of the crowd (ten thousand) at the Amphidrome, a wooden building and the first arena in the United States built specifically for hockey. It was the largest crowd in all of Michigan.

The next day's headline in the *Marquette Mining Journal* proclaimed, "Big Bull Moose's U. P. Tour a Continual Triumph; Colonel Acclaimed by Cloverland Citizens from Early in the Morning until Late at Night." The reference to Cloverland was an attempt by Russell and other regional boosters

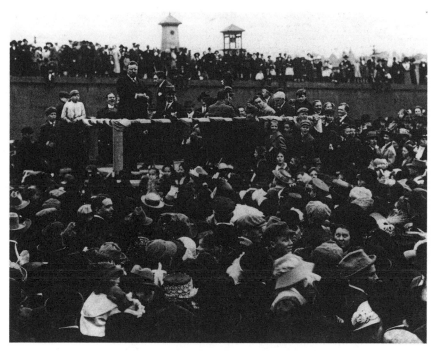

Theodore Roosevelt campaigning in Marquette, Michigan, 1912.
Courtesy of the Marquette Regional History Center.

to rebrand the Upper Peninsula and market the region's cutover lands to ranchers, farmers, and immigrants.

Russell effused in his lead paragraph, "Colonel Theodore Roosevelt, the great warrior of modern times for human rights, the greatest quickener of the public consciousness the country has known since Lincoln, a man who the country has honored with its richest prize, and the most unusual estate among men the world has been pleased to honor came to the Upper Peninsula yesterday in one of the most significant fights in his full career, carrying the message of the Progressive Party to the electorate of the Twelfth District of Michigan."

The Republican papers tried to downplay what was clearly a successful campaign swing through the peninsula. George Newett, the editor of the *Iron Ore*, a weekly in Ishpeming, was the voice of Old Guard Republicanism in the region. He served on the Republican state central committee and his good friend, Olin H. Young, who had represented Northern Michigan in Congress for four terms, was up for reelection. Because of Roosevelt's jump to a third party, there was a real danger that Young would lose to a Progressive candidate.

In 1912, the *Iron Ore* had a circulation of just three thousand, but it reflected the views of the mining and steel conglomerates in the mining districts of Michigan, Colorado, Montana, Arizona, and Nevada. Newett had a reputation for strong political opinion backing the big trusts.

"Mr. Newett wields a merciless pen. His editorial columns lashed his opponents. . . . He has gone his way for years, leaving victims strewn around him," the *New York Times* wrote.

Newett was a teetotaler, too, who had "strong convictions on this subject." He did not use tobacco either.

On October 12 in a scathing editorial headlined "The Roosevelt Way," Newett wrote that the ex-president was an intemperate, profane man who had problems with anyone who disagreed with him.

According to Roosevelt, he is the only man that can call others liars, rascals and thieves, terms he applied to Republicans generally. . . . If anyone calls Roosevelt a liar, he raves and roars and takes on in an awful way and yet Roosevelt is a pretty good liar himself. Where a lie will serve to advance his position, he employs it. Roosevelt lies and curses in a most disgusting way; he gets drunk, too, and that not infrequently and all his intimates know it.

. . . he acts like a madman if anyone dares criticize him. He must do all the swearing and abusing of people; no one else can question him. All who oppose him are wreckers of the country, liars, knaves and undesirables. He alone is pure and entitled to a halo. Rats. For so great a fighter, self-styled, he is the poorest loser we ever knew.

Strong words and plainly stated.

Most attacks were sly and insinuating like one from the *Marquette Chronicle*—a newspaper leaning toward the Old Guard—describing a brief stop Roosevelt's train made at Munising Junction, a rural crossroads where a group of five hundred lumberjacks, workers, and ladies gathered to see the ex-president.

Something was evidently wrong with Roosevelt, something more than there generally is. He acted as a man who was not himself. For some reason or other, his speech was thick and he had to stop from time to time for words and thoughts. He was unable to speak at once directly or clearly. Those in the party, though not Bull Moosers, who had been friendly toward the man were disgusted. They could not understand what was the matter. The entire party regretted that it had taken the time away from work to hear him.

The report was unattributed and vague, but readers got the gist—Roosevelt was intoxicated.

Newett's mistake was being unambiguous and retelling as fact all those rumors regarding alcohol. He wrote for local consumption out of anger and the desire to help his friend Representative Young, who had been telling Newett that all of Washington knew Roosevelt was a drunkard.

On October 14 while he was dining in a Chicago hotel, Roosevelt was given a copy of the *Iron Ore* by the secretary of the Progressive Party. Progressive sources had done a bit of inquiry about the paper and Newett's character. The *Iron Ore* was a small but reputable weekly. Newett was a man of good standing in the community and of means. He could pay damages.

Roosevelt, still nursing his sore throat, reportedly whispered, "Let's go at him."

It was a historic, fateful day for TR and the Progressive Party, but not because of this decision. After breakfast, Roosevelt took a train to Wisconsin for a speech at the Milwaukee Auditorium. While he stood up in a car to wave at the crowd, John Schrank, a barkeeper from New York, stepped out and fired a .38 caliber bullet into Roosevelt's chest. He had stalked the candidate for three weeks through eight states.

"Any man looking for a third term ought to be shot," Schrank said, later revealing to police that the ghost of William McKinley had dispatched him to shoot McKinley's former vice president.

The slug tore through a steel eyeglass case and a folded fifty-page speech in Roosevelt's suit coat and then lodged in the chest wall, missing his internal organs. The old hunter coughed, spit, and made a self-diagnosis: no blood, so the bullet likely missed his lungs. Despite pleas by doctors, Roosevelt went on stage, waved the bloodstained manuscript with a bullet hole through the sheets and proclaimed to the hall, "You see. It takes more than that to kill a Bull Moose."

He nearly keeled over during the speech and spent eight days in the hospital. The bullet was never removed.

While Roosevelt was in the hospital, Shiras sent him a flashlight picture of a beaver repairing the dam. The inscription on the back read, "Here is the answer to your question of October 9."

The attempted assassination effectively ended TR's campaign.

Marquette County voted overwhelmingly Progressive; the Colonel won the twelfth district by more than five thousand votes. His coattails helped elect William McDonald and throw out H. Olin Young. Roosevelt won the popular vote in Michigan, too, but Woodrow Wilson became president with 41.8 percent of the national vote. Roosevelt received 27.4, Taft 23.2, and the socialist Eugene Debs 6 percent.

On October 25, just before the election, Roosevelt's lawyers filed a $10,000 criminal libel suit at the Marquette County Courthouse against George Newett and the *Iron Ore*.

Newett was arrested that afternoon "on a capias" warrant, essentially an order to appear in court. The *New York Times* reported, "Mr. Newett is quite wealthy and he was released on his own recognizance on promising to appear to-morrow morning for arraignment. He has given no hint what his defense will be. If Col. Roosevelt gets a judgment for $10,000 there will be no difficult in collecting it."

Newett's best defense was to prove the charges of drunkenness were true. Alternatively, he could claim that he was simply repeating what was common knowledge and had a right to comment on the character of a public person running for public office. Later in the twentieth century, after Supreme Court decisions such as *New York Times Co. v. Sullivan* (1964), which allowed for criticisms of public officials and figures, the latter would have been sufficient. In fact, the libel suit would have been thrown out by a judge on summary judgment and never gone to trial.

But in 1912 with Victorian ideals about honor still in play, libel suits were much more common. Even public figures whose reputations certainly could have survived the rantings of an editor of a tiny weekly newspaper in a relatively empty quarter of the United States had a right to sue—even a moral obligation, according to societal norms. The latter attitude was expressed in *The Outlook* by editor Lawrence Abbott, who said of the lawsuit and Roosevelt: "This seemed to him to be not only a duty to himself and his family but a duty to the country. It has been a matter of shame and regret to all decent Americans that their presidents from the time of Washington down to the present have visited insidious gossip about their private lives and character."

Several close associates of Roosevelt, including George Shiras 3d and editor Frank Russell, thought the libel suit unwise. It could invite a humiliating defeat or hung jury. The Marquette County sheriff, the jury commissioner, and other court officials were Old Guard Republicans, part of the local anti-Roosevelt clique and, Shiras warned, they would work to pick an "unfair jury."

Roosevelt scoffed and wrote to Shiras from New York, saying "the issue was plain and I would not hesitate to go before a jury in any decent community demanding a hearing of my case."

In the months prior to the trial, a flurry of correspondence passed between the two friends. Shiras invited Roosevelt and his party to stay at his summer home in Marquette during the trial. Shiras was at Ormond Beach that winter but would come up to Marquette to open and prepare the house. He did not want to miss the spectacle.

On January 21, 1913, Roosevelt accepted the invitation, thinking he would come north with two or three people. He wrote, "I am very indignant at this scoundrel Newett. When he started these libels against me, he may not have known that they were false, but he must know it now if he has made any inquiry."

Shiras told TR he was certain Newett was receiving help and encouragement from "outside the district . . . the local office holders and political machine will be against you, backed secretly by cunning politicians throughout the United States."

Yet Shiras doubted it would come to a trial, "because Newett will offer you an apology when he hears you are going to attend the trial or if you decline to accept the same that he will plead guilty and throw himself on the mercy of the court."

Roosevelt hired James Pound of Detroit to represent him. Pound was a corpulent, aggressive man who wanted Roosevelt to ask for more damages.

Roosevelt asked Shiras, "Is he the right man? May I send part of your letter to him? I would especially like to present to him what you say about taking care of the jury."

There was still room to talk about their mutual interest in conservation. In the letter, Roosevelt enclosed a copy of his review of William T. Hornaday's just-published book, *Our Vanishing Wildlife*, which proved to be an important book in the fight to save wildlife. In it, Hornaday credits the Shiras bird bill as the prototype for federal protection of wildlife.

On January 28, TR wrote Shiras again, saying Pound was coming to New York for consultations. He also asked that Frank Russell come to see him. "It looks as if we should have a very big fight. Undoubtedly, the scoundrel who is responsible for the libel is now being backed by outside money. He is sending around the country to get depositions."

In fact, Newett had obtained nearly forty depositions, mostly from people on the campaign trail who said they had seen Roosevelt drunk while making a speech or stumbling through crowds supported on both sides by his bodyguards. Some depositions simply stated it was common gossip in Washington that Roosevelt drank to excess.

Frank Russell warned that Roosevelt should not come to Marquette with a bunch of outsiders. And after meeting with Russell in New York, Roosevelt hired James Belden, a Marquette attorney. Russell wrote to Shiras, "Now that I felt that we at least have called this matter to the Colonel's attention and so he will be informed that at least in some minds there is a question whether his case will be in the best of hands. That lets us out."

Newett's lawyers worked for Cleveland Cliffs Iron Company, part of the big steel trust Roosevelt had railed against. Ironically, Shiras was friends with William Mather, its president. The Shiras family owned a good deal of stock in the company, too.

Shiras came north in early May, first to New York where he went out to Sagamore Hill to talk over trial strategy and Progressive politics. Roosevelt wanted to know how things were in Florida because he had his eye on running again in 1916.

Shiras's son, George IV, then twenty-three years old, accompanied his father to Marquette for the trial. Fanny remained in Florida. On the afternoon of May 23, TR and his party boarded the Lake Shore Limited at Grand Central Station in New York. They switched trains in Chicago and went north through Wisconsin along the Lake Michigan shoreline.

The Colonel brought along an impressive entourage of supporters and character witnesses. The New York Central attached a Pullman car especially for the Roosevelt party, which included William Loeb Jr., his White House secretary; Alexander Lambert, his personal physician; James Sloan, a secret serviceman; Jacob Riis, photographer and social reformer; Robert Bacon, the former secretary of state; and Philip Roosevelt and Emlen Roosevelt, cousins of the president. He also brought along Edwin Emerson, the regimental clerk for the Rough Riders; Edward Heller, a naturalist at the Smithsonian Institution; and Frank H. Tyree of the Secret Service, who guarded Roosevelt when he was president. Also included were Gifford Pinchot and James R. Garfield, who had lost their jobs in the Taft administration.

From the *New York World*: "To support his civil action, there have gone with him into that distant quarter a small army of notable divines, family physicians, eminent blood relatives, ex-governors of states, collectors of ports, ex-ambassadors, distinguished sociologists and real editors. Over the fate of this mighty expedition set out to crush a country editor the nation sits in anxious interest."

Hearing that Roosevelt had left New York, Newett issued a statement that "he would not listen to the word compromise."

Interest in the trial was high—a cause célèbre—with wire services, major newspapers, and even foreign newspapers sending correspondents to the Upper Peninsula. Special telegraph wires were put into the courthouse so reporters could quickly file their stories. Messengers ran dispatches. Prior to Roosevelt's arrival, reporters nosed around town.

From the *New York World*:

The home of George Shiras whose guests the party will be has the facilities for the utmost comfort of the visitors. For several days, decorators, furnishers and other artisans have been at work. Accommodations for thirty people were provided. The mansion was stocked liberally with food. The visiting party will find many things in the house to interest them.

The Colonel will find a congenial atmosphere in the Shiras home. It is a charming old house, roomy, rangy, perched upon the brow of a hill overlooking the lake. Mr. Shiras, who has followed the calling of naturalist for forty years (without nature faking) has probably one of the country's best collections of prints, photographs, and books on the subject.

The *New York Times* wrote, "Col. Roosevelt will be the guest of his friend, George Shiras, who is famous as a photographer of wild animals in their native jungles."

As the wire services disseminated the story and photographs of the Peter White mansion, Shiras began receiving "heavy mail." Most letters came from people begging for money. One asked Shiras if he would pay his installment on his farm. Other letters to Roosevelt and Newett offered advice on the trial.

At 7:45 a.m., the train pulled into the station at Negaunee, a mining town not far from Marquette, where the entourage was met by Shiras and several hundred people. The men came down to Marquette by automobile. As they entered town and saw Lake Superior, the guests noticed the people on the streets were wearing overcoats and woolen hats. Despite it being nearly June, the cool breeze off the lake made straw hats impractical.

There was a grand breakfast in the "Peter White mansion," and then the men took up quarters in the main house and the nearby homes of Shiras's nieces and nephews. Reporters noticed a courier arriving carrying a box that contained "medicated milk," and there was a great deal of speculation what this could be. In *The Outlook*, Lawrence Abbott had previously written that Roosevelt drank only milk and coffee to excess.

Roosevelt v. Newett was tried in the Marquette County Courthouse, a stately building erected in 1904 with the best Victorian touches: gold stenciling, Beaux Arts columns, copper-clad dome, ceramic tiling, Italian marble wainscoting, and a hardwood interior.

Richard C. Flannigan, a young, scholarly judge who later served on the Michigan Supreme Court, proved to be stern, fair, and capable on the bench, keeping good order in what was nearly a circus atmosphere. One of his first moves was to seat all the women on the left side of the courtroom and ask the men to fill the galleys because "it would be more gallant."

Despite all the attention, Flannigan took the cases in order, hearing misdemeanor cases first. Then at two p.m. jury selection began for *Roosevelt v. Newett*. Voir dire took until eleven p.m., and the cast of characters provided plenty of colorful copy for the reporters.

One potential juror was excused when it was learned he had been beating up any man in town who spoke against Roosevelt. Another came to court with a Bull Moose button on his lapel but assured the lawyers he could be objective. He was excused. To the astonishment of nearly everyone in the courtroom, one man said he didn't read newspapers and had never heard of the case. He was chosen.

The jury was seated with four miners, three teamsters, two farmers, a blacksmith, a lumberjack, and a locomotive fireman. In this era before women's suffrage, all jurors were male. The jury was sequestered, sleeping on cots in an anteroom and eating its meals under the eyes of court officials. They were "deprived of newspapers."

The common practice in a libel suit was to force the defendant to prove his allegations by calling witnesses and presenting evidence, but this was a show trial and Roosevelt asked to go first. The world was to be enthralled by what the *New York Times* called "the spectacle of the ex-president accounting in public with laborious pains the way in which he spent his time while at the head of the nation, describing his private life and answering questions about life in his own home among his guests."

On the second day, Roosevelt led off, standing in the witness box just a few feet from the jury.

He declared he had never drunk a highball or cocktail. He didn't like beer and limited his drinking to light wine and champagne, mainly at party and state functions. He occasionally took a little brandy under doctor's orders and had once carried a flask of whiskey for medicinal purposes when he was a ranchman in the Dakotas—as most cowboys did—but then found he didn't need it.

When asked if he kept brandy and whiskey in the White House, he said the alcohol stock was a leftover from the McKinley administration. Through all the questions, Roosevelt was unequivocal, "I have never been drunk or in the slightest degree under the influence of liquor."

He did, however, express a fondness for mint juleps, explaining there was a fine bed of mint at the White House and he would ask a servant to fix him a fresh drink, especially when relaxing and reading on the porch during hot, humid days in Washington. He estimated he drank maybe a dozen a year.

When this appeared in the next day's papers, tourists in DC immediately asked White House police to show them the bed of mint, which was located beside latticework on which laundresses hung clothes to dry. It had been planted at the request of President McKinley.

From the very beginning, the defense was having a hard time. Roosevelt was a commanding figure and not at all cowed by cross-examination.

Newett's lawyers desperately tried to keep out all references to his colorful past: his war record, ability as a hunter, and even the assassination attempt in Milwaukee—all of which they felt would prejudice the jury.

It was an impossible task because so much of his life was wrapped up in big events. At one point, when the testimony ranged on his drinking habits as a Rough Rider during the Spanish-American War, Roosevelt rolled up his sleeve and showed a scar on his forearm where he had been shot. That was news in itself. It was not common knowledge. During a recess, he explained to reporters that he had never gone to an aid station but had someone wrap the wound in a bandage and pressed on.

The defense objected when Roosevelt referred to an event during the Progressive campaign by prefacing "after I was shot."

Frank Russell wrote in the *Marquette Mining Journal,* "If the sturdy-looking man who spent several years of his life in the duties of the presidency of the United States saw anything curious in his position of explaining to twelve simpler toilers of the woods and the mines that he was not really a drunkard, his confidence and his manner did not betray it."

A *New York Times* reporter thought it advantageous that the jury was seated so close to the plaintiff where they could observe his curious demeanor and gesticulations, which during the campaign led some listeners to think he was under the influence of something.

"There are certain peculiar mannerisms of his, known to all who have seen him often, such as a muscular action of the jaw which bares his teeth when he is speaking very earnestly, and a falsetto sound in his voice when he seeks to be emphatic . . .

"Those who hear him speak imagine that these are intended as efforts of humor on his part, but they are natural, unconscious and unavoidable."

As the parade of character witnesses testified, everyone watched Roosevelt's reactions. His eyes glistened as old friend Jacob Riis testified to the strength of his character.

Riis said he'd known the president for more than two decades, had accompanied him on trips, and never heard Roosevelt use an oath stronger than "Godfrey"—which Riis didn't think was blasphemous. As for the Colonel being a drinking man, it was a "monstrous lie."

Surgeon General Presley Rixley said he had attended Roosevelt nearly every day in seven and a half years of his presidency and had never smelled liquor. On hunting and camping trips, the Colonel shot his rifles with an exceedingly steady hand, Rixley added. No drinking man could be such a marksman.

By the end of the second day, Republican leaders in Marquette County were aghast, certain the trial would end in victory for Roosevelt and put their party on the scrap heap. They were depending on former congressman H. Olin Young to testify about how rumors regarding Roosevelt's drinking habits were rife and common knowledge in Washington, DC, but Young had made himself scarce. He wasn't even in Michigan.

For those intimates of Roosevelt, the trial and accommodations in Marquette turned out to be a smashing good time. On the second evening during dinner at the Shiras home, George 3d sat at the head of the table with Roosevelt to his right and Jacob Riis on the left.

Roosevelt looked at Riis and said, "Jake, it was a fine thing for you to make this long trip on my behalf. You knew me when I was police commissioner and probably knew my habits better than anyone else in that city. I consider your testimony of the greatest value."

Then he told Robert Bacon, who had also testified that day, that he was grateful. Bacon said Roosevelt was a "special chum" at Harvard and had been a temperate young man.

The Colonel looked about the table and obviously was moved with a transfixed expression. The silence was thick until Shiras quipped, "Colonel, if this testimony keeps up a few days longer, you will believe it yourself." Reportedly, the laughter and shouting rattled the china. Roosevelt blushed and joined in.

According to the *Pittsburg Press*, the Colonel was "elated over the huge library and wonderful collection of animal pictures he found in the Shiras home."

Later that day, nearly everyone but Shiras and Roosevelt left to go to the theater. After seeing them off, Shiras wandered into the library and found the Colonel writing a letter.

Looking up, TR asked, "Shiras, can you guess whom I am writing to?"

"That's easy. You are writing to a very fine and very anxious wife you left behind."

"Not a bad guess at all," remarked Roosevelt. "Only you have the wives mixed up, for I am writing to yours."

His letter to Fanny thanked her for the use of her home and invited the Shirases to visit soon at Sagamore Hill on Oyster Bay.

"All of your guests are having a delightful time; but we do wish our hostess were here. . . . Your husband is the best of hosts; the table is so delicious that I have been overeating scandalously; and my room is the kind of room I most like; and so the result as a whole is that what would otherwise be a peculiarly irritating and indeed mortifying experience has become almost a spree."

As *The Outlook* reported in its June issue, "The witnesses who went out to Northern Michigan prepared to endure the discomforts of ordinary travel in their support of their friend, the plaintiff, found themselves members of most delightful house party so that the week in Marquette was really a vacation in charming surroundings."

The next day Gifford Pinchot and other intimates testified.

Pinchot spoke like a true Progressive and the father of the Forest Service's doctrine of multiple use. "I have always been especially interested in questions of efficiency. If I saw a man who was capable of unusual work, who was very efficient, I wanted to observe what he ate, what he drank, how much he slept, everything that might have a bearing on the questions of these things which make for or take from efficiency. I never in my life met any man who can do as much work as Colonel Roosevelt. That's why I kept my eye on him."

The young Roosevelt cousins talked about going on camping excursions and trips with TR while growing up. They took any intimation of drunkenness as personal affronts.

Philip Roosevelt admitted that liquor was kept at Sagamore Hill.

"A regular collection of liquor?" asked one of Newett's lawyers.

"A regular gentlemen's cellar," said Philip Roosevelt.

Later the butler testified there was very little use of the "gentleman's cellar."

It all was a hoot to the newspapermen—and to the country, too, who eagerly read the newspaper dispatches. The term "gentlemen's cellar" got a lot of copy. The lawyers wrangled over the definition of a drink: What was liquor and what was wine? How does one make medicated milk punch to soothe a sore throat?—apparently, a spoonful of brandy and a tumbler of milk.

"It was enough to make a New York bartender tear out his hair," one reporter wrote.

Newett's lawyers were trying to show that TR had been drunk in Ohio during a campaign swing where he reportedly had to be helped through the crowds by his bodyguards.

Anticipating this tack, Pound and Belden called Judge A. Z. Blair, a prominent figure in the anti-saloon league of Ohio. He accompanied Roosevelt on the campaign train.

In a time before television, the reporters used observation and metaphors to give readers a picture of the actors in this courtroom drama. The *New York Times* reporter wrote, "Judge Blair is a sharp-eyed man, with a gray crest like a hawk, a nose like an eagle's beak, a strong voice and a Western roll to the letter R. His eyes are black and protected by gold-rimmed glasses."

Blair saw no evidence of drinking on the train.

It was Roosevelt's bodyguards and the Secret Service that sealed the deal and provided a behind-the-scenes look at the presidency. James Sloan testified that he always sat within arm's length of the president and carefully watched what he ate and drank. The Secret Service frequently planted agents at head tables and dressed one as a waiter, who either served the president himself or helped keep an eye on the other waiters.

Sloan never saw the president "half seas over."

As for moving through crowds with assistance? Well, that was because he could be overwhelmed by the mob and obviously needed protection—after all, three presidents had been assassinated in the past forty years, and Roosevelt had been shot in Milwaukee. Sloan would take the president's arm "because he was very near sighted and could stumble."

On Decoration Day, the "Roosevelt Army" at the Shiras home broke into little groups and took long walks through Marquette. TR accompanied Shiras for a ten-mile automobile ride into the farming district, the part of the county away from the chill of Lake Superior where they might see deer.

The Colonel declined to give a Decoration Day speech at the Opera House, thinking it would be impolitic considering the trial. But he met with veterans of the Grand Army of the Republic at the Shiras house. Pictures were taken on the front steps with the gray-haired and bearded ex-soldiers. Two were brothers who fought on opposite sides of the Civil War. Roosevelt remarked that it was the first time he had met such men.

The Newett crowd caucused back in Ishpeming, agonizing over their bleak prospects. None of their witnesses were intimates of Roosevelt. Their knowledge was secondhand and based on observation and innuendos.

Their most powerful potential witness had been James Martin Miller, a newspaperman who said in a deposition before trial that he saw Roosevelt drunk in St. Louis at the seventieth birthday party for "Uncle Joe" Cannon. The Colonel already conceded that he attended the party and toasted Cannon but said he was never drunk. After giving his deposition, Miller's credibility was ruined when he wrote several bad checks in New York and fled to Canada to escape prosecution.

Representative H. Olin Young continued to be missing in action.

The *New York Times* quipped, "Mr. Newett has been sending out S. O. S. and C. Q. D. calls for a week but his wireless apparatus hasn't been strong enough to reach Mr. Young's station."

Newett and his lawyers feared the jury might award the full $10,000. They contacted James Garfield, who was a lawyer as well as a Roosevelt confidant, intimating they were interested in a settlement. The lawyers got together the next morning along with the judge and worked out the details.

In the courtroom, Newett stepped to the witness stand and read a four-page statement. There was a tense silence.

He wrote his editorial, he said, because he felt Roosevelt had made unjust attacks on Olin Young while speaking in Marquette. He had believed Young when told of the Colonel's drinking, and while taking depositions that winter, his lawyers had found witnesses who were willing to swear they saw Roosevelt drunk during campaign appearances, but now these same witnesses were unwilling to testify.

"It is fair to the plaintiff to state I have been unable to find in any section of the country any individual witness who is willing to state that he had personally seen Mr. Roosevelt drink to excess," Newett read. "I have been profoundly impressed during the progress of this trial by the nature and extent of the evidence produced by the plaintiff to the effect he did not in fact use liquor to excess on any occasion."

He now believed all the eminent people who testified. Obviously, they had more access to TR than any of his witnesses. They had no reason to lie: "We have reached the conclusion that to continue to express or implicitly assert that Mr. Roosevelt drank to an excess or actually became intoxicated as set forth in the article would be to do him an injustice."

As Newett read the statement, it was obvious to everyone that he was throwing in the towel. There was a shuffling of messengers as reporters began scribbling dispatches and tried to beat their competitors to the wires.

Roosevelt got up, moved to a chair, and whispered in the ear of his attorney, who afterward asked the judge if his client could make a statement.

Roosevelt rose and said in a ringing voice, "I ask the court to instruct the jury that I desire only nominal damages. I did not go into this suit for money. I did not go into it with a vindictive purpose. I wished once and for all during my lifetime thoroughly and comprehensively to deal with these slanders so that never again will it be possible for any man in good faith to repeat them. I have achieved my purpose and I am content."

As he uttered his last sentence, Roosevelt thrust a clenched fist over his head. The judge called a recess, and the spectators in the courtroom leaped over the banisters and waved handkerchiefs in the air.

"We put it through by George," Roosevelt shouted, trying to shake both hands with the crowd.

A reporter wrote, "He was in the center of a struggling mass that near tore him apart and kept him swishing and swirling about like a chip on a billow. The reporters finally made a flying wedge and got through with a brutal disregard of the feelings of the population of Marquette County."

Flannigan came back and charged the jury to find for the plaintiff the least possible amount, which in Michigan was six cents. One reporter noted it would cover the price of a "good newspaper."

Pound grumbled to reporters about his client's magnanimity. He felt damages should have been paid simply to reimburse Roosevelt for all his expenses. Newett's lawyers tried to characterize the capitulation as merely a settlement, but the Roosevelt side called it a complete vindication. The *New York Times* did, too.

"Theodore Roosevelt was vindicated to-day in the most thorough and complete manner of the charge of drinking to an excess."

The headline read:

"Newett Admits He Was Wrong and Makes Full Apology on the Stand
Colonel Waives Damages Verdict for Six Cents
Follows Admission that Drinking Charge Was Most Unjust"

Roosevelt drove off in the Shiras automobile, tipping his hat to the "Chautauqua salute" (a waving of white handkerchiefs) being given by the crowd on the courthouse steps. Because the trial was expected to last up to ten days, the two men had planned a weekend trip to the camp on White-fish Lake. But the sudden conclusion of the trial changed plans. Eager to get back to New York, Roosevelt decided to leave on the evening train.

Consequently, he never visited Whitefish Lake, which must have been a disappointment to Shiras—perhaps to Roosevelt, too.

That evening as the train passed through the cutover lands of northern Wisconsin, TR sat in his room and wrote a letter to his sister, Anna Roosevelt Cowles: "The libeler finally capitulated. I deemed it best not to demand money damages; the man is a country editor and while I thoroughly despise him, I do not care to seem to persecute him . . . the way my friends rallied has been really very touching. We have been very comfortable for we have been staying in the big pleasant house of George Shiras, who is a trump if ever there was one."

Later when he got back to New York, TR wrote to Shiras from his office at *The Outlook*. "It is very hard on one's friends to be dragged into irksome and uncomfortable proceedings; but it is a mighty pleasant thing for a man to find out that he has friends who will stand the strain. My dear fellow, I have long valued your friendship, but I think I appreciate its full worth now. You have done invaluable service for me in this suit, and moreover by your openhanded hospitality you made our stay in Marquette a pleasure instead of a penance."

18 | THE CRUSADE TO SAVE BIRDS

HAD THEODORE ROOSEVELT recaptured the White House, he might have signed the most sweeping national law ever enacted to protect wildlife. Instead, it fell to Howard Taft, who didn't know that an appropriations bill he signed on his last day in office—March 4, 1913—would empower the federal government to take jurisdiction over the nation's birds. The migratory bird bill, officially known as the Weeks-McLean Act, was snuck into the bill as a rider because proponents knew Taft considered it unconstitutional. The president, hurrying to meet President-Elect Woodrow Wilson and ride to the capitol for the swearing in, signed the appropriations bill without realizing it contained the Weeks-McLean Act.

The great moral crusade to save birds was well underway when Shiras wrote his bird bill in 1903. His friend George Bird Grinnell started the first Audubon Club in the late 1880s and promoted it in *Forest and Stream*. A decade later, women in Boston's high society formed the Massachusetts Audubon Society and called on women nationwide to boycott fashions—especially hats—that used feathers and stuffed birds as decorations. The Audubon movement quickly spread to other states where women accounted for the majority of the membership. In 1901, the state clubs joined in a loose federation, which in 1905 incorporated as the National Association of Audubon Societies for the Protection of Wild Birds and Animals. William Dutcher became its first president.

Mabel Osgood Wright, a nature writer and president of the Connecticut Audubon, wrote several influential children's books and field guides, including *Citizen Bird*. In 1895, Frank Chapman produced his first edition of *The Handbook of Birds of Eastern North America*, which helped popularize the study and observation of birds by citizens. *Observation* is a key word because previously bird enthusiasts—including a youthful Theodore Roosevelt—collected birds by bringing them down with shotguns.

As early as the 1880s, the American Ornithologists' Union had presented a model law to state legislatures to stem the slaughter of birds. It organized efforts to hire wardens to protect sea- and shorebird rookeries in Florida. Some of the first wardens were murdered by plume hunters in what became known as the Feathers War.

When Shiras served on the Public Lands Committee, he admired and tried to emulate its chairman John Lacey. Shiras often talked birds with TR and supported the president's move to create habitat refuges.

Although Roosevelt set aside fifty-one refuges by executive action during his tenure, birds were still in trouble when he left office. The passenger pigeon and the Carolina parakeet were on their way to extinction, and likely to follow were snowy egrets, great egrets, herons, trumpeter swans, white and brown pelicans, and roseate spoonbills. Rookeries up and down the East Coast were raided repeatedly for feathers. On Cobb's Island in Virginia, hunters for the millinery trade killed fourteen hundred least terns in just one day. Wood ducks were so low in number that biologists were certain they would go extinct. Canada geese and snow geese were equally scarce.

It had become obvious, too, that the number of passerine, or perching birds—purple martins, vireos, swallows, warblers, waxwings, and other neotropical migrants—were on the decline. In the South, where each winter American robins gathered in great flocks, farmers killed the birds by the millions and fed them to hogs. The robin, a choice and beloved songbird in the backyard of northern residents, was in the South simply fodder for animals. One could walk through a marketplace in any major city and see wildlife for sale. Punt gun hunters in the Chesapeake region supplied markets with the duck hearts, livers, and gizzards that sold for twenty-five cents a bucketful. In Louisiana in 1910 an estimated 3.1 million ducks were killed. E. V. Visart, a game warden in Arkansas, reported that in October 1911, an estimated ninety thousand ducks were shipped to eastern city markets from just one county on the Mississippi River.

"Unless we get federal protection of all migratory birds, they like the pigeon, will be exterminated," said Visart.

Spring shooting was especially devastating. A migratory shorebird, duck, brant, or goose might only have a few weeks of protection during the entire year or perhaps none at all. Along the Pacific flyway, Washington and Oregon had fairly adequate laws on spring shooting, but California had no protection for geese. Ducks could be killed there until March. Snipe, curlew, and plovers could be shot until May 1.

North Dakota, Wisconsin, and Minnesota had some restrictions on spring shooting, but states to the south where nesting occurred did not. In the spring of 1912, cold fronts and high winds slowed the migration of wildfowl heading north to the pothole regions of the Dakotas and the Canadian prairies. The birds piled up in Iowa, which had no restriction against spring shooting. In an editorial, the *Waterloo Courier* commented on the ease with which hunters shot the emaciated and mated birds. The paper estimated fifty thousand ducks were killed in just two weeks

The editor lamented, "If permitted to pass on to their breeding grounds unmolested, these birds and their progeny would furnish fine sport next fall."

The southern states, such as Texas and Arkansas, were the worst offenders with year-round shooting of waterfowl. However, the game departments in the southern states were almost uniformly in support of a migratory bird act. They understood the toll more than the politicians. And it was not just hunting to blame. Deforestation, draining of wetlands, conversion of grassland to farms, and pollution of waterways had all attributed to the decline.

Shiras, the hunter, had become quite a birdwatcher himself. He kept lists of observations in Ormond Beach, a new home in Wesley Heights in DC, and at Marquette and Whitefish Lake. His bird bill initially only protected game birds, but as it evolved, the law was broadened to encompass all birds with exceptions of hawks, kingfishers, owls, crows, eagles, and blackbirds, which were considered to be pest species and deserving of elimination on sight—another example of good versus bad animals.

During his last months in the House of Representatives, Shiras prepared a legal brief that was published on November 24, 1906, as a special supplement in *Forest and Stream*.

It was a rather odd document to appear in what was essentially a "hook and gun magazine" for sportsmen. The magazine's masthead displayed two gentlemen, nattily clad in suit and tie, seated next to a lake, holding a shotgun and a bamboo fishing pole. A shoulder-and-head mount of a moose hung over the two men as if nailed on the wall of the sky. Little forest creatures—fox, rabbit, and squirrel—peered at the men from the bushes. The words *Forest and Stream* were fashioned from woody logs and twigs. The subtitle read *A Journal of Outdoor Life, Travel, Nature Study, Shooting, Fishing, and Yachting.*

It was a whimsical masthead, designed to evoke the romance of the age, the love of the outdoors, and its target audience—gentlemen sportsmen. The special supplement, however, carried a weighty, cumbersome title: "Federal Protection of Waterfowl: The Existence of a National Police Power, Inclusive of Federal Control for the Protection of Migratory Wildfowl and of Fish in the Interstate Public Waters of the United States."

The brief ran some forty thousand words, a document dense with legalese but still largely readable, although it required a degree of learnedness from its readers as well as patience. The editors, Grinnell and Charles Reynolds, had attempted to cut it down but then decided it should run in its entirety.

Grinnell, who wrote an accompanying editorial in the front of the magazine, believed that bird lovers and sportsmen had their moral convictions well in hand but needed to understand the regulatory footing required to bring the bird bill to reality.

The one obstacle which has seemed to stand in the way of attaining this end has been a popular acceptance of the belief that all game protection was an exclusive function of the State, and one in which Congress could have no part. The task to which Mr. Shiras has set himself is to show that this popular notion is erroneous and that Congress rightly may and should legislate for migratory fowl. He has sought to demonstrate this by showing that in numerous instances the national government already does have that police power in which the branch of authority game and fish protection belongs.

Grinnell also sought to establish Shiras's sporting and legal credentials by giving a synopsis of his life as a legislator, hunter, photographer, lawyer, and son of a Supreme Court justice.

"It hardly needs to be remarked that the paper contains evidence of having been written by one who is not only a student of constitutional law but a sportsman as well, and one deeply concerned in the subject from a sportsman and naturalist's point of view . . . thus it will be seen that his environments have been peculiarly favorable to the development of such a study as that which the present paper is concerned; and that the brief is not the outcome of hastily conceived notions."

Shiras argued that the states were incapable of protecting birds and fishes. The power the states supposedly held in their game and fish laws was incapable of being exercised; therefore, it was a "legal fiction" that state law was supreme over federal law.

"A power that can only be partially exercised cannot be infringed upon when the same is made full effective by the assistance of the central government," he wrote. "The centralization of power by the national government and the decentralization by states are co-existent forces working in entire harmony within a true republic—one extending downward, in a hundred directions in the effort to reach the lowest form into which our governmental system may be satisfactorily divided—the other developing upward, concentrating the diverse minor powers into a central medium, representing the nation at large and like a sturdy tree depending on its roots to withstand the gales and tempest."

He cited a laundry list of federal involvement: immigration law, international quarantine, the Sherman Antitrust Act, the Impure Food and Drug Importation Act, and even the Oleomargarine Act of 1886—a federal statute that taxed oleo by the pound if it was stained yellow to imitate butter. There were examples of conservation legislation, too: the Lacey Act, of course, and the Act to Protect Birds and Their Eggs in Game and Bird Preserves, which gave the feds jurisdiction over game animals on federal preserves even though those preserves were within state boundaries.

Several laws carried the stamp of Progressivism and were enacted during the Roosevelt era of trustbusting and the regulation of meat and food, drugs, child labor, and the petroleum industry. Muckraking journalists may have investigated many of these problems and raised the indignation of the public, but reforms required muscular action by the executive and Congress. Nearly all the laws had been upheld in the Supreme Court.

Consequently, Shiras felt on firm ground legally, and as a Progressive, he endorsed activist government. After leaving public office, he was in a better position to make the case for the bird bill. He wrote, "My assertions would have seemed dogmatic when I was in Congress but as a private citizen, I can be regarded as earnest in behalf of a good cause."

Snippets of the legal argument were picked up by other sporting publications and some newspapers, which editorialized on the need for a bird law. The League of American Sportsmen, the Explorers Club in New York, and the Camp-Fire Club naturally fell behind the effort. They were joined by the National Farmers Union after William Dutcher and T. Gilbert Pearson of the Audubon clubs suggested that protection be extended to include songbirds and insectivorous birds (insect eaters).

An array of statistics and assertions were cited by the Audubon clubs about the agricultural benefits of birds. Cricket plagues in Utah, tent caterpillars in New England, and locusts in Nebraska might be arrested or lessened by insectivorous birds.

The premise was not without merit, especially in an era before chemical pesticides and insecticides. The US Agriculture Department reported that insectivorous birds destroyed "thousands of tons of noxious weed seeds and billions of harmful insects. These birds are the deadliest foe yet found of the boll weevil, the gypsy and brown-tailed moths and other like pests." The value of a single meadowlark in a ten-acre field of cotton, corn, or wheat was estimated to be five dollars annually. The Biological Survey had examined the crops of thirty-five hundred birds and found on average 30 grasshoppers and 250 caterpillars in cuckoos and 38 cutworms in a blackbird.

Shiras lobbied, wrote articles, and spoke to groups of sportsmen. The League of American Sportsmen met in Norfolk, Virginia, in May 1907 and Shiras as the keynote speaker denounced an attempt by Congressman James Wadsworth of New York, an opponent of the bird bill, to abolish the Biological Survey.

The *Virginia Pilot* newspaper noted, "The sportsmen were keyed up to a high pitch of enthusiasm when they adopted the condemnatory resolution. They had been listening to the address of former Congressman Shiras of Pennsylvania, who has been the champion of the game birds, beasts, and fish in the national legislation and whose bill calling for a Federal game law was sidetracked during the last session . . . the speech came as a relief to the delegates. They received it enthusiastically and applauded it to the echo."

Although bird lovers and farmers certainly were instrumental, it was hunters and fishermen who pushed the law through and ultimately came up with mechanisms—fees on licenses, firearms, and ammo, mainly—to fund protection and, later, to purchase important wildlife habitat.

The American Game Protective and Propagation Association (AGPPA)— now no longer in existence—led the charge under the direction of its dynamic president, John Bird Burnham. The organization helped write legislation, craft regulations, lobby politicians, and work with government agencies that were new (or just new to conservation). George Shiras 3d and George Grinnell served on the AGPPA board of directors for many years. Shiras was the organization's vice president through the years of the Great War and into the 1920s.

The AGPPA was the brainchild of Billy Clark, the advertising manager for the Winchester Repeating Arms Company. In 1910, Clark brought the idea to Harry S. Leonard, the company vice president, under the premise that it was good insurance, publicity, and business to support the survival and increase of game animals.

Leonard initially thought the company should contribute to one of the existing state game protective agencies. He wanted to make it solely a "Winchester project" but was rebuffed by state agencies, who were reluctant to take funds from a gun company. Instead, he convinced eleven firearm and ammunition manufacturers to pledge a starter fund of $125,000 to be paid in installments of $25,000 per year to further game protection and propagation. They set up the AGPPA, drew up a constitution, and passed bylaws. George Shiras 3d and other notable conservationists were recruited to serve on the board. The mission was to enact game laws, help organize societies and clubs with like-minded goals, and educate the public that "propagation is a feasible and practical means of increasing the sports and general food supply." As Leonard put it: "the concerns which provided the means for killing game had a duty to the public and a special obligation to maintain and restore the supply of game." Theodore Roosevelt publicly supported the organization, which immediately gave it legitimacy and clout.

Headquartered in the Woolworth Building in New York City, the well-funded AGPPA soon made itself known on the national stage. President John Burnham was an entrepreneur, adventurer, journalist, and influential proponent of wildlife conservation in the late nineteenth and early twentieth centuries.

In 1891, Burnham joined the staff of *Forest and Stream*, where he wrote articles in support of game laws and game preserves. He eventually became an associate editor and the business manager, but in 1897, itching for adventure and in an apparent effort to overcome a bout of depression, he joined the Klondike Gold Rush. He stayed in Canada just a couple of years but earned a reputation as a bold and skilled river man on the Yukon.

When he came home, he established a home in the Adirondacks and was given a position in the New York Department of Conservation after writing an article that condemned the practice of "hounding deer," or running deer with dogs. The practice was already illegal, but no one was enforcing the statute.

Burnham was named a game protector, or warden, in 1903; named the state's chief game protector in 1906; and in 1910, he served on a three-member commission that codified game laws in New York. In his private life, he helped organize the Crater Club, a summer retreat for families on Lake Champlain. He and his wife manufactured Adirondack Mountain Creams, a maple sugar confection packaged in birchbark boxes with a romantic picture of a canoe and pine tree under the moonlight. It was a popular and expensive candy shipped nationwide.

Throughout his life, John Burnham was a restless, driven man with a mission to save animals and preserve habitat. He loved to hunt, saw sportsmen as natural conservationists, and believed wild game was a renewable resource that humans could manage and harvest sustainably.

He led the American Game Protective and Propagation Association from 1911 until 1928. During those years, he traveled tens of thousands of miles, wrote prodigiously, cajoled and nudged decision makers, and fought the interests arrayed against protection—most notably market hunters and the millinery industry. The AGPPA sought publicity, and Burnham was not shy about making the aims of the organization known or apologizing for them, either. The gun and ammunition companies had a vested self-interest in increasing the supply of game, but in his opinion that only boded well for wildlife. At times, he fought bitterly with William T. Hornaday, who felt the AGPPA, "funded by gunners," had no legitimate place in conservation circles. Hornaday—a vain man who attacked the motives of other conservationists or anyone else who disagreed with him—helped found the Camp-Fire Club of America as an alternative to the wealth and social standing required for membership in the Boone and Crockett Club. The only condition of eligibility was "to have camped on the ground in a howling wilderness and to have killed or painted big game."

Burnham's greatest success was helping to make the Weeks-McLean Act the law of the land, and in that aim he was willing to work with anyone— including Hornaday—and if necessary use subterfuge to reach his goals.

After Shiras left Congress, his bird bill was amended and carried forward by Rep. John Weeks of Massachusetts in the House and by George Payne McLean of Connecticut in the Senate.

Both were Republicans with substantive accomplishments in conservation issues. McLean had been governor of Connecticut before being elected to the US Senate by the state assembly in that period before direct election of senators. He was a member of the Boone and Crockett Club and well known to Shiras.

In 1911, Weeks successfully authored the Weeks Act, also known as the Appalachian Bill, which directed the US Department of Agriculture to purchase lands in the eastern United States—where there were no large federal tracts—for conservation and flood control purposes. Flooding in the East, especially in the city of Pittsburgh, had been exacerbated by deforestation upstream, and conservationists, including Gifford Pinchot, had been calling for the establishment of eastern national forests to protect watersheds. The Weeks Act led to the creation of several new national forests, including the Allegheny in Pennsylvania and the Ottawa and Hiawatha National Forests in Michigan's Upper Peninsula, where the federal government purchased millions of acres of cutover land.

There was growing support for the migratory bird bill.

In 1910 and 1911, the National Conservation Congress, an annual forum started by Roosevelt for discussion and debate among public and private conservation leaders, had passed unanimous supporting resolutions. The New York legislature passed a resolution supporting the bird bill. The resolution read, "There is a very general sentiment in this State in favor of such protection, and an urgent request for the enactment of such a law has been made, as appears by numerous petitions, received."

In late 1912, at a hearing before the combined House and Senate Agricultural Committee, more than thirty organizations offered testimony and gave their support to the bird bill. Oddly enough, the most well-known detractor was Hornaday, who thought that waterfowl should be removed from the bill entirely—that these birds were only of interest to sportsmen and not a valuable economic asset to the rest of the people.

It was a rather bizarre notion, but Hornaday could be cocksure of his own convictions—at least those he held at the time. He once displayed an African pygmy at the Bronx Zoo as an example of primitive man.

Shiras appreciated all that Hornaday had done in saving the American bison and promoting conservation, but he considered the man difficult and unduly confrontational. In his book *Our Vanishing Wildlife: Its Extermination and Preservation*, Hornaday had railed against overhunting and declared that repeating arms would be the doom of most game species. He got a lot of pushback from sporting groups and shooting clubs, who saw the book as a screed against sport hunting.

One night in 1912, Hornaday asked Burnham to give an update on the status of the bill to a group of a dozen or so conservationists in New York City. Hornaday sat at the head of the table that evening and, according to Burnham, frequently interrupted him: "Several times during the course of my talk, he tried to make me admit that the prospect of passing the bill was hopeless. I did not agree with him in this, but on the contrary stated that I felt confident the measure would pass at that session of Congress."

As soon as Burnham left the meeting to catch an overnight train, Hornaday opined that the bill was at an impasse and the only way to rescue it was to abandon protection of waterfowl species and start a new campaign through farming organizations to protect nongame species only.

That did not happen.

Burnham and the AGPPA used the organization's treasure chest to travel, buy publicity and, most importantly, lobby in Congress. When Weeks introduced the measure in the House in 1912, opposition was tiny and muted. Out of 435 members, only a half-dozen were opposed, one being the infamous representative Frank Mondell of Wyoming.

Mondell—the same politician who opposed expanding Yellowstone

Park and had sat on the Public Lands Committee with Shiras—called the act the most revolutionary, most far-reaching federal legislation he had ever seen. He was outraged: "Pass this bill and every barrier standing against the assert of Federal police control in every line and with regard to every act and activity of the American people is broken down, and we no longer have a government of self-governing states but are well on our way to an empire governed from this capital."

In the Senate, the measure passed unanimously.

But the bill had come up late in the Sixty-Second Congress, and proponents were afraid it would once again die. There was no guarantee the president would sign it. Howard Taft had been badly beaten in the 1912 election and throughout the campaign had been assailed by Progressives who said Taft's feelings for conservation were lukewarm.

Taft was well aware of the bill and, as a lawyer who would later become the chief justice of the Supreme Court, had great doubts as to its constitutionality. He would have vetoed it on that basis alone had it appeared on his desk as a single issue.

Burnham worked to have it attached as a rider to a larger appropriations bill, but Rep. Weeks said the strategy would not work. Taft had clearly said on several occasions that he also would veto any appropriations bill that came with riders.

Only the Senate Committee on Agriculture and Forestry could do the work. It was headed up by Senator Henry Burnham of New Hampshire, who was a distant relative of John Burnham. The two men had hit it off when they found a common relative had come to New England on a ship in the early 1600s.

The senator was well aware of Taft's threat to veto riders, but he also liked the bird bill. It was his last term in Congress, and he was open to taking a risk.

As John Burnham recalled, "He had an opportunity to take action that would add luster to his exit from public life."

He asked the senator: If the committee saw fit to add the bird bill as a rider to the Agricultural Appropriations Bill, would he object?

The senator smiled broadly and replied, "How can I object to a bill I heartily favor?"

Afterward in the hall, John Burnham directed a delegation of a half-dozen Camp-Fire men who had come to lobby for the bill. He had them visit all the other members of the committee with the request to attach the bird bill as a rider.

Undoubtedly, the first question from the other senators would be, "What does the chairman think?" They were instructed to assure them that the chairman would have no objection to the addition.

With the groundwork prepared, the appropriations bill with the rider went forward. On January 22, 1913, the bill passed the Senate.

Burnham met Shiras on the street in Washington and told him of the successful passage.

Shiras proclaimed, "You are joking!"

Burnham assured Shiras he was not. "On being assured it was fact, he rejoiced to think his idea, after a delay of many years, had been approved and was in a fair way to become a law," Burnham remembered.

The bill reached Taft's desk in the White House and, in the confusion and distraction of inauguration day, he signed it into law. Woodrow Wilson, who had worked against the millinery trade when he was governor of New Jersey, affirmed his support of the Weeks-McLean Act soon after entering office. He instructed the Department of Agriculture through the Biological Survey to draw up specific regulations. A division of the Ag Department, the Biological Survey had moved from a research organization concentrated on field studies to a bureaucracy helping frame laws it would later administer. Its director was C. Hart Merriam, Roosevelt's good friend and another member of Boone and Crockett and the Cosmos Club.

The act was short on specifics and the wording little changed from Shiras's original language except to include more species: "All wild geese, wild swans, brant, wild ducks, snipe, plover, wood ducks, rail, wild pigeons and all other migratory game and insectivorous birds which in their northern and southern migrations pass through or do not remain permanently the entire year within the borders of any State or Territory, shall hereafter be deemed within the custody and protection of the Government of the United States and shall not be destroyed or taken contrary to regulations."

Those regulations would be controversial, so the secretary of agriculture appointed a fifteen-member advisory board of "leading sportsmen, game protectionists, and field naturalists." The names were familiar: George Shiras 3d, John Burnham, George Grinnell, John Lacey, William Temple

Hornaday, T. Gilbert Pearson (secretary of the National Association of Audubon Societies), and Marshall McLean (president of the Camp-Fire Club). Nearly all remaining members were the heads of state game and fish departments who would understand local and regional conditions. Burnham was named chairman of the Advisory Board on Migratory Birds.

Shiras accepted his appointment with a letter to the secretary of agriculture on March 27, 1913, written from Ormond Beach: "It is natural that I should feel a certain responsibility for the successful operation of the law and especially for those provisions taken from the first bill."

He warned, "It is of the utmost importance that both the necessity and the legality of such legislation should be clearly understood and therefore the regulations of your Department should be so drawn as to produce the best immediate results and at the same time avoid any unnecessary antagonism."

The advisory board was to act as a buffer between the government and all those affected by the bill, to lessen the impact of a supposedly bureaucratic dictatorship. The bill was not just sparse on details—it authorized only a paltry $10,000 annually from the US Treasury to carry out the act.

After several months of wrangling, the government issued the rules: The Weeks-McLean Act prohibited spring hunting of waterfowl. It banned shooting before sunrise and after sunset, making punt gun or any other nighttime forays illegal. Some hunting zones and seasons were allowed but with bag limits. For species nearing extinction, hunting was banned outright. Insectivorous birds were permanently protected.

The main opposition came from the millinery trade, but feather fashion was already on its way out, and the lack of market demand eventually put an end to plume hunting. Market hunters were outraged. Along the Atlantic flyway and in Florida and Louisiana they had made a good living supplying ducks for the table. Hunt clubs and resorts, such as Revel Island, would have to change their practices of unlimited shooting, although the crashing population of many game birds was already having an effect on business.

States' rights advocates saw the law as federal overreach. Others viewed it as elitist sportsmen tramping on the rights of common folk who hunted for subsistence or pleasure and were accustomed to taking what they wanted.

The attorney general of New York, bucking the trend in his state, said the federal government had no right to classify some game as migratory and take ownership. At the same time, he admitted states were likely incapable of providing the necessary protection. To him, however, it was a point of law: "It would be better to submit to an ineffective exercise of power of a state in regard to a subject over which the state has recognized jurisdiction than submit to a much more effective exercise of power on the part of the Federal government in relation to a subject over which it had no jurisdiction."

This was the antithesis of Shiras's legal understanding.

Shiras commented, "The federal jurisdiction in the bill instead of arousing the jealousy or opposition of the state game wardens was declared to be the only effective means of saving the migratory birds and few stronger friends of the measure came to its support than the men officially selected by the states to enforce the game laws."

He acknowledged the constitutional question of jurisdiction would bring excitement and objections but added "while we may assume that most of these objections are made in good faith, it is well to remember that behind such objections will come trailing a vast hoard of market hunters, spring shooters, the owners of a certain class of sportsmen's resorts and others."

The shooting and slaughter did not stop overnight. Poaching was too lucrative. Punt gunners continued to go out at night. A market for illegal trade in feathers sprung up but, over time, behavior began to change. Scofflaws were fined and imprisoned. The Weeks-McLean Act, although fragile and underfunded, probably saved several bird species that would have gone extinct.

After passage, there was still a need to prop up the bill, defend against its detractors, and build a case for the court challenges likely to come.

In early 1914, the American Game Protective and Propagation Association and Shiras produced a pamphlet entitled *Necessity for and Constitutionality of the Act of Congress Protecting Migratory Birds*. Beneath Shiras's name on the cover was the qualifier, "Author of the Original Bills Putting under Federal Control Migratory Birds and Migratory Fishes." The document ran thirty pages. Printed on heavy card stock, it was designed for distribution to sportsmen at meetings and conventions and to be used by lobbyists in their work with legislators.

Shiras considered it a pivotal piece of work and, years later, when he donated some of his papers to the National Geographic Society, his hand-written note on its cover read "Very Important."

Much of the contents were based on the original brief in *Forest and Stream*, but also added was testimony from the congressional hearings and anecdotes in letters sent to the AGPPA.

Shiras argued that states were the "proper custodians of local game" such as grouse, deer, wild turkey, quail, or trout that are present year around. Game departments and legislatures certainly had the right to establish game refuges or set short or longer hunting seasons to manage such populations, but when it came to birds or fishes that migrated across state boundaries only federal oversight would be effective.

Local game was often protected for ten months a year, he noted, while migratory species were open to hunting throughout most of the year as they moved from state to state. Two-thirds of all waterfowl received no protection at all: "Local hunters regard the visiting migrant as one to be killed when conditions best favor its destruction . . . the fact that several states have closed seasons on geese, ducks and snipe after they have left their territory is, of course, a legislative joke and a sad one at that."

Spring shooting was especially devastating to any wildlife population, and he noted that "the idea of killing local game in the nesting period when it is about to bear its young is naturally revolting because it is as improvident as it is indecent."

He also presented some specious arguments that may have resonated at the time of the Great War. The United States had an estimated four million hunters out of a population of ninety-two million people. The loss of game animals would idle "the greatest army of marksmen in the world, who self-reliant, endured to hardships and educated on the use of firearms now stand in reserve for the defense of the country and thus save hundreds of millions of dollars to the tax payers should we maintain a standing army compatible with the size and interests of our nation."

Despite Shiras's legal theories, appeals to morality, or a martial call for marksmen militia, the new law—at the time of its adoption anyway—rested upon shaky constitutional ground. The fight would go on for years and finally be settled by the US Supreme Court.

19 | THE SHIRAS BEAR

A FEW WEEKS after the libel trial and the publishing of his piece on the white sheep of Alaska, Shiras wrote to Gilbert Grosvenor saying he had stayed close to Marquette all summer to be with his dying mother.

He had gone no further afield than the camp on Whitefish Lake and the game preserve on Grand Island. Despite all of the personal business, it had been an especially productive season for camera trapping: "I have gotten a large amount of flashlight pictures taken by animals pulling a string, including does, fawns, muskrats, skunks, raccoons, otters, rabbits, and, best of all, a beaver preparing its dam. This matter will prove valuable for the next article."

George had become an important member of the National Geographic Society, both as a contributor to the magazine and as an adviser. In 1912 on Grosvenor's recommendation, Shiras was named a member of the board of managers, joining such luminaries as C. Hart Merriam, Alexander Graham Bell, and David Fairchild, the botanist and explorer. Beneath Shiras's name on the masthead was the title "Formerly Member U.S. Congress, Faunal Naturalist and Wild-Game Photographer." He would remain on the board for the next twenty-eight years, giving legal advice, approving funding requests for expeditions, and making investment decisions, including convincing the society to purchase corporate bonds issued by the Cleveland Cliffs Iron Company.

His photography work over the previous decade had been technically groundbreaking and exceedingly valuable to the magazine as it transitioned from a gray, stodgy scholarly journal to a popular illustrated magazine with a worldwide reputation. In 1905, the magazine published just 10,000 copies per month. By 1912, the circulation, or membership, was more than 250,000. As a source of science information, the society had influence with lawmakers in Washington and credibility with scientists. It had the financial resources to fund expeditions and support important exploratory work to distant parts of the earth. Through its articles and state-of-the-art photography, *National Geographic* magazine had captured the popular imagination.

Once again, Grosvenor filled an entire issue with the images and writings of George Shiras 3d. The July 1913 number, with sixty-seven images, featured the article "Wild Animals that Took Their Own Pictures by Day and by Night." In the editor's note, Grosvenor writes little about the photography—it speaks for itself—but goes into detail about Shiras's role in the fight to save migratory birds: "The bills have received hearty approval of the leading game and fish protective associations in the United States and Canada, while the author's extensive brief in support of such constitutional power has met with the approbation of many leading jurists and lawyers. Within the next year, active steps will be taken to enact these into law."

The National Geographic Society was clearly on the side of conservation and wildlife preservation, and George Shiras 3d was one of its own. The suite of images in the magazine celebrated his mastery of the camera trap and knowledge of the habits of animals.

In 1912, the society published *The Book of Birds: Common Birds of Town and Country and American Game Birds*, which brought together Shiras and some of its other luminaries to create a beautifully illustrated field book for backyard birdwatchers. The book featured 250 color paintings by Louis Fuertes. In the chapter "How Birds Can Take Their Own Portraits," Shiras described how he had adapted camera traps to photograph quail and vultures in Florida. Clearly, the society was capitalizing on the public's desire for bird watching, natural history, and preservation. Throughout the book, there is a strong call to support federal protection of game and common songbirds. The last passenger pigeon would die a year later in the Cincinnati Zoo, and Fuertes wrote a prophetic obituary saying, "The history of the passenger pigeon from the first settlement and to including our own reads like a romance, but a romance tinged on every page with man's cruelty, rapacity, and shortsightedness."

Shiras had published five articles and hundreds of images in the magazine. Grosvenor wrote on September 25, 1913, "We have here enough for a book and I want to urge very seriously upon you the revision and enlargement of these articles during the coming winter . . . let us get this book out now and surprise the Colonel."

That fall, Shiras again set off for Alaska on a National Geographic expedition. This time he brought along his son and namesake, George IV, who like his father and Uncle Winfield, had completed prep school in Massachusetts and was bound for Yale.

The young man loved the outdoor life, had spent much time at Whitefish Lake and, like his father, grew up hunting and fishing with boys from Marquette. He was, however, a frail youth, plagued with a "weak constitution." Exactly what health problem plagued him through childhood isn't clear. He may have had a weak heart. Whatever it was, poor health often laid him low during his teenage years and would eventually take his life as a young man.

But in 1913, he was in good enough shape to undertake what was plainly a strenuous and adventure-filled trip to Admiralty Island, where the Shirases went to hunt and kill a brown bear. Much of what is known about the trip comes from young George's journal, and it shows how difficult conditions were during a September visit to the ninety-six-by-thirty-mile island in the rain-soaked coastal forests of Southeast Alaska.

The trip did not start well. The two Georges and guides Charlie Anderson and John Hammer caught a train out of Marquette, but a few hours later the locomotive slammed into a giant white pine that had blown across the tracks during a thunderstorm. The engine derailed and rolled over, killing the fireman, the engineer, and two trainmen in another car. The father and son and their guides made their way through the wreckage to gawk at the overturned locomotive while rain fell and lightning flashed through the woods. Nothing was going to get through for some days, so they went back to Marquette and rescheduled for the following week. They eventually got a steamer out of Seattle and reached Juneau via the Inside Passage.

In Juneau, they connected with Allen Hasselborg, a local guide recommended by C. Hart Merriam. For several years, Hasselborg had been killing bears for collectors and scientists who were intrigued by the variety of brown bears *Ursus arctos* found on islands in that part of Alaska. Some biologists—including Merriam—considered the color of fur and skin as a defining morphology of new species and subspecies. As the country's leading biologist, Merriam had been naming new subspecies of several animals, including bears from the Inside Passage. Theodore Roosevelt often disagreed with Merriam and considered many of his proclamations—particularly regarding bears—in error. TR believed fur coloration mostly superficial, and he was right. The Alaskan brown bear is a grizzly bear that grows to enormous size on the coast by consuming a rich diet of salmon.

One of the naturalists in Washington, DC, cautioned Shiras prior to his trip: "For heaven's sake don't bring back with you a new species of bear or Merriam will never finish his book."

Shiras never identified who offered the warning. Was it the Colonel or perhaps E. W. Nelson, about to take over the Biological Survey? Certainly, it was someone who disagreed with Merriam's penchant for finding new species and subspecies. And it's evidence that Shiras went to the region with the predisposed notion that new discoveries were yet to be made.

Merriam cautioned Shiras that Hasselborg was a peculiar man—a competent Alaskan guide, good with bears, but not so good with people. Hasselborg had arrived in Alaska a few years after the Klondike Gold Rush and lived off the land by trapping, fishing, and guiding. He later built a cabin on Admiralty Island and came to Juneau a couple of times a year to sell furs and get supplies. Sometimes, he rowed the entire way, about two hundred miles round-trip, over a period of three weeks. His hermit-like existence and affinity for bears earned him the nickname "the Bear Man of Admiralty Island." He lived on Admiralty until his death in 1951.

Shiras and company immediately experienced Hasselborg's eccentricities. In Juneau, the guide refused to enter the hotel to discuss the coming expedition, claiming public houses were cold and injurious to good health. He met the men in the harbor on his motor launch, which was cramped, jury-rigged, and serving as the guide's home. He must have cut quite a figure, recovering from injuries received the year earlier when he shot a grizzly on a steep slope. The bear grabbed him and the two rolled to the bottom of a gulch, with the dying bear clawing and badly lacerating his arm.

The next day the four men from Michigan crowded onto the launch and set off for Admiralty Island under clear and stunning skies with the blue-white glaciers between the mountaintops contrasting with the heavily forested slopes. Orcas hunted in the sea and bears prowled the wild shorelines. Long after dark, they arrived at Admiralty Island and set up camp in a cove of Pybus Bay.

"Our confinement all day in the small cabin of the motor boat had nearly stifled us and we proceeded at once to put up the tent," George 3d wrote.

Shiras had been lured to this spot by his Boone and Crockett friend Charles Sheldon, who had been the driving force behind Denali National Park. When daylight arrived, they found the remains of Sheldon's 1909 camp, where he had spent several weeks with his new wife. In his book on Alaska, Sheldon had written about enduring eighteen consecutive days of rain and fog, so Shiras was not surprised when Hasselborg looked about and said, "If you want to take some pictures of the surroundings, you'd better do it now for rain and fog can soon be expected."

Within a few hours, poor weather engulfed the camp and except for a break of five hours and later another of seven hours, it did not lift for the next nineteen days. Conditions were miserable for photography. One day, Shiras erected a camera trap on a stream where bears were fishing for salmon. He returned to find the watercourse flooded and the camera submerged, held fast in the current by the strong trip wire. The fiber box was ruined but he was able to salvage the lens, which had sentimental value. It had taken his first pictures of deer twenty-five years earlier at Whitefish Lake.

The canvas tents didn't hold up much better, although they were considered "waterproof" for the period. The two Georges had set up their tent beneath a copse of enormous red cedars. Unfortunately, when the wind blew, the trees shed gallons of water. The repeated pounding on the canvas roof forced rain inside, where it pooled on the floor. Sometimes, they actually had to bail out the tents.

The cook tent occupied by Hammer had been treated heavily with paraffin. It also had a cook stove, which warmed the men and dried their clothing and sleeping bags. Some nights when he awoke to a pool of water on his sleeping bag, young George moved to the relative comfort of the cook tent. Hammer was well provisioned with wooden crates of canned food. There was game to kill, too. In the coming days, they dined on ptarmigan, Sitka deer, geese, ducks, black turnstone, salmon, and trout.

Young George recalled arriving at camp wet and discouraged after a disappointing day on the hunt, but he felt better after "a hearty meal of roast goose, boiled potatoes, apple sauce, prunes, rice pudding and cups of coffee."

Tides at Admiralty ran high. At times, their rowboats could not reach the campsite. At low tide, they would walk or drag boats across a hundred yards of muddy flats. But they were rugged, stoic men and had come to the wilderness for adventure. While his father pursued what photography he could under such conditions, George IV focused entirely on bagging a brown bear and a trophy Sitka black-tailed deer.

While motoring along the shore in the launch, the men spotted several bears more black in appearance than brown, although the size of the animals and the distinctive hump on their backs indicated they were grizzlies and not a species of black bear. Intrigued by these "black brown bears," young George set off with Hasselborg. His hunting uniform consisted of a rubber rain slicker, puttees, and a pith helmet. Typically, they landed a small rowboat at the mouth of a salmon stream and climbed the steep slopes to reach some sort of plateau or meadow where there might be deer. Along the way, they hoped to jump a big bear. The bears of Admiralty Island were numerous and had tramped game trails through the thick scrub alders. Despite these trails, the landscape was steep, difficult to walk, and often required climbing using both hands and feet.

Young George wrote in his diary, "In places it was so steep that it was impossible for me to retain my foothold and I would slide 15 to 20 feet at a time, clutching wildly at bushes as I went. In places here and there, the slope dropped away sheer for 150 to 200 feet and we had to work cautiously around these cliffs. This was nervous work for me."

Hasselborg appears to have been kindhearted to his young charge but not always patient. More than once, he reached camp ahead of George, who struggled in the thick growth of the rain forest. One of the other guides would shout into the forest to keep him moving in the right direction toward the shoreline.

On September 4, the young hunter went out with Charlie Anderson. They hiked up a mountainside, grabbing onto scrubby alders and shoving their feet into toeholds. George heard "snorting, growling, and hissing sounds," and then rocks started rolling on either side of him. He cocked his gun and yelled out to Charlie, alerting the bear to his presence just before it was about to run him over. The bear veered off. Though it was just a few feet away in the thick undergrowth, he never saw it.

The rain let up in the afternoon, but they were soaked from the wet leaves and branches. It took an hour to make just three hundred yards in what George described as a "heart breaking tangle of dense brush."

After a few hours, they started back to camp but descended the wrong slope and lost their way. They became chilled, their teeth chattering. They had failed to put their matches into a waterproof container, but starting a fire would have been nearly impossible in the dampness anyway. By late afternoon, they were in the throes of hypothermia, clumsy and desperate, stumbling through the wet brush and falling over hidden logs. George was exhausted when they emerged on shore just four hundred yards from camp.

"Our relief was tremendous," he wrote in his diary.

Hasselborg and Shiras had gone out looking for the men but were brought back to camp by a gunshot from Hammer indicating the pair had returned. Charlie and young George had been eleven hours in the field.

On September 9, when it stopped raining for a few hours. Hasselborg and young George crossed to the other side of the bay, followed a salmon stream into the interior, and came upon a big brown bear on the opposite bank. George dropped to one knee and fired at its neck. The bear fell and rolled over and over, roaring and bellowing with rage and pain.

Hasselborg shouted, "He's a dead bear . . . shoot again."

George hit it again in the shoulder, and the bear took off into the bush. They followed the blood trail cautiously with rifles in hand but the bear, although bleeding badly, could not be found before dark. Hasselborg said they would return in the morning and certainly find a dead bear, probably not far from where they stood.

The stars were shining when they finally made it back to camp, but it began raining hard at midnight and by morning, the blood trail had disappeared. The wounded bear was never found. It was not exactly the kind of clean killing advocated by the Boone and Crockett Club.

George wounded another bear five days later when they circled the mountain behind camp and came upon a grizzly in midstream, a flopping salmon held crosswise in its mouth. George crept within one hundred yards and fired. The first two shots were high. The third hit the bear in the hindquarters. It stood up and tried to climb a tree. Another shot hit it in the paw before it ran off. They followed, finding pools of blood where the bear lay down, but each time it heard them coming, the bear moved a little further away. Again, they lost the blood trail in the rain and returned to camp. They searched again the next day but found nothing.

Later that same day, they spotted another big bear just fifteen feet below them. George fired four shots into its side, one into the rump, and another into its lower jaw. The bear staggered thirty feet and died.

It was a male, entirely black. They gutted the animal and took measurements—six foot eight inches from nose to tail. The hind foot with claws was fourteen inches long.

They left the carcass and returned to camp.

As George 3d remembered it, "Upon their return later, it was apparent at a glance that my son had been successful. He had killed an old male of the big, black-colored animals, which we had been seeing but were previously unknown to Hasselborg."

The next day was clear and the entire camp hiked up to the dead bear, where ravens perched in the trees after feasting on the entrails. They cleared the brush around the carcass and George posed his son standing with his rifle, wearing the pith helmet and looking down at the bear. They skinned the carcass, took off the head, and cut off the great paws.

The trip was a success as a hunt and expedition with his son, but it was not much for making pictures. Besides the dead animal, George never got a picture of any other bear—only ptarmigan, some spawning salmon, and the men posing in their boats and about camp. Rather than hunting with a camera, he had picked up a gun and brought in game for the table: "With the skies almost continually overcast and the air filled with rain and fog, I had little chance to picture the birds on or about the island. Many of these appeared on a different kind of plate where a knife and a fork instead of developing powder came into use."

They left the island on September 20 and immediately ran into a serious storm whipping up fierce seas. Hasselborg ran the launch to a small wooded island and a deserted trapper's hut. There was no way to land, so the two Shiras men and guides set off in rowboats. Hasselborg sought refuge in another cove on the other side of Admiralty Island.

He indicated he would be back as soon as the weather let up. The next day dawned bright and sunny and, as planned, the men packed their gear and waited on the beach—all day. By late afternoon, they were worried, and the two guides went looking in the rowboats.

They spent another night in the cabin and then waited again the next day until they were sure some mishap had occurred. Finally, at sundown Hasselborg came chugging up with several large logs of Sitka spruce strapped onto the launch. He had spent the time cutting several trees for a boat he was building.

When he expressed astonishment that they would worry and be interested in his welfare, Shiras corrected him, "We made it plain that our anxiety had more to do with our situation."

The Alaskan guide could not understand that either, and they left it alone.

But they had lost the good weather. The next day in big swells, the overloaded launch rolled heavily. In open water, the motor gave out and took several minutes to restart. They were on the verge of capsizing before Hasselborg repointed the bow into the waves. Already, they had offloaded their smaller rowboats to lighten the load and had attached them to the stern with a towline. Hasselborg considered cutting the boats loose, but that would have left the men without a lifeboat. When the passengers suggested they return to Admiralty Island to wait out the storm, Hasselborg shrugged, "We got to meet our fate some time, so why worry?"

During that worrisome day, Shiras saw a steamer passing in the distance on its way to Seward, "I must confess that I had a great desire to be on board her."

In the afternoon, the towline broke and they were forced to make a wide circle in the heavy swells to recover the boats. Finally, they sought shelter in a little cove, and just as they entered the calmer waters, the motor quit again. With John Hammer, the mechanic, helping, it took four hours to make repairs. Had the motor quit in the middle of the channel, the boat would have likely capsized, Shiras recalled. "It is needless to say that all in our party were much relieved when we finally came alongside the wharf at Juneau, although Hasselborg appeared quite unconcerned at the time."

They were glad to get shut of the man, and despite all the rain, discomfort, danger, and lack of decent images, they relished in the adventure and the big bear. Young George had his trophy.

Weeks later back in Washington, Shiras presented the bear skull, skin, and front paws to C. Hart Merriam at the Biological Survey. True to predictions, Merriam determined that the "black bears" of Admiralty Island were indeed a novel subspecies. In a letter to Shiras on July 1, 1914, he wrote: "Your bear turned out to be a splendid new species, which it has given me the pleasure to name *Ursus arctos shirasi*. We previously had several young specimens of it but none old enough to show the adult skull characteristics."

In the technical narrative of the proceedings of the Biological Society of Washington, under "Descriptions of New Bears from North America," the Shiras animal is described as entirely black except for the full brown muzzle and a brownish streak along the back: "*Ursus shirasi* is a very large member of the Brown Bear Group. Whether or not it is always black, like the type specimen, it is not known."

George 3d was obviously proud of his son and until the end of his life, both in magazine articles and in his big book *Hunting Wild Life with Camera and Flashlight*, he held *Ursus arctos shirasi* on par with *Alces americanus shirasi*, the Shiras moose of the Rocky Mountains. But even by the 1930s, it was clear that the Shiras bear was not novel but simply a form of *Ursus arctos*. Today, there is no mention of it in the literature. The Shiras moose, however, remains a distinctive subspecies—the moose of the Rocky Mountains.

In 1978 Admiralty Island was declared a national monument under the Antiquities Act, and two years later Congress added wilderness designation. Managed by the Tongass National Forest, the island's virgin forests of western hemlock, Sitka spruce, and western red cedar are within the largest temperate rain forest left on the entire Pacific coast. Its streams and estuaries support great runs of wild salmon. Known as "the fortress of the bear," the island still supports the greatest density of brown bears in North America.

20 | GATUN LAKE AND PANAMA

IN EARLY 1914, Shiras went to Central America for *National Geographic* to write about the completion of the Panama Canal and the filling of Gatun Lake, the impoundment encompassing thirty-two miles of the fifty-mile waterway.

The Panama Canal was an audacious piece of engineering and construction, the enterprise of Theodore Roosevelt's presidency. Its opening in August would give the story currency in *National Geographic* magazine. Shiras had been hearing about the region and its abundant wildlife from Frank Chapman and other scientists who visited Panama during the ten years of construction.

The expedition, largely financed by Shiras and the National Geographic Society, lasted about six weeks during February and March. The scientists who accompanied him from the Smithsonian and the Museum of Natural History in New York always referred to the trip as the Shiras Expedition. Shiras had been a life member of the museum in New York since 1908 and had access to all the laboratories and workrooms. He was chair of the section of mammals. Throughout his life, he contributed to the museum to support other expeditions, including a fund to collect specimens of Shiras moose from the Rocky Mountains. Once, he gave the museum fifty dollars toward a marble bust of his friend, Frank Chapman.

As was customary, Shiras brought along a guide and helper from Marquette, this time Charlie Anderson. The men arrived at Colon on the Atlantic side of the isthmus and amused themselves for a few days by touring the new locks, the power plant, worker housing, hospital wards, and other sights of the Canal Zone. Construction had just been completed and ships were making test runs through the locks.

As a renowned naturalist and a former congressional representative who voted for the canal project while he was in office, Shiras had stature. He arrived with a letter of introduction from Henry Stimson, the US secretary of war, which he presented to George Goethals, chief engineer of the canal and first governor of the Canal Zone. He also met Colonel William Gorgas, the physician who made construction of the canal possible by controlling the mosquitoes spreading yellow fever and malaria. Both men offered advice on his explorations and gave him quarters in the village of Gatun, the site of the massive earthen dam.

Created by damming the Chagres River, Gatun Lake was the heart of the system, forming the main passage between the seas. Ships were raised or lowered eighty-five feet from the oceans via the locks and then sailed thirty-two miles across the lake. The dam supplied fifty-two million gallons of water needed to fill the locks for each passage. It generated hydropower to operate the locks and electrify the entire infrastructure in the Canal Zone. It also supplied drinking water.

Gatun was the largest man-made impoundment in the world and, as its waters filled valleys and drowned forests, villages, and plantations, the flooding forced animals out of the lowlands and onto hilltops, some of which became islands. The lake inundated 180 square miles. Although it was a disaster for the land creatures—monkeys, ocelots, tapirs, armadillos, sloths, iguanas, snakes, peccary, and jaguars—Shiras looked at it as the necessary price of civilization as well as a fascinating spectacle.

Exploring Gatun Lake, he wrote, was the "most novel of all my wilderness experiences."

In this early period, no one knew the lake's exact shape. The waters were full of detritus: logs, tens of thousands of uprooted trees, and floating masses of vegetation—water hyacinth, orchid, ferns and vines, and palm fronds. The debris piled up in windrows and choked the new bays and coves. Some former rivers and tributaries could only be followed by the crowns of trees still breaking the surface. All was in flux and decay. The water temperature was in the eighties, the air hot and humid, and the fecund odors of dying and rotting vegetation filled the nostrils.

Old foot trails had been inundated, and the best way to get to the interior was by boat. For the expedition, Shiras decided to fashion a houseboat—akin to what he used on Whitefish Lake and the Halifax River in Florida. The scientists lived on the boat while tying up at various locations and exploring on foot.

He and Anderson found a zinc-roofed, nine-by-thirty-foot floating tool shed used during canal construction. They put in a floor, built bunks and tacked up screening from floor to roof. A thirty-gallon drum was installed to hold fresh water and an oil stove to cook food. There was a hinged table for eating and a work surface to prepare museum specimens.

They were joined by Harold E. Anthony, a scientist for the Museum of Natural History. He was just twenty-four years old but tough and experienced in the bush. He had been in Panama for some weeks, hiking into the mountains and collecting animals. He welcomed the opportunity to cruise along in a boat.

Anderson and Anthony proved to be congenial companions, and Shiras noted in his *National Geographic* article how much he enjoyed their company.

While they waited for the houseboat to be completed, the men took day trips into the rain forest, employing as guides former construction workers who remained to work as trappers and market hunters.

The flooding opened up the nearly impenetrable jungle to easy exploration and exploitation. The canal workers, familiar with the topography just beneath the water, operated the gas launches at high speed and swerved through the drowned forests with confidence. In places, the water was ninety feet deep.

One day, they went up the main channel of the Chagres to the Chillibro River to explore interconnecting limestone caves harboring several species of bats, including the vampire bat with a wingspread of twenty-six inches.

The boat brought them within a mile of the caves at a point where the river emptied into the lake. As they walked into the forest, Shiras marveled at the number of game trails and the tracks around the river pools where tapirs, peccary, deer, opossums, capybara, ocelots, and jaguars came to drink. The rising waters concentrated the animals. The forest was alive with the sounds of toucans, parrots, and parakeets and the grunts and screeches of howler monkeys—a memorable medley for someone from the north. The caves were equally exotic, with stalactites dripping water, enormous black beetles crawling across a floor thick with guano, and bats hanging from the walls and ceilings.

Anthony wanted specimens. The guides, eager to help, took off their belts and began to beat the critters and knock them off the walls. The scientists put a stop to that, but when they began throwing rocks to dislodge some of the vampire bats hanging from the ceiling, a guide became impatient and let loose with a booming blast of a shotgun.

Shiras recalled, "A few mangled and useless bodies fell and then a black stream of bats circled noiselessly overhead creating a perceptible current of air as they flew continuously back and forth through the connecting caverns. Finally, they attached themselves to the roof and we were able to obtain a sufficient number for our purpose."

A dark cave full of bats was well suited for a wildlife photographer specializing in flashlights, and he captured some of his best images of the trip this day. Most dramatic was a shot of Anderson and two guides seated on rocks, arranged about ten feet apart in a triangle. Anderson wears leather gaiters to protect his legs against snakes. A knife dangles from his belt and his hands cradle one of Shiras's cameras. The guide at the top of the frame holds a chemical flashlight in his outstretched arm, much like Shiras would do in a boat when approaching a deer.

The picture captures the moment the Blitz Pulver explodes into a burst of light. In its archives, *National Geographic* labels the photograph as "three scientists inside a fire-lit bat cave" but the light—nearly three feet across—does not resemble so much a torch as an exploding star. In anticipation of the flash, the men shut their eyes.

In early March, a crowd of natives and workers gathered to watch the launch of the houseboat. It had no power and had to be towed. It rode low and, in any kind of wave action, water rolled onto the decks. They had to be careful. A long fetch of open water, wind, and swells imperiled the journey.

They hired a pilot, identified only as Captain Brown, to take them up what had been the Trinidad River where a plantation operated just outside the confines of the zone. It was the least explored area of the lake. Frequently they resorted to a compass to get their bearings. They traveled for

Flashlight explosion
in bat cave, Panama,
1914. George Shiras 3d;
Courtesy of National
Geographic Creative.

hours and, as darkness fell under a half moon, all hands turned out and stood at the gunnels with oars and boat hooks to push floating logs out of the way and watch for deadheads.

Just before dawn, they tied up to a large tree on the edge of the plantation where they picked up two native guides, or "native boys," using the paternalistic parlance of the period—this despite the fact that the guides were grown men.

Anthony was after specimens for the museum, and he went inland with steel traps, rifles, and shotguns. Shiras walked up dry creek beds—scoured clear by strong flows during the rainy season—and looked for pools where he could place camera traps. They stayed at the location for several days, hacking their way with machetes and amassing what Shiras called "a wonderful collection of ticks and red bugs and other insect pests."

Troops of black howler monkeys frequented the forest, and their guttural growls, heard for miles, were otherworldly. Anthony, conceding that he felt "a pain of regret," brought down a large male who crashed into a bees' nest the size of a bushel basket, making retrieval of the body a nasty business. Shiras stretched the body out on a log, took a photograph, and posed the monkey in such a way that it requires a second look to understand that it is dead.

As a land bridge between two continents, Panama contained then and now exceedingly diverse flora and fauna. The area harbored fifty types of bats, more than one hundred species of mammals, and numerous amphibians and reptiles.

The men were opportunistic when it came to specimens. As they passed a floating mass of debris, they saw a boa constrictor curled in the branch of a dead tree. "Since this snake was regarded as a good museum specimen, we put a rifle ball just back of its neck. With a convulsive movement, the snake hurled itself toward the bow of the launch, but fortunately it slid into the water . . . only a crimson circle on the surface and a string of bubbles marked its way to the bottom where it was beyond recovery."

In daytime Shiras was able to take illustrative pictures for his articles: the houseboat tied to a tree, the men skinning animals, and native Panamanians gliding by in dugout canoes. Flashlight photography proved difficult. He hoped to capture images of a big cat: mountain lion, jaguar, or ocelot. He baited the camera traps with skinned carcasses of animals collected by Anthony, but the carrion mainly drew scavengers: "The moment darkness fell I could hear the reports from the scattered flashlight machines and always there was a possibility of their having been fired by marsupials."

Opossums, mostly, but also night rails, large rodents like the paca, and even flying bats sprung the traps. In the daytime, vultures dropped in to take the bait. Still, the images of these animals were excellent. The explosion and light of one flashlight so frightened an opossum that it fell into a coma-like state, also known as playing possum. Another time a falling tree buried a camera. The trees, partially submerged, rotted at the trunks. Weighed down by lianas, or climbing vines, they frequently broke apart, so much so that the men were careful where they tied up the boat.

Humidity was the biggest impediment to photography. Plates left in the cameras for more than a day spoiled due to fast-growing mildew, and often it would be two or three days before Shiras could return to the scene.

He missed a jaguar that tried to carry off the skinned carcass of an opossum. The camera fired, but the plate was so mildewed it could not be developed. Claw marks on the bank clearly showed signs of a big cat. All Shiras could do was to fire a daylight picture of the brushy site and explain what happened to magazine readers under a legend that read, "Here the Author Almost Achieved a Triumph."

However, Shiras was prescient in the trap's future utility as a tool for biologists: "Undoubtedly flash photography is the ideal way of getting pictures of larger size and mostly nocturnal animals of South America, where dense brush prevents any possibilities of daylight pictures unless the subjects can be cornered or treed by hounds."

The men also tried to jacklight animals from the houseboat, first for the purpose of photography and then as a way to collect specimens. "We occasionally caught glimpses of glowing eyes back from the waters' edge but floating logs and tottering trees made the approach so difficult that before we could come within range, the mysterious beast we were eager to photograph had always disappeared."

Anthony, of course, did not need to get so close. He shined a spotlight into a tree, saw a pair of red eyes and fired a bullet, thinking he might bag an ocelot, but instead a goatsucker, a type of nighthawk, tumbled to the ground. Another time on shore, he was about to fire into a tree when a big boar peccary nearly knocked him over. The pig, which he was able to kill, had been fleeing a jaguar, which roared in the face of the frightened hunters before running off into the forest.

Rising waters concentrated the animals. Some made it to large landforms but others were marooned on small islands, left there to starve, be eaten by predators, or be picked off by native hunters. Captain Brown made pets of an owl monkey and deer he found marooned on floating masses of vegetation. Shiras took a flashlight picture of the monkey and so frightened the animal that it wouldn't approach him again.

Wherever he went, Shiras saw animals being killed for food or simply for the sake of shooting and so-called sport. One morning, he watched native hunters open up on flocks of parrots: "No effort was made to preserve even the ornamental birds of the country. The well-earned outings of the canal employees were too often signalized by their using the harmless, nongame animals and birds as targets."

Over the next few weeks, the Shiras Expedition collected scores of animals, which were skinned and prepared for taxidermy. Anthony later published two papers about his collections in Panama and declared that the Shiras Expedition found new species of a rabbit and a marsupial.

Sometimes the men ate the meat of the specimens, mostly peccaries. One night after Anderson cleaned a peccary on the floor of the cabin, he woke up covered with several large ticks that had come off the pig's body. Shiras recalled "raiding ants in daytime, fever-bearing mosquitoes at night and vicious red bugs and ticks at all times." The air temperature rarely dropped below the mid-seventies and got up to ninety during the day. Water temperature, however, remained around eighty degrees. When they jumped into the lake for a dip to cool off or wash, the men were nipped by small biting fish.

Still it was a great adventure. *National Geographic* timed the release of the article and photographs for the canal's official opening later that year. "Nature's Transformation at Panama: Remarkable Changes in Faunal and Physical Conditions in the Gatun Lake Region" appeared in the August 1914 issue. The article was accompanied by thirty-six illustrations and two colored maps. Unfortunately, the attention of the world had turned toward Europe as the old powers and monarchies of the continent stumbled into the Great War, a conflict that was to change everything. The war overshadowed the canal's actual opening.

In the article, Shiras proposed that the Canal Zone should serve as a great international park and suggested Barro Colorado—also known as West Island, the largest land form not inundated by the lake—be reserved as a natural park, a place to study tropical wildlife: "I was so impressed by the richness of the flora and fauna about the shore of Gatun Lake, especially the mammals, birds and reptiles, that it appeared to me to be an ideal place for a center of research by scientists."

He wasn't the first naturalist to make the suggestion, but saying so in a magazine read by Washington decision makers certainly helped the cause. In 1923 hunting was banned on the island, and the Smithsonian Institution established a biological research station there. Over the ensuing decades, the remaining rain forests around Gatun Lake and inside the Canal Zone were put under protection. Today the sixteen-hundred-acre island adjoins Panama's fifty-four-thousand-acre Soberania National Park and another ten thousand acres of surrounding mainland peninsulas. The Barro Colorado Tropical Research Institute has hosted thousands of scientists and made the area one of the most studied tropical environments in the world.

Frank Chapman built a cottage at the research station and spent several winters there in the 1920s and '30s, producing a book called *My Tropical Air Castle*. In a copy owned by Shiras, Chapman wrote: "To George Shiras 3d, whose work with a camera laid the foundation on which this book reared."

Chapman realized Shiras's dream of capturing a big cat on film using a camera trap. Learning flashlight photography from Shiras, Chapman set out camera traps to do a "census of the living" on Barro Colorado, determining what animals were in the reserve. He successfully photographed mountain lions, ocelots, and coatimundis and even used the images and markings to differentiate between individuals. He was the first biologist to use remote photography to do a biological survey of animals, a technique that was cumbersome and expensive until the modern trail camera emerged in the 1990s.

21 | THE BULLET IS ON THE WAY

AFTER GEORGE RETURNED from Panama, his son took sick, left college, and wintered with the family in Ormond Beach. George IV's illness was serious, and he had weakened over the course of many months.

Shiras wrote Grosvenor from the Hotel Ormond and asked that copies of the halftone prints selected for the Panama article be sent to him so he could begin to write the legends. "We have been here about two weeks and find that George's condition is improving. Should he have a return of his complaint, we will return to Washington. Both Chapman and I have gotten over our colds and are having a good time."

Strangely, however, it was not Shiras's son who died first but Grosvenor's fourth child, Alexander Graham Bell Grosvenor, who was just five years old. He died in March 1915.

Shiras, not knowing what was coming himself, wrote to Grosvenor. "I was about to write you a business letter last week when word came of your great loss. It was fortunate that you have other children to ease the blow later on, though for the present time, this will not be so apparent. Mrs. Shiras and I extend our deepest sympathy to you and your wife."

He immediately follows with several paragraphs about the Panama article, asking for more copies of halftones and wondering which would be the best month for the article to run.

It is a sympathetic letter, but the business portion comes off as a bit less than sensitive. Perhaps there had been other expressions of sympathy—likely a telegram.

George IV was not improving. In April, they brought him to their home in Wesley Heights in DC. In the last two weeks of his life, his father read young George newspapers regarding another Roosevelt libel trial, this time in Syracuse. TR was being sued by the editor of the *Albany Times-Union* after Roosevelt called him a "political boss of the most obnoxious type." The trial lasted five weeks and, to Roosevelt's surprise, the jury found for him.

In a letter to the Colonel, Shiras said young George wanted all the papers saved so he could read them later.

"The verdict brought tears to his eyes and was a great satisfaction," wrote Shiras.

George IV died at home on May 27. He was just twenty-six years old.

Fanny wrote in her diary, "Our dear George left us this morning. It has been to us a very, very sad day. We went into his room at three o'clock. It was peaceful for him. Ellie [her daughter, Ellen Kennedy Shiras] and I stayed in the room. George 3d could not bear it—so walked back and forth."

The family brought the body back to Marquette for the funeral and burial, where according to an obituary in the *Mining Journal*—probably written by Frank Russell—it was said, "Marquette was his favorite place of residence and it was here that he had his dearest friends . . . his acquaintanceship was large, bearing witness to his fine democratic instincts and the wide range of his interest in his fellows."

A Washington friend added, "Gentle and manly always, quietly and without hesitation he helped those who asked and more often anticipated the needs of his friends. Now that his sufferings are over, we cannot but feel that he kept much to himself that he knew would cause anxiety to those nearest him."

Roosevelt sent a telegram: "It is dreadful to lose one's son and especially such a fine and gallant fellow. There has never been a stauncher and more loyal friend than you and we mourn with you with all of our hearts."

Fanny wrote in her diary, "George 3d had a very sympathetic telegram from Col. Roosevelt. It pleased us all. George Peter had so much feeling for Col. R."

George 3d sought solace at Whitefish Lake. Fanny wrote, "George came up from camp. He went down yesterday—needed a change—poor dear—he has been so depressed. Everything was beautiful at camp and restful. G. wants me to go out."

Obviously to lose his only son and namesake was a crushing blow. Fanny's distress had seriously affected her health. Ellie wasn't much better.

In a letter thanking Grosvenor for his sympathy, Shiras said, "the expressive note of yours came just at the right time."

Then in the last paragraph, he again mentions the Panama piece. "Should you desire the article for the July number, let me know, as I can finish any time and it will be a relief in having something to occupy my mind at the present time."

He wrote on June 27 to Grosvenor with changes and suggestions on the Panama article. In it, he mentioned that "Mrs. Shiras is steadily improving and we leave for my camp in the middle of the week."

He mentions how young George, in recent years, had become much more of a companion and a fellow sportsman: "He inherited to a marked degree the traits of his paternal ancestors and the love of the woods and the betterment of political conditions."

There was another exchange of letters in which Shiras mused that he might try to get started on a monograph of white-tailed deer, perhaps as a prelude to working on his big book. He needed distraction and invited E. W. Nelson to come to the Upper Peninsula and visit him at camp. Perhaps they could work on the monograph together. He expected to spend the summer and fall in Marquette.

Word must have gotten to Roosevelt, who wrote from Oyster Bay, saying he was "delighted" that Shiras had agreed to write a "biography" of the white-tailed deer. He didn't want any "foreigners" doing the serious work of natural history. "There isn't anyone who can do as well as you the kind of work that just at this time needs doing. I earnestly hope you sit right down to that white-tailed deer biography and not let up until it is finished."

It was vintage TR. If Shiras needed a model on how to keep going after a tragedy, he could look to Roosevelt, whose wife and mother died the same day, in the same house, just a few rooms apart. The grief drove him to take up ranching in the Dakota Badlands and then charge back into politics. Work, adventure, and continual action chased away depression.

In the years after his 1912 defeat, the pugnacious politician sought distraction: giving speeches, writing, and traveling. In 1913, he eagerly accepted an opportunity to descend an unexplored river in Brazil. Sponsored by the American Museum of Natural History, the expedition seemed moderately difficult but turned into a thousand-mile-long dangerous exploration of wilderness complete with hostile natives. The explorers could not find game, ran low on food, and were plagued by insects and treacherous river conditions. Three men died, and the aptly named River of Doubt nearly killed the president, too, when he came down with malaria and a bacterial infection from a gash in his leg.

When Roosevelt got back and limped off the boat at New York, he looked terrible, having lost nearly sixty pounds.

On a warm evening on May 26 in Washington, Shiras was in the audience when a gaunt TR gave a lecture on the expedition to the National Geographic Society. It was attended by more than four thousand people crammed into Convention Hall, the largest auditorium in the district.

The Colonel perspired heavily in the heat and appeared to be in pain but gave a lively lecture. Months later he turned out a book, *Through the Brazilian Wilderness*. In it, he made reference to George Shiras 3d: "Nowadays there is a growing proportion of big-game hunters and sportsmen who are of the Schilling, Selous and Shiras type. These men do work of capital value for science. The mere big-game butcher is tending to disappear as a type. On the other hand, the big-game hunter who is a good observer, a good field naturalist, occupies at present a more important position than ever before."

The fact that Roosevelt wrote a book so quickly after his expedition and in poor health demonstrated his powers of concentration and desire to document his work. Whenever he harangued Shiras to write a book, he wasn't just talking.

The wound from the 1912 assassination attempt, the recurrence of malaria (he'd first caught it in Cuba), and the rigors of the Brazilian expedition took their toll on the ex-president. The damaged leg never healed properly and occasionally became reinfected. Rheumatoid arthritis caused him great pain. In his late fifties, the Colonel was not in good health.

In early 1918, he contracted a throat infection, which spread to both ears. Doctors pierced his eardrums to drain the infection. One ear recovered, the other did not. Now, he was blind in one eye and deaf in an ear. He spent weeks in Roosevelt Hospital in New York.

Having read about Roosevelt's condition in the newspapers and hearing from mutual friends, Shiras sent a telegram inviting the Colonel and Edith to come to Ormond for a period of convalescence. It was cosigned by Frank Chapman and Henry Fairfield Osborne.

Shiras followed up with a heartfelt letter, "You will be welcomed into a quiet little family that probably knows just how to manage matters in your period of inactivity."

The letter, written on stationery of the Ormond Beach Property Owners Association, of which Shiras was the president, draws a relaxing picture of Ormond in a way that would appeal to a naturalist: "Broad verandas in an orange grove, birds in sight all of the time, fine drives on the beach or river front and trails throughout the forest with continuous sunshine, balmy air, and appreciative friends at your disposal at any time. Here you will find a quiet place for the rest and surroundings needed now."

J. M. Stucker, Roosevelt's secretary, wrote back, "Both Colonel and Mrs. Roosevelt thank you and appreciate to the full your very kind invitation. But Colonel Roosevelt will not be able to go even to Oyster Bay for at least three weeks and he says he is more anxious to get home than any place else."

A few days later, Gilbert Grosvenor and his wife visited Ormond and stayed with the Shirases on their way to Miami to visit botanist and plant explorer David Fairchild, who was a member of the board of managers and married to the sister of Grosvenor's wife. Earlier that month, letters had been exchanged between Grosvenor and Flavel S. Luther, president of Trinity College in Hartford, Connecticut. Luther was an old friend of Roosevelt's and had invited him to speak at the June 1918 commencement. Luther also wanted to award TR an honorary degree, but he knew the president was not fond of such honoraria. One way to convince him, Luther thought, would be to invite another eminent naturalist and award both of them degrees.

Shiras had been suggested by Joseph Buffington, a federal judge in Pittsburgh, and William Mather, president of Cleveland Cliffs and the architect of the Grand Island Game Preserve. Both were Trinity alumni. Luther wrote to Grosvenor to get confirmation of Shiras's qualifications and was delighted with what he heard from Grosvenor, the photographic work he had seen in National Geographic, and Shiras's personal relationship with TR. After extending the invitation, Luther exchanged letters with Shiras and waxed romantically about his feelings of viewing the flashlight images and how much fun he once had with some other Trinity men when Mather arranged for them to take an iron ore steamer between Cleveland and Marquette.

While recuperating at Oyster Bay, Roosevelt accepted the invitation, pleased that Shiras would be joining him and also receiving an honorary science degree. After the commencement, the men lunched at Luther's house and that afternoon accepted an invitation by the chapter of Alpha Delta Phi to sign the members' registry book at the fraternity house. The two former fraternity members posed for pictures in their caps and gowns with the college president and other luminaries who had come to see Roosevelt.

When it was time to take pictures of the honorees only, Roosevelt bellowed out, "Nature fakers to the front."

It was another reference to their old fight.

Later, Roosevelt pulled Shiras to one side and urged him again to write his "big book": "I really think you are getting along very well in the serial publication of the material for your book but I want to warn you that we are no longer young."

Then he said with emotion, perhaps because of his own precarious health, "The bullet is on the way for each of us and may not be very far off."

When he recalled the warning, Shiras wrote, "A sad prophecy . . . six months later his voice was silenced—but his deeds will continue to speak with a thousand tongues."

At the Trinity ceremony, TR was in pain and old beyond his years. Another catastrophe was about to strike. The following month, he would lose his youngest son, Quentin, a twenty-year-old aviator, to the Great War.

The Colonel had been warmongering since 1914, demanding the United States enter on the side of the Allies. He wanted to return to the battlefield and lead men himself, but Woodrow Wilson would not allow it. So TR encouraged all of his sons to go in his place. He understood the risks, of course, but Quentin's death was a blow from which the heartbroken father would never recover.

Receiving honorary degrees at Trinity College in Hartford, Connecticut, 1918.
From left: college president Flavel S. Luther; Theodore Roosevelt; R. J. Coles,
a field naturalist; and George Shiras 3d.
Courtesy of National Geographic Creative.

Shiras and Roosevelt signed the guestbook in the fraternity house, and then Shiras bid his old friend goodbye. He had a train to catch to Washington. His last words to TR were, "I leave you in good hands and we are all quite agreed that you are the most distinguished and respected member of the society."

By that, he meant the Alpha Delta Phi fraternity, but his feelings extended far beyond.

After Quentin's death, Shiras sent condolences and Roosevelt answered with a short note, "My dear Shiras: We thank you and Mrs. Shiras. You have both always been true friends to us."

It was their last correspondence.

That fall, TR traveled to North Dakota to visit old friends and see the Badlands again, hoping his psyche might once again be soothed by nature. He was in anguish both mentally and physically. The jostling of the train and other aspects of the trip caused his leg to become reinfected and the trip was cut short.

Roosevelt died at Sagamore Hill in Oyster Bay on January 5, 1919. He experienced breathing problems, went to bed, and around four a.m. a blood clot detached from a vein and traveled to his lungs. He was just sixty years old.

Thomas Marshall, vice president of the United States, notably said, "Death had to take Roosevelt sleeping, for if he had been awake, there would have been a fight."

Eulogizing began at once as did talk of memorials.

Two days following Roosevelt's death, Shiras was in New York for a directors' meeting of the American Game Protective and Propagation Association and proposed that it work toward a memorial reflecting TR's interest in game conservation and natural history.

A committee of Burnham, Shiras, E. W. Nelson and Charles Sheldon came up with "The Theodore Roosevelt Foundation for the Conservation of Wild Life." Shiras wrote the proposal, saying the object would be "the conservation of wildlife, mainly in America but secondarily in other parts of the world. The wildlife to be thus conserved being principally the native bird and mammal faunas." Styled after the Carnegie Institution with a board of directors, the foundation would act as a clearinghouse of information, establish a reference library, fund research, and do educational outreach. The AGPPA estimated that it alone could raise $2 to $3 million toward the foundation.

Other organizations had different ideas. T. Gilbert Pearson of the Audubon Societies proposed a memorial fountain be built in Washington at the cost of $200,000.

To sort it all out, the Roosevelt Permanent Memorial National Committee formed in New York to determine how the ex-president should be remembered by the country. Henry Cabot Lodge, Elihu Root, Leonard Wood, John Sargent, Gifford Pinchot, Philander Knox, and William Howard Taft served on the committee.

The committee published a *Book of Suggestions* to present the many proposals to the press, the public, and the Roosevelt family. Shiras made a strong case that the wildlife institution was "urgently needed and would epitomize the Colonel's penchant for the outdoors and the strenuous life.

"His delight in wild things of the forest and plain and his intimate association and fellowship with naturalists, big game hunters and others interested in wild life have been well known for years. . . . The perpetuation of wild game is an insurance for the opportunity of healthful out-of-door activity, such as those which transformed Colonel Roosevelt from a weakly youth to the magnificent physique which all admired."

Burnham and the AGPPA already had approached the family on the wildlife foundation. Carl Akeley, an AGPPA director and the taxidermist who accompanied Roosevelt to Africa, took the proposal to the Roosevelt family. Edith Roosevelt gave her approval. Burnham set up a lunch with Hermann Hagedorn, the secretary for the Permanent Memorial Committee. He sent out letters, made phone calls, and began a lobbying effort.

The permanent committee, however, had its own ideas, which went beyond conservation. In the weeks immediately after Roosevelt's death, the main thought was to give citizenship to all immigrants living in the United States—an Americanization idea.

The committee would meet in open session at the Waldorf Astoria on March 24 to hear oral presentations. Then it would vote at the conclusion of the meeting. Shiras was in Ormond Beach at his cottage. Burnham and Nelson urged him to come north to make the presentation, but Shiras begged off, apparently not feeling well enough for the trip.

"Its success or failure depends in large measure on its proper presentation and no other man can do this so well as you can," Burnham wrote.

Meanwhile, Burnham sent out press releases to newspapers to pressure the committee. Under the title "Noted Naturalists Present Project to Memorial Committee," the press release referred to the sponsors as "a group of Colonel Roosevelt's friends, naturalists, and sportsmen."

The release read, "They contend that because of Colonel Roosevelt's well-known interest in nature throughout his life, both as one of the keenest and most observant of American field naturalists and as a hunter of big game, no memorial could be devised which he himself would have looked upon with greater appreciation and pleasure."

Burnham wasn't wrong and, of all Roosevelt's policies, conservation certainly became his most enduring legacy. However, this was 1919, and there was politics to consider. The Great War had just ended. TR, despite his poor health, had contemplated another run for the White House. He had been stirring things up in the Republican Party and loudly opposing the League of Nations.

For many members of the committee, birds and wildlife were not exactly front and center. Even Gifford Pinchot wanted a more inclusive type of conservation memorial, not one just focused on wildlife.

The committee met and immediately nixed the Americanization idea, which would have required an act of Congress. However, Senator Frank Kellogg of Minnesota declared, "Americanism as believed in and preached by Colonel Roosevelt should be taught in every college and high school in the country."

Nelson and Burnham were given five minutes to present the wildlife fund. Burnham read Shiras's proposal to the committee. At the end of the day, Theodore Roosevelt Jr. spoke and gave the family's endorsement of "suggestions that came concerning the preservation of wildlife."

But there would be no foundation for wildlife. Instead the committee prioritized three projects: (1) a suitable memorial in Washington, DC, on par with the Lincoln Memorial or Washington Monument; (2) the acquisition of land for a park in Oyster Bay and eventually the preservation of the Roosevelt home (Sagamore Hill) on the same level as George Washington's Mount Vernon and Abraham Lincoln's home in Illinois; and (3) incorporation of a society "to promote the development and application of the policies and ideals of Theodore Roosevelt for the benefit of the American people."

The latter, the Theodore Roosevelt Association, was a genericized version of the wildlife foundation. Still in existence today and based in Oyster Bay, it gives out awards for public speaking and police bravery and service. The association also sponsors "strenuous life adventures" for people who want to visit places made famous by Roosevelt, such as Medora, North Dakota. It has little to do with conservation.

Burnham was disappointed—actually disgusted—with the committee, which he felt had ignored the desires of the Roosevelt family. In a letter to Shiras, he blamed Elihu Root: "The presentation made by Mr. Nelson and myself was wasted. The committee hearing was dominated by Root and Root then, as always, opposed anything being done for wild life conservation. I am sorry to have to send this report. I think we have done all that could be done, under the circumstances."

Hagedorn, who was to become president of the Theodore Roosevelt Association and write eight books on the Colonel's life, later invited Shiras to meet with him in New York and present a scaled-down version of the foundation to the association. Nothing came of it.

The memorial association also asked Shiras to write down some anecdotes of his dealings with Roosevelt on wildlife issues. He sent copies of his personal correspondence. Later, Shiras served on its national committee and joined the Michigan branch of the Roosevelt Memorial Committee, which met annually in Detroit. He was on the Honorary Adviser Council of the Roosevelt Wild Life Forest Experimental Station at the New York State Forestry School in Syracuse.

There were other small remembrances. In *Bird-Lore*, Helen P. Childs, secretary of the Audubon club in the District of Columbia, noted that at a meeting, "Mr. Shiras is anxious to have our society undertake the regular feeding of the Pigeons in one or more of our Public Parks as a memorial to ex-president Roosevelt. This we have been striving to do."

The great TR was gone, and Shiras felt the loss of his friendship and the extraordinary eminence and spirit the Colonel had brought to the causes of conservation and Progressivism. In his presidency alone, Roosevelt established 51 federal bird reservations, 4 national game preserves, 150 national forests, 5 national parks, and 18 national monuments. He created the National Forest Service and protected 230 million acres of public lands. He made conservation of natural resources a vital and enduring national issue.

Like many sportsmen and naturalists, Shiras wondered how the cause of wildlife conservation would go forward, although he was certain it would. Still, it was the end of the era.

For many years afterward, he and Fanny stayed in touch with Edith Roosevelt, exchanging letters and holiday cards. George sent her a photograph, "Innocents Abroad," of a doe and two fawns from the *Midnight Series*, which she put in Roosevelt's office at Sagamore Hill in Oyster Bay.

She wrote, "There could not be a greeting such as yours and I couldn't describe my pleasure which it has given me. I am trying to imagine how you felt when catching that unconcerned mother and the interested, but unalarmed twins. All of the spirit of the northern woods is there. I shall keep it in the library where I always seem to see Theodore busy at his desk."

In 1926 Shiras gave a speech in Marquette to the Rotary Club, reminiscing about his sixteen-year friendship with the Colonel. He read from letters and related how TR kept "everlasting at" him to write a big book.

He recounted an evening spent as a guest at Oyster Bay after Roosevelt left the presidency in which the two men retired to the porch after dinner and discussed the meaning of the word "genius." It had frequently been used to describe the president—and Shiras, too—but Roosevelt told Shiras he found the term "most inapplicable and objectionable."

When telling the anecdote then, or later when he wrote it out in his unfinished autobiography, Shiras recounted the conversation as if he had recorded it verbatim. Perhaps he did write it down later that evening. More likely, he simply reconstructed the conversation and Roosevelt's manner of speech.

TR allegedly said, "If there is one thing that may have exemplified my career, it is what can be accomplished by most persons through hard work and making the best of every opportunity. My rule is a simple one—do the best you can with what you have and do it now.

"Why I have been a second or third rater in everything I have tried to do and any accomplishment must be credited to industry and not to any providential endowment arbitrarily separating me from the rest of the community."

"Innocents Abroad," from the *Midnight Series*. George Shiras 3d;
Courtesy of National Geographic Creative.

Shiras protested that Roosevelt was being too modest. He ticked off a
litany of TR's achievements:

> Nevertheless, you are a genius and a conspicuous one at that. . . .
> author, editor, historian, lecturer, legislator, ranchman, sportsman,
> naturalist and explorer, athlete, police commissioner and coworker
> with Jacob Riis in social betterment, rehabilitator of the Navy, a
> successful military leader and a foremost promoter of international
> peace, the chief executive of a great state and of the nation, a
> conservator of national resources, a statesman and active political
> leader, the foe alike of capitalist tyranny or industrial demagoguery,
> a human link between all grades of mankind from kings to pugilists
> and finally one who, by his exemplary private life and moral
> teachings, made an impress on the country and the world in general

quite as valuable as his successful discharge of his many public duties.

In conclusion, Shiras pointed out that, while Roosevelt may not have taken a first prize, allotted only to the specialist or the peculiarly endowed, he had taken so many second and third prizes that he outpointed any competitor and therefore was, in fact, a genius in versatility—the greatest of all from the standpoint of mentality or of public service.

It was quite an expression of hero worship—perhaps something Roosevelt was accustomed to hearing. TR chuckled and reportedly said, "Well, I'm glad to see you admit that I never stood at the top in any one of the many things I endeavored to do."

22 | THE BIRD TREATY

ELIHU ROOT NEVER believed the Migratory Bird Act could pass constitutional muster, and he repeatedly told Shiras and Burnham that the law was
likely to be overturned by the US Supreme Court. Root, who had served as
TR's secretary of state and then was elected to the US Senate in 1909, suggested that the way to avoid a constitutional challenge was to establish a
treaty with the Dominion of Canada and Great Britain.

It made sense—biologically as well as politically. Birds knew international borders no more than they did state borders. Considerable parts of
their lives were spent in Canada, Mexico, and the Caribbean, too, so there
were compelling reasons to expand the law and extend protection across
North America.

From a legal standpoint, said Root, a treaty with Canada would invoke
the supremacy clause of the US Constitution, which requires international
treaties be the supreme law of the land. Once approved by the Senate, the
treaty would require another law, or enabling act, to enforce it. By then it
would be untouchable, because treaties were clearly in the bailiwick of the
federal government. No state could interfere with a treaty made with
another country.

Shiras didn't think the legal underpinnings were so weak, but Root was also a lawyer—former counsel to Andrew Carnegie—and a shrewd Washington power player. Though he was at times an irksome opponent of conservation, his viewpoint could not be ignored.

Root introduced a treaty resolution in the Senate on March 4, 1913, even before the Weeks-McLean Act took force, but it failed to pass. McLean successfully reintroduced it a year later, and President Wilson began negotiations with Canada.

The hotbeds of resistance to the Migratory Bird Act were states in the Midwest along the Mississippi River and in the South along the Atlantic and Gulf shores where the hunting of ducks and shorebirds was tradition—particularly spring shooting.

It was also a matter of regionalism and class, of North versus South, of Easterners versus the Middle West, of rural states versus urban centers, and of common folk accustomed to subsistence hunting versus moneyed men hunting for sport.

Coleman Blease, governor of South Carolina, declared, "This is only an effort to protect a certain set of Northerners. They establish their hunting clubs, which are often nothing more than barrooms and gambling dens, put fences around their hunting preserves, and say to our people, 'Stay Out.' The United States government because these people are rich is attempting, in their interest, to deprive the people of our state their God-given liberty and right to hunt and fish for game and fish, which an all-wise Providence has provided free to all mankind."

The challenge came in Arkansas in early 1914 when a young man by the name of Harvey C. Shauver of Jonesboro was arrested for shooting two coots out of season. Shauver planned to plead guilty before a federal judge but the local game warden instead asked him to plead not guilty in order to create a test case. Shauver agreed to do it as a patriotic duty.

In May, the federal district judge in Arkansas found Shauver not guilty, saying the state not the national government owned the wildlife within its borders and the feds had no jurisdiction to regulate shooting. It simply was a matter of states' rights. The judge declared the Weeks-McLean Act unconstitutional, as did another judge in Kansas in 1915. The Kansas legislature passed a bill demanding that the state attorney general defend any hunters prosecuted by federal game wardens.

As laid out in Shiras's legal brief, the fight was about federalism and police powers. After the decisions in Arkansas and Kansas, James Clark McReynolds, the US attorney general under Woodrow Wilson, sought legal advice and strategy from Shiras and William Haskell, the legal counsel and a vice president for the American Game Protective and Propagation Association. The Boone and Crockett Club and the New York Zoological Society filed an amicus brief that AGPPA sent out to dozens of conservation organizations to get them to sign on.

In 1915 McReynolds argued the case in front of the US Supreme Court, but it stalled without a decision. There is some mystery why. Some members of the court may have been absent, and the court ordered rearguments but never scheduled them—probably because the justices were well aware that treaty negotiations were underway with Canada.

The AGPPA—mainly Burnham, Haskell, and Shiras—wrote the actual draft of the treaty and submitted the language to the Department of Agriculture. Once the State Department was on board, the treaty was revised by Dr. T. S. Palmer, head of the US Biological Survey. Then it was up to Dr. C. Gordon Hewitt, the Canada Dominion consulting zoologist, to take to the rails, travel to all the provinces, and sell the treaty to politicians. There was opposition. Many local politicians saw no need for a treaty—birds seemed plentiful and safe in Canada—and the provinces had been handling their own game laws. To the provinces, Dominion control from Ottawa was as suspect as Washington federalism was in the United States. Because of the Great War and all the efforts to supply men and materiel to the allies, some provincial governments simply weren't interested in talking about birds.

In 1916, E. W. Nelson became the new head of the Biological Survey and collaborated with AGPPA's lobbying efforts. Burnham logged more than forty thousand miles on "mission work" talking with Canadian lawmakers, sportsmen, and the powerful railroads that held much sway in Canada. It was tedious work. Each province had to sign off on the treaty before it could be submitted to the Dominion government and finally to the king of England.

As well, there were numerous conferences and negotiations in Washington between Canada, the states and provinces, and the Agriculture Department. Revisions allowed Inuit to kill birds in spring for subsistence, and language was inserted that allowed for the killing of birds if they became detrimental to agriculture. The latter helped secure support from farmers.

The US Senate ratified the treaty on August 29, 1916. It was proclaimed by President Wilson on December 8, 1916. The Supreme Court immediately dropped Shauver's case when the Weeks-McLean Act became moot.

William T. Hornaday wrote Senator McLean and called it "the greatest victory for birds ever achieved anywhere. It is enough to make any man famous for a lifetime."

Shiras and AGPPA stayed busy working on passage of the enabling act. In 1917, Shiras wrote an opinion column in the *New York Sun*, "Congress Right to Aid Wild Fowl: National Welfare Demands Protection for Migratory Birds," and a week later he penned another opinion with the headline "Wild Fowl Law for the Public Good—Reasons Why the Federal Government Owns Migratory Game Birds." Both pieces were amalgams of his legal brief and a moral plea to save birds for future generations.

The enabling act did not pass until July 1918. Once again, the AGPPA did some hard lobbying and literal strong-arming. Burnham recalled one night when he visited a House office and waited until midnight while an unnamed congressman played poker. The politician slipped out, purposefully avoiding Burnham.

Burnham returned the next day and followed the politician to a committee room where he overheard him scheming with other legislators about how "they were going to punish a postmaster who didn't campaign for the party in the last election."

The men realized Burnham was eavesdropping on their conversation, and the leader left his chair, strode over to where Burnham was sitting, and demanded, "Who are you and what do you want?"

Burnham started to explain, but the man waved him aside with what Burnham recalled "a grand gesture."

"When our boys are dying in France, I cannot talk about birds," he declared.

"The hell you can't!" Burnham exclaimed, grabbing the congressman by the coat lapels and swinging him around. "You can stay up all night playing poker, and you can frame a little postmaster while are boys are dying in France—so why can't you talk about birds?"

Burnham recalled the congressman "was visibly shaken by my anger and stood perfectly still while I told what I wanted of him."

"'Yes, yes,' he said. 'I've heard about that bill. It is excellent and I'll see that it passes.'"

The AGPPA members were considered zealots, and Burnham's tactics and strident talk sometimes got him into trouble with other conservation groups. He and William T. Hornaday had an ongoing feud that erupted a few years later in a libel case.

Yet AGPPA was in the leadership role. Burnham chaired the advisory board of the Migratory Bird Treaty. Shiras, vice president of AGPPA, served on the committee as well.

It was a hard-knuckle fight to the end. Senator James Reed of Missouri had pushed hard against the treaty because his state still had a free-market economy for wild game and birds. Hunters were accustomed to spring shooting there because birds were more plentiful at that time of year as they staged on lakes and rivers waiting for the weather to ease up north. During fall migration, the birds either bypassed the Middle West or didn't linger long as they flew south.

When the enabling act became law, the Missouri state legislature—like Kansas had done—passed a bill instructing Frank McAllister, the state attorney general, to defend anyone charged under the law in order to create a test case to take to the US Supreme Court. A group of duck-hunting and shooting clubs pledged money for a defense fund.

McAllister, a duck hunter himself, urged Missourians in defiance of the law to pursue traditional spring shooting. In speeches and interviews in newspapers, he taunted the federal game wardens, employed by the US Biological Survey, to make arrests.

The wardens did. They took in two men near Kansas City for shooting mallards, but the most significant bust came a week later when Ray Holland, the federal warden in that region, got wind that McAllister and friends were going duck hunting on the Kansas border.

On February 25, 1919, after his deputies observed the men shooting birds, Holland drove out to the duck club and personally arrested the attorney general and four other members. McAllister had in his possession forty-two pintails, twenty-three mallards, three green-winged teal, and one blue goose. The arrest took place in his duck blind, and the surprised and flustered McAllister compounded his problems by giving a false name. The men were arraigned and released after posting $1,000 bail.

McAllister himself became the test case.

He immediately asked for a federal restraining order, declaring the law violated the Tenth Amendment, which says powers not delegated to the United States by the Constitution, nor prohibited to it by the states, are reserved to the states or to the people.

The district judge dismissed the suit, and in May of that year, Senator Reed tried to nominate McAllister to become the federal judge of the eastern district. It was a bizarre move, and George Bird Grinnell as president of the Boone and Crockett Club wrote the US attorney general in Washington pointedly reminding him that McAllister had been arrested for violating a federal law: "We, therefore, protest against his consideration for the appointment as a federal judge, where he would have an opportunity to pass upon the law which he holds in contempt and we trust that you will not recommend his appointment to the president."

Missouri appealed the arrest of McAllister and the other duck hunters to the US Supreme Court in the case *Missouri v. Holland.* Some thirty conservation organizations filed briefs with the court and, according to the National Geographic Society, the most important brief was one prepared by Shiras.

During oral arguments, McAllister represented Missouri and thus himself. He claimed the state had a pecuniary interest as the owner of birds within its borders. He tried to use the Shauver decision as precedent, but that was rejected.

Chief Justice Oliver Wendell Holmes delivered the court's decision against Missouri on April 19, 1920. The vote was seven to two.

Citing the supremacy clause, the majority held the law constitutional.

In his opinion, Holmes made reference to what was later christened "the concept of the living Constitution," meaning it is a document open to interpretation by the courts—that the founders of the country could not have foreseen all the ways the Constitution would be applied to the needs of the country in the future.

When the Constitution was written, wild fowl and birds were plentiful. Clouds of passenger pigeons darkened the skies. The great auk could still be found on the coast of New England. But in the early twentieth century, there was real risk for birds everywhere, said Holmes.

He referred to the peril and the transitory nature of wildlife that does not recognize state or country demarcations:

Wild birds are not in the possession of anyone; and possession is the beginning of ownership. The whole foundation of states' rights is the presence within their jurisdiction of birds that yesterday had not arrived, tomorrow may be in another state and in a week, a thousand miles away. . . .

Here a national interest of very nearly the first magnitude is involved. It can be protected only by rational action in concert with that of another power. The subject matter is only transitory within the State and had no permanent habitat therein. But for the treaty and the statute there soon might be no birds at all for any powers to deal with. We see nothing in the Constitution that compels the Government to sit by while a food supply is cut off and the protectors of our forests and our crops are destroyed. It is not sufficient to rely upon the States.

The decision put an end to the legal challenges. McAllister pleaded guilty in Joplin and was fined. Ray Holland resigned as game warden and took a position with the AGPPA—another indication of the closeness between the organization and the Biological Survey. Holland hung a picture of McAllister in his AGPPA office to remind himself of the victory. Violators in Missouri, Kansas, and places like the Chesapeake Bay continued an underground trade in waterfowl, but public opinion had turned to protecting the birds. Women no longer found feathers fashionable. Hunting ethics changed and the food market for birds dried up. A new era had arrived. In later years, the treaty was extended to Mexico, the Soviet Union, and Japan.

The bird law first envisioned by George Shiras proved to be an exceptionally powerful and effective federal environmental statute.

Forest and Stream editorialized the treaty as "the biggest accomplishment in wildlife conservation ever achieved on the continent." It was not hyperbole—then and now. With the exception of the Endangered Species Act passed by Congress decades later, no other law had a more profound effect on the conservation of wildlife.

There was plenty of credit to go around, and each group, including the AGPPA and the Audubon Societies, laid some claim to the law's development and passage.

In *Bird-Lore*, T. Gilbert Pearson made sure his members understood the role the Audubon Societies played in altering the original bird bill: "The bird bill of Shiras contemplated the protection of migratory game birds only. The President of this Association urged its author to change the wording so as to include all migratory birds. This bill did not become law but its principles were embodied in the bird bill introduced years later . . . that migratory non-game birds are protected in Canada and the United States by Treaty is a direct result of policies and activities of the National Association of Audubon Societies and this should never be forgotten."

Grinnell telegrammed Shiras, telling him of the court's decision, "Your crown has come at last. Heartiest congratulations."

That same day he followed with a letter praising Shiras as the originator of the idea. The prose is especially laudatory: "I offer you congratulations on having really come into your own. You have taken your place among those who have done well for their country and whose services are acknowledged by all. You have seen your ideas triumph in a comparatively short time. Few men, working for a great novel principle, have attained success so swiftly. You are greatly to be congratulated and those who love you rejoice for and with you. We are all heartily glad."

Nelson at the Biological Survey was more businesslike. His telegram to Shiras read, "Yesterday Supreme Court rendered decision sustaining constitutionality migratory bird act." By mail, he sent a copy of Holmes's written decision.

Holland sent Shiras editorials from the *New York World*, the *New York Sun*, and the *New York Herald*, all mentioning Shiras as the originator of the bill and congratulating him, Weeks, and AGPPA on the "long, hard uphill fight." Holland included a note, "although the AGPPA had not the slightest doubt as to the ultimate outcome of the Missouri case, it is very gratifying that the constitutionality of this law has been upheld . . . if this law is kept on the statute books and we can prevail upon Congress to appropriate sufficient funds for its rigid enforcement, I am convinced we will have waterfowl and shore bird shooting for all time to come."

The *American Game Protective and Propagation Association Bulletin*, the group's official publication, ran a portrait of Shiras under a headline "Conclusion of 15-Year Fight."

The article stated,

While many have worked to secure the passage of the law and deserve credit for what they have done, it seems fitting at this crowning moment of the success to call attention to the fact that the result would not have been possible except for the genius of George Shiras 3d . . . it all seems sensible and simple now and a part of the common knowledge like the telephone and wireless telegraphy, but no one had thought of such an idea before or sensed its potentialities. He had the vision of a Bell or Marconi.

On May 1, 1920, Shiras wrote to Grinnell telling him that he would be in New York City to attend a meeting of the American Association of Mammalogists. He would stay at the Wolcott, an elegant hotel on West Thirty-First Street, and he hoped that they could get together and discuss how, now that the law had been sustained, he might "put in written form the history of the whole affair."

He addressed Grinnell's praise regarding his own participation: "When I wrote to you from Ormond in acknowledgment of your telegram, I was on my way to Daytona and sent only a brief reply. On returning several hours later, I found your letter originally addressed to Washington and felt quite overcome by the generous and affectionate tribute contained therein. In fact, I value such a letter more than any I have received from any friend on any subject."

Early the next year, Grinnell organized a tribute to Shiras. He wrote letters to several organizations—the Audubon Society, the Camp-Fire Club of America, the Boone and Crockett Club, and the AGPPA—soliciting funds to present a gift to Shiras.

Grinnell bought a silver tea and coffee service, had it engraved with a note of thanks, and delivered it to Shiras's home in Washington—apparently with Fanny Shiras's knowledge.

On May 6, 1921, Shiras wrote a thank-you letter to all four clubs and described how on the previous evening, he came into the dining room, sat down to dinner and saw a beautiful silver tray holding the coffee. Fanny asked him to pour that evening. Apparently, this was her normal function at dinner.

Shiras recalled,

I inquired of Mrs. Shiras if she was in any way incapacitated. She answered by saying she was feeling quite well, in fact unusually happy and she hoped I would read the inscription on the tray. On doing this, I was quite overcome—for such a gift from such sources was most unexpected. After recovering somewhat, the reading of the letter accompanying the remembrance produced additional emotion.

I must disclaim any honor in this final achievement. For while furnishing the seed, it is those who tilled the soil and knew how to gather the crop that should receive the thanks of the sportsmen, nature lovers and agriculturists of our country . . . alongside the gift let me place the successful endeavors of your respective organizations, for otherwise this silver token could not have been awarded to one who, while unfurling the flag, did not wage the battle.

In a *Forest and Stream* editorial, Grinnell offered a more public thanks, so his readers would understand Shiras's contributions: "With characteristic breadth of vision, he saw the right moves to be made. And with his usual energy, he set about seeing to it that they were made.

"While it is true that no single man may claim all the credit for bringing about the beneficent change, yet to the leader—to him who raised the banner that many so hastened to follow—must be given the chief honor."

23 | YELLOWSTONE DAM FIGHT

ONE CLEAR LEGACY of Theodore Roosevelt was the establishment of several national parks, most notably Wind Cave and Crater Lake. He also declared Grand Canyon a national monument with the expectation that it too would gain park status.

But what was a national park? In the early twentieth century, there was no unified management, budget, or philosophy. Some parks were watched over by the army and other parks by political appointees.

Developers, agricultural and mining interests, and western politicians did not see the parks as untouchable, but more akin to national forests—which they did not much like either—with the multiple-use doctrine that allowed for grazing and water storage.

In 1918 Woodrow Wilson signed an executive order creating the US National Park Service to administrate and protect the fourteen parks and eighteen national monuments that had proliferated since the establishment of Yellowstone in 1872.

The first director of the Park Service was Stephen Mather—no relation to William Mather, president of Cleveland Cliffs—although he too was a wealthy industrialist, having made his money mining borax in the West. Stephen Mather was a preservationist and had campaigned for the new agency with that mission in mind. Run out of Interior rather than the Ag Department, the Park Service was to be a different type of agency than the Forest Service.

Mather immediately encouraged the formation of the National Parks Association, a lobbying group to rally conservation organizations and the public around the new agency and its mission. George Shiras was named a director and participated in the agency's first major battle against developers. It was an early but defining moment for the Park Service.

After the closing of the frontier, the West grew into a sparsely populated but settled region. The homestead acts opened land to settlement, and railroads reached remote locations and provided farmers and ranchers a means to get their livestock and other products to market.

As agriculture proliferated, the demand for irrigation became more intense, as did pressure on public lands to provide that water. Federal officials—including Theodore Roosevelt and Gifford Pinchot—were eager to help. Much of their justification for national forests was preservation of watersheds. Congress created the Bureau of Reclamation to help bring water to arid lands for agriculture, hydropower, and recreation. Rivers and watersheds all over the West were studied for their storage potential.

Agriculture interests in Idaho and Montana had been eyeing Yellowstone Lake and other watersheds within the park for some time. In 1920, Senator Tom Walsh of Montana collaborated with a group known as the Yellowstone Irrigation Association to propose building a twenty-five-foot earthen dam at Fishing Bridge or a short distance downriver from the outlet. It would store spring runoff, release it for use in summer, and open a million acres in Montana to irrigation.

In 1916 the government allowed the flooding of Hetch Hetchy Valley in Yosemite National Park to supplement the water supply for San Francisco.

That same year, a concrete and earthen dam was approved across the Snake River to create Jackson Lake Reservoir. Grand Teton National Park did not yet exist, but the project showed that the federal government—through the Bureau of Reclamation—was quite willing to push for impoundments in even the most scenic country.

Much of the reasoning for Hetch Hetchy stemmed from the earthquake of 1906 and the resulting fires that destroyed the city. San Francisco was still recovering and beginning to grow again. The inundation of Hetch

Hetchy—a stunning, scenic valley—had been a terrible blow to preservationists, including John Muir. They vowed to fight hard for Yellowstone Lake.

George Shiras had often been pragmatic, even forgiving, regarding development of pristine lands. He had witnessed the settlement of the Upper Peninsula—including the devastation of its mature pine and hardwood forests—and his feelings had largely been resignation and even approval in that the cutover lands benefited game species: deer, rabbits, and grouse. But he had also watched the loggers throw up temporary dams on rivers and creeks, constructing impoundments and swelling inland lakes with spring runoff, so they could later dynamite the dams and release giant floods to drive the logs down to Lakes Michigan and Superior. The torrents tore away banks, scoured riparian forests, washed several feet of sand and silt into the rivers, and damaged whole fisheries—including speckled coaster brook trout. The trout, which had been so abundant when the Shiras family first came north, were by 1920 reduced to scattered small remnants. Dams did ugly stuff, including turning beautiful wooded lakes into little more than bathtubs.

The Yellowstone dam would enlarge the lake, flood nine thousand acres of forest, inundate the white pelican rookery on Molly Island, drown the thermal features at West Thumb, and ruin all that wonderful moose habitat in the Yellowstone delta.

Shiras saw no reason the American people, the true owners of the park, should stand by and let such a violation happen. In this fight, he was clearly a preservationist. No park would be safe if Yellowstone were violated. It was important to establish the Park Service's mission to preserve the land and ecosystem for future generations.

Several newspapers and magazines—including the influential *Saturday Evening Post*—editorialized against the dam. George Bird Grinnell, who had fought hard for park designation years earlier, published an article from Shiras in the February 1921 issue of *Forest and Stream.*

In "The Yellowstone Dam: How It Would Affect the Scenery, Wild Life, and Public Usefulness of Yellowstone Lake and the Surrounding Country," Shiras cited his fifty years of experience in exploring and observing inland lakes from a "recreational and economic standpoint." The potential damage to Yellowstone Lake, he said, was beyond the public's comprehension, otherwise "it would be almost unanimously opposed."

He focused on the southeast bay, where the river delta was 3.5 miles wide and contained small lakes and ponds full of aquatic vegetation. It was critical habitat for moose, which by 1920 were spreading to other areas of the park. *Alces americanus shirasi* would become abundant in other Rocky Mountain states, he predicted, if the herd and habitat remained protected. Rising water behind a dam would drown those wetlands as well as cover sand beaches, coves, and islands. Thousands of trees would die, and at that altitude with its short summer, dead timber would stand for decades. Ill-smelling mudflats, bleached rock, and bathtub rings would greet tourists. The shoreline would not recover for hundreds of years. It was a bleak but not inaccurate picture. When Jackson Lake was drawn down in late summer and fall, a muddy moonscape of dead trees was revealed.

Shiras filed a legal brief against the dam with the US House of Representatives. He also testified in front of the Rules Committee arguing that a national park was a public trust over which the states had no rights—even if the park resided within its borders. Shiras, like many dam opponents, was incensed that Walsh's bill would grant Montana or organizations it would designate (mainly ranchers) the perpetual use of the dam site and overflow territory. Essentially, they would have control of the lake and leave the new Park Service impotent.

In the brief, "Yellowstone National Park Now in the Inalienable Possession of The Citizens of the United States," he pointed out that the park was created when Wyoming, Montana, and Idaho were territories, not states, and determined it was more like the District of Columbia: "Today it is regarded as the most scenic wonderland in the world . . . our people in a legal way, are joint tenants with the right of the survivorship in future generations. In a moral sense, at least, there had never been a more clearly developed public trust intended for perpetual use or in which the right of the public have been more clearly vested."

By early 1921, Walsh attempted to push a bill through Congress. He invited all the irrigators and dam proponents to testify at a hearing. Opponents were shut out. It was a public relations blunder because the tide against the dam—against any dam in a national park—was turning. The conservationists were winning in the court of public opinion.

Shiras wrote, "No plainer test of vested public rights against selfish private privileges could be imagined than this threated invasion."

In 1922, the bills for the dam were defeated. Then President Warren Harding established a policy that national parks would be maintained in "absolute, unimpaired form for the present and all time to come." He visited Yellowstone that summer and stated "commercialism will never be tolerated here so long as I have the power to prevent it." Harding died later on that trip in San Francisco of cerebral hemorrhage, but his successor, Calvin Coolidge, pledged to continue the policy.

The Park Service had overcome the precedent of Hetch Hetchy.

24 | KAIBAB PLATEAU

BY 1921 GEORGE Shiras had summered in the Upper Peninsula for more than fifty years. The rustic camp at Whitefish Lake where he and the guides once stored their coffeepot and cookware in a hollow log had morphed into a ten-room house. Shiras built a separate cabin for John Hammer, who assumed caretaker duties over the camp and hundreds of acres of surrounding land where the family timbered commercially and tapped up to three thousand trees to produce maple sugar for sale. The old walking trail from the railroad had turned into the Peter White Road, and George and his extended family reached the camp from Marquette by automobile in less than an hour.

For the August issue of *National Geographic* magazine that year, George produced a paean to the Upper Peninsula: its geology and geography, its wildlife, and his family's long history with the region. The article, "The Wildlife of Lake Superior, Past and Present," ran eighty pages with seventy illustrations.

Prior to the publishing of his big book, the magazine piece represented his accomplishments as a wildlife photographer, his feeling for the land and intimate knowledge of the region honed through exploration and close observation.

Camp of the Fiddling Cat, Whitefish Lake, circa 1920s. Courtesy of the John Hammer family.

The storytelling was anecdotal and the photographs intimate.

In one image, Jack La Pete—circa 1880s—stands in rumpled street clothes off to one side of a group of Ojibwa people posing in front of a bark wigwam on Presque Isle. Led by Chief Charles Kawbawgum, the stoic-looking band were the last Native Americans to live on the island before Peter White purchased the land and donated it to the city for a park. When Kawbawgum died of typhoid fever in 1902, he was buried in the park and a memorial erected.

Not far from the wigwam was the mouth of the Dead River, where Shiras and boyhood friends first camped and imagined that the Indian dog dragging away breakfast was a ferocious bear. He remarked how much had changed at that location in the ensuing decades: "The largest charcoal furnace in the world is now in operation on one side of the river, which is spanned by a steel bridge, and beyond is the largest concrete ore dock where leviathan freighters six or seven hundred feet long have replaced the birch bark canoe. A shore driveway with its multitude of automobiles occupies the sand beach which once registered the tracks of many wild animals."

He tells of hiking with La Pete and seeing Whitefish Lake for the first time, shooting his first deer, and camera hunting with Jake Brown and John Hammer.

There were night images of deer raiding the camp gardens. He set up camera traps and then flashlights without cameras to chase away the marauders, but the deer grew tame and accustomed to the noise and lights. Late at night, he recalled looking out the windows "to see shadowy figures moving about noiselessly."

In his mind, the true marauders at camp were predators. One winter image shows four dead gray wolves hanging by their hind feet from a horizontal pole. A pair of rawhide-and-wood snowshoes protrudes from a nearby snowdrift. Back in 1900, the picture had run in the *Detroit Journal* with the headline "Peter White Fighting Wolves on His Great Game Preserve."

There had been attempts to poison the wolves using strychnine and cyanide of potassium, but it wasn't until John Hammer hung poisoned hunks of meat on sticks thrust into the ice on the lake that they had success. A day or so later, Hammer and Charlie Anderson were on the lake, cutting blocks of ice to put in the icehouse, when they saw that "evidence of distress was plentiful." They dragged two bodies off the ice and followed the tracks into the woods where they found the wolves dead or finished them with a gun. Although war had been waged on gray wolves for many years—the bounty in 1921 ran thirty to fifty dollars per hide—Shiras ruefully noted that there were still wolves in the Upper Peninsula.

He admired their tenacity. On the other hand, he called them "distrustful, cunning, skulking in the shadows of the night intent upon rending to pieces any less powerful animal. . . . However much the other animals of the forest may stand in awe of them, man is ever their relentless and successful enemy and only by the exercise of all their high developed senses can they hope to escape the same miserable death they so ruthlessly inflict on their prey."

In the article, he also addresses human fear of wolves—taking another shot at the nature fakers as well as outdoor sporting publications of the day,

Poisoned gray wolves at Whitefish Lake, 1900. George Shiras 3d;
Courtesy of National Geographic Creative.

which so often depicted on their magazine covers a hunter facing down a
furious bear, cougar, or wolves: "Never in America have I been able to get
an authentic account of a man being deliberately pursued or injured by
wolf . . . on detecting the presence of a traveler in the woods it is not likely
to attack him in the flesh since it shrinks in terror whenever discovering
anything indicating human scent."

By this point in his journey as a faunal naturalist, Shiras was a skilled
observer, expert in the habits of the "forest folk" about the camp. Whitefish
Lake was his open-air laboratory in which he recorded nibbles on trees by
beavers, dusting depressions of grouse in the yard, nesting hawks in the
outbuildings, and the calls of owls and whippoorwills from the night woods.
Using entries from the camp journal and his camera diary and the

memories in his head, the article evoked a sense of place and emotional attachment.

Gilbert Grosvenor was immensely pleased: "The members of the Society I am confident will regard this as the most valuable and interesting of your contributions to the Magazine . . . I am frank to say that I regard this article as one of the most outstanding publications of the *National Geographic* magazine in recent years. It is the kind of article that as editor, I look back upon as it will have the most useful influence and helps to accomplish those altruistic and patriotic purposes for which the Society and magazine exists."

In his early sixties, Shiras's physical strength was not what it once was, and his big expedition days were behind him. Still, he was an experienced naturalist and able to get out in the field with his camera.

In 1923 the US Biological Survey asked him to investigate an unfolding wildlife disaster on the Kaibab Plateau in Arizona, where the population of mule deer had exploded in recent years. The situation had a profound impact on the science of game management and taught wildlife biologists hard lessons about maintaining a balance between predators and prey.

The Kaibab, about sixty by forty miles in extent, lies just to the north of the Grand Canyon. It is part of the Greater Colorado Plateau with an elevation between six and nine thousand feet. The Kaibab is mostly forested with extensive tracts of ponderosa pine and, at the higher elevations, blue Engelmann spruce and Douglas fir interspersed with clusters of quaking aspen. Although arid, the region receives monsoonal flows in late summer and fall and substantial snows in winter. It is like a landed island with natural barriers—the north rim of the Grand Canyon, the Colorado River, and high desert—that make the deer herd there relatively isolated and singular.

The Kaibab Plateau was set aside as a forest preserve in 1893 under President Benjamin Harrison. In 1906, Theodore Roosevelt created the Grand Canyon Game Preserve on the Kaibab to protect what he called the "finest deer herd in America."

When the Kaibab National Forest was created in 1908, and the Grand Canyon was protected as a national monument, there were an estimated four thousand deer in the herd. Sheep, cattle, and horses had overgrazed the plateau and eliminated most tall grasses. However, game managers believed if livestock grazing was reduced, hunting banned, and predators controlled, the carrying capacity of the range could be increased to thirty thousand mule deer.

Over the next thirty years, the Forest Service and Biological Survey killed 7,388 coyotes, 816 mountain lions, 500 bobcats, and 20 wolves. Using specially trained hounds, a game warden on the North Rim personally killed more than 400 lions. As a private citizen, Theodore Roosevelt came to the Kaibab in 1913 to hunt mountain lions and aid the cause.

In 1919 when Grand Canyon National Park was established, the Park Service supported the policy because it was important for tourists to see deer, turkey, and elk. Deer were especially popular because they were cute and, in the early twentieth century when game animals were diminished in much of the nation, many people were not accustomed to seeing a deer in the wild.

By the early 1920s, however, deer were everywhere and, with few predators left, the herd exploded to between eighty and one hundred thousand animals. Population and habitat surveys were still crude and inaccurate, but the Biological Survey and other federal authorities knew the animals outstripped the carrying capacity of the land. They just didn't know what to do about it—and they were hamstrung by ingrained ideas of game management, including protecting the good animals from the bad animals—or predators.

E. W. Nelson, then head of the Biological Survey, asked Shiras to make a report. John Hammer and Shiras set off for the Kaibab in September 1923. They arrived at Lund Station in Utah's Escalante Valley on the Union Pacific Railroad and then switched to a branch line to Cedar City, which the railroad opened that year to encourage travel to Zion National Park and the Grand Canyon. The men were met by an "assistant predatory animal inspector"—in other words, a hunter of varmints—from the Kaibab National Forest. He drove them in a touring car to the VT Ranch, about fifteen miles from the north rim of the Grand Canyon.

A private ranch with a lodge and cabins for visitors and "dudes," the VT was located at one end of De Motte Park, a sprawling narrow meadow, two miles wide and ten miles long. The VT was a favored stop for tourists because hundreds of mule deer emerged from the surrounding forest in the mornings and evenings to feed in the meadow and drink from water holes. The VT promoted itself as "The place where the deer meet the tourists."

De Motte Park is at an elevation of eight thousand feet surrounded by hills dark with spruce and fir. As their car climbed up to the ranch, Shiras admired several smaller meadows whose edges were ringed with the whitish trunks of quaking aspen. The contrast of their pale bark and the fluttering green leaves against the darker conifer forest was quite beautiful, he thought.

At the VT, however, he examined the forest edge and discovered why the aspens were so distinct. They were denuded of branches as high as deer could reach. There was no understory, no young trees. Seedlings, suckers, and root sprouts from existing aspens were devoured before they had a chance to grow, which is why those white trunks were so conspicuous. His black-and-white photographs from the trip plainly show the contrast.

In the following days, he saw more evidence of overbrowsing. The meadows were extraordinarily uniform, the grass cropped to a half-inch in height much like a golf course. When he joined the tourists that first evening to gawk at the hundreds of deer emerging on De Motte Park, he was reminded of livestock.

"The changed forage conditions here had forced the deer to become grazers instead of browsers," he wrote. "They fed with heads continually held down, just like a flock of sheep and so closely did they crop this vegetation that it never came to seed."

The next day he and Hammer explored along the forest edge to find locations for their camera traps. Shiras brought a chunk of rock salt for bait, but VT was a working ranch. Horses and cattle grazed the open range of the meadow and would crave salt as much as any wild animal. He didn't want livestock tripping his camera traps. Instead, they cut down a couple of aspen trees and hacked off leafed-out branches to use for bait.

They set up several cameras, attaching a strong but fine thread between a branch and the triggering mechanisms. They retreated from the meadow, but before they were back to the ranch, several does and fawns approached one of the camera sets. Through binoculars, Shiras observed the deer "acting like a pack of hungry dogs." Each one seized a branch and then ran a short distance away to consume the leaves and twigs by itself. Four big bucks came along, bearing large antlers in velvet. Immediately, the males chased the others away and began to fight among themselves. One took a short leap and caught a trip wire with his hoof. A blaze of light, a puff of white smoke, and then a resounding boom came across the meadow.

It was a rare and delightful event to see the camera trap in action. Shiras knew immediately he had captured something special. When he developed the plate back in Marquette, the negative showed an eight-point buck in full leap, head up, muscles tensed, and all four feet in the air. At the explosion, the bucks took flight, but to his astonishment, they ran only a short distance and, when the smoke cleared, approached the bait again. These were opportunistic deer, and they weren't leaving behind a rare meal of browse.

The men crossed the meadow again, drove the deer away, and reset the camera. Before they reached camp, there was another explosion. They heard two more flashlights go off while they were in the lodge having dinner.

Although the Kaibab deer seemed tame, they were not easily approached in the open. Daylight pictures proved impossible. Shiras and Hammer could get no closer than a few hundred yards before the deer went bouncing back to the forest for cover.

With no shortage of subjects, he fired all his flashlight cartridges in a few days. The images were some of his best of deer. Several images were exposed just before sunset, and the ambient light conveyed a sense of twilight, illuminated details of the forest, and provided a depth of field often missing from the nighttime shots in which the animals were rather flat and brightly lit against a black background. In Arizona, the flashlight acted mostly as fill and created a more naturalistic mood. Because the animals were jostling for the browse and frequently chasing one another, there is a dynamism and sense of motion, too.

From the VT Ranch, they made a day trip on a new road to the Colorado River. All brush cut by the construction workers had been eaten by the deer almost as soon as it was tossed into piles. Another day on the North Rim of the Grand Canyon, he noticed that a fenced-off area near the tourist cabins had mature grass and clover and scrub oaks full of acorns. Everywhere else, pickings were slim. Finally, he ran into cowboys rounding up cattle in the national forest. The drive was being made earlier each year, they said, because the forage was so sparse. The cattle would lose weight before market. One older hand remembered when grass in upland meadows was stirrup high, even in fall—but no more.

Evidence of an overpopulation of deer was everywhere, but what to do about it?

Shiras went back East and wrote his report: "My observations convinced me that this game refuge was dangerously overstocked, and that unless there was a prompt reduction in the number of deer, a progressive deterioration in the forage production would be followed by starvation on a large scale."

His solution was to allow hunting and cull the herd. Although other game managers had proposed revisiting the policy of predator removal, Shiras had not changed his beliefs regarding varmints. He clearly saw what was being done to the land and understood the herd was not functioning normally, but he did not quite make the connections to what had been a disastrous predator policy.

He wrote, "To me the idea of leaving surplus deer to become the prey of predatory animals or victims of starvation seems an unworthy means of solving such problems as had developed on the Kaibab."

His report spurred Henry Wallace, head of the Department of Agriculture, which oversaw the Forest Service, to appoint a commission of sportsmen and conservationists to make recommendations. The Kaibab Investigating Committee included John Burnham of the AGPPA, Heywood Cutting of the Boone and Crockett Club, and T. Gilbert Pearson of the National Audubon Societies—all professional associates of Shiras.

The committee went to the Kaibab in 1924 but could not agree on any quick solution.

They suggested capturing and shipping live animals to other locations, allowing limited hunting by sportsmen, and, as a last resort, culling the herd by the use of government hunters. But those recommendations could not be implemented quickly. The mandate of the Park Service was not to allow hunting on its lands, and the Forest Service took the position that it didn't have the legal right to cull the herd with government hunters, although it had no problem continuing its predator control program. Limited hunting by sportsman in 1924 removed just six hundred–some animals in the national forest, probably only one-tenth of the number of deer born that spring.

Nelson had been advocating more shooting, and he was very opposed to the Park Service's policy of no hunting. Writing to Charles Sheldon, he said, "The conditions are so bad from overgrazing that Goldman thinks there will be very heavy losses from starvation in the coming winter. This is a fine object lesson of the reckless futility of trying to carry on game con-servation by sentimentalists."

Nelson was pleased to learn that Mather had given up his opposition to shooting surplus deer in Grand Canyon National Park: "He evidently appreciates the arrival of an embarrassing situation. It is evident that the Kaibab affair will strengthen the hand of those advocating game adminis-tration and may result in preventing further interference in such cases by sentimentalists."

By the mid-1920s, the die-offs were dramatic. Perhaps as many as sixty thousand deer starved to death in 1925 and 1926. In 1930, the Park Ser-vice moved sixty fawns from the Kaibab to the South Rim to provide wildlife for the growing crowds taking the train up from the town of Williams. But with the lack of hunting and predators, the animals soon proliferated there and required supplemental feeding. The learning curve was long.

The deer problem on the Kaibab became a famous case study for mis-management and a controversial chapter in the history of the Forest Ser-vice in the Southwest. Aldo Leopold, who had graduated from Yale and was working those years as a forester in the Southwest, saw the Kaibab die-offs and began to question the agency's position on killing so-called vermin. Leopold was to become one of the most important voices in the conserva-tion movement in coming decades.

Conservationists were learning the hard lessons of systems ecology—that a missing component can have a profound effect. The reluctance to reverse thinking about predators and take a more holistic approach isn't surprising, considering how ingrained the idea of good animals and bad animals was at the time.

When he got back to Michigan and began working on his report that winter, Shiras thought about the effect the deer were having on the small critters of the Kaibab Forest—the birds, the squirrels, and even the grubs, worms, and ants. He remembered how there were few grouse and wood-land birds on Grand Island and Isle Royale—other places where he had watched populations of ruminants thrive and then crash: "When one real-izes what effect the absence of ground vegetation or of saplings, bushes bearing buds, berries and seeds, has on the food supply and shelter of many birds and animals, it is not strange that they have deserted such places."

In his subsequent writings on the Kaibab, Shiras almost sounded like an ecologist: "When the equilibrium maintained by nature is thrown out of balance, it disrupts a system of interdependence based upon centuries of mutual adjustment. This must be recognized if we are to get at the foundation of many problems now confronting the zoologist or game conservationist."

As he was writing his report, Shiras went out to Whitefish Lake and did a bit of hunting with the gun. He still liked to shoot—ducks and grouse mostly—but deer, too, if he stayed long enough into fall for deer season. When he brought home game, Fanny joked that he was "backsliding."

Although George Junior was ninety years old that summer, he came to Marquette and made his last trip out to Whitefish Lake. For the previous ten years, he lived in Pittsburgh with Winfield, who was still practicing law at the old firm. A male nurse attended him for many of those years and reported that Junior was unhappy with Prohibition. He had to depend on his doctor to prescribe the glass of rye whiskey he habitually drank just before dinner and bed each evening. Any other medicine he was apt to throw out the nearest window.

Mentally, he was still quite sharp. However, when he went back to Pittsburgh that autumn, he fell at Winfield's home and fractured his hip. In the hospital, he caught pneumonia, fell into a coma, and lingered for two days with his sons at his bedside.

Toward the end, during a moment of semiconsciousness, he asked, "What is it doing outside? Which way is the wind?"

In the biography he wrote of his father, George 3d mused about all the changes Junior had seen, having been born in the stagecoach-and-canal era and finished up being ferried about in automobiles in a Pittsburgh transformed by steel and the blast furnace. Up in Michigan, he had seen Marquette, a rough-hewn village, turn into a busy and prosperous town. He had experienced the virgin forest of the Upper Peninsula and then watched steam barges tow millions of feet of lumber down the lake in the annihilation of the pine and hardwood forests. There had been the advent of telegraphy, railroads, motion pictures, photography, wireless communication, airplanes, and telephones.

George 3d wrote,

There is a curious fascination as to what goes on in the mind of a very old man who sits looking at a view and gazing with what seems to be rapt attention into the distance. For instance, what went on in Shiras's mind as he sat on his back veranda in Marquette, looking out through a frame of birch trees at the beautiful blue bay that is a part of Lake Superior? Did he actually see the moving ships, the flashing gulls, the ruffled water, the stirring leaves? . . . There was much for him to remember at ninety as he sat rocking and watching the ore boats loading in Marquette harbor with raw ore to feed the furnaces and steel mills in his native Pittsburgh a thousand miles away.

In his obituary in the *Marquette Mining Journal*, Frank Russell wrote that Junior's outdoor life on Lake Superior and the summers spent in Marquette benefited his health. "There was hardly a bay or point on Lake Superior, on either shore where he has not cast a fly or sometimes camped for weeks in the sixty-five years he visited this region. Retirement from the bench doubtless had much to do with his reaching such an unusual age."

25 | FINAL BIRD BATTLES

IN THE NORTH *American Review* in July 1928, John Burnham wrote an essay titled "Conservation's Debt to Sportsmen":

> I am writing to disabuse the mind of those who still hold to the colonial New England view that a sportsman is a man too lazy to work and not smart enough to steal; also that other set of good people who believe the Victorian idea of old Webster's dictionaries that sportsmen are jockey or gangster types skilled in field sports, also of a later day who class them as bloodthirsty assassins of wildlife. None of these classifications will fit George Bird Grinnell, William Dutcher, George Shiras, Theodore Roosevelt, men who have worked to save wildlife and wild nature in this country.

The article was a response to William T. Hornaday and others who had fomented several years of bitter infighting among the coalition—hunters, scientists, museums, birdwatchers, fishermen, naturalists, foresters, state game managers, businesses, and congressmen—that had come together earlier in the century to save waterfowl and migratory birds. Burnham's essay, defending the leaders of the American Game Protective and

Propagation Association and hunters in general, served as a kind of coda for the Progressive Era of conservation.

By the late 1920s, it was over.

Disputes in those years revolved around the politics of the Advisory Board on Migratory Birds, the policies of the US Biological Survey, and the best ways to protect waterfowl and rebuild their populations. In other words, where do we go from here?

E. W. Nelson, who had become chief of the Biological Survey in 1918, believed that waterfowl populations—mainly ducks and geese—could sustain harvest by hunters. After approval of the Migratory Bird Treaty, the agency set a bag limit of twenty-five ducks and eight geese per day during the hunting seasons. The greatest threat came not from hunting, said Nelson, but the draining and filling of wetlands and the lack of wildlife refuges to provide breeding habitat.

Hornaday, always distrustful of hunting interests, was aghast at the bag limits. He feared a growing army of "gunners" with new automatic and pump guns and the capability to reach shooting grounds by automobile. His evidence regarding declining populations was largely anecdotal—he often cited a train journey he took across the northern tier in which he saw only a handful of ducks in the prairie potholes—but his convictions were firm and confidence in his own opinion was unassailable. He wanted less killing by sportsmen and called for a reduction in bag limits. Nelson, who had just twenty-four federal wardens nationwide, didn't believe he could enforce a reduction but noted that states could lower bag limits within their boundaries. Many did so.

In 1922 Hornaday proposed to fellow members of the Advisory Board on Migratory Birds that bag limits and hunting seasons be reduced by 50 percent. When it was rejected by a vote of sixteen to two, the zookeeper resigned, feeling he had been treated with contempt. His old nemesis John Burnham and most other members—including Shiras—were under the influence of gun and ammo makers, he said. The AGPPA, too, was just a front for the "gunners."

Others in the conservation community agreed, but no one had the credentials, fame, and zealotry to launch a personal crusade. Hornaday, with access to wealthy donors, formed the Permanent Wildlife Protection Fund—essentially an organization of one—that enabled him to lobby, travel, and speak. He also wielded a poison pen in letters to other conservationists and the newspapers. He criticized the AGPPA relentlessly and was especially angry at T. Gilbert Pearson, the head of the Audubon Societies, who had "sided with the gunners." He frequently referred to "the Burnham-Nelson-Pearson combine" as being in cahoots against him.

Nelson was of the opinion that Hornaday was not getting anywhere. The secretary of the Ag Department was ignoring him.

Nelson wrote to Charles Sheldon from the Cosmos Club in September 1924, "I do not think we need worry over Hornaday's campaign. So far as I can size up he has made his big explosion and the thing will die down. . . . The Sporting magazines are fracturing and in fact they hardly mention it so I can't see what he is accomplishing."

Shiras wrote to Hornaday asking that he consider rejoining the advisory board: "I'm afraid that you are disposed to split away from the only set of men who have game protection at heart."

Hornaday scoffed, "If I cannot find in Washington and in the Department of Agriculture, men who feel keenly about the better preservation of wildlife, who have courage for meeting the crisis of the hour, and are willing to take occasionally a sporting chance, then I must look elsewhere for colleagues and allies who will do those things."

What exacerbated the situation was the introduction in Congress of a Game Refuge and Public Shooting Grounds Bill that would create more sanctuaries but allow for public shooting. Hunters would be required to purchase a one-dollar federal hunting license, which would function as the funding mechanism to purchase or lease additional habitat.

Burnham and Nelson drafted the legislation. Refuges previously set aside by Roosevelt and subsequent presidents were relatively small and inadequate. The US Treasury alone could not generate enough cash for land acquisition, and Congress couldn't be depended upon to fund what was needed, they said. Sportsmen could provide the money.

Allowing hunting on new refuges immediately raised suspicion and derision from opponents. Why set up refuges for wildlife and then allow killing? Some congressmen objected to the precedent of a federal hunting license; western legislators saw it as another land grab by elitist eastern sportsmen. To Hornaday, it was evidence the AGPPA, advisory board, and Biological Survey were doing the bidding of the gun and ammunition manufacturers. It was true that the money to finance lobbying and publicity efforts came from the manufacturers.

A compromise was suggested to strip hunting from the refuge bill, but Burnham disagreed vehemently. AGPPA believed in the notion of public hunting grounds. In the past, sportsmen had to be wealthy to join duck and hunting clubs—such as Revel Island—that controlled vast areas. Public refuges would provide opportunities for poorer people. Game could be managed and propagated to restore populations and create a surplus for hunting. There was no conflict between controlled hunting and wildlife propagation, he said.

In his *North American Review* essay, Burnham wrote, "We are now in the constructive era. We have learned the fundamentals of game administration, and we know how to put our experience to practical use."

As a director in AGPPA, Shiras organized a meeting in New York City of publishers of the leading sporting journals—*American Shooter, Field and Stream, Forest and Stream, Outdoor Life,* and *Sportsmen's Review*—where he proposed a "More Game" movement. Readers would pay a marginally greater price for their annual subscription, say from $1 per year to $1.50, and the difference would be donated to the causes of game management. Eventually this proposal through the 1920s raised some $1 million. Its aims included "the divorcement of politics from the administration of game laws" and "the establishment of sanctuaries in every community where birds may breed undisturbed."

During the 1920s, Shiras lent his name and expertise to a number of organizations. He was named honorary vice president of the Quetico-Superior Council, which urged Minnesota to purchase a million acres of cutover lands from bankrupt farmers in the northeast part of the state, reforest the area, and create a vast public shooting ground. Attempts to drain lakes and marshes in the region failed, and the region eventually became part of Boundary Waters Canoe Area—the premier wilderness in the Midwest.

In 1924 Shiras also served on the executive committee of the National Conference on Outdoor Recreation called by President Calvin Coolidge that brought together three hundred representatives of 128 conservation organizations. Coolidge's charge was to come up with a national policy on recreation and address the growing population of the country and its increased mobility by automobile. The standing committee on wildlife, on which Shiras served, heartily endorsed the concept of public shooting grounds with the statement, "The present Game Refuge bill is too vital to the welfare of the country to have it obstructed by good intentions based on a lack of understanding of it."

The Game Refuge and Public Shooting Grounds Bill lost in the House of Representatives, a defeat orchestrated by the infamous Frank Mondell of Wyoming who, having lost his Senate seat, got himself back into Congress by winning the state's only House seat. A bill Hornaday championed to decrease bag limits and shooting also failed.

Both sides wanted to reintroduce their bills. To assuage Hornaday, Nelson agreed to survey game officials and wardens in the various states and come up with baseline numerical evidence on populations. The sciences of sampling and wildlife management were still new.

In 1925 Nelson announced the result of the survey and concluded—much to Hornaday's dismay and prediction—that the bag limits were reasonable, that wildlife was in fact increasing, but that progress would not continue unless more refuges were created. Nelson had much invested in the refuge bill, which promised his department funding, power, and autonomy from Congress.

Hornaday wrote Nelson, "You remind me of the fireman who refused to save a rich man's house, saying, 'He's got plenty more houses. The loss of this one won't ruin him. Let her burn!'"

Nelson's feeling about Hornaday was summed up in a letter he wrote to Charles Sheldon:

> It appears to me to be almost unbelievable that any man having conservation at heart should take the course Hornaday is pursuing. There is not a single fact indicating any emergency which demands immediate action in the reduction of bag limits. The entire matter is being worked about Hornaday. If he had his way it would destroy all sensible methods of handling conservation and would reduce it to an arbitrary dictatorship by Hornaday . . . I regret very much that our efforts to placate Hornaday and get him to work with us have failed so completely.

Headlines in the *New York Herald Tribune* on June 4, 1926, declared "Gun

Factories Back Bird Bill. Utah Senator Declares Biological Survey Tool of Manufacturers. Contends Aim Is to Establish Hunting Grounds Instead of Preserves. Supports Hornaday's View."

In the article, Hornaday is quoted saying the Biological Survey was in the grips of "the manufacturers of shotguns and shotgun shells . . . the proposed refuges for birds are not to be bird sanctuaries or sanctuaries for game in the proper sense, but, in fact, to be public shooting grounds where birds and game will be destroyed without limit."

Hornaday and his congressional allies got hold of internal memos and letters of AGPPA, showing there was pressure from the gun companies. Burnham in his correspondence to the gun companies had complained about the "sentimentalists" who were opposed to hunting.

Hornaday and his allies raised a ruckus at the annual meeting of the Audubon Clubs. Many club members couldn't understand why T. Gilbert Pearson defended hunting. In response, he said sportsmen and organizations like the AGPPA had been critical to passing of the bird act. As for the banning of hunting—that was utopian. He was dealing with the world as it existed.

The fight got personal. Hornaday's rhetoric became so shrill, sarcastic, and reckless that the trustees at the New York Zoological Park warned him to tone it down. His attacks on T. Gilbert Pearson were upsetting to Frank Chapman and people in leading museums. Hornaday, however, didn't respond well to criticism. His cause was righteous.

Through the years, Shiras had a ringside seat. He knew all the fighters and congressional leaders, too. Although he was never close to Hornaday, the zoo director had praised both his advocacy and his photography. Shiras was especially pleased with a magazine piece Hornaday had written called, "Masterpieces of Wild Animal Photography." In a letter written to Hornaday from Marquette, in which Shiras suggested they sit down and talk about some "game conservation matters," he said, "I want to thank you for the kind manner in which you refer to my particular work."

In their discussions, he tried to reason with Hornaday, but when the zoo director testified at a Senate hearing and attacked Burnham and the advisory board—calling them "sordid"—Shiras wrote a long, angry letter to the committee.

He zeroed in on what many people felt about Hornaday—the man was full of himself. "While Dr. Hornaday is to be praised for much of his earlier work in game conservation, as he has grown older he has shown a marked disposition to discredit every conservation measure in which he is not the leader. . . . To continually reiterate the charge that Mr. Burnham, the chairman of this board, controlled the vote or action of the other members of this board is a most unworthy accusation but is in line with Dr. Hornaday's belief that no one can be trusted but himself."

In the end, it was a standoff.

The refuge bill never passed, and Hornaday did not get his bag limits. After years of bitter debate and bad publicity, the gun and ammo companies pulled funding from AGPPA. Burnham left the organization in 1927. Nelson resigned as chief of the Biological Survey the same year. Hornaday retired from the zoo in 1926, to the relief of trustees who had tired of his hyperbole and rhetoric. Burnham sued Hornaday for his public remarks and won a libel suit in March 1928. In 1931 Hornaday published a book whose title reflected his blamelessness and bitterness: *Thirty Years' War for Wildlife: Gains and Losses in the Thankless Task.*

After the main combatants—and their egos—were out of the way, compromises were possible. In 1928, the Biological Survey reduced the bag limit to fifteen ducks and four geese per day. The following year, Congress passed the Migratory Bird Conservation Act, which called for new refuges without hunting or licensing fees. But the stock market crash in 1929 and the resulting Great Depression left the country bereft of money for birds.

In 1934 the Federal Duck Stamp program—essentially AGPPA's idea of a federal waterfowl license—was signed into law by Franklin Roosevelt. Falling land prices during the Depression enabled the government to buy up habitat and create a system of national wildlife refuges with money from sportsmen. Hunting became a management tool on refuges, and wildlife management itself grew into a scientific discipline to be practiced by trained professionals.

The American Game Protective and Propagation Association faded from the scene and was absorbed by the American Wildlife Institute, and the era of Progressive conservation was over. Important work had been done and there was legacy to record. In 1927 Shiras published his final pamphlet, *History of the First Migratory Bird Bill and Its Subsequent Enactment.*

26 | THE BIG BOOK

WHEN HE TURNED seventy years old, Shiras started work on his big book, which he initially foresaw as a three-volume set. It was a task he could put off no longer. Despite his father's longevity, George assumed the bullet could not be far off for him.

He gifted his photographic collection to the National Geographic Society. He had discussed it with Gilbert Grosvenor but to make it official, he addressed a letter in November 1928 "giving all my best wild life negatives, covering a period of half a century and totaling a thousand or more scenes in the wilderness.

"The original flashlight negatives were the first of their kind and therefore have an historic interest apart from any other value. In case the Society accepts this gift. it might be understood that scientific societies, government bureaus, and naturalists and sportsmen of good standing be permitted to make limited use of this material in accordance with regulations made by the Society."

Two days later, Grosvenor accepted the gift and put on record the society's promise to carefully index the negatives, store them in fireproof safes, and make them available for "future generations desiring to study natural life as it was in its original wilderness."

I take this opportunity to convey to you once more what I have and the other members of the staff have inadequately expressed, namely, our deep gratitude to you for your devotion to the work and interests of the National Geographic Society, which has continued unswerving for twenty-three years. The first collection of pictures which you gave this Society enabling it to print that historic number, *Photographing Wild Game with Flashlight and Camera,* in 1906 started the organization on a path of usefulness in the promotion of public interest in natural and scenic and wild-life resources of the United States that has brought the Society much credit and greatly assisted these worthy interests.

Taking its title from his 1906 article, his "big book" would include hundreds of images published in *National Geographic* and a compilation of his eight magazine articles. Much of the text would run verbatim but required transitions between chapters and insertions of new material to update information. He would include a few new chapters to give historical perspective to his work and weave in anecdotes about his friendships with Theodore Roosevelt, Frank Chapman, Charles Sheldon, John Burnham, and E. W. Nelson. He would reminisce about his years of observing and photographing at Whitefish Lake, the Upper Peninsula, and Ormond Beach. And he would authenticate his legacy as an early conservationist, recounting his legal work for the Migratory Bird Act, his service in Congress, and his long tenure as a trustee for the National Geographic Society and the AGPPA.

Hunting Wild Life with Camera and Flashlight: A Record of Sixty-Five Years' Visits to the Woods and Waters of North America would be his definitive opus and realization of his life's work.

There was writing to do, of course, but the initial and daunting task was to sort and catalogue his wildlife negatives and images—and to biologically classify the animals depicted.

It was a task he could not do alone—or at least, felt he could not do alone despite his reputation as an expert faunal naturalist. Perhaps he just wanted encouragement and company. And there was his health. He was ailing, apparently with rheumatism, arthritis, stomach problems, and a radium burn to the ear, which caused him pain and kept him awake at night. His ear problems went back as early as 1923. Exactly what happened with his ear is unknown, but doctors were known at that time to use beads of radium to shrink tumors or kill tissue. It was an early and crude form of radiation therapy that sometimes went awry.

He hired E. W. Nelson to help him sort his negatives, edit the narrative for scientific accuracy, and choose images to run in the book. The images alone would run to nine hundred.

Nelson was in his late seventies. He had retired to a ranch in California but still spent time in Washington to work on projects. Shiras handwrote a contract anticipating about twelve to eighteen months' work to be done in Washington, Ormond Beach, and Marquette: "My Dear Nelson, Judging from the present situation, I think you shall receive a minimum of $8,000 and a maximum of about $10,000 in the revision work you are doing for me, provided you are able to complete it."

By then Nelson had already written a foreword to the book in which he gave a biographical overview of the Shiras clan, their sojourns and integration into Michigan's Upper Peninsula, and George's evolution from a gun to a camera hunter. He set out all of Shiras's photographic firsts:

1) the first to photograph in daytime wild animals or birds from a canoe or blind 2) the first to get automatic daylight pictures of wild animals by touching a string across a trail or pulling a bait attached to a string operating the shutter of the camera 3) the first to operate a camera at a distance by a string running from a blind 4) the first to invent a means for picturing animals from a canoe by a hand flashlight 5) the first to invent a means to obtain automatic flashlight photographs for which the animals or birds fired the flash 6) the first to use two flashlights and two cameras, one set picturing the animal when quiescent and the other set, a second later, showing the animal in action when alarmed by the explosion of the first flashlight 7) The first to practice wing shooting with camera by means of a specially devised apparatus by which wild fowl and shore birds can be photographed when flying from fifty to seventy-five miles an hour.

The foreword ran nearly seven thousand words or eleven pages, but for a book that would total nine hundred pages and two hundred thousand words, it was not so long.

Grosvenor approved. In July 1929, he wrote to Shiras in Marquette: "Dr. Nelson came out to the house last evening and we discussed at considerable length your plans for the publication of your material. I think you have been very wise to engage Dr. Nelson to cooperate with you. No one else has his unique experience . . . I have read Dr. Nelson's foreword and I think it is excellent."

Several months later, Shiras and Nelson delivered 155 wooden boxes containing 2,054 glass negatives and 349 film negatives. The catalogue included the geographic location, date, and subject of each image.

Nelson sat down at the Cosmos Club, where he did much of his correspondence, and wrote directions to the photographic division. It was to print four copies of each negative. One set would enable the naturalists to winnow down the collection to about two thousand images, which would then become the property of the National Geographic Society: "I trust the entire set of prints will be made early in April so I can get Shiras to work with me in preparing the final catalog—which you appreciate as I do is essential to give the negatives their full value."

The following year, Nelson spent weeks with Shiras in Ormond Beach and nearly a month in Marquette during the summer. He had been a guest at the Florida home before, but only for a short time. Now there was much work to be done. He was there during that year's national census, which counted him as a guest. It also recorded, in addition to George and Fanny, two servants: Daisy Shelton, a cook, and Louisa Brown, a maid, who worked for the family in DC and wintered with them in Florida.

Shiras and Nelson focused on completing volume 1—subtitled *The Lake Superior Region*—that would cover his years in the Upper Peninsula and Canada. Shiras described his pioneering camera work and filled the pages with his most iconic flashlight images—in particular, the *Midnight Series*.

They delivered volume 1 at the end of that year but received little feedback from the staff at the Geographic. Shiras wrote to Nelson on December 11 wondering if "we had somehow offended Gilbert Grosvenor or overwhelmed him" with thousands of prints and requests for galleys and proofs.

Concurrently, Shiras submitted for publication a magazine article covering trips to photograph ducks and shorebirds in the wetlands of the Atlantic and Gulf Coasts. The trips were not recent, the story was lengthy

Wing-shooting ducks in Louisiana marshes, circa 1920s. George Shiras 3d; Courtesy of National Geographic Creative.

and rambling, and many images weren't that spectacular—at least, as compared to his previous work and what was possible with daylight photography in the 1930s. The staff passed the article between editors and sent it back to Shiras for revisions. He thought they were dawdling.

He wrote Ralph Graves, an assistant editor, "I trust the article is now in shape so that with any necessary editing in your office, it can be printed in one of the fall numbers of the magazine. It is now more than eight years since I have had an article in the magazine, and I would like to see it out of the way, so that with my remaining strength I can work on the book."

Shiras was not in good shape and had been unable to go into the office to see Grosvenor personally. He asked Grosvenor to come and see him. Twice the editor promised to do so but then begged off, claiming he was too busy.

Mystified by Grosvenor's seeming disinterest or neglect, Shiras finally wrote a letter wondering what was the matter.

Grosvenor went to Wesley Heights the very next afternoon, apologetic, not realizing his absence had caused Shiras such anxiety. Over lunch, he listened to Shiras's passionate pleas to move the work along on both the book and the pending article.

Shiras related the conversation to Nelson: "I spoke an hour or so going over the situation, describing the value and usefulness of the wild life negatives at some length, and he seemed much impressed."

The editor assured him the work would be done, that the book was a noteworthy project, and that Shiras and Nelson should proceed with volume 2, with the subtitle of *Wild Life of Coasts, Islands and Mountains*. It would cover all his expeditions outside of the north woods as well as his efforts on conservation issues. Grosvenor would order halftone engravings and edit the magazine piece himself.

Shiras's physical condition, especially the pain in his ear, had been hard on him mentally.

He told Nelson, "The increased pain interferes with much rest at night and I hope that something can be done to relieve it."

He was set to go to Johns Hopkins Hospital in Baltimore for what he deemed a small operation, but obviously he was worried. There were economic anxieties, too. The stock market crash the year earlier had hurt his investments. Then Nelson presented him with a bill for his services—nearly $12,000. It exceeded what Shiras thought they had agreed upon. Worse, he did not have the cash.

In a letter written to Nelson on New Year's Day 1931, Shiras said he could send only $1,000; otherwise he would have to borrow money. He expressed surprise at "your shifting the nature of our previous agreement." He presented a long analysis of the work the two men had done over the past year and concluded he was being overcharged.

Of the nineteen months of billing, there were five months where no work was done when Nelson was hospitalized for heart problems, took vacations, returned to his ranch in California, or worked on other projects, Shiras recounted. Even when they were together, the pace was hardly torrid:

Take, for example, the two months spent in Marquette. There we
had a late breakfast; then you often worked about three hours in
the morning and in the afternoon, a nap was in order and then an

automobile ride and none in the evening as I recall it. For these two
months, I am charged $1,250 and the total outlay of $1,700. In the
two summers in Marquette and the two winters in Florida, the work
was about the same. However, I told you that I not only wanted to
be just, but to be liberal and to this end, I have given you credit for
fourteen months on the basis of seven hours a day.

The letter went on for several pages. What is clear is that Shiras wanted
to pay a lump sum of about $10,000 and forget about a counting of hours.

Apparently, neither man kept good records of their time together—
Shiras because he felt he did not have to and Nelson because, perhaps,
he never imagined his veracity would be questioned.

Shiras concluded with, "Now I don't want the above analysis to hurt your
feelings because in the absence of records you didn't fully realize that the
shift of the contract rate would result in a disproportionate consideration.
. . . I want you to know that I appreciate our long and pleasant friendship
and your great aid at a critical time."

The operation at Johns Hopkins was delayed because Shiras had a head
cold. Grosvenor took the train over to Baltimore and visited him in the
hospital, where Shiras related the compensation debacle and the editorial
disagreements he and Nelson had over volume 1—particularly the classification of some animals. Shiras wanted to separate rabbits and hares from
the rodent family but Nelson "vigorously objected." He also wanted to
group muskrats with beavers and Nelson was against that, too. As one of
the country's leading biologists, Nelson was known to be headstrong and,
at that time, distinctions between groups were still up for debate in the
biological community.

Afterward, Shiras felt some remorse for his remarks to Grosvenor and,
in case he did not survive the operation, he did not want this criticism to
be the last word on his old friend. Grosvenor would need Nelson to finish
the work if Shiras died.

He wrote to Grosvenor from Johns Hopkins with Fanny taking dictation:

I regard him as one of the greatest of our living naturalists, for he
has had fifty-five years of experience in the field . . . we have been
associated more or less for twenty-five years and today he has a better

knowledge of my experiences and my materials than any other man. He examined all my wild life negatives and properly grouped them and is familiar with all the pictures made from these negatives as well as those that should be enlarged. . . . We must primarily depend on Dr. Nelson's assistance for I know he is most anxious to make this an outstanding work of the period and while differences may arise over some of the minor details the task would be a hopeless one if turned over to strangers.

While Shiras convalesced back home in Washington, a letter arrived from Nelson. He had been sick himself and hospitalized for a month with influenza. The three-and-a-half-page handwritten letter of dense cursive defended his billing and provided line after line of detail regarding the work done: "For the last year, I have been so desirous to get the work done both for your sake and in order that I might be free to get at my own that it put me in a more worse condition than I have felt in years. It has been with reluctance that I felt it necessary to give the foregoing detailed statements."

Shiras responded with a few rejoinders but grudgingly acquiesced. He sent a check for the unpaid balance to "clear up the situation" and asked Nelson to join him in Florida to get on with the work. He packed all his materials for volume 2. "I shall try to hold out the best I can but can't do much in your absence."

Several of his Marquette relatives were already at Ormond Beach and reported the hotel was only half filled due to "the financial anxiety and the deepening recession."

At the *National Geographic*, Grosvenor wrote a memo to Franklin Fisher, chief of the Illustrations Division, and told him to send the photographs for Shiras's magazine article to the engravers, although he added, "it will be a difficult task, as some of these photographs are inferior to Mr. Shiras' usual standard."

He added a paragraph regarding Shiras's health: "I spent a good part of yesterday afternoon with Mr. Shiras. He is in a terribly depressed condition and greatly weakened, being obliged to spend twenty hours of the twenty-four in bed. I'm afraid he will not be with us much longer."

Fisher read the article and told Grosvenor "it was hardly suitable for a *Geographic* article unless considerably abridged."

Much of the natural history and geography had been reported by other writers. The magazine, for example, had covered the Great Flood of 1927 on the Mississippi River. Yet the article was salvageable, Fisher noted, and could run as a memoir of a great naturalist. "Much of Mr. Shiras's story is reminiscent and for that reason is interesting . . . I feel that his story would hold the attention of many people but duck hunters most of all . . . there's a vast army of the public interested in wild life and most of them are members of N.G.S."

Fisher sent proofs of the images to Shiras so he could write the legends. Shiras's response shows how aware he was of the skimming habits of *Geographic* readers, many of whom looked at the pictures but did not read the text. The legends and titles, therefore, needed to tell a story on their own, he said: "The preparation of the titles and legends is difficult but important. They must be readable and wholly accurate. Every member examines the pictures closely, even if a good many do not read all the text. Any error therefore in a legend sticks out like a sore toe."

Nelson did not rejoin Shiras until later in the spring in Washington. Shiras was physically weak but eager to get through the manuscript. He fashioned another contract, this time more specific on hours and covering only twenty-six days. Neither old friend wanted another financial disagreement.

Grosvenor had been looking over volume 1 and was having second opinions about Nelson's involvement. Shiras leaned too much on Nelson's advice and gave undeserved deference to his editing of the manuscript. Some of the prose read like a government report. Nelson was editing prose already published in the magazine, which Grosvenor saw as unnecessary and presumptuous.

Shiras thought he might die before volume 2 was complete and fretted the society could lose money on the project. He told Grosvenor he did not want royalties on the books and would insure the society against any financial loss—a commitment binding to his heirs and estate.

He also suggested before publication that the work be submitted to an independent, disinterested, but experienced committee made up of "a leading mammalogist, ornithologist, a general authority on natural history and some leader or author representing the sportsmen of the country . . . unless such a committee with practical unanimity finds that the work submitted is of an outstanding character and that it is interesting, informative and of an apparent permanent value, I certainly think that you should not publish the work."

Then he underlined, "I have always wanted to be regarded as a benefactor of the society instead of a liability."

Grosvenor, however, was enthusiastic about the books, certain they would be a hit with the membership. In a letter, he again reminded Shiras how much he had done for the National Geographic Society over the years and how valuable photography had become to the magazine: "This generous offer on your part accords with your similar generosity to the Society extending back to your first donation in 1906 of the extensive series of selections from your collection of photographs. As I have stated many times to you, the Society is under lasting obligations for the great contributions which you gave the Magazine at a time when other periodicals were offering you bigger prices for your unique and priceless material."

Grosvenor set a price of five dollars for the two volumes, which would guarantee sales of twenty-five hundred copies to the nation's libraries alone. Pages would be laid out in "Geographic style" with the text in double columns. Legends would accompany each picture.

Finally, he gives a warning regarding Nelson's editing: "You have a charming style which exactly suits your purpose. My advice is to let Dr. Nelson pass on the accuracy of your observations, but don't let him take liberties with your methods of expression. Your command and use of English is unusual; hold to it."

Then he added a personal note, likely due to Shiras's allusions to death: "Your friendship has always been an inspiration to me and I value it as one of my most cherished acquisitions. You gave help, encouragement, and sound advice when I was just beginning. I can never forget it."

Grosvenor left for his summer home in Nova Scotia taking the magazine article with him for editing. "In the past, I have personally prepared your articles for the magazine and I wish to continue this pleasant privilege."

The article ran September 1932 with the title "Wild Life of the Atlantic and Gulf Coasts: A Field Naturalist's Photographic Record of Nearly Half a Century of Fruitful Exploration." The piece proved popular and, in the succeeding weeks, Shiras and the magazine received scores of letters from readers and hunters.

By 1932 Shiras was back in Washington and getting closer to a final revision of volume 2. Nelson, who had heart problems, was hospitalized in California and could not come back to Washington until fall. Shiras worked alone and in a letter to Grosvenor on June 23, took satisfaction in his progress: "I have done this work better than in putting any of the responsibility elsewhere."

Grosvenor responded, "I have the highest respect for Dr. Nelson's scientific ability, not so high an estimate of his editorial ability. You possess an unusual literary gift. Everything you write breathes of the woods and the natural surroundings which you love so much and to which you have devoted much of your life. When you rely too much on Dr. Nelson's guidance, much of the freshness and popular appeal of your manuscript disappears."

The manuscripts were complete, but the books would not be published for another three years. During that time, scores of letters, memoranda, and telephone conversations passed between Shiras, Grosvenor, and other editors as they went through the laborious tasks of editing, rewriting, proofing, discussing—and debating—the contents of the books. It was exacting work, and sometimes aggravatingly slow, especially when Shiras and Grosvenor were not in Washington. Then the galleys and proofs had to be prepared for shipment, and days were lost waiting for the mails.

Incredibly, Shiras's health improved and he did revisions with the help of stenographers hired in different locations as he traveled between his three homes. However, in April 1933, he had unexpected complications from an abdominal rupture, which had been bothersome but tolerable for several years. It developed into a strangulated hernia, and he underwent immediate surgery in Washington. He had to remain in bed for the wound to heal. By June, he was able to take the train to the Upper Peninsula.

He had a good summer in Marquette, although his activities other than reading and writing were confined to "automobile drives in the afternoon."

He made two overnight visits to Whitefish Lake, where he got an "exceptionally fine" picture of a black-billed cuckoo and, later, a Harris's sparrow that was migrating through Michigan. He added both images to the volumes still in progress. His eyesight was failing and he told Grosvenor in a letter, "These efforts probably represent my last work with the camera in Northern Michigan."

That year, *The Auk*, the magazine of the American Ornithologists Union, published a book reviewing the first fifty years of the organization, including the effort by scientists to document bird life through photography.

Of Shiras, it said "his phenomenal achievements have placed him in the forefront ranks of nature photographers . . . among his photographic trophies are making striking pictures of bird life. The invention of the flashlight has made possible the photography of birds and mammals under poor lighting conditions and at nighttime. It has opened up a fascinating field of photography."

Shiras was still a member of the board of managers and, in a letter to Grosvenor, he asked how the National Geographic Society's investments were faring in what had become a full-blown economic depression. In America, 1933 was an especially desperate year. About a quarter of all workers were unemployed, millions of people were on the move—some living in shanty towns—banks had failed, and there was no clear way out of the economic morass.

Franklin Roosevelt had just taken office, and many of the public works projects of the New Deal were underway. Although he had been a Progressive, Shiras was still a Republican, a wealthy man, and he felt that Herbert Hoover had been doing the best that he could under the circumstances. He was wary of the Democrats and all the new "make-work" projects: "The many experiments of the Administration seem to be slowing matters up, but we are all hoping for the best."

Despite the economic stress, Grosvenor expected membership in the society would go over nine hundred thousand, a considerable achievement.

One reason Grosvenor felt the Shiras book would sell well was the large, captive audience of *National Geographic* readers. The book would not be offered in stores, only through mail order direct from the society.

The following year E. W. Nelson died of heart problems. Grosvenor and his staff winnowed down the material, eliminating chapters on the nature faker controversy, a trip Shiras made to Hawaii, and more than a dozen pages where Shiras mused about the weather in the Upper Peninsula and in Lake Superior. He theorized that winds in the middle of the lake never exceeded sixty miles per hour due to its lack of topography while along the shoreline they often hit eighty—sometimes one hundred miles per hour—during storms in November.

In the foreword of the book, Shiras and Nelson claimed that he was the first to take photographs of wild animals and birds. It was a claim that the National Geographic Society took pains to research, sending editors to the Smithsonian, the Library of Congress, and the Museum of Natural History in New York. Memos went back and forth, and eventually letters were sent to Berlin to investigate the claims of European photographers, including the German Charles Schillings who had published *Rifle and Flashlight.*

Evidence emerged that some daylight pictures of deer and birds had been taken by members of the Smithsonian staff nearly ten years before Shiras. There may have been other photographers as well, but their efforts were not well documented.

The question became: Was Shiras the first to take pictures of animals in their "natural environments" as opposed to some enclosure or zoo? Shiras had been adamant about not doing the latter and disdainful of so-called wildlife photographers who did so. He was a camera hunter, one who went into the wilds and stalked animals with a camera, not a gun.

Shiras's claims were not necessarily overblown, but enough ambiguity existed in the record that the Geographic editors finessed the wording of the foreword and references to "firsts." Clearly, George Shiras 3d was a major pioneer in wildlife photography and, without doubt, the first person to take pictures of wildlife at night. At Whitefish Lake, he invented the camera trap and perfected techniques with trip wires and flashlights. And he was the first wildlife photographer to have images appear in *National Geographic,* which in his lifetime evolved into the premier magazine of its kind in the world.

Shiras sometimes objected to the rewording and deletions. The nature faker saga—which had always been important to him—ought to be in the book, he insisted. The controversy had raged in periodicals of the day, but had never been covered in book form and consequently had faded from the memory of sportsmen and conservationists. He also believed the foreword ought to contain several paragraphs about his early political battles in Pittsburgh, including the stolen election and the Bayne affair.

Grosvenor, however, was adamant that the volumes focus on Shiras's expeditions, camera hunting, and his thoughts about game management. Other subjects had little place in such a work. When Shiras asked twice to keep the weather section, Grosvenor became exasperated, saying he wanted to hear no more about it. The editors had already fact-checked his conclusions with government meteorologists and found them erroneous. Shiras was an expert on mammals, not on weather, he said.

It all worked out in the end, although Shiras worried that he had been a trying author and had hurt his friendship with the editor.

He apologized in a letter: "Had I retained my health in the past two years, I could have dropped into your office every few weeks, as was customary previously, and any difference of opinion could have been smoothed over in a few minutes. As it is, I most sincerely hope that I have done nothing to lessen our friendship, even though, at times, I must have tried your patience."

He certainly had, but Grosvenor was a friend, and he understood that Shiras was an exacting man—as he was himself. The photographer also was elderly and ailing.

Shiras looked back at his life when he wrote the introduction to the book: "No printed page can do more than stimulate one's interest for the sheer joy of life and its marvels, which goes with a sympathetic visitor to the wilder places. Everywhere he finds awaiting him birds and beasts and other forms of life in a marvelous variety of form, color, and habit that are an endless source of enchantment. The more one delves into this world, the greater is his interest for not a day passes that fails to add its quota to his store of pleasing memories."

He thanked Fanny for her work on his manuscript, Grosvenor for encouragement, and finally John Hammer. Of the latter, he said, "I desire also to record my indebtedness to my guide, John Hammer, for his many years of faithful service in the field, which have contributed so much to my photographic success."

Grosvenor was thrilled to have the project completed and satisfied with the result.

There would be a first run of ten thousand copies of a seven-by-ten-and-a-quarter-inch hardback book. The cost of the two volumes was $3.76 plus additional advertising and marketing. Shipping was estimated at $1.50 for both volumes.

The target price of $5 was obtainable.

Hunting Wild Life with Camera and Flashlight: A Record of Sixty-Five Years'

Visits to the Woods and Waters of North America, published in October 1935, was dedicated: "To the memory of Theodore Roosevelt, sportsman, naturalist, explorer, statesman, and conservator of wild life."

The magazine advertised the books in the October number in an elaborate five-page circular. The customarily white spaces of the pages—such as the margins—were printed pure black to give the illusion of night. The text itself was white. The Shiras books would "fascinate and interest the growing boy or girl who likes to tramp through the woodland or meadow. They will prove their worth to the sportsman and vacationist. A gift that will delight your friends."

Another text block proclaimed, "Although they might be reasonably expected to sell for $20.00 a price of $5.00 is made possible because neither the author nor the Society makes any profit."

Under the headline "Theodore Roosevelt Urged the Writing of This Book" there was a quote from the 1906 letter TR wrote to Shiras after first seeing his pictures in the magazine.

The circular included iconic images from the *Midnight Series,* raccoons and alligators in Florida, bears in Yellowstone, deer in Michigan, and ducks exploding into the air from a Louisiana marsh.

The *Pittsburgh Press* ran a review on its Books page in the Sunday paper on December 15, 1935. Under a picture of a mother and two fawns on Whitefish Lake was the caption: "Shot! But they will live forever." And beneath an image of ducks, "Picture Nimrod Got Them."

Like Grosvenor, the reviewer found Shiras's prose charming and accessible: "The writing, while undoubtedly of scientific worth, isn't for a moment heavy or dull. It is rather that of a man with a consuming love for the wild places and creatures, a man who writes not for the student but also for those of us to whom *Ursus horribilis* is just a grizzly bear."

The hundreds of halftones—all monochromatic (no color prints)—were reproduced on what the printer called "Geographic Coated" paper, which gave them an exceptionally rich saturation and appearance. Because the negatives were relatively large—including five-by-seven-inch glass negatives—the images were sharp and detailed.

The *New York Times Book Review* called it a book of "incomparable beauty and interest."

The reviewer noted:

Into this noble and very beautiful two-volume George Shiras 3d, internationally known for his lifetime of enthusiastic study of wild life and work for its conservation, has gathered some of the most important things he has done with pen and camera toward that end.

. . . The two fine volumes will stand as a monument to his devoted labor for the preservation for future generations of Americans of the wilderness and his native creatures. They deserve the reading and admiration of those who are interested in these things.

The journal *Nature* called it "an outstanding work of its kind and must be looked upon as a classic in the history of wild life photography. Its author, George Shiras, born in Pittsburgh in 1859, is the pioneer of American nature photographers."

Sales were brisk and the volumes soon became known as *the Shiras books*, purchased by libraries and sportsmen. Despite the efforts of the editors, there were mistakes and typographical errors—several that distressed the fastidious Shiras—but because the books sold well, plans were made to publish a second edition, which came out with revisions and corrections in September 1936.

A third edition was considered but never executed.

27 | LAST DAYS

DURING THE PRODUCTION of the books, a letter arrived at the society addressed to "Friend George" from Jake Brown, his former guide who had moved to Idaho in 1894 and then left for Alaska with a pack train and partner.

No one had heard from Jake in all those years. They assumed he had died in the Canadian Rockies after arguing with and abandoning his partner just as a brutal winter was coming on. But Brown had crossed the Rockies on foot, killed animals, lived off the land, and eventually made it to Alaska.

In 1929, he was seventy-two years old and living in the San Juan Islands off the coast of Washington. "I write you a few lines to see if you are still living. I live on Whidbey Island, thirty-five miles north of Seattle. You passed a half mile from my cabin when you went to Alaska . . . I am about played out, can hardly get around to look after myself, am laid up most of the time in winter with rheumatism."

Shiras replied immediately, "Your letter of May 3rd caused as much excitement in the family as if the chimney had fallen in, though we were pleased by this surprise . . . Only last year I wrote a chapter . . . for a book which gave you a good sendoff but depicted your bones as being scattered by the four winds or wild beasts on top of the Canadian Rockies."

He asked Brown to write back about his adventures so he could update the chapter. Brown told of a rugged life of hunting, prospecting for gold, trapping in the winter, and working as a timber cruiser in both Alaska and the Northwest Territories. He spent eighteen years trapping for the Hudson's Bay Company in the headwaters of the Mackenzie River. He and a partner killed wood buffalo for their hides: "That country beats any place for wild fowl that I ever saw. We used to gather eggs by the canoe load, pack them in spruce needles and they would keep for six weeks. Any amount of moose and bear. In the winter, millions of caribou came down from the north. The railroad goes through that country now; all game will soon be gone."

He moved to the San Juan Islands around 1920 and lived alone in a cabin. His nearest neighbor was a half mile down the beach. After exchanging several letters, Brown sent Shiras a photograph of himself taken by visitors passing in a boat. It shows an old man with a white beard, gripping a rifle, standing next to a cabin of rough-cut boards. The attached woodshed is as big as the cabin. Shiras sent him the reprint of the 1921 article on the Lake Superior region that featured references to Whitefish Lake, Jack La Pete, and Brown, too.

Jake wrote back, "Do you have any hunting there now?" he asked. "I showed the *National Geographic* to my friends here and nearly all of them have seen your name in print. Will have to put the book away. With these old timers thumbing through it, it won't look very well."

He added, "I have knocked around a whole lot but never found a place I liked half as well as Whitefish Lake, but I am all right here now."

In another letter he said, "I am mighty glad to hear from you and John Hammer. I would like to be back again on Lake Superior, but I am in no condition at my age to be of any real service, so the curtain had better fall on me here now."

In November 1932, Shiras received a letter from the prosecuting attorney in Coupeville, Washington, informing him of Brown's death. Jake was seen walking on the beach one day, but apparently never made it back to his cabin. The sheriff and neighbors searched the premises, the beach, and the woods but didn't find the guide, who was so badly crippled he could not row his boat or venture far in the woods. It is likely, the attorney wrote, that Brown was stricken on the beach and his body carried out with the tide. Finding Shiras's letters in the cabin, the attorney decided to write him in case he might have additional information. Apparently, Brown had no one else.

It was a distressing end.

In his revised chapter, Shiras eulogized, "Doubtless Davey Jones' locker now contains the mortal remains of my old and faithful guide. The ebb and flow of the mighty ocean will be commemorative of this restless and venturesome spirit who left the windswept shore of his island retreat for a haven of eternal rest."

In 1933, Shiras found himself referenced in a peculiar short story by Ernest Hemingway, whose literary light shined especially bright in that period. "Homage to Switzerland," published in *Scribner's* magazine, is not one of Hemingway's most well-known stories, but the piece is remarkable for its complicated experimental structure—three nearly identical vignettes of an expatriate American sitting in a train station, teasing a waitress, talking to locals, and waiting for the late express to Paris. Critics believe Hemingway was riffing on the theory of relativity—creating a fluid reality, using time and trains as symbols, and setting the scenes in Switzerland where Einstein developed his theories. The form was so enigmatic that the story was rejected by *Colliers* and then picked up by *Scribner's*.

In the third version, a gentleman approaches an American named Harris in the train station and asks,

"I beg your pardon, if I might intrude but it just occurred to me that you might be a member of the National Geographic Society. Have you seen the number with the colored plates of the North American Fauna?"

"Yes, I have it in Paris."

"And the number containing the panorama of the volcanoes of Alaska?"

"That was a wonder."

"I enjoyed very much, too, the wild animal photographs of George Shiras three."

"They were damned fine."

"I beg your pardon?"

"There were excellent. That fellow Shiras—"

"You call him that fellow?"

"We're old friends," said Harris.

"I see you know George Shiras three. He must be very interesting."

"He is. He's about the most interesting man I know."

"And do you know George Shiras two? Is he interesting?"

"Oh, he's not so interesting. You know, a funny thing. He's not so interesting, I've often wondered why."

"H'm," said the gentleman. "I should have thought anyone in that family would be interesting."

For today's readers, the reference to the Shirases would be obscure, but at the time many knew of Hemingway's passion for big game hunting and his connections to Michigan's north woods, where he set several of his autobiographical "Nick Adams" stories. One of his most famous short stories, "Big Two-Hearted River," takes place sixty miles west of Marquette near the lumber town of Seney where Nick, an emotionally scarred veteran of trench warfare in Europe, hikes over cutover and burnt land to reach the solace of a tree-shaded trout stream. In the story, the burnt-over land functions as metaphor, but Hemingway paints a literary portrait of the Upper Peninsula at the end of the logging period.

Fires caused by lightning strikes, sparks thrown off from passing steam locomotives, or settlers burning off the growth to promote blueberries burned and smoldered uncontrolled throughout the summer months. Extinguished only by winter snows, the fires hampered the regeneration of a second-growth forest.

In the first decades of the twentieth century, the cutover lands attracted dreamers and schemers. Regional boosters—including Frank Russell of the *Mining Journal*—tried to rebrand the region by calling it Cloverland and marketing the so-called "seven million fertile acres" to ranchers, farmers, and immigrants.

Homesteaders came north and from Europe to turn the stump lands into farms. It was mostly wishful thinking, and at its worst, hucksterism. The soils were poor, the latitude too far north for most agriculture, the cold and snow impossible to overcome. By the 1930s, thousands of farms were abandoned, a trend hastened by the Great Depression. Northern Michigan was mainly suited to grow trees. Shiras said so himself in the introduction to volume 1: "The Upper Peninsula, with little prospect of any great development in agriculture or manufactures, seems destined to a long future as a recreational wilderness area."

The Hiawatha and Ottawa National Forests were established in the Upper Peninsula, and the hard economic times enabled the US Forest Service and the state of Michigan to buy up tens of thousands of abandoned acres and denuded forests—often for the price of back taxes.

Then came the Civilian Conservation Corps, also known as Franklin Roosevelt's "Tree Army." Part of the New Deal to give work to the unemployed, the CCC played a crucial role in reforesting the Upper Peninsula. In the ten years between Roosevelt's inauguration and the beginning of World War II, the young men of the CCC planted nearly 500 million trees in Northern Michigan, more than any other state. They built fire towers and access roads to suppress fires. They rehabilitated streams, constructed campgrounds, and built marshlands—including the sprawling Seney National Wildlife Refuge.

Having experienced the destruction of the virgin forest and alteration of ecosystems, Shiras, at the end of life, witnessed large-scale environmental restoration—a continuation of conservation policies begun by the Progressives.

His last magazine article appeared in the *Michigan Sportsman* in July 1933, with the prosaic title: "I Photograph Deer in the Dark." The editor's note read, "We consider it a real privilege to be able to present in this issue reproductions of the fine photographs by George Shiras III and the story of how they were made."

It was a nostalgic article, but the photographic technology and techniques were not obsolete.

Flash powder and chemical flashlights were still in use in 1933. The first flash bulbs had been introduced in Germany in 1929. They were filled with aluminum foil and oxygen under pressure. When a current passed through priming wires inside the base, the foil instantly combusted at a speed of 1/50 of a second. At first, there was no means of synchronizing the flash and camera shutter. The "open flash" technique required the photographer to place the camera on a tripod, open the shutter, set off the flash, and then close the shutter—much like Shiras had done decades earlier at Whitefish Lake. There is no evidence that Shiras ever used a flashbulb, and in the early 1930s, his "powder speed" method was superior but still hazardous.

The editor ran three full-page images of the *Midnight Series* printed full frame and horizontally. Many of the anecdotes previously appeared in *National Geographic*. In today's parlance, it was a repurposed, cut-and-paste article.

But a few paragraphs summed up his life's work: "Persistent pursuit and the trial of many methods finally suggested ways of getting pictures with ease and certainty, for in the end few wild animals can escape the gun, the trap or the camera when hunted with care and energy."

In summer 1935, Shiras walked into the editorial offices of the National Geographic Society, carrying what he considered to be his most important papers. He wanted them preserved in the society's archives. In a note to Grosvenor, he speculated about a "future biographer."

The contents included tattered clippings from the *Marquette Mining Journal*, *Forest and Stream*, and the *New York Independent*. There were pristine copies of the influential pamphlets he had authored on the passage of the Migratory Bird Act, batches of speeches given before the Marquette Rotary Club, a legal brief on tariffs, and a treatise on the failure of the League of Nations. He left a book of scientific papers from the University of Michigan's "Shiras Expedition to Whitefish Point in the Upper Peninsula," which he financed in the 1920s.

Grosvenor's secretary created a bibliography of the materials under the title, "Very Valuable—Original Papers of George Shiras 3d." At the bottom Grosvenor wrote, "Place in a Fireproof Safe. These pamphlets are not to be taken away." They remain in the *National Geographic* archives today. However, not all of the wildlife negatives that he donated were preserved. In 1963 when the society was trying to save physical space, the photographic division decided to discard all unpublished negatives and images.

In 1935, Shiras went to Ormond Beach and asked John Hammer to build a feeding platform for birds in the orange grove on his property. The family had a pavilion there where he and Fanny liked to sit, read, and picnic. The pavilion was about one hundred yards behind the house in a forty-foot clearing surrounded by bushes and trees with two orange trees in the center. The grove had long been a place to observe birds.

The two men baited the feeding station with seeds, slices of citrus, and other morsels. For background, Shiras placed a white screen behind the platform and decorated the bench with palmetto leaves, longleaf pine, Spanish moss, and bits of sand, rocks, and seashells to create a diorama of sorts. Then he set up a camera with his "fourteen-inch long lens." His vision was poor, so he measured the distance with a tape and preset the focus and aperture.

All there was left to do was get into the blind, wait, and trip the shutter.

Over several days, he shot portraits of scrub jays, eastern towhees, mockingbirds, cardinals, catbirds, mourning doves, brown thrashers, and red-bellied woodpeckers. Before going up to the house at night—where he watched the January sun going down on the Halifax River—he and John set out camera traps and for a few nights, the neighbors heard the familiar explosions emanating from the dark. He captured two pictures: a feral tabby cat and a skunk.

These were his final photographs, and he was making a ceremony of it as he recalled his grandfather, at eighty-eight, and his father, at ninety, had done when they could no longer go into the field as hunters and fishermen. They bundled up their rods, guns, gear, and passed them down to their sons. George, of course, had lost his son, but there was still tradition.

"I felt I should with equal serenity, bid farewell to the use of my cameras . . ."

Both he and Fanny were thinking about posterity and undertaking philanthropy that would do good work decades after their deaths. In the early 1920s, they had purchased a wood frame home next to the Peter White Public Library in Marquette to be used as a clubhouse for the Marquette Federation of Women's Clubs. They also funded construction of an outdoor pool on Presque Isle and donated thousands of feet of Lake Superior shoreline to the city to create Shiras Park. At the mouth of the Dead River, where George and his pals had first camped in 1870, they paid for construction of a rock and water garden. With a group of investors—mostly members of his extended family—they rescued the stalled project of the one-hundred-room Northland Hotel in the heart of downtown Marquette. The stone foundation had been laid but sat unfinished for years because of the Depression. It was an eyesore in the downtown district. The Northland became a first-class hotel that served as the social center of the city between the 1930s and 1960s.

Their most enduring legacy, however, was the creation of the Shiras Institute, a trust fund with an endowment of $100,000 to "benefit in the fields of beautification, recreation and cultural activities in the city of Marquette Michigan and the Upper Peninsula of Michigan in the broadest and most liberal manner."

The *Milwaukee Journal* ran a headline in September 1937: "Peninsula City Given Big Gift." In succeeding years, the institute provided millions to build a planetarium, a hockey rink, and a local history center. It has given grants to youth soccer leagues and civic clubs. In 2017, it had assets of $1.5 million.

On September 16, 1938, Fanny Shiras died suddenly of a heart attack at her ancestral home on Ridge Street. She was seventy-seven years old. The *Mining Journal* wrote, "When she failed to answer the usual morning summons, it was found that she had passed away quietly in her sleep."

Shiras returned to Washington and in early February 1939 began closing up his house. Some items were shipped to Marquette, but much of the furniture he gifted to intimate friends. He sent a china cabinet to John Oliver La Gorce, the editor at *National Geographic* magazine. La Gorce wrote a thank-you letter that relates how he had recently met a Polish count in Washington on an urgent diplomatic mission to get help for his country. The Nazis had annexed Czechoslovakia, and Germany would invade Poland that September and begin the Second World War.

When the Count learned that La Gorce worked for the magazine, he immediately began praising "the Shiras books."

La Gorce continued,

An American friend had sent him the volumes as a gift knowing of his great interest in wild life that he contacted all over the world and in excellent English he said that your books were his prized possessions among the library of natural history subjects he had brought together . . .

It must be a real source of satisfaction to you to know how splendidly received your volumes are and the incalculable amount of pleasure and education that your work has given thousands . . . My dear Mr. Shiras, I remember as though it were but yesterday that day nearly thirty-four years ago when you first walked into our offices.

In June, Shiras wrote to Grosvenor asking for help in putting his affairs in order. He was wondering if there was any more material that he should be leaving the society.

"Last night was a very poor one for me, and I became quite discouraged. You are a person of good judgment, and, I believe anxious to help out in every way . . . It has proved a most difficult task to decide on just what papers and records to take with me to Marquette."

Melville Grosvenor, who was working at the magazine, sent his father the letter with a handwritten note on the top, "Wonder if I could handle it or do you wish to see the old boy?"

Shiras returned to Marquette for the last years of his life, where he was cared for by servants and nieces and nephews. Ellie had married Frank Russell in November 1925. It was his second marriage and her first. She was thirty-nine years old. Frank had a son and namesake from a previous marriage who had taken over the *Mining Journal.*

Ellie and Frank moved to Iron Mountain, fifty miles southwest of Marquette, where Frank started an afternoon newspaper, the *Iron Mountain Daily News.* They lived close enough so she could visit her father frequently.

George began writing a biography of his father and in it planned to tell the story of his family going back to the Revolutionary War. He also wanted to clear his father's name over the income tax case. Junior had been blamed by the press for changing his vote and delaying for many years the application of an income tax. The implication was that he was protecting men of wealth, such as his friends in Pittsburgh. The resulting imbroglio may have led to Junior's retiring from the court after what was a relatively short tenure. The criticism still stung after all these years.

He got assistance in these literary endeavors from Frank Russell and a local stenographer. Most importantly, he enlisted the help of his nephew Winfield, the son of his brother in Pittsburgh. Winfield Jr. was a book editor in New York, and he edited chapters via the mails and occasionally came to Marquette to work on the book with his uncle.

George also penned a political autobiography of sorts, recounting his time in the Pennsylvania legislature and his involvement in the Pig Iron and Quay affairs. If he intended these memoirs for a book, it is difficult to say, but he set them down for posterity. It was only in these pages that he revealed his authorship of the *Pig Iron* pamphlet.

He occasionally exchanged letters with Gilbert Grosvenor, who sent him advance copies of the magazine and asked for his opinions. In 1940, Hermann Hagedorn, president of the Theodore Roosevelt Association, wrote to Grosvenor asking him for suggestions of possible candidates for a distinguished service Roosevelt Medal. The association awarded three each year.

Grosvenor enthusiastically recommended George Shiras 3d. He sent copies of the Shiras books and pointed out their dedication to TR and the long friendship between the two men. Shiras was then eighty years old and unaware his name was being suggested. Previous medal winners were Frank Chapman, George Grinnell, Elihu Root, Gifford Pinchot, and C. Hart Merriam. He certainly would have fit with this eminent group, but in 1940, the association awarded medals to a newspaper editor, a social welfare advocate from New York, and the head of the Selective Service, who was quite busy in preparation for the next war.

Just three months after the Japanese attack on Pearl Harbor, Shiras died of pneumonia at home in Marquette on Thursday, March 24, 1942. He was buried in Park Cemetery next to Fanny and his son. Gilbert Grosvenor and Frank Chapman served as honorary pallbearers.

In the obituary, the *New York Times* hit the salient events of his life:

George Shiras, Eighty-Three, Noted Naturalist
  Pioneer in Taking Flashlight Photos of Wild Animals Is Dead in Marquette, Mich.
  Once a Representative
  Wrote Bill that Put Migratory Birds and Fish Under Federal Control—Also an Author.
  The Rotary Club of Marquette, of which Shiras was an honorary member, passed a resolution stating, "We loved George Shiras. There was about him a dignity that approached austerity, but beneath that exterior, there was a soft appreciative feeling for nature, God's creatures, and mankind that made him loved by all who knew him. A fern, a bit of moss, a doe with her young, a moose, a man in need were each a tremendous thing to him."

The *Milwaukee Journal* captured his importance to sportsmen and the fact that he had faded to near obscurity by the time of his death.

Conservation lost a good friend Thursday when the scholarly George Shiras III died at Marquette Michigan. Not so widely known to outdoorsmen of the last decades, Shiras nevertheless was big enough to deserve a place among most of the national conservation leaders of this generation. Shiras was of an old school and a good school. . . .

In an era when fast camera lenses were not obtainable, when synchronized speed guns and easily handled flashbulbs were unknown, Shiras went into the woods of the Midwest and made flashlight pictures at night that have never been better.

The tall, scholarly Shiras was easily one of the greatest outdoorsmen of his time, full qualified by his many contributions to wildlife knowledge to have a place in posterity with Burroughs, Muir and others.

EPILOGUE

George Shiras died before finishing the biography of Junior, but his nephew Winfield completed the manuscript using notes, letters, and early drafts. The University of Pittsburgh Press published *Justice George Shiras Jr. of Pittsburgh* in 1953. In the book's preface, Winfield recounted one of his last visits to Marquette.

Charlie Anderson, the guide, came to the house on Ridge Street to take George duck hunting on Whitefish Lake. It was a raw day in early November with winds gusting and snowflakes periodically filling the sky.

"At least once a year, he would exercise his fondness for wildfowling," wrote Winfield. "The day certainly seemed unsuited to so frail an octogenarian. We helped to bundle him into the car and we worried about him during the day. Darkness had fallen before he came home triumphantly bringing six or seven ducks and a fine Canada goose."

John Hammer lived to be ninety-eight years old. When he died in 1957, the *Mining Journal* editorialized, "Using the crudest of equipment, he and Shiras succeeded in obtaining some of the finest photographs of wildlife that have ever been put on negatives . . . Now Mr. Hammer is gone after a full and eventful life. Perhaps he will be remembered, in a manner of speaking, as a great man in his own right who lived in the shadow of another great man." The State of Michigan named a picnic area after him at Laughing Whitefish Falls, which today is a state scenic area.

Ellen Shiras and Frank Russell never had children. Russell's son came to own four of the eight daily newspapers in the Upper Peninsula and started the region's first television station. Frank turned his Progressive tendencies into lifelong boosterism of all things Upper Peninsula. He headed the Shiras Institute and the Northland Hotel group, helped start hospitals, and advocated for labor rights in editorials. He died of a heart ailment in Daytona Beach in March 1947.

Upon her death in 1963, Ellen donated her $1.2 million estate to charities and organizations in Ormond Beach, Marquette, and Iron Mountain. Recipients included hospitals, high schools, libraries, country clubs, Episcopal churches, the Shiras Institute, and Northern Michigan University. The big clapboard homes in Ormond passed out of family ownership and made way for even bigger homes on Riverside Drive where the live oaks and the Halifax River are still magnificent. The Ormond Beach Hotel was razed in 1992 after sitting empty for a number of years.

Florida 1A, or Ocean Boulevard, bisects the peninsula between the beaches of the Atlantic Ocean and the Halifax River, where George once set out his camera traps and took strolls with Frank Chapman. From Ormond through Daytona, the highway is lined with high-rise hotels, T-shirt and beachwear shops, and all the concrete and commercial sprawl of tourist Florida. It's impossible to imagine what the area was like in Shiras's day except to visit the Canaveral National Seashore to the south or Tomoka State Park to the north, where something of natural Florida still exists.

In the West in the twentieth century, *Alces americanus shirasi* repopulated much of the northern Rockies aided by decades of modern game management, including capture and release in which surplus moose were moved to new locations. In northwest Wyoming in recent years, however, the moose herd has declined precipitously. Biologists believe parasites and climate change may be partly to blame. The Yellowstone fires of 1988 removed much of the forest cover the moose had used to stay cool in summer. There's evidence too that predators—especially introduced gray wolves—have reduced the herd.

In the Upper Peninsula, gray wolves were extirpated by the 1960s, abetted by unrestricted varmint hunting, poisoning, and trapping. Then in the 1980s, animals migrated from Minnesota, where a robust population survived in the wilderness of the Superior National Forest. The Upper Peninsula and northern Wisconsin were undiscovered country for wolves, with vast tracts of forest and plenty of prey—beaver, deer, and moose. By 2018, perhaps one thousand animals had set up packs in the region, and a few lone wolves have crossed the ice into the Lower Peninsula.

Because of the wolf's return, old debates and passions erupted. Some

Rock carving at camp on Whitefish Lake. Photograph by the author.

people viewed gray wolves as dangerous predators, ruthless killers of game. Others waxed sentimental and held up wolves as magnificent endangered creatures, symbols of the wild. Although never fond of predators himself, George Shiras today might embrace a middle ground favored by biologists— that when adequate numbers are reached, remove wolves from endangered/ threatened status, designate it a game animal, and hold a limited hunt. Then wolves would become just another critter—like lake trout, fishers, bald eagles, peregrine falcons, moose, and mountain lions—who have returned to the north woods after being extirpated or nearly so during settlement.

Agriculture never got much of a foothold in the Upper Peninsula. Today, 98 percent or about 8.4 million acres of the region is forested. It is a young forest—much of it held in national and state ownership—and still in recovery, gradually maturing. There is little old growth left and not much actual wilderness. Forest roads, off-road vehicle trails, and overgrown logging trails cut through the woods, but vast expanses are isolated, sparsely populated and primitive.

In the early twenty-first century, the Upper Peninsula of Michigan retains its physical insularity, remote from the rest of the Midwest—a sliver of land between Lakes Huron, Michigan, and Superior. Most Americans would be hard pressed to locate it on a map, or might identify it as an arm of Wisconsin or perhaps a province of Canada. Of Michigan's 9.9 million people, just 300,000 live north of the Mackinac Straits.

Marquette is the largest town, with thirty thousand residents, where the mammoth ships still leave the docks next to the Dead River loaded with iron ore from Cleveland Cliffs mines. The company sold Grand Island to the Forest Service, and the island is now a national recreation area popular with mountain bikers. Pictured Rocks is a national park.

Whitefish Lake remains a secluded, private lake deep in the woods. Descendants of Peter White remodeled the camp since its heyday. The caretaker house of John Hammer collapsed several years ago. The root cellar, too. The gardens are gone, although foxgloves raised by Jake Brown have seeded and gone wild on the property. The camp is still off the grid but can be rented out by the public for overnight and weekend stays. Not far from the main cabin, a lichen-and-moss-covered boulder displays a deep etching where George Shiras 3d left his mark: *G. S. 1871.*

A few years ago, the family donated half the acreage around the lake to the Nature Conservancy, which created the George Shiras 3d Discovery Trail, a 1.5-mile walking path with interpretive signage telling of his photography and conservation work. The Laughing Whitefish Lake Preserve is a rare property for the organization, which typically preserves land and waters for wildlife and rare habitats, but important events in America's conservation history happened on Whitefish Lake.

By the time of George's death, photography had moved well beyond chemical flashes and black-and-white imagery. Camera traps were quaint anachronisms, complicated to rig up and not really worth the trouble. But in the late 1990s, the digital revolution eliminated film, ushered in electronic sensing, and miniaturized components.

Trail cameras became accessible, simple to use, and affordable not only for photographers and scientists but deer hunters and anyone just curious about what is moving about on the land at night. Trail cameras documented the journey of a gray wolf that over several weeks wandered from Montana to California. A hunter in the Upper Peninsula strapped a camera on a tree next to a deer carcass and videotaped a feeding mountain lion. Biologists using trail cameras have discovered rare leopards in China, rhinos in Java, deer in Malaysia, jaguars in Arizona. The camera trap is now the tool of conservation Shiras once envisioned.

If he returned to Whitefish Lake today, Shiras could paddle up on a deer standing mesmerized in the slough, flinch at the slap of a beaver's tail on the water, and hear the wail of tenacious gray wolves in the darkness.

What he would have to work with is a trail camera in a waterproof plastic case with superb optics, wide-angle view, deep depth of focus, strobes synched to high shutter speeds, a laser motion detector effective to one hundred feet, and digital storage capable of capturing sound, hundreds of still photos, or minutes-long video. He could uplink it to his mobile device or a satellite.

Imagine what George Shiras 3d might have done with such technology.

ACKNOWLEDGMENTS

In 2010, when I considered writing a biography of George Shiras 3d, I drove to Pittsburgh to see what I could find in archives and libraries. At the University of Pittsburgh, which I attended in the 1970s, I discovered a graduate thesis from the 1950s on the political life of George 3d, the young reformer and Progressive who helped bring down the Magee-Flinn machine. There was scant information regarding his photography and conservation work, but the student's bibliography referenced the George Shiras 3d Papers at the University of Pittsburgh. When I asked to see the papers at the reference desk of Hillman Library, the perplexed librarians found nothing in the catalogue. And as good reference librarians do, they went on the hunt.

Two days later, just as I was about to leave the city, they called. Three boxes had been located in a warehouse in the suburbs. The boxes hadn't been opened in decades. Inside, we found an unfinished autobiography, old newspaper clippings, scrapbooks, and personal letters—including handwritten missives between Shiras and Theodore Roosevelt. Here was enough primary source material to begin a book.

The University of Pittsburgh eventually gifted the papers to the Central Upper Peninsula and Northern Michigan University Archives, where in the ensuing years we've added to the Shiras collection. Just before I finished the manuscript, a homeowner in Marquette found a fragile, dry-as-dust scrapbook in a garage once owned by a hunting guide. It contained decades of letters and newspapers that George preserved from his battles over the fight for migratory birds. This Shiras scrapbook was marked No. 7, so there may be more out there.

Rejoicing in such discoveries, exploring archives and libraries, and visiting locations where George Shiras 3d once set up his camera traps were the true joys of writing this book.

I had plenty of help along the way.

I want to thank John Hansenjager of the American Wildlife Conservation Foundation for sending me a copy of the history of the American Game Protective and Propagation Association. Thanks also to Paul Sweet, collection manager of the Department of Ornithology, and Mai Reitmeyer, librarian, at the Museum of Natural History in New York City.

I spent several days at the National Geographic Society in Washington, ably assisted by Cathy Hunter, archivist, and Renee Braden, manager of Archives and Special Collections. In addition to letters and memos between Shiras and Gilbert Grosvenor, they dug up those special papers that Shiras donated for safekeeping in the 1930s. They also told me that "someone really ought to write a book about George Shiras."

One September, I drove out to Yellowstone National Park and sorted through material at the Yellowstone Heritage and Research Center in Gardiner, Montana, where I was assisted by archivists Brian Davis and Anne L. Foster and historian Lee H. Whittlesey. In Jackson Hole, I interviewed biologists at the Game and Fish Department about Shiras moose.

I visited the Ormond Beach Historical Society in Florida and toured town with Charles DuToit, a biologist and historian, who located the site of the Shiras cottages and talked to me about the Ormond Hotel. I birded with David Hartgrove and the late Chuck Tague of the Halifax River Audubon chapter. Meret Wilson, a naturalist and bird bander, showed me Tomoka State Park and advised that I visit Canaveral National Seashore to see the coast as it was in Shiras's day.

Over the years, I did research at the Library of Congress, the National Archives, the Smithsonian Institution, Yale University, and Historical Society of Western Pennsylvania Senator John Heinz Pittsburgh Regional History Center in Pittsburgh.

Back in Michigan, Peggy Frazier and Alice Reynolds, descendants of Peter White, allowed me access to the lands and camp around Whitefish Lake. Alice graciously let me view the logbook for the Camp of the Fiddling Cat.

B. J. Olds, grandson of John Hammer, showed me photographs, documents, and the many artifacts that his grandfather saved from that time, including the actual cameras and mechanisms used to take flashlight pictures on Whitefish Lake.

Tina Hall, director of land resources for the Nature Conservancy in Michigan, first made me aware of the George 3d Discovery Trail and led my nature writing classes there on field trips. Also thanks to Jack Deo, owner of Superior View, who sells vintage photographs of the Upper Peninsula, including iconic images from the *Midnight Series*. Jack has promoted the Shiras legacy in the Upper Peninsula for many years.

Appreciation also to the staffs at the Marquette County Historical Society and Peter White Public Library. The Shiras Room in the library holds the personal book collection of George 3d. The library, overlooking the town and Lake Superior, is a delightful space to write.

At Northern Michigan University, I'm appreciative of Melissa Matuscak, director of the art museum, Diane Kordich, curator of Lee Hall Gallery, Russell Managhi, professor emeritus of history, Michael Broadway, former dean of the College of Arts and Sciences, and Marcus Robyns, the university archivist.

And finally, my appreciation to the institution itself. Northern Michigan University generously supports faculty research and conferred on me the Peter White Scholar Award. Given annually to an NMU professor, the Peter White was originally endowed by Ellen Shiras-Russell upon her death in 1963. Consequently, it was seed money from the Shiras-White fortunes that made this book possible.

NOTES AND REFERENCES

PREFACE

In the 1890s on Whitefish Lake: George Shiras 3d, *Hunting Wild Life with Camera and Flashlight*, vol. 1 (Washington, DC: National Geographic Society, 1935).

It was a crude setup, but one that yielded extraordinary images: Grant Harris, Ron Thompson, Jack L. Childs, and James G. Sanderson, "Automatic Storage and Analysis of Camera Trap Data," *Bulletin of the Ecological Society of America* 91, no. 3 (July 2010): 352–60, https://doi.org/10.1890/0012-9623-91.3.352.

At the turn of the twentieth century, the future of many wildlife species—including whitetail deer—appeared bleak: Robert J. Brulle and Robert D. Benford, "From Game Protection to Wildlife Management: Frame Shifts, Organizational Development, and Field Practices," *Rural Sociology*, 77, no. 1 (2012), 62–88, https://doi.org/10.1111/j.1549-0831.2011.00067.x.

Much of the Upper Peninsula was cutover country: George N. Fuller, ed., *A History of the Upper Peninsula of Michigan* (Dayton, OH: National Historical Association, 1926).

Market hunters riding the new railroads killed tens of thousands of deer: "Deer Management History in Michigan," Michigan Department of Natural Resources, www.michigan.gov.dnr.

They packed the meat into barrels: *Role of Railroads*, J. M. Longyear Research Library pamphlet, Marquette Regional History Center, Marquette, MI (hereafter MRHC).

It was not until the coming of the Progressive Movement: Brulle and Benford, "From Game Protection to Wildlife Management."

George Shiras was a native of Pittsburgh, Pennsylvania: "Obituary of George Shiras 3d," *Marquette Mining Journal*, March 25, 1942.

At his father-in-law's "game preserve" on Whitefish Lake: "Peter White Fighting Wolves on His Great Game Preserve," *Detroit Journal*, January 27, 1900.

one of the Progressives in the early twentieth century who saved several species of wildlife: George A. Cevasco and Richard P. Harmond, eds., *Modern American Environmentalists: A Biographical Encyclopedia* (Baltimore: Johns Hopkins University Press, 2009).

As a congressional representative, Shiras introduced and established the legal foundations: Shiras 3d, *Hunting Wild Life*, vol. 1.

CHAPTER 1

The two boys trudged through the woods most of the day: Shiras 3d, *Hunting Wild Life,* vol. 1.

George and Winfield were keen to go: George Shiras 3d, "The Wild Life of Lake Superior, Past and Present: The Habits of Deer, Moose, Wolves, Beavers, Muskrats, Trout, and Feathered Wood-Folk Studied with Camera and Flashlight," *National Geographic* magazine, August 1921.

following game trails that coalesced into wide "deer runways": Aldo Leopold, "Report on a Game Survey of the North Central States" (Madison, WI: Sporting Arms and Ammunition Manufacturers' Institute, 1931).

The boys had come to hunt big game: Shiras 3d, *Hunting Wild Life,* vol. 1.

When Jack and Winfield came into camp: Shiras 3d, *Hunting Wild Life,* vol. 1.

Nearly fifty years later he wrote: Shiras 3d, *Hunting Wild Life,* vol. 1.

Eventually, the practice of fire hunting or jacking a deer: Shiras 3d, *Hunting Wild Life,* vol. 1.

CHAPTER 2

That first visit to Whitefish Lake occurred during the Gilded Age: William Nesbitt, *How to Hunt with a Camera: A Complete Guide to all Forms of Outdoor Photography* (Boston: E. P. Dutton, 1926).

The city was known as "Hell with the lid off": Shiras 3d, *Hunting Wild Life,* vol. 1.

The family's relationship with the Pittsburgh region went back a couple of generations: George Shiras 3d and Winfield Shiras, *Justice George Shiras Jr. of Pittsburgh* (Pittsburgh: University of Pittsburgh Press, 1953).

in the cooler, cleaner climes of the Great Lakes: "Shiras Urges Lake Superior Booster Move," *Marquette Mining Journal,* June 12, 1936.

In those days, manufacturing beer and liquor or keeping a tavern: Shiras 3d and Shiras, *Justice George Shiras Jr.*

He purchased a hundred-acre farm with fine springs of clear water: Shiras 3d and Shiras, *Justice George Shiras Jr.*

Settlers also destroyed the flocks of passenger pigeons: Joel Greenberg, *A Feathered River across the Sky: The Passenger Pigeon's Flight to Extinction* (New York: Bloomsbury, 2014).

George Sr. had settled into a life as a gentleman farmer and sportsman: "'Lone Fisherman' Shiras Rates as Marquette's First Tourist," *Marquette Mining Journal,* September 7, 1963.

At the Soo, Shiras found a village of about five hundred residents: Shiras 3d and Shiras, *Justice George Shiras Jr.*

The speckled trout sought by George Sr.: "Status of the Brook Trout in Lake Superior," Report for Lake Superior Technical Committee, the Brook Trout Subcommittee, US Fish and Wildlife Service, March 1996.

Shiras beheld a mature forest of mixed hardwoods: Fuller, *History of the Upper Peninsula.*

It was a forest more advantageous to moose and woodland caribou: Louise Verme, "Some Background on Moose in Upper Michigan," Report No. 2973, Michigan Department of Natural Resources, 1984.

which were the top ungulates: Leopold, "Report on a Game Survey."

He traveled two hundred miles to the tip of the Keweenaw Peninsula: "'Lone Fisherman' Shiras," *Marquette Mining Journal.*

He stayed a few days and then made his way back to the Soo: Shiras 3d and Shiras, *Justice George Shiras Jr.*

The Harmonites had come from Germany in 1804: Brochure of Harmonist History, Old Economy Village, Ambridge, Pennsylvania.

when he and his followers: Arthur Versluis, "Studies in American Esotericism, Western Esotericism and the Harmony Society," *Esoterica* (1999): 20–47.

The Shiras boys were well educated for the period: Shiras 3d and Shiras, *Justice George Shiras Jr.*

Junior returned to Pittsburgh in 1853 and set up a law practice: Contemporary Biography of Pennsylvania, Library and Archives Division, Historical Society of Western Pennsylvania, Pittsburgh, Pennsylvania.

By this time, George Sr. had made several trips to the region: George Shiras Sr. to Mr. Gormly, July 19, 1856, J. M. Longyear Research Library, MRHC.

White ran a store and the post office: Ralph D. Williams, *The Honorable Peter White: A Biographical Sketch of the Lake Superior Iron Country* (Cleveland, OH: Penton Publishing, 1906).

The iron deposits of the upper Great Lakes were a critical resource for the Union: George N. Fuller, ed., *Historic Michigan: Land of the Great Lakes, Its Life, Resources, Industries, People, Politics, Government, Wars, Institutions, Achievements, The Press, Schools and Churches, Legendary and Prehistoric Lore* (Dayton, OH: National Historical Association, 1925).

The Mathers put local dynamo Peter White in charge: Williams, *Honorable Peter White.*

In 1857, Peter White married Ellen Sophia Hewitt: Reynolds Family Tree, Courtesy of the descendants of Peter White, Marquette, MI.

In 1852, Marquette shipped just six barrels of iron ore to New Castle, Pennsylvania: Fuller, *Historic Michigan.*

At first, the ore came out of the hills in raw chunks of reddish stone: Williams, *Honorable Peter White.*

Already, two of his wife's sisters: Shiras 3d and Shiras, *Justice George Shiras Jr.*

George Jr. was a leading counsel for the Baltimore and Ohio and the Junction Valley Railroads: Contemporary Biography of Pennsylvania.

He had the reputation of being "an able debater": Shiras 3d and Shiras, *Justice George Shiras Jr.*

organized the private club to cater to the industrialists and the business elites: Jean Horne, "The Duquesne Club: An Exclusive Retreat for the Corporate Elite," *Pittsburgh Tribune-Review,* January 26, 2011, https://triblive.com/x/pittsburghtrib/lifestyles/s_718227.html.

As one historian wrote: "Living it Up: The Elite Private Club," *Bloomberg News,* April 21, 1997, https://www.bloomberg.com/news/articles/1997-04-20/living-it-up-the-elite-private-clubs.

He joined the club's "Number 6 Group": Shiras 3d and Shiras, *Justice George Shiras Jr.*

CHAPTER 3

In 1869 when George was ten and Winfield nine: Shiras 3d, "Wild Life of Lake Superior."

The campers transferred to yawls: Shiras 3d, "Wild Life of Lake Superior."

Their first adventure together: Shiras 3d, *Hunting Wild Life,* vol. 1.

Normally the boys were accompanied by a guide: Shiras 3d, *Hunting Wild Life,* vol. 1.

George Sr. called La Pete: Shiras 3d and Shiras, *Justice George Shiras Jr.*

Brown, born in New York's Finger Lakes region: Shiras 3d and Shiras, *Justice George Shiras Jr.*

The preferred camp cook was Samson Noll: Shiras 3d and Shiras, *Justice George Shiras Jr.*

In the 1870s, Noll accompanied George: Shiras 3d, *Hunting Wild Life,* vol. 1.

Such seasonal migrations had occurred for centuries: Shiras 3d, *Hunting Wild Life,* vol. 1.

The deer populations exploded: "Deer Management History," www.michigan.gov.dnr.

In 1880, seventy thousand deer were taken in Michigan: "Deer Management History," www.michigan.gov.dnr.

As it was with the bison on the Great Plains: John Burnham, Proceedings of the National Parks Conference, 1917.

the game was there for the taking: Editorial by George Shields, *Shields'* magazine, January 1908.

Noll and his young charges rode the train out of Marquette: Shiras 3d, *Hunting Wild Life,* vol. 1.

The boys were alarmed: Shiras 3d, *Hunting Wild Life,* vol. 1.

The next week in Marquette: Shiras 3d, *Hunting Wild Life,* vol. 1.

George and his family were never as profligate: Logbook from the Camp of the Fiddling Cat, courtesy of the descendants of Peter White, Marquette, MI.

The coming of the railroads: Role of Railroads pamphlet.

Jacking deer at night: Original galley with handwritten corrections of Shiras 3d, *Hunting Wild Life with Camera and Flashlight,* Edward William Nelson and Edward Alphonso Goldman Collection, circa 1873–1946 and undated, Smithsonian Institution Archives, Washington, DC (hereafter Nelson and Goldman Collection).

Buck fever and an itchy trigger finger: Shiras 3d, *Hunting Wild Life,* vol. 1.

went fishing off the mouth of the Sand River: Shiras 3d and Shiras, *Justice George Shiras Jr.*

Outdoor adventures were mostly for men: Shiras 3d, *Hunting Wild Life,* vol. 1.

The men brought earthworms from Pittsburgh: "Obituary of George Shiras Jr.," *Marquette Mining Journal,* August 22, 1924.

there were no Lumbricus terrestris in the Upper Peninsula: Lee E. Frelich and Peter B. Reich, "Will Environmental Changes Reinforce the Impact of Global Warming on the Prairie–Forest Border of Central North America?" *Frontiers in Ecology and the Environment* 8, no. 7 (2009), https://doi.org/10.1890/080191.

Where they established themselves, earthworms changed the ecosystem: Lee E. Frelich, Cindy M. Hale, Stefan Scheu, Andrew R. Holdsworth, Liam Heneghan, Patrick J. Bohlen, and Peter B. Reich, "Earthworm Invasion into Previously Earthworm-Free Temperate and Boreal Forests," *Biological Invasions* 8, no. 6 (September 2006): 1235–45, https://doi.org/10.1007/s10530-006-9019-3.

The coming of the railroads: Role of Railroads pamphlet.

In 1879 when crews reached: Charles A. Symon, ed., "A History of Onota Township," *Alger County: A Centennial History 1885–1985* (Munising, MI: Alger County Historical Society, 1986).

He came to Marquette every September: Shiras 3d and Shiras, *Justice George Shiras Jr.*

they stopped and observed six pileated woodpeckers: Original galley, Shiras 3d, *Hunting Wild Life with Camera and Flashlight.*

It was the last time they camped at Jack's lean-to: Shiras 3d, *Hunting Wild Life*, vol. 1.

Some of George's first photographs: Shiras 3d, *Hunting Wild Life*, vol. 1.

CHAPTER 4

the school was a well-established destination for American boys of privilege: History of Phillips Andover Academy, www.andover.edu

In 1877 Shiras entered Cornell University: The *Pittsburg Index* (a social register of the city's movers and shakers), Library and Archives Division, Historical Society of Western Pennsylvania, Pittsburgh, Pennsylvania, 1898.

The fraternity also brought about Shiras's first meeting with Theodore Roosevelt: George Shiras 3d, "Autobiography of George Shiras 3d" (unpublished manuscript), Central Upper Peninsula and Northern Michigan University Archives, Marquette, MI (hereafter CUP-NMU).

Cayuga Lake (one of New York's Finger Lakes): Shiras 3d, *Hunting Wild Life*, vol. 2.

The ducks were goldeneye, which tend to be solitary, wary birds: Shiras 3d, *Hunting Wild Life*, vol. 2.

He rented a room at a boarding house near the mouth of the East Haven River: Shiras 3d, *Hunting Wild Life*, vol. 2.

He purchased a Barnegat sneak boat: Robert B. White, "History of the Barnegat Bay Sneakbox," *Forest and Stream* magazine, April 3, 1874.

At Yale, his most intellectually stimulating activity: Shiras 3d, unpublished autobiography.

taken notice of Frances or "Fanny" White: Obituary of Frances "Fanny" Shiras, *Marquette Mining Journal*, September 16, 1938.

They married October 31, 1885, in St. Paul's Cathedral: *Marquette Mining Journal*, November 1, 1885.

the reception held at Peter White's mansion on Ridge Street: "Brilliant Nuptials," Milwaukee Sentinel, November 1, 1885.

the presents were "handsome and very costly": *Detroit Journal*, November 1, 1885.

The young couple boarded the train to Chicago: *Marquette Mining Journal*, November 1, 1885.

CHAPTER 5

Shiras recalled those night hunts with fondness and detail: Shiras 3d, *Hunting Wild Life*, vol. 1.

he took a streetcar or cab livery into the downtown offices of Shiras and Dickey: Pittsburg Index.

George was a busy attorney, married man, and a father: "George Shiras at Marquette," *Chicago Tribune*, August 23, 1889.

to form a hunting and fishing club near Cheat Mountain: "History of Cheat Mountain Club," www.cheatmountainclub.com.

In breathless hyperbole: "Favored of Diana: The Spot Chosen as a Preserve by the Cheat Mountain Association," *Pittsburg Press*, May 22, 1888.

"The Cheat Mountain Association is flourishing": "Pittsburg Pickings: Lively Notes on Western Pennsylvania Sportsmen," *Sporting Life*, January 1, 1888.

During his visits, George always saw deer at the slough: Shiras 3d, *Hunting Wild Life*, vol. 1.

Like many photographers of the period: Shiras 3d, *Hunting Wild Life*, vol. 1.

Many years later, Shiras wryly noted: Shiras 3d, *Hunting Wild Life*, vol. 1.

the first commercially produced handheld camera: *Enhancing the Illusion: The Process and Origins of Photography* (pamphlet), Technology Archive of the George Eastman House, Rochester, New York.

Patented in 1883 by William Schmid of Brooklyn: William Schmid, *Photographic Camera*, US Patent 270,133, January 2, 1883.

the camera had a reflex viewfinder: Eaton S. Lothrop Jr., *A Century of Cameras: From the Collection of the International Museum of Photography at George Eastman House* (New York: Morgan and Morgan, 1973).

Shiras, too, was chagrined about so badly wounding the deer: Shiras 3d, *Hunting Wild Life*, vol. 1.

A camera hunter had to get close: Shiras 3d, *Hunting Wild Life*, vol. 1.

He was camera hunting: Matthew Brower, "Trophy Shots: Early North American Photographs of Nonhuman Animals and the Display of Masculine Prowess," *Society and Animals* 13, no. 1 (March 1, 2005): 13–32.

George was regularly emerging from the new darkroom: Shiras 3d, *Hunting Wild Life*, vol. 1.

Deer weren't his only subjects: Shiras 3d, *Hunting Wild Life*, vol. 1.

In following seasons, he purchased more equipment: Nesbitt, *How to Hunt with a Camera*.

In June 1891, Shiras came up with what he called the "camera set": Harris, Thompson, Childs, and Sanderson, "Automatic Storage and Analysis of Camera Trap Data."

Bear, foxes, wolves, and deer were more wary: "Took His Own Picture: Astonishment of a Bear When He Photographed Himself," *New York World*, October 30, 1908.

Shiras had to ignite flash powder: *Flash Photography, Flash Powder* (pamphlet), George Eastman House, Rochester, New York.

Such pyrotechnics involving magnesium powder: Michael Peres, ed., "Flash Powder," *The Focal Encyclopedia of Photography: Digital Imaging, Theory and Application, History and Science* (Taylor & Francis, 2007).

Vacuum flashbulbs sparked with electric current wouldn't be perfected until the 1930s: "The First Flash Bulb," *Image: Journal of Photography of the George Eastman House*, September 1953, http://www.luminous-lint.com/libraryvault/GEH_Image/GEH_1953_02_06.pdf.

Eventually, George Shiras 3d became a master at using flashlights: Nesbitt, *How to Hunt with a Camera*.

If the Schmid Detective camera could be considered a precision machine: Schmid, *Photographic Camera*.

Being back on the lake in the blackness: George Shiras 3d, "A Harmless Sport—Hunting with the Camera," *New York Independent* 52 (June 7, 1900): 1364–68.

When he developed the plate back at the cabin: Shiras 3d, *Hunting Wild Life*, vol. 1.

The answer again lay back in Pittsburgh: George Shiras 3d, "The Shiras Game Pictures," *Outdoor Life,* February 1900.

Fortunately, his boots were damp from the portage: Shiras 3d, *Hunting Wild Life,* vol. 1.

it was clear Shiras needed to be more careful: *Hunting Wild Life,* vol. 1.

To fire Blitz Pulver instantly and safely: *Hunting Wild Life,* vol. 1.

He took out a patent on the device: Photographic Technology Patents, www.vintage-photo.tv/patents.

According to the patent, the portable flashlight could be whipped from the pocket: "Shiras Game Pictures," *Outdoor Life.*

Shiras never produced the device commercially: George Shiras 3d letter to Eastman Kodak Company, January 8, 1912, CUP-NMU.

It's not likely any detectives adopted his camera trap: "First Flash Bulb," Image.

but the patent proves he had created a portable flashlight mechanism: Gilbert Grosvenor memo to Leo Borah, July 1, 1935, National Geographic Library and Archives, Washington, DC (hereafter NGLA).

In 1893 when Jake Brown was unavailable as a guide: "Hammer Recalls Scenes from Adventurous Life," *Marquette Mining Journal,* February 13, 1953.

Over the following forty years: "John Hammer Won Fame as Guide to George Shiras 3d," *Kalamazoo Gazette,* January 22, 1947.

Hammer, the machinist and inventor: Shiras 3d, *Hunting Wild Life,* vol. 1.

They were clever but complicated: "John Hammer Won Fame," *Kalamazoo Gazette.*

The men became friends: George Shiras 3d letter to John Hammer, October 30, 1904, courtesy of the John Hammer family, Marquette, MI.

In a 1903 entry from the camp journal: Camp of the Fiddling Cat logbook.

Success for Shiras the nighttime game photographer came that summer: Shiras 3d, *Hunting Wild Life,* vol. 1.

Photoelectric light meters were decades away: "Exposure Meters," *Early Photography,* http://www.earlyphotography.co.uk/site/meters.html.

Exposures were made on dry plates: Rudolf Kingslake, *Rochester Camera and Lens Companies* (Rochester, NY: Photographic Historical Society, 1974).

The cameras were primitive yet elegantly simple: David Silver, *The 1892 Folding Rochester* (San Francisco: International Photographic Historical Organization, 2012), http://www.photographyhistory.com/CS06/foldingrochester.html.

For some night shots, George employed a stereoscopic camera: Shiras 3d, *Hunting Wild Life,* vol. 1.

the company's patented Unicum Shutter: Rudolf Kingslake, *A History of the Photographic Lens* (Boston: Academic Press, 1989).

Introduced in 1897, the Unicum leaf shutter could shoot from 1/2 to 1/100 of second: "Diaphragm or Leaf Shutters," The Living Image Vintage Camera Museum, www.licm.org.uk.

Shiras also owned a Goerz Dagor lens: "Diaphragm or Leaf Shutters," Living Image Vintage Camera Museum.

His first article and recognition as a camera hunter: George Shiras 3d, "Still Hunting with a Camera," Forest and Stream Amateur Photography Competition, *Forest and Stream* magazine, September 1892.

when he entered several daytime pictures in the magazine's amateur photography competition: Shiras 3d, "Still Hunting with a Camera."

Forest and Stream was a highly influential magazine: George Bird Grinnell and Charles Sheldon, *Hunting and Conservation: The Book of the Boone and Crockett Club* (New Haven, CT: Yale University Press, 1925).

George Bird Grinnell, a historian, anthropologist, and naturalist: Chris Madson, "The Invisible Conservationist," *Wildfowl* magazine, November 2010.

He lived an extraordinary life: George Bird Grinnell Symposium, http://gbgsymposium. homestead.com.

Both Chapman and Grinnell, who later became close friends with Shiras: Frank Chapman letter to George Shiras 3d, February 10, 1904, CUP-NMU.

The contest offered prizes for images of game and fish: Shiras 3d, "Still Hunting with a Camera."

Just four years earlier, he and Grinnell had founded the Boone and Crockett Club: Grinnell and Sheldon, *Hunting and Conservation*.

A letter from Shiras served as the accompanying article: Shiras 3d, "Still Hunting with a Camera."

were not mere snapshots but elegant images of animals in nature: Brower, "Trophy Shots."

One summer night—when the last of twilight faded away: Shiras 3d, *Hunting Wild Life*, vol. 1.

CHAPTER 6

In 1892 President William Harrison nominated George Shiras Jr. to the US Supreme Court: *Contemporary Biography of Pennsylvania*.

in defiance of the Pennsylvania Republican political machine: "Senator Cameron Objects: Trying to Defeat the Confirmation of George Shiras Jr.," *New York Times*, July 22, 1892.

Newspapers generally approved of Shiras: *Muncie Morning News*, May 17, 1892.

Despite being appointed a Supreme Court justice: "Anecdotes of Justice Shiras, George Shiras 3d," *Marquette Mining Journal*, August 1, 1954.

Corruption had an ethnic component: Eugene Thrasher, "The Magee-Flinn Political Machine 1895–1903" (master's thesis, University of Pittsburgh, 1951).

George 3d, whose feelings about politics came from his father and grandfather: Shiras 3d, unpublished autobiography.

of Matthew S. Quay, the state treasurer: Leila H. Rupp, "Matthew Stanley Quay in Pennsylvania State Politics" (master's thesis, University of Pittsburgh, 1928).

Reformers such as Shiras were livid: George Shiras 3d, *A Pig Iron State and Pygmy Statesmen*, pamphlet, 1887, CUP-NMU.

Aside from name-calling: Shiras 3d, *Pig Iron State*.

The affair whetted Shiras's appetite for reform: Shiras 3d, unpublished autobiography.

I came to the conclusion: Shiras 3d, unpublished autobiography.

A few days before he was to leave for Harrisburg: Shiras 3d, unpublished autobiography.

Shiras wrote, "the measure should have been entitled": Shiras 3d, unpublished autobiography.

John Hood, a member of the Feed and Flour Exchange in Pittsburgh, wrote: "Shiras vs. Graham," Campaign Circular of the Citizen's Party, 1902, CUP-NMU.

The following exchange Shiras recalled in detail: Shiras 3d, unpublished autobiography.

Shiras was not always so accommodating: Shiras 3d, unpublished autobiography.

He suspected Judge White and Graham had colluded: Shiras 3d, unpublished autobiography.

His opponent was Colonel Thomas M. Bayne: George Shiras 3d, letter to Gilbert Grosvenor, December 4, 1934, NGLA.

Even the Republican papers: Pittsburgh Commercial Gazette, December 5, 1891.

Stone sent an emissary to Shiras: Shiras 3d, unpublished autobiography.

The party convention was a sham: Shiras 3d, unpublished autobiography.

The police chief "threatened to break any man's head": Pittsburgh Dispatch, September 3, 1902.

With Shiras in the background: Pittsburgh Leader, January 22, 1892.

When the case was heard, the jury came back with a guilty verdict: Pittsburgh Commercial Gazette, April 23, 1902.

A special election was held and Colonel William M. Kennedy: Pittsburgh Commercial Gazette, April 23, 1902.

he posed his grandfather and father in front of a library of books: Shiras 3d, Hunting Wild Life, vol. 1.

CHAPTER 7

In August 1885, just two months before his marriage: Shiras 3d, Hunting Wild Life, vol. 2.

Typically, pigeons arrived in the Lake Superior region in May: Shiras 3d, Hunting Wild Life, vol. 2.

Once the pigeons established breeding colonies: Shiras 3d, Hunting Wild Life, vol. 2.

Baited traps, decoys, nets, whatever the method: Greenberg, Feathered River.

There had been several spectacular and tragic fires: http://peshtigofiremuseum.com/.

Shiras was on the Yellow Dog Plains in the middle of berry patches: Shiras 3d, Hunting Wild Life, vol. 2.

Northern Michigan and western Ontario: Greenberg, Feathered River.

It was a terrible, emblematic loss: Ann E. Chapman, "Nineteenth Century Trends in American Conservation," National Park Service, https://www.nps.gov/nr/travel/massachusetts_conservation/nineteenth_century_trends_in_%20american_conservation.html.

The country at the end of the nineteenth century was learning hard lessons: Burnham, 1917 National Parks Conference.

Natural resources were finite: Brulle and Benford, "From Game Protection to Wildlife Management."

Whitetail deer were no longer common: Grinnell and Sheldon, Hunting and Conservation.

The American bison was gone from the plains entirely: Ernest Harold Baynes, secretary of the American Bison Society, letter to Samuel B. M. Young, superintendent of Yellowstone National Park, December 14, 1907, Archives at the Yellowstone Heritage and Research Center, Gardiner, Montana.

There were many causes: Burnham, 1917 National Parks Conference.

the Shirases became charter members of the Revel Island Shooting Club: Shiras 3d to Hammer, October 30, 1904.

Today the area is part of the Nature Conservancy's Virginia Coast Reserve: www.nature.org/
ourinitiatives/regions/northamerica/unitedstates/virginia.

In the 1890s the area was a shooting gallery for waterfowlers: William G. Thomas, Bruce
Miles Barnes, and Tom Szuba, "The Countryside Transformed: The Eastern
Shore of Virginia, the Pennsylvania Railroad, and the Creation of a Modern Landscape," *Southern Spaces*, 2007, https://southernspaces.org/2007/
countryside-transformed-eastern-shore-virginia-pennsylvania-railroad-and-
creation-modern.

Local guides—even whole families—carved decoys: Shiras 3d, *Hunting Wild Life*, vol. 2.

Locals made extra money as "eggers": Shiras 3d, *Hunting Wild Life*, vol. 2.

Market hunters used sneak boats and punt guns: White, "History of the Barnegat Bay
Sneakbox."

The so-called sportsmen of the day were nearly as profligate: William T. Hornaday, *Our
Vanishing Wildlife: Its Extermination and Preservation* (New York Zoological Society,
1913).

During spring and fall migrations at Revel Island: Shiras 3d, *Hunting Wild Life*, vol. 2.

As George 3d remembered it, every clubhouse from Virginia to New Jersey: Shiras 3d, *Hunting
Wild Life*, vol. 2.

Perhaps the best indication of his greater appreciation: Shiras 3d, *Hunting Wild Life*, vol. 2.

CHAPTER 8

Mary, who had married A. O. Jopling: Alvah L. Sawyer, "Biographical Sketch of A. O.
Jopling," *A History of the Northern Peninsula of Michigan and Its People* (Chicago:
Lewis Publishing, 1911). J. M. Longyear Research Library, MRHC.

The primitive camp of logs at Whitefish Lake: Shiras 3d, "Wild Life of Lake Superior."

The evolution logically followed: Symon, "History of Onota Township."

A description of the camp from a biography of Peter White: Williams, *Honorable Peter White*.

Camp life was carefully recorded: Camp of the Fiddling Cat logbook.

Canned goods and other supplies: Symon, "History of Onota Township."

After that, there was the old cabin: Camp of the Fiddling Cat logbook.

John Hammer's occasional journal entries: Camp of the Fiddling Cat logbook.

The houseboat was moored: Map from plat book and logging survey of Peter White
holdings, Section 34, Township 4, Range 22, circa 1910, CUP-NMU.

When the women wrote in the journal: Camp of the Fiddling Cat logbook.

Edwin W. Smith, a member of the Duquesne Club: Shiras 3d, *Hunting Wild Life*, vol. 1.

At camp, the men sailed Certain Death: Camp of the Fiddling Cat logbook.

described the difficulty of making "flashlight pictures": Camp of the Fiddling Cat logbook.

Although an 1887 law made it illegal to use dogs or lights for taking deer: "Deer Management History," www.michigan.gov.dnr.

Typically, Jake Brown or John Hammer rowed the hunters: Shiras 3d, *Hunting Wild Life*, vol.
1.

Always, White kept score in the camp journal: Camp of the Fiddling Cat logbook.

They did just that: Shiras 3d, *Hunting Wild Life*, vol. 1.

One evening, a party ate dinner on the houseboat: Camp of the Fiddling Cat logbook.

Flash powder was a volatile substance: Shiras 3d to Eastman Kodak Company, January 8, 1912.

By the late 1890s, Jack La Pete could no longer do the hard work of a camp man: Shiras 3d, *Hunting Wild Life,* vol. 1.

Jake Brown left Michigan in 1894: Shiras 3d, *Hunting Wild Life,* vol. 1.

Henry's Lake proved a deliverance for Jake: Shiras 3d, *Hunting Wild Life,* vol. 2.

Samson Noll died in 1898 in a cabin near Whitefish Lake: Shiras 3d, *Hunting Wild Life,* vol. 2.

He looked for ways to automate the process: Shiras 3d, *Hunting Wild Life,* vol. 1.

Hammer, the machinist: Shiras 3d, *Hunting Wild Life,* vol. 1.

Typically, Shiras placed one half to three quarters of an ounce: Peres, "Flash Powder."

George wrote, "Lying beside a blazing camp fire that accentuates the darkness": Shiras 3d, *Hunting Wild Life,* vol. 1.

Hammer, with Shiras's encouragement, took out patents on the air pump mechanism: John H. Hammer, *Photographic-shutter-operating mechanism,* US Patent 762,711, June 14, 1904.

A. O. Jopling, Shiras's brother-in-law, was an engineer and partner in the hardware business: Sawyer, "Biographical Sketch of A. O. Jopling."

He was a published author and a photographer of growing reputation: George Shiras 3d, "Hunting with a Camera," *New York Sun,* July 8, 1895.

The following year, he produced: The Famous "Midnight Series" of Wild Game Photographs, marketing booklet, 1901.

He published sets of bromide enlargements: Famous "Midnight Series" marketing booklet.

It was not quite wildlife photography: Matthew Brower, *Developing Animals, Wildlife and Early American Photography* (Minneapolis: University of Minnesota Press, 2010).

the pictures were entirely novel: Finis Dunaway, *Natural Visions: The Power of Images in American Environmental Movement* (Chicago: University of Chicago Press, 2008).

The editor of Recreation *magazine:* Famous "Midnight Series" marketing booklet.

Shiras estimated he earned more than $20,000: George Shiras 3d letter to Gilbert Grosvenor, November 16, 1934, NGLA.

one hundred years later would be the equivalent of nearly $500,000: Consumer Price Index, Bureau of Labor Statistics, https://www.bls.gov/cpi/.

In 1900, the US Forestry Division: Draft of foreword to *Hunting Wild Life with Camera and Flashlight,* Nelson and Goldman Collection.

The four wildlife images in the American Pavilion: Sonia Voss and Jean-Christophe Bailly, *George Shiras: In the Heart of the Dark Night* (Paris: Editions Xavier Barral, 2015).

In 1900, in Outdoor Life: "Shiras Game Pictures," *Outdoor Life.*

On another night that season, he let Hammer pursue a fawn: "Hammer Recalls Scenes," *Marquette Mining Journal.*

the guide ended up with a bloody nose: Shiras 3d, *Hunting Wild Life,* vol. 1.

As time went on, Shiras gained: New York Independent, November 11, 1900.

CHAPTER 9

Although George Shiras 3d was gaining a national: Nesbitt, *How to Hunt with a Camera.*

The Progressive Era—as it came to be known: David Stradling, ed., *Conservation in the Progressive Era: Classic Texts* (Seattle: University of Washington Press, 2004).

Progressivism started in the 1890s: Overview of the Progressive Era, www.digitalhistory. uh.edu.

Muckraking journalists—Ida Tarbell, Lincoln Steffens: Doris Kearns-Goodwin, *The Bully Pulpit: Theodore Roosevelt, William Howard Taft and the Golden Age of Journalism* (New York: Simon and Schuster, 2004), 303–8.

In December 1901, the Citizen's Party was born: Shiras 3d, unpublished autobiography.

The movement was a serious challenge to the Ring: Shiras 3d, unpublished autobiography.

His nephew later wrote: Shiras 3d and Shiras, *Justice George Shiras Jr.*

He was a Republican, too: Joan Marie Ellis, "Law, Lawmakers and Politics: The Life and Times of George Shiras 3d" (master's thesis, University of Pittsburgh, 1955).

The Shiras-Graham fight was close all the way: Ellis, "Law, Lawmakers and Politics."

The Citizen's Party distributed thousands: "Shiras vs. Graham," Campaign Circular of the Citizen's Party, 1902.

On Election Day, turnout was heavy: "Shiras vs. Graham," Campaign Circular of the Citizen's Party, 1902.

Shiras met Roosevelt at a reception: Shiras 3d, unpublished autobiography.

In 1902, Philander Knox, the US attorney general: Letters between George Shiras 3d, Philander Knox, and George Cortelyou, March 12 and 13, 1902, CUP-NMU.

As a reformer, he did not curry favor with Joe Cannon, the powerful Speaker of the House: History, Art, and Archives, US House of Representatives, http://history.house.gov/.

It was an impressive group headed by the renowned John Lacey: Madson, "Invisible Conservationist."

The Lacey Act of 1900 made it illegal to kill game: Lawrence H. Chamberlain, *The President, Congress, and Legislation* (New York: Columbia University Press, 1946)

Just as he took office, an outbreak of typhoid fever: James A. McKee, ed., "The 1903–1904 Typhoid Fever Epidemic in Butler, Pennsylvania," *20th Century History of Butler and Butler County* (Chicago: Richmond-Arnold, 1909).

In the nineteenth century, typhoid outbreaks: Andrea Hektor, Stephanie Arbelovsky, and Christina Hynes, "Typhoid in America 1840–1940," Report for Monroe Weber-Shirk Civil and Environmental Engineering, 2004, ceeserver.cee.cornell.edu/ mw24/Archive/04/cee454/typhoid/TyphoidFunPH.doc.

Typhoid is a bacterial infection: Jesse Ausubel, Perrin Meyer, and Iddo K. Wernick, "Death and the Human Environment: The United States in the 20th Century," Report for the Program for the Human Environment, Rockefeller University, Technology in Society, 2001.

Pittsburgh led the nation in cases of typhoid fever: Ausubel, Meyer, and Wernick, "Death and the Human Environment."

Partly what motivated Shiras was the Supreme Court decision: "Obituary of George Shiras Jr.," *Marquette Mining Journal.*

Shiras called upon Surgeon General Walter Wyman: George Shiras Papers, History of Medicine Division, National Library of Medicine, National Institutes of Health, Bethesda, Maryland.

In the brief, Shiras made a case for federal oversight: Efficiency of Public Health and Marine Hospital Service, Report Number 2000 to the US House of Representatives, Sixtieth Congress, 1909.

He also made a speech on the House floor: Speech by George Shiras 3d in US House of Representatives, February 23, 1905.

His conclusions would impact his thinking: George Shiras 3d, *History of the First Migratory Bird Bill and Its Subsequent Enactment*, pamphlet, July 1, 1927.

Being a member of the Public Lands Committee: Shiras 3d, *Hunting Wild Life*, vol. 2.

Enlarging Yellowstone National Park was not a new idea: Christina M. Cromley, "Historical Elk Migrations around Jackson Hole, Wyoming," *Yale F&ES Bulletin* 104 (2008): 53–65.

In the year prior to Shiras's visit: Shiras 3d, *Hunting Wild Life*, vol. 2.

Shiras and John Hammer arrived on the Northern Pacific Railway: Shiras 3d, *Hunting Wild Life*, vol. 2.

the US Army was in charge of the park: Baynes to Young, December 14, 1907.

Shiras and Hammer stayed at the clubhouse for several days: Baynes to Young, December 14, 1907.

Shiras wrote to William Loeb, Theodore Roosevelt's secretary: George Shiras 3d letter to William Loeb, January 26, 1905, CUP-NMU.

In 1912, the National Elk Refuge was established: Cromley, "Historical Elk Migrations."

In the second session of the Fifty-Eighth Congress: Reports of the Public Lands Committee, House of Representatives, Fifty-Eighth Congress, United States National Archives.

Another report recommended giving North Dakota: Fifty-Eighth Congress Second Session, House of Representatives, Committee on Public Lands Reports, United States National Archives, Washington, DC.

In his pursuit of conservation, Theodore Roosevelt frequently acted unilaterally: "The Conservationists of the Progressive Period," in Stradling, *Conservation in the Progressive Era.*

Uncle Joe Cannon did much to slow down: History, Art, and Archives, US House of Representatives, http://history.house.gov.

Under executive order: Theodore Roosevelt letter to George Shiras 3d, February 1, 1905, CUP-NMU.

Protecting land under the jurisdiction of the federal government: Chapman, "Nineteenth Century Trends."

When he became president, Roosevelt named his friend Gifford Pinchot: US Forest Service History, www.foresthistory.org.

Their aggressive actions were an inspiration: Migratory Bird Bill, H.R. 1560, 59th Cong. (1904).

The states were inadequate to protect birds: Migratory Bird Bill, H.R. 1560.

Forest and Stream offered support for the bill: Editorial, *Forest and Stream* magazine, January 1905.

Charles Bingham Reynolds, the editor, sent the bill to several state game commissioners: Charles Bingham Reynolds letter to George Shiras 3d, January 11, 1905, CUP-NMU.

On letterhead of the Committee of Public Lands: Shiras 3d to Loeb, January 26, 1905.

Speaking for the Audubon Society: George Shiras 3d, *Necessity for and Constitutionality of the Act of Congress Protecting Migratory Birds*, 1914 pamphlet, NGLA.

The bird law was not produced in a vacuum: Caspar Whitney, "The Sportsman's View-Point," *Outing: An Illustrated Monthly Magazine of Recreation*, February 1905.

The Businessman's League of Rockport: Scrapbook of George Shiras 3d, CUP-NMU.

Shiras's office in Washington received a letter: Scrapbook of George Shiras 3d.

Members and their club wardens: Sam B. Woods, "The First Hundred Years of Lake County, as Lived and Acted by Bartlett Woods and Family and by Sam B. Woods and Family," 1938, http://genealogytrails.com/ind/lake/tollestongunclub.html.

U. J. Hindert, a farmer from Minonk, Illinois: Scrapbook of George Shiras 3d.

Roosevelt wrote to Shiras from the White House: Roosevelt to Shiras 3d, February 1, 1905.

Roosevelt, a bird-watcher: Frank Chapman, *Autobiography of a Bird-Lover* (New York: D. Appleton-Century, 1933).

True to his word, Shiras declined to run: Scrapbook of George Shiras 3d.

Later, Shiras expressed pride in his friend's longevity in office: Scrapbook of George Shiras 3d.

In 1903 George Junior retired from the Supreme Court: Shiras 3d and Shiras, *Justice George Shiras Jr.*

In 1895 Junior received unfavorable publicity: Charles Fairman, "Reviewed Work: Justice George Shiras, Jr., of Pittsburgh: A Chronicle of His Family, Life, and Times by George Shiras, 3rd, Winfield Shiras," *Yale Law Journal*, January 1954.

George 3d, Fanny and the children, however, established a home in Wesley Heights: Shiras 3d, unpublished autobiography.

He joined the Cosmos Club, a private social club for men on Lafayette Square: www.cosmos-club.org/History.

He held the organization and its ideals in high regard: Shiras's personal copy of *American Big Game in Its Haunts: The Book of the Boone and Crockett Club*, edited by Theodore Roosevelt (Forest and Stream Publishing, 1904), Peter White Public Library, Marquette, MI (hereafter PWPL).

the club elected Shiras an associate member: Shiras 3d, unpublished autobiography.

The men of Boone and Crockett and the Cosmos Club held high positions in the government: Chapman, *Autobiography of a Bird-Lover*.

Discussions and ideas at the clubs: George Bird Grinnell Papers, Yale University Library, New Haven, Connecticut (hereafter GBGP).

As Shiras later wrote: Shiras 3d, *Hunting Wild Life*, vol. 1.

CHAPTER 10

The entire staff of the magazine: John Oliver La Gorce letter to George Shiras 3d, October 4, 1938, NGLA.

The National Geographic Society had been founded in 1888: www.nationalgeographic.com/about-national-geographic/milestones.

Meanwhile, consumer magazines of all types were booming: Muckraking magazines, Periodicals Department Collection and State Library Resources, Enoch Pratt Free Library, www.prattlibrary.org.

The technologies of photography and printing were going through a revolution: "First Flash Bulb," Image.

When Hubbard died in 1897: www.nationalgeographic.com/about-national-geographic/milestones.

It was the first time the magazine had a full-time editor: Obituary of Dr. Gilbert H. Grosvenor, *New York Times*, February 4, 1966.

The men embraced photography as a way to popularize the magazine: Volkmar K. Wentzel, "Gilbert Hovey Grosvenor, Father of Photojournalism," www.comosclub.org/web/journals/1998/wentzel.html.

"the word photograph *had become as musical to my ear"*: Wentzel, "Gilbert Hovey Grosvenor."

After the publicity of the World's Fair: Lectures on Wild Beasts, *Washington Herald*, November 27, 1910.

However, the fame derived from the National Geographic Society: George Shiras's Wildlife Photographs, National Geographic Timeline 1900–1909, The National Geographic Society, Washington, DC, http://press.nationalgeographic.com/milestones/.

It would make Shiras a seminal figure of the early conservation movement: Norma Olin Ireland, Index to Scientists of the World from Ancient to Modern Times: Biographies and Portraits (Boston: F. W. Faxon Co., 1962).

of being a renowned faunal naturalist: John Oliver La Gorce letter to George Shiras 3d, March 27, 1922, NGLA.

These were the first wildlife photos ever published in the magazine: 1906: Wildlife Photography Comes to the Magazine, National Geographic Timeline, The National Geographic Society, Washington, DC.

By this time, Shiras had accumulated nearly three thousand glass negatives: George Shiras 3d letter to Theodore Roosevelt, February 27, 1906, CUP-NMU.

To illustrate his camera hunting technique: George Shiras 3d, "Photographing Wild Game with Flashlight and Camera: With a Series of 70 illustrations of Wild Game—Deer, Elk, Bull Moose, Raccoon, Porcupine, Wild Cat, Herons, Ducks, Snowy Owls, Pelicans, Birds In Flight, Etc." *National Geographic* magazine, July 1906.

Other images represented Shiras's wide interest: Chapman to Shiras 3d, February 10, 1904.

This time Grosvenor got guff from the society's stodgy board of managers: Mark Collins Jenkins, *National Geographic 125 Years: Legendary Photographs, Adventures, and Discoveries That Changed the World* (Washington, DC: National Geographic, 2012), 85–88.

Grosvenor, however, remembered the July 1906 "number": Gilbert Grosvenor letter to George Shiras 3d, 1928, NGLA.

Theodore Roosevelt was so impressed: Theodore Roosevelt letter to Gilbert H. Grosvenor, July 14, 1906, Archives at the National Geographic Society, Washington, DC.

That same day, Roosevelt dictated a letter: Theodore Roosevelt letter to George Shiras 3d, July 14, 1906, CUP-NMU.

I have just been looking through your photographs: Roosevelt letter to Shiras 3d, July 14, 1906.

Although he had been doing taxidermy since he was a child: Gerald Carson, "T. R. and the 'Nature Fakers,'" *American Heritage* magazine, 1971.

Roosevelt was not formally trained: J. Emmett Duffy, ed., "History of the Pelican Island National Wildlife Refuge," US Fish and Wildlife Service, 2006, http://www. eoearth.org/view/article/153519/.

The letter was not the first occasion Roosevelt had urged Shiras to write a book: Series of letters between George Shiras 3d and Theodore Roosevelt, 1906–1918, CUP-NMU.

Shiras proved to be a perfectionist: George Shiras 3d letter to Gilbert Grosvenor, July 6, 1921, NGLA.

When the July 1906 number appeared: George Shiras 3d letter to Theodore Roosevelt, July 28, 1906, CUP-NMU.

In the National Geographic article: Shiras 3d, "Photographing Wild Game."

Yet he set himself apart: Shiras 3d, "Photographing Wild Game."

Shiras defended true sportsmen: Shiras 3d, "Photographing Wild Game."

As the article was being published: Shiras 3d, *Hunting Wild Life*, vol. 1.

Frank Chapman, when he saw these pictures, felt the images were rather artificial: Original galley, Shiras 3d, *Hunting Wild Life with Camera and Flashlight*.

The explosions were powerful: Shiras 3d, *Hunting Wild Life*, vol. 1.

By 1906 Shiras was not only the camera hunter working with nighttime photography: Shiras 3d, *Hunting Wild Life*, vol. 1.

CHAPTER 11

In 1903 Roosevelt signed an executive order: Duffy, "History of the Pelican Island National Wildlife Refuge."

Five weeks after Roosevelt declared the island protected: Shiras 3d, *Hunting Wild Life*, vol. 2.

In 1905 he returned to the island with Frank Chapman: Chapman, *Autobiography of a Bird-Lover*.

It could be a dangerous business: Ruth Shippen Musgrave and Judy Flynn-O'Brien, "Federal Wildlife Law of the 20th Century," *Federal Wildlife Laws Handbook with Related Laws* (Government Institutes, 1998).

One year, he went to the Big Green Swamp: Shiras 3d, *Hunting Wild Life*, vol. 2.

Built in 1887 by some of the town's pioneer families: Alice Strickland, *Ormond-on-the-Halifax: A Centennial History of Ormond Beach* (Ormond Beach Historical Trust, 1980).

the hotel was a sprawling, all-wooden structure: Donald Spencer, *Hotel Ormond: A Lost Treasure* (Ormond Beach, FL: Camelot, 2002)

members of the New York and New England social set: "Social Events at Springtime Resorts," *New York Times*, March 31, 1912.

Henry Flagler, one of the founders of Standard Oil: Alice Strickland, *Ormond's Historic Homes: From Palmetto-Thatched Shacks to Millionaire's Mansions* (Ormond Beach Historical Trust, 1992).

He added a casino, swimming pool, and golf course: Strickland, *Ormond's Historic Homes*.

In 1895 Ormond had just four hundred permanent residents: Michael G. Schene, Hopes, Dreams, and Promises: A History of Volusia County, Florida (Daytona Beach, FL: News-Journal Corporation, c. 1976).

In the early 1900s, the hotel's telegraph office frequently announced: Strickland, *Ormond's Historic Homes.*

The location proved pleasant: Daytona *Gazette-News,* January 16, 1904.

The cottages were sprawling, two-story clapboard homes: Daytona *Gazette-News,* January 18, 1908.

Ormond became a gathering point: Daytona *Gazette-News,* December 25, 1909.

They attended and donated generously to the Episcopal Church: Strickland, *Ormond-on-the-Halifax.*

In retirement, Junior spent many a happy winter: Shiras 3d and Shiras, *Justice George Shiras Jr.*

George 3d discovered a wealth of critters living behind his winter home: Shiras 3d, *Hunting Wild Life,* vol. 2.

The cameras and booming flashlights at first alarmed the neighbors and guests: Shiras 3d, *Hunting Wild Life,* vol. 1.

Few animals escaped his camera: George Shiras 3d letter to Gilbert Grosvenor, February 26, 1912, NGLA.

It is clear from his field notes and copious observations: Shiras 3d, *Hunting Wild Life,* vol. 2.

He surmised correctly that it was a specialist: Canaveral/Merritt's Island National Wildlife Refuge, map and description, US Department of the Interior.

Close to Ormond, the Tomoka River became a favorite haunt: Tomoka State Park Description, Florida Division of Recreation and Parks, https://floridastateparks.org/.

After taking his family on one of these picnic excursions: Shiras 3d, *Hunting Wild Life,* vol. 2.

Shiras also maintained a houseboat on the Halifax: Shiras 3d, *Hunting Wild Life,* vol. 2.

Frequently they took the boat down the river: Quarterly Newsletter of the Ponce de Leon Inlet Lighthouse Preservation Association, January 2014.

what many years later became the space center: "Ponce de Leon Inlet Light Station and Museum," brochure, Ponce de Leon Inlet Lighthouse Preservation Association.

They'd been hit by a seventy-five-foot scow: Shiras 3d, *Hunting Wild Life,* vol. 2.

Shiras and Frank Chapman spent many nights at Oak Lodge: Chapman, *Autobiography of a Bird-Lover.*

"Ma" Latham, who ran the lodge: Duffy, "History of the Pelican Island National Wildlife Refuge."

It was a good life for gentlemen and naturalists: George Shiras 3d letter to E. W. Nelson, February 17, 1922, Nelson and Goldman Collection.

E. W. Nelson of the Biological Survey would stay for a few days: George Shiras 3d letter to Gilbert Grosvenor, March 21, 1923, NGLA.

Norman McClintock, a fellow Pittsburgher: Obituary of Norman McClintock, *The Auk,* 1938.

to film birds on the beach and in nearby marshes: "Bird Life in Movies: Norman McClintock's Films Delight National Geographic Society," *Washington Post,* April 7, 1917.

Over the years, Shiras helped finance: George Shiras 3d letter to Gilbert Grosvenor, March 18, 1920, NGLA.

Frank Chapman chose Ormond Beach as a winter home: Chapman, *Autobiography of a Bird-Lover.*

the Casements, across the street from the hotel: Strickland, *Ormond-on-the-Halifax.*

But Frank Chapman was quite friendly with Rockefeller: Chapman, *Autobiography of a Bird-Lover.*

Chapman and George 3d were often seen strolling: Chapman, *Autobiography of a Bird-Lover.*

CHAPTER 12

In the spring of 1907, Frank Chapman invited Shiras on an expedition: George Shiras 3d letter to William Loeb, February 10, 1908, CUP-NMU.

They met up in Miami and boarded the fifty-eight-foot yacht of the Marine Biological Laboratory: Shiras 3d, *Hunting Wild Life,* vol. 2.

Chapman planned to arrive at Cay Verde at the height of nesting season: Frank Chapman, "A Report on Expeditions Made in 1907 under the North American Ornithology Fund," *American Museum Journal* 7 no. 8 (December 1907): 121–32, Archives of the American Museum of Natural History, New York City (hereafter AMNH).

The calm did not last: Chapman, "Expeditions Made in 1907."

They laid up for two days, pumping out the bilges: Chapman, "Expeditions Made in 1907."

The boobies were amazingly tame: Chapman, "Expeditions Made in 1907."

Shiras set up his camera within inches of a nest: George Shiras 3d, "One Season's Game-Bag with the Camera," *National Geographic* magazine, June 1908.

Some of his most striking images revealed frigates in midair: Shiras 3d, "One Season's Game-Bag."

Two years later, the men joined up for another adventure: Chapman, *Autobiography of a Bird-Lover.*

They were joined by Louis A. Fuertes: http://www.birds.cornell.edu/.

He illustrated the field guide Citizen Bird: www.latinonaturalhistory.biodiversityexhibition.com.

Shiras was in eminent company: Shiras 3d, *Hunting Wild Life,* vol. 2.

They identified eighty-eight species of birds during their stay: Shiras 3d, *Hunting Wild Life,* vol. 2.

Sunset found the men short of their goal: Chapman, *Autobiography of a Bird-Lover.*

"Shiras, a far more experienced camper": Chapman, *Autobiography of a Bird-Lover.*

In the evenings, Fuertes sketched the specimens: Shiras 3d, *Hunting Wild Life,* vol. 2.

paintings could be more lifelike and better studied by ornithologists: *The Auk,* January 1911.

He had observed Chapman taking scoops: Shiras 3d, *Hunting Wild Life,* vol. 2.

The men had fun in camp: Shiras 3d, *Hunting Wild Life,* vol. 2.

CHAPTER 13

"After studying the law of men, I wanted to study the law of nature": Shiras 3d, "Wild Life of Lake Superior."

In 1908 the Museum of Natural History in New York named Shiras chair: Frank Chapman letter to George Shiras 3d, December 19, 1911, AMNH.

He joined the Explorers Club: Chapman to Shiras 3d, December 19, 1911.

a literary war of words against authors of so-called realistic animal stories: Ralph Lutts, *The Nature Fakers: Wildlife, Science, and Sentiment* (University Press of Virginia, 2001).

Beginning in the 1890s: Shiras 3d, unpublished autobiography.

Two trips Shiras took to Newfoundland: George Shiras 3d letter to Theodore Roosevelt, June 25, 1907, CUP-NMU.

In September 1906 he went north to witness the migration: Shiras 3d, *Hunting Wild Life*, vol. 2.

Shiras went north by train and ferry with John Hammer: Shiras 3d, *Hunting Wild Life*, vol. 2.

Foxes were numerous even in daytime: Shiras 3d, *Hunting Wild Life*, vol. 2.

He shot a wonderfully sublime image of Hammer: Shiras 3d, *Hunting Wild Life*, vol. 2.

Back in the States that winter: Brochure of Canadian Club Dinner, New York City, November 1907, GBGP.

He had missed the migration: Shiras 3d, *Hunting Wild Life*, vol. 2.

One evening, three college boys came into camp: Shiras 3d, *Hunting Wild Life*, vol. 2.

As they paddled back to the railroad: Shiras 3d, *Hunting Wild Life*, vol. 2.

Rudyard Kipling had started the trend of animal fiction in 1894: Lutts, *Nature Fakers*.

When he arrived back in Washington: George Shiras 3d letters to Robert T. Morris and George Bird Grinnell, November 11, 1907, GBGP.

He dashed off a letter to Robert T. Morris: Shiras 3d to Morris and Grinnell, November 11, 1907.

To understand the rancor of the nature-faker debate: Chapman, "Nineteenth Century Trends."

People felt divorced from nature: Grinnell and Sheldon, *Hunting and Conservation*.

Peter White convinced the federal government to cede the three-hundred-acre peninsula: Maps and Information to Presque Isle (City of Marquette brochure, 2016).

For decades, Burroughs wrote from his farm in the Catskill Mountains: John Burroughs Association, www.research.amnh.org.

An early practitioner was Ernest Thompson Seton: Famous "Midnight Series" marketing booklet.

In the prologue, he claims: Ernest Thompson Seton, *Wild Animals I Have Known* (New York: Grosset & Dunlap, 1898).

William Long, pastor of the Congregationalist Church: Carson, "T. R. and the 'Nature Fakers.'"

By summer 1903, John Burroughs had enough of this excess sentimentalizing: Chapman, *Autobiography of a Bird-Lover*.

But it was Burroughs's stature as the most eminent naturalist of the day: "Veteran Naturalist Analyzes Dr. Long's Animal Stories," *New York Tribune*, June 9, 1907.

In the Atlantic article, he disparaged this "yellow journalism of the woods": "Real and Sham Natural History," *Atlantic Monthly*, March 1903.

In this post-Darwinian period: Lutts, *Nature Fakers*.

Seton was chastened by the criticism: Carson, "T. R. and the 'Nature Fakers.'"

Both Frank Chapman and Mabel Osgood Wright: Chapman, *Autobiography of a Bird-Lover*.

He offered another example: "Veteran Naturalist," *New York Tribune*.

He once saw a woodcock with a fractured leg: "Real Naturalists on Nature Faking: President Roosevelt and Seven of the Most Eminent American Naturalists Riddle the Pretensions of the Nature Fakers," *Everybody's* magazine, September 1907.

Animal behavior was so diverse: Barney Nelson, "Nature Faking," *Range* magazine, Spring 2002.

These wild claims were met with derision: Chapman, *Autobiography of a Bird-Lover*.

That summer Roosevelt invited Burroughs: Lutts, *Nature Fakers*.

At the Cosmos Club and in scientific circles: Chapman, *Autobiography of a Bird-Lover*.

Roosevelt publicly held his tongue until early 1907: Carson, "T. R. and the 'Nature Fakers.'"

The president gave an interview to Edward B. Clark: Edward B. Clark, "Roosevelt on the Nature Fakirs," *Everybody's* magazine, June 1907.

Roosevelt cited the expertise of his friend: Clark, "Roosevelt on the Nature Fakirs."

with an angry Dr. Long ready to fight back: "Roosevelt Only a Gamekiller—Long; Stamford Naturalist Strikes Back at Criticism of His Nature Books," *New York Times*, May 23, 1907.

Long prepared an open letter to the president: "Long Writes Roosevelt: Says His Article is Noticeable for Bad Taste and Cowardice," *New York Times*, May 24, 1907.

In Washington, Shiras read the papers with a mixture of alarm and amusement: George Shiras 3d letter to William Loeb, May 30, 1907, CUP-NMU.

Still, Shiras worried Long was getting more press: "The Nature Controversy," *New York Times*, June 8, 1907.

He wrote a long letter to Roosevelt: George Shiras 3d letter to Theodore Roosevelt, May 30, 1907, CUP-NMU.

Nevertheless, Long was good at dishing it out: Associated Press, 1907.

It all made good copy: Theodore Roosevelt letter to George Shiras 3d, June 7, 1907, CUP-NMU.

When The Outlook *ran another letter from Long*: Roosevelt to Shiras 3d, June 7, 1907.

Roosevelt had a soft spot for The Outlook: Scrapbook of George Shiras 3d.

On June 8 Shiras wrote the president that he was postponing a trip to Canada: George Shiras 3d letter to Theodore Roosevelt, June 8, 1907, CUP-NMU.

On June 9 Roosevelt invited Shiras to lunch at the White House: Theodore Roosevelt letter to George Shiras 3d, June 9, 1907, CUP-NMU.

Remarkably, it may have been the last time an accomplished ornithologist: Greenberg, *Feathered River*.

At lunch that day, Shiras and TR were joined: Shiras 3d, unpublished autobiography.

But the more immediate issue for the president was nature faking: Letters and telegrams between George Shiras 3d, E. W. Nelson, William Loeb, Edward Clark, and Theodore Roosevelt, July 1907, CUP-NMU.

When Roosevelt wrote Shiras from Oyster Bay: Theodore Roosevelt letter to George Shiras 3d, July 22, 1907, CUP-NMU.

Things were moving fast: Theodore Roosevelt letter to George Shiras 3d, July 29, 1907, CUP-NMU.

Nelson wired Shiras from Washington: E. W. Nelson and Edward Clark telegrams to George Shiras 3d, July 25, 1907, CUP-NMU.

Shiras was at Whitefish Lake: George Shiras 3d letter to E. W. Nelson, July 27, 1907, Nelson and Goldman Collection.

he was dictating an essay "on the mendacity of Dr. Long": George Shiras 3d letter to Theodore Roosevelt at Oyster Bay, NY, July 29, 1907, CUP-NMU.

William Loeb wrote on July 31 from Oyster Bay: William Loeb Jr. letter to George Shiras 3d, July 31, 1907, CUP-NMU.

A teaser on page one proclaimed: "Real Naturalists on Nature Faking," *Everybody's* magazine.

The symposium, Clark wrote in the introduction: "Real Naturalists on Nature Faking," *Everybody's* magazine.

On his last trip through New Brunswick and Newfoundland: "Real Naturalists on Nature Faking," *Everybody's* magazine.

George was harking back to the Bible: "Real Naturalists on Nature Faking," *Everybody's* magazine.

Then it fell to Roosevelt to strike Long dead: "Real Naturalists on Nature Faking," *Everybody's* magazine.

After extolling the virtues and expertise of his fellow naturalists: Maurice Garland Fulton, ed., *Roosevelt's Writings: Selections from the Writings of Theodore Roosevelt* (New York: MacMillan, 1920).

The next day, the New York Times ran an article: "Roosevelt Whacks Dr. Long Once More, Seven Hall-Marked Naturalists Write a Symposium on Nature Fakers," *New York Times*, August 21, 1907.

Long never recovered from the onslaught: Carson, "T. R. and the 'Nature Fakers.'"

The bellicose Long never forgave Roosevelt: Lutts, *Nature Fakers*.

That was a reference to the rumor being spread by the "Old Guard" Republicans: Lawrence Abbott, *Impressions of Theodore Roosevelt* (New York: Doubleday, 1920).

CHAPTER 14

When his friendship with the Colonel: Shiras 3d, *Hunting Wild Life*, vol. 1.

Shiras began getting invitations to the White House: Series of letters between George Shiras 3d, Theodore Roosevelt, and William Loeb Jr., 1905–1907, CUP-NMU.

Shiras never knew who might share the table: Shiras 3d, unpublished autobiography.

The youngsters turned out to be William Howard Taft: Shiras 3d, *Hunting Wild Life*, vol. 1.

Shiras told a tale about a friend: Shiras 3d, *Hunting Wild Life*, vol. 1.

Over the years, there were many such social occasions: Series of letters between George Shiras 3d and Theodore Roosevelt, 1904 to 1915, CUP-NMU.

In 1907, National Geographic magazine published a rather odd story: George Shiras 3d, "A Flashlight Story of an Albino Porcupine and of a Cunning but Unfortunate Coon," *National Geographic* magazine, August 1907.

The mere presence of a raccoon at Whitefish Lake: Leopold, "Report on a Game Survey."

For the next two weeks, he set camera traps: George Shiras 3d, "A Raccoon Explores New Country," *Forest and Stream* magazine, January 1920.

In June 1908 National Geographic magazine: George Shiras 3d, "One Season's Game-Bag with the Camera," *National Geographic* magazine, June 1908.

That year, National Geographic *published*: "Scenes from Every Land," special edition from *National Geographic* magazine, 1908.

Another read, "New Brunswick, Caribou stag with symmetrical horns": "Scenes from Every Land," National Geographic magazine.

That actually wasn't quite true: "Camera Hunt in the Wilds of Alaska," *Seattle Post-Intelligencer*, September 22, 1911.

the heavily forested island in Lake Superior had been stocked with exotic animals by William Mather: "Grand Island Experimental Game Refuge for Many Years," *Marquette Mining Journal,* 1951.

Mather's stated purpose on Grand Island was to create "a second Yellowstone": Lawrence Rakestraw, Fred Stormer, and Christopher R. Eder, "A Second Yellowstone," *Journal of Forest History* 21, no. 3 (July 1977): 158–60.

The island was wonderfully scenic: "Grand Island," *Marquette Mining Journal.*

most frank expression regarding his personal feeling toward predators: "Grand Island," *Marquette Mining Journal.*

Grand Island already had deer: Rakestraw, Stormer, and Eder, "A Second Yellowstone."

The Grand Island Game Preserve experiment: Rakestraw, Stormer, and Eder, "A Second Yellowstone."

George Shiras Jr. and Lillie summered every year on Ridge Street: Shiras 3d and Shiras, *Justice George Shiras Jr.*

Peter White frequently visited Washington: Williams, *Honorable Peter White.*

In June 1908 White was in Detroit: "Peter White Drops Dead," *New York Times,* June 7, 1908.

White was a beloved figure in the town: Obituary of Peter White, *Marquette Mining Journal,* June 9, 1908.

Shiras would in the future always describe Whitefish Lake as "my camp": Sawyer, "Biographical Sketch of A. O. Jopling."

CHAPTER 15

Military authorities in Yellowstone Park: Shiras 3d, *Hunting Wild Life,* vol. 2.

even from the period of the mountain men in the 1820s: Dale E. Toweill and Gary Vecellio, "Shiras Moose in Idaho," *Alces* 40 (2004): 33–44.

In July 1872 the Hayden expedition to Yellowstone: Douglas G. Brimeyer and Timothy P. Thomas, "History of Moose Management in Wyoming and Recent Trends in Jackson Hole," *Alces* 40 (2004): 133–44.

Now there was this sighting: Shiras 3d, *Hunting Wild Life,* vol. 2.

In July he and Hammer put up at the Mammoth Hot Springs Hotel: Shiras 3d, *Hunting Wild Life,* vol. 2.

When the men arrived at the outlet of Yellowstone Lake: Billy Hofer, "Montana," *Forest and Stream* magazine, August 1920.

It was a rough, white-knuckle trip with sudden gusts of wind: Shiras 3d, *Hunting Wild Life,* vol. 2.

Around noontime, they paused on a sand bar: Shiras 3d, *Hunting Wild Life,* vol. 2.

Banned since the military took over jurisdiction, weapons were to be "sealed": Lt. Colonel S.

B. M. Young (Calvary, Acting Superintendent) letter to Dwight E. Hollister of Wapiti, Wyoming, August 28, 1911, Archives at the Yellowstone Heritage and Research Center, Gardiner, Montana.

When he wrote to Roosevelt about the trip: George Shiras 3d letter to Theodore Roosevelt, June 23, 1908, CUP-NMU.

Over the next three days, making some sixteen river miles: Shiras 3d, *Hunting Wild Life,* vol. 2.

Finally, the flimsy oars broke: Shiras 3d, *Hunting Wild Life,* vol. 2.

He and Frank Chapman recently had established the League of Wild Life Photographers: Bird-Lore, National Audubon Society, 1920.

He expressed such to Roosevelt: George Shiras 3d letter to Theodore Roosevelt, June 23, 1908, CUP-NMU.

When he wrote about the trip in Forest and Stream: George Shiras 3d, "Silver-Tip Surprises: During a Hunting Trip for Big Game with the Camera on the Upper Yellowstone River," *Forest and Stream* magazine, July 10, 1909.

Shiras was being a bit of a purist: "Camera Hunt in the Wilds of Alaska," *Seattle Post-Intelligencer.*

Shiras did take one picture of a scavenging grizzly bear: Shiras 3d, "Silver-Tip Surprises."

Shiras let out a loud hiss, and the bear ran away: Shiras 3d, "Silver-Tip Surprises."

Shiras and Hammer returned the following year: Shiras 3d, *Hunting Wild Life,* vol. 2.

They soon saw moose: "Wyoming or Yellowstone Moose," *Wildlife Series No.* 2, Jackson Hole Wildlife Park, New York Zoological Society and Wyoming Game and Fish Department, 1964.

In the valley, moose had everything required: "Wyoming or Yellowstone Moose," Wildlife Series No. 2.

Consequently, the moose of the Thorofare had been relatively hidden: David DeLancey Condon, "Feet More than a Foot on a Moose," report by ranger, Archives at the Yellowstone Heritage and Research Center, Gardiner, MT.

When Shiras and Hammer got back to Gardiner: Shiras 3d, *Hunting Wild Life,* vol. 2.

A letter in the Yellowstone Archives: F. E. Gorton letter to Theodore Roosevelt, December 28, 1904, Archives at the Yellowstone Heritage and Research Center, Gardiner, MT.

In 1910 he and Hammer returned to Yellowstone Park for a final trip: Shiras 3d, *Hunting Wild Life,* vol. 2.

One young bull was knocked into the mud: Shiras 3d, *Hunting Wild Life,* vol. 2.

It wasn't until July 1913 that Shiras wrote about his Yellowstone experiences: George Shiras 3d, "Wild Animals that Took Their Own Pictures by Day and Night," *National Geographic* magazine, July 1913.

In Washington, E. W. Nelson at the Bureau of Biological Survey: E. W. Nelson, "Description of a New Subspecies of Moose from Wyoming," Proceedings of the Biological Society of Washington, April 25, 1914.

Nelson, a man who loved to be in the field: Edward Goldman, "Edward W. Nelson—Naturalist 1855–1934," *The Auk,* April 1935.

At the time, the color of an animal's fur was perceived to be an important—even defining—difference: Frank Baker (superintendent of National Zoological Park,

Smithsonian Institution) letter to Samuel B. M. Young, superintendent of Yellowstone National Park, April 8, 1908, Archives at the Yellowstone Heritage and Research Center, Gardiner, MT.

The male served as the type for the new subspecies: Baker to Young, April 8, 1908.

Although Alces americanus shirasi *can reach eight hundred pounds:* Randolph Peterson, *North American Moose* (University of Toronto Press, 1955).

And this may have allowed for the expansion of the moose's range: M. L. Wolfe, K. R. Hersey, and D. C. Stoner, "A History of Moose Management in Utah," *Alces* 46 (2010): 37–52.

Shiras moose—as they are still known today: Brimeyer and Thomas, "History of Moose Management in Wyoming."

By the early 1920s, Wyoming was issuing one hundred licenses annually to kill bull moose: Brimeyer and Thomas, "History of Moose Management in Wyoming."

not all the progeny resulted from the core group in the Thorofare Region: Moose Count, District Ranger Report, August 17 to 22 1936, National Park Service, Archives at the Yellowstone Heritage and Research Center, Gardiner, MT.

CHAPTER 16

New Nationalism would be the platform of the Progressive Party in 1912: "TR: Presidential Politics," *American Experience,* https://www.pbs.org/wgbh/americanexperience/features/tr-politics/.

Shiras continued, "While it is true that I began this analysis of Federal powers partly as the result of my interest in health legislation": "Federal Control of Fish in the Great Lakes by Treaty and by Direct Federal Action," *Marquette Mining Journal,* January 15, 1911.

From the canoes, Shiras spotted several bulls: Shiras 3d, *Hunting Wild Life,* vol. 2.

Determined to get a closer picture: Shiras 3d, *Hunting Wild Life,* vol. 2.

They set up a small tent above tree line: Shiras 3d, *Hunting Wild Life,* vol. 2.

They moved to a ledge overlooking a meadow full of snow: Shiras 3d, *Hunting Wild Life,* vol. 2.

A few days later, after another stalk: Shiras 3d, *Hunting Wild Life,* vol. 2.

In early 1914, the American Game Protective and Propagation Association and Shiras produced a pamphlet: Shiras 3d, Necessity for and Constitutionality of Protecting Migratory Birds.

Construction of a railroad into the interior had stalled at mile seventy: "Skilak Pictures Worth 100 Years—Early Photographs a Hit in National Geographic," *Redoubt Reporter,* Soldotna, AK, January 18, 2012.

The remaining pictures were mainly of snow fields, rocky crags, dark meadows: "Skilak Pictures," *Redoubt Reporter.*

Although he had a rather disdainful attitude regarding the threat of bears: George Shiras 3d, "Savage Beast A Nature Fake: Domestic Animals Kill More Persons in Season Than Wild Ones in 50 Years," *Detroit Free Press,* October 21, 1911.

quotes from the faunal naturalist had appeared in some newspapers: "Camera Hunt in the Wilds of Alaska," *Seattle Post-Intelligencer.*

CHAPTER 17

but his father had his doubts about its dogmas and reforms: Shiras 3d and Shiras, *Justice George Shiras Jr.*

Yet people were reading the muckrakers: Overview of the Progressive Era, www.digitalhistory. uh.edu.

Taft forced out Secretary of the Interior James Garfield: Goodwin, *Bully Pulpit.*

A muckraking article in Colliers magazine: Goodwin, *Bully Pulpit.*

What became known as the Ballinger-Pinchot controversy: Goodwin, *Bully Pulpit.*

When Roosevelt agreed to challenge Taft: Goodwin, *Bully Pulpit.*

One day in 1907, Shiras was lunching with Roosevelt: Shiras 3d, unpublished autobiography.

His odd behaviors had nothing to do with alcohol: Jay G. Hayden, "Teddy Roosevelt's Day in a Michigan Court," *Detroit News,* March 28, 1965.

He swept all the primaries: Hayden, "Teddy Roosevelt's Day."

In Toledo, he boarded the train carrying TR to the convention: Hayden, "Teddy Roosevelt's Day."

It was a harbinger of the animus toward Roosevelt: Shiras 3d, unpublished autobiography.

He also served on the Committee of Resolutions and Platforms: "TR," https://www.pbs.org/ wgbh/americanexperience/features/tr-politics/.

Roosevelt gritted his teeth: Hayden, "Teddy Roosevelt's Day."

When Roosevelt began his third-party campaign: Hayden, "Teddy Roosevelt's Day."

was a forthright Progressive: Obituary of Frank J. Russell, Iron Mountain Daily News, March 19, 1947.

He had exchanged letters with Roosevelt: Letters between George Shiras 3d and Theodore Roosevelt, April–May 1913, CUP-NMU.

Shiras tied a string between a camera trap and birch branch: Shiras 3d, "Wild Life of Lake Superior."

Roosevelt began October 9, 1912: Marquette Mining Journal.

He was well aware that his friend had been in the woods: George Shiras 3d letter to Gilbert Grosvenor, October 22, 1912, NGLA.

A man stood up in his car and called the president a liar: James Chace, 1912: Wilson, Roosevelt, *Taft and Debs—The Election that Changed the Country* (New York: Simon and Schuster, 2004).

"He tore the hide off the man's words": Roosevelt vs Newett: A Transcript of the Testimony Taken and Depositions Read at Marquette, Mich (published by W. Emlen Roosevelt, 1914).

He recovered somewhat by the time he reached the Keweenaw Peninsula: Marquette Mining Journal.

Russell effused in his lead paragraph: Marquette Mining Journal, October 10, 1912.

The Republican papers tried to downplay: C. Fred Rydholm, *Superior Heartland: A Backwoods History* (Winter Cabin Books, 1989).

Most attacks were sly and insinuating: Marquette Chronicle, October 10, 1912.

while he was dining in a Chicago hotel: "Civil Suit for $10,000 Started in Circuit Court Yesterday," *Marquette Mining Journal,* October 26, 1912.

The attempted assassination effectively ended TR's campaign: Theodore Roosevelt, Letters from Theodore Roosevelt to Anna Roosevelt Cowles, 1870–1918 (New York: Charles Scribner's Sons, 1924).

Marquette County voted overwhelming Progressive: *Marquette Mining Journal*, November 4, 1912.

just before the election, Roosevelt's lawyers filed a $10,000 criminal libel suit: "Roosevelt Going on With His Libel Suit," *New York Times*, October 26, 1912.

Newett was arrested that afternoon "on a capias" warrant: "Roosevelt Suing for Criminal Libel," *New York Times*, October 26, 1912.

The latter attitude was expressed: Roosevelt Libel Suit (staff correspondence), *The Outlook*, June 14, 1913.

Shiras told TR he was certain: George Shiras 3d letter to Theodore Roosevelt, January 22, 1913, CUP-NMU.

Roosevelt scoffed and wrote to Shiras: Theodore Roosevelt letter to George Shiras 3d, January 24, 1913, CUP-NMU.

a flurry of correspondence passed between the two friends: Series of letters between Theodore Roosevelt and George Shiras 3d, January to April 1913, CUP-NMU.

Yet Shiras doubted it would come to a trial: Roosevelt and Shiras 3d letters, January to April 1913.

There was still room to talk about their mutual interest in conservation: Hornaday, *Our Vanishing Wildlife*.

Russell wrote to Shiras: Frank Russell letter to George Shiras 3d, January 29, 1913, CUP-NMU.

On January 21, 1913, Roosevelt accepted the invitation: Theodore Roosevelt letter to George Shiras 3d, January 21, 1913, CUP-NMU.

He also asked that Frank Russell come to see him: Theodore Roosevelt letter to George Shiras 3d, January 28, 1913, CUP-NMU.

In fact, Newett had obtained nearly forty depositions: "To Testify for Colonel: Dewey and Others to be Witnesses—Defense Has Story of Drinking," *New York Times*, May 16, 1913.

Newett's lawyers worked for Cleveland Cliffs Iron Company: Rydholm, *Superior Heartland*.

Shiras came north in early May: Shiras 3d, unpublished autobiography.

TR and his party boarded the Lake Shore Limited: "Colonel and Party off to Libel Trial: Special Milk Supply on Train," *New York Times*, May 25, 1913.

The New York Central attached a Pullman car: "Colonel and Party," *New York Times*.

The Colonel brought along an impressive entourage of supporters and character witnesses: Abbott, *Impressions of Theodore Roosevelt*.

William Loeb Jr., his White House secretary: Scrapbook of George Shiras 3d.

"To support his civil action": *New York World*, May 25, 1924.

Interest in the trial was high: Roosevelt Libel Suit (staff correspondence), *The Outlook*.

Prior to Roosevelt's arrival, reporters nosed around town: "Case Opens Today: Roosevelt to be Guest of Naturalist," *New York World*, May 26, 1913.

Shiras began receiving "heavy mail": *New York World*, May 27, 1913.

There was a grand breakfast in the "Peter White Mansion": Shiras 3d, unpublished autobiography.

Roosevelt v. Newett was tried in the Marquette County Courthouse: Kenyon Boyer, *Historical Highlights Roosevelt-Newett Trial* (Marquette County Historical Society pamphlet, 1965).

Richard C. Flannigan, a young, scholarly judge: Peter W. Strom and Paul L. Strom, "Trials in History, Rough Rider Clears Name in the U.P.: Theodore Roosevelt vs. George A. Newett Hon. Richard C. Flannigan, Presiding," *Michigan Bar Journal,* May 2001.

the cast of characters provided plenty of colorful copy for the reporters: "Jury Will be a Problem: If Republicans and Moosers are Barred It Will be Hard to Fill the Box," *New York Times,* May 25, 1913.

One potential juror was excused: Rydholm, *Superior Heartland.*

The jury was seated: "Jury Obtained to Rule on Sobriety of Mr. Roosevelt," *Ishpeming Iron Ore,* May 25, 1913.

The common practice in a libel suit was to force the defendant: Roosevelt Libel Suit (staff correspondence), *The Outlook.*

this was a show trial and Roosevelt asked to go first: Abbott, *Impressions of Theodore Roosevelt.*

On the second day, Roosevelt led off: Rydholm, *Superior Heartland.*

He declared he had never drunk a highball or cocktail: Roosevelt vs Newett (published by W. Emlen Roosevelt).

Through all the questions, Roosevelt was unequivocal: Roosevelt vs Newett.

He did, however, express a fondness for mint juleps: Roosevelt vs Newett.

When this appeared in the next day's papers: "Never Drunk in All My Life," *New York Times,* May 28, 1913.

Frank Russell wrote in the Marquette Mining Journal: *Marquette Mining Journal,* May 25, 1913.

"There are certain peculiar mannerism of his": "Never Drunk in All My Life," *New York Times.*

Riis said he known the president for more than two decades: Roosevelt vs Newett.

the trial and accommodations in Marquette turned out to be a smashing good time: Jacob Riis letter to George Shiras 3d, June 26, 1913, CUP-NMU.

On the second evening during dinner at the Shiras home: Shiras 3d, unpublished autobiography.

Later that day, nearly everyone: Shiras 3d, unpublished autobiography.

His letter to Fanny thanked her for the use of her home: Theodore Roosevelt letter to Frances "Fanny" Shiras, May 27, 1913, CUP-NMU.

The next day Gifford Pinchot and other intimates testified: Roosevelt vs Newett.

Philip Roosevelt admitted that liquor was kept at Sagamore Hill: Roosevelt vs Newett.

It was Roosevelt's bodyguards and the Secret Service: Roosevelt vs Newett.

On Decoration Day, the "Roosevelt Army" at the Shiras home: "Veterans Meet Col. Roosevelt," *Marquette Mining Journal,* May 29, 1913.

The Newett crowd caucused back in Ishpeming: Abbott, *Impressions of Theodore Roosevelt.*

The lawyers got together the next morning along with the judge: "Roosevelt-Newett Suit is Ended," *Ishpeming Iron Ore,* May 25, 1913.

In the courtroom, Newett stepped to the witness stand: Roosevelt Libel Suit (staff correspondence), *The Outlook.*

Roosevelt rose and said in a ringing voice: Roosevelt vs Newett.

TR sat in his room and wrote a letter to his sister: Theodore Roosevelt letter to Anna Roosevelt Cowles, May 31, 1913, Letters from Theodore Roosevelt.

Later when he got back to New York: Theodore Roosevelt letter to George Shiras 3d, June 2, 1913, CUP-NMU.

CHAPTER 18

The great moral crusade to save birds: Chapman, "Nineteenth Century Trends."

His friend George Bird Grinnell started the first Audubon Club: Grinnell Symposium, http://gbgsymposium.homestead.com.

The Audubon movement quickly spread to other states: Duffy, "History of the Pelican Island National Wildlife Refuge."

Mabel Osgood Wright, a nature writer and president of the Connecticut Audubon: Chapman, *Autobiography of a Bird-Lover.*

Some of the first wardens were murdered by plume hunters: William Souder, "No Egrets," *Smithsonian* magazine, March 2013.

In Louisiana in 1910 an estimated 3.1 million ducks were killed: Shiras 3d, History of the First Migratory Bird Bill.

published on November 24, 1906, as a special supplement in Forest and Stream: Shiras 3d, History of the First Migratory Bird Bill.

The magazine's masthead displayed two gentlemen: Forest and Stream magazine, November 24, 1906.

Grinnell, who wrote an accompanying editorial in the front of the magazine: Forest and Stream magazine, November 24, 1906.

Shiras argued that the states were incapable: Forest and Stream magazine, November 24, 1906.

protection be extended to include songbirds and insectivorous birds: Shiras 3d, History of the First Migratory Bird Bill.

The premise was not without merit: "Protect Birds and Save Crops," *Washington Post,* Sunday, May 16, 1915.

Shiras lobbied, wrote articles, and spoke to groups of sportsmen: Scrapbook of George Shiras 3d.

The League of American Sportsmen met in Norfolk: Virginia Pilot, May 23, 1907.

The organization helped write legislation, craft regulations, lobby politicians: Historical Highlights, American Wildlife Conservation, http://www.awcf1911.org/history.htm.

The AGPPA was the brainchild of Billy Clark: William S. Haskell, *The American Game Protective and Propagation Association, A History* (pamphlet), 1937.

means of increasing the sports and general food supply: Bulletin of the American Game Protective and Propagation Association (an insert published in *Outer's Book* magazine), February 1918 (Chicago: Outers Book Company).

John Burnham was an entrepreneur, adventurer, journalist: Bulletin of the AGPPA, February 1918.

Burnham was named a game protector, or warden: Bulletin of the AGPPA, February 1918.

At times, he fought bitterly: Bulletin of the AGPPA, February 1918.

helped found the Camp-Fire Club of America: Jeffrey Gronauer, "The Camp Fire Club of America," *Fair Chase* magazine, 2011.

Weeks successfully authored: Shiras 3d, History of the First Migratory Bird Bill.

In 1910 and 1911, the National Conservation Congress: Shiras 3d, History of the First Migratory Bird Bill.

In late 1912, at a hearing before the combined House and Senate Agricultural Committee: Hearings before the House Committee on Agriculture on H.R. 36 and H.R. 4428, Sixty-Second Congress, March 1912.

It was a rather bizarre notion, but Hornaday could be cocksure of his own convictions: Hornaday, *Our Vanishing Wildlife*.

Hornaday had railed against overhunting: Stradling, *Conservation in the Progressive Era*.

One night in 1912, Hornaday asked Burnham to give an update on the status of the bill: Maitland C. De Sormo, *John Bird Burnham: Klondiker, Adirondacker, and Eminent Conservationist* (Saranac Lake, New York: Adirondack Yesteryears, May 1978).

Mondell—the same politician who opposed expanding Yellowstone Park: Sixty-Second Congress, House Agriculture hearings on H.R. 36 and H.R. 4428.

But the bill had come up late in the Sixty-Second Congress: Sixty-Second Congress, House Agriculture hearings on H.R. 36 and H.R. 4428.

Only the Senate Committee on Agriculture and Forestry could do the work: De Sormo, *John Bird Burnham*.

Afterward in the hall, John Burnham directed a delegation: De Sormo, *John Bird Burnham*.

Burnham met Shiras on the street in Washington: De Sormo, *John Bird Burnham*.

The bill reached Taft's desk in the White House: Shiras 3d, Necessity for and Constitutionality of Protecting Migratory Birds.

the secretary of agriculture appointed a fifteen member advisory board: Associated Press Wire Service, July 21, 1913.

Shiras accepted his appointment: Shiras 3d, History of the First Migratory Bird Bill.

The main opposition came from the millinery trade: Souder, "No Egrets."

The attorney general of New York: Shiras 3d, Necessity for and Constitutionality of Protecting Migratory Birds.

the shooting and slaughter did not stop overnight: D. C. Adams letter to George Bird Grinnell, June 8, 1914, GBGP.

Shiras considered it a pivotal piece of work: Shiras 3d, Necessity for and Constitutionality of Protecting Migratory Birds.

Spring shooting was especially devastating: Shiras 3d, Necessity for and Constitutionality of Protecting Migratory Birds.

CHAPTER 19

A few weeks after the libel trial: Shiras 3d to Grosvenor, October 22, 1912.

George had become an important member of the National Geographic Society: Gilbert Grosvenor letter to George Shiras 3d, March 15, 1920, NGLA.

Once again, Grosvenor filled an entire issue: Shiras 3d, "Wild Animals."

giving legal advice: Letters between R. J. H. DeLoach (legal counsel for Ernest Harold Bayne) and George Shiras 3d, January–February 1921, NGLA.

approving funding requests for expeditions: Gilbert Grosvenor letter to George Shiras 3d, April 22, 1920, NGLA.

making investment decisions: Gilbert Grosvenor telegram to George Shiras 3d, March 16, 1923, NGLA.

His photography work over the previous decade: Cevasco and Harmond, *Modern American Environmentalists*.

The National Geographic Society was clearly on the side of conservation and wildlife preservation: Henry W. Henshaw, ed., *The Book of Birds: Common Birds of Town and Country and American Game Birds* (Washington, DC: National Geographic Society, 1912).

Throughout the book, there is a strong call to support federal protection: Henshaw, *Book of Birds*.

Shiras had published five articles and hundreds of images: Gilbert Grosvenor letter to George Shiras 3d, September 25, 1913, NGLA.

That fall, Shiras again set off for Alaska: Shiras 3d, *Hunting Wild Life*, vol. 1.

As the country's leading biologist, Merriam had been naming new subspecies: C. Hart Merriam, "Description of Thirty Apparently New Grizzly and Brown Bears from North America," Proceedings of the Biological Society of Washington, August 13, 1914.

Merriam cautioned Shiras that Hasselborg was a peculiar man: Shiras 3d, *Hunting Wild Life*, vol. 2.

Hasselborg had arrived in Alaska: John Howe, *Bear Man of Admiralty Island: A Biography of Allen E. Hasselborg* (Fairbanks: University of Alaska Press, 1996).

Shiras and company immediately experienced Hasselborg's eccentricities: Shiras 3d, *Hunting Wild Life*, vol. 2.

Shiras had been lured to this spot: Shiras 3d, *Hunting Wild Life*, vol. 2.

Young George recalled arriving at camp wet: Shiras 3d, *Hunting Wild Life*, vol. 2.

Hasselborg appears to have been kindhearted: Shiras 3d, *Hunting Wild Life*, vol. 2.

The stars were shining: Shiras 3d, *Hunting Wild Life*, vol. 2.

The trip was a success as a hunt and expedition with his son: George Shiras 3d letter to Gilbert Grosvenor, October 14, 1913, NGLA.

They left the island on September 20: Shiras 3d, *Hunting Wild Life*, vol. 2.

During that worrisome day: Shiras 3d, *Hunting Wild Life*, vol. 2.

Weeks later back in Washington: Shiras 3d, *Hunting Wild Life*, vol. 2.

In the technical narrative: Merriam, "Description of . . . New Grizzly."

George 3d was obviously proud of his son: Shiras 3d, *Hunting Wild Life*, vol. 2.

In 1978 Admiralty Island was declared a national nonument: National Park Service: https://www.nps.gov/glba/learn/nature/admiralty-island-province.htm.

CHAPTER 20

Shiras had been hearing about the region: Frank Chapman, *My Tropical Air Castle: Nature Studies in Panama* (New York: Appleton, 1931).

The expedition, largely financed by Shiras and the National Geographic Society: The Shiras Expedition, AMNH.

Shiras had been a life member of the museum: H. E. Anthony, curator, letter to museum director G. H. Sherwood, November 1, 1933, AMNH.

He was chair of the section of mammals: Chapman to Shiras 3d, December 19, 1911.

As was customary, Shiras brought along a guide: Shiras 3d, *Hunting Wild Life*, vol. 2.

As a renowned naturalist and a former congressional representative: Shiras 3d, *Hunting Wild Life,* vol. 2.

In the village of Gatun: Shiras 3d, *Hunting Wild Life,* vol. 2.

Exploring Gatun Lake, he wrote: Shiras 3d, *Hunting Wild Life,* vol. 2.

Old foot trails had been inundated: George Shiras 3d, "Nature's Transformation at Panama: Remarkable Changes in Faunal and Physical Conditions in the Gatun Lake Region," *National Geographic* magazine, August 1914.

They were joined by Harold E. Anthony: American Society of Mammologists, http://www.mammalogy.org/uploads/Harold% 20Anthony.pdf.

The boat brought them within a mile of the caves: Shiras 3d, *Hunting Wild Life,* vol. 2.

A dark cave full of bats: Shiras 3d, *Hunting Wild Life,* vol. 2.

Troops of black howler monkeys frequented the forest: Shiras 3d, "Nature's Transformation."

as a land bridge between two continents: Richard Condit et al., "The Status of the Panama Canal Watershed and Its Biodiversity at the Beginning of the 21st Century," *BioScience* 51, no. 5 (May 2001): 389–98.

In daytime Shiras was able to take illustrative pictures for his articles: Shiras 3d, "Nature's Transformation."

Humidity was the biggest impediment to photography: Shiras 3d, *Hunting Wild Life,* vol. 2.

Wherever he went, Shiras saw animals being killed for food: Shiras 3d, *Hunting Wild Life,* vol. 2.

Anthony later published two papers about his collections in Panama: H. E. Anthony, "A New Rabbit and a New Bat from Neo-Tropical Regions," Bulletin of the Museum of Natural History, June 9, 1916.

Sometimes the men ate the meat of the specimens: Shiras 3d, "Nature's Transformation."

Still it was a great adventure, Shiras 3d, "Nature's Transformation."

He wasn't the first naturalist to make the suggestion: Frank Chapman letter to George Shiras 3d, December 14, 1929, Shiras book collection, PWPL.

In 1923 hunting was banned on the island: https://siarchives.si.edu/history/smithsonian-tropical-research-institute.

the remaining rain forests around Gatun Lake: Condit et al., "Status of the Panama Canal Watershed."

In a copy owned by Shiras: Frank Chapman personal note to George Shiras 3d, Shiras book collection, PWPL.

Chapman realized Shiras's dream: Chapman, *My Tropical Air Castle.*

Chapman set out camera traps: James Sanderson and Mogens Trolle, "Monitoring Elusive Animals, Unattended Cameras Reveal Secrets of Some of the World's Wildest Places," *American Scientist* 93, no. 2 (March–April 2005): 148–55.

He was the first biologist to use: Jeremy Hance, "Camera Traps Emerge as Key Tool in Wildlife Research," YaleEnvironment360, December 5, 2011, https://e360.yale.edu/features/camera_traps_emerge_as_key_tool_in_wildlife_research.

CHAPTER 21

After George returned from Panama: George Shiras 3d letter to Gilbert Grosvenor, February 24, 1915, NGLA.

Strangely, however, it was not Shiras's son who died first: George Shiras 3d letter to Gilbert Grosvenor, March 14, 1915, NGLA.

Shiras, not knowing what was coming himself: George Shiras 3d letter to Gilbert Grosvenor, March 11, 1915, NGLA.

George IV was not improving: George Shiras 3d letter to Theodore Roosevelt, June 30, 1915, CUP-NMU.

George IV died at home on May 27: District of Columbia Deaths 1874–1959, George Peter Shiras, www.familysearch.org.

Fanny wrote in her diary: Frances "Fanny" Shiras, personal diary, MRHC.

The family brought the body back to Marquette: "Justice George Shiras Interesting Subject for Biography by Son," *Marquette Mining Journal,* December 12, 1953.

according to an obituary in the Mining Journal—probably written by Frank Russell: "George P. Shiras Is Much Mourned, Obituary of George Peter Shiras IV," *Marquette Mining Journal,* June 22, 1915.

A Washington friend added: "George P. Shiras Is Much Mourned," *Marquette Mining Journal.*

Roosevelt sent a telegram: Theodore Roosevelt telegram to George and Frances Shiras, May 31, 1915; Shiras 3d, unpublished autobiography.

George 3d sought solace at Whitefish Lake: Frances "Fanny" Shiras, personal diary.

Obviously to lose his only son and namesake was a crushing blow: George Shiras 3d letter to Gilbert Grosvenor, June 2, 1915, NGLA.

He needed distraction: George Shiras 3d letter to E. W. Nelson, July 19, 1915, Nelson and Goldman Collection.

There was another exchange of letters: George Shiras 3d letter to Gilbert Grosvenor, June 9, 1915, NGLA.

In the years after his 1912 defeat: Edmund Morris, *Colonel Roosevelt* (New York: Random House, 2010).

Sponsored by the American Museum of Natural History: Chapman, *Autobiography of a Bird-Lover.*

and the aptly named River of Doubt nearly killed the president: Candice Millard, *The River of Doubt: Theodore Roosevelt's Darkest Journey* (New York: Broadway Books, 2006).

"Nowadays there is a growing proportion of big-game hunters": Theodore Roosevelt, *Through the Brazilian Wilderness* (New York: Scribner's and Sons, 1920).

The wound from the 1912 assassination attempt: Morris, *Colonel Roosevelt.*

Having read about Roosevelt's about his condition in the newspapers: George Shiras 3d letter to Theodore Roosevelt, February 18, 1918, CUP-NMU.

J. M. Stucker, Roosevelt's secretary, wrote back: J. M. Stucker (private secretary to Theodore Roosevelt) letter to George Shiras 3d, February 21, 1918, CUP-NMU.

A few days later, Gilbert Grosvenor and his wife visited Ormond: Shiras 3d, "Wild Animals."

Shiras had been suggested by Joseph Buffington: Shiras 3d, unpublished autobiography.

Luther exchanged letters with Shiras: Shiras 3d, unpublished autobiography.

After the commencement, the men lunched at Luther's house: Shiras 3d, unpublished autobiography.

When it was time to take pictures of the honorees only: Shiras 3d, unpublished autobiography.

Shiras and Roosevelt signed the guestbook: Shiras 3d, unpublished autobiography.

After Quentin's death, Shiras sent condolences: George Shiras 3d telegram to Theodore Roosevelt, July 26, 1918, CUP-NMU.

That fall, TR traveled to North Dakota: Morris, *Colonel Roosevelt.*

proposed that it work toward a memorial: George Shiras 3d letter to George Adams, February 5, 1921, GBGP.

Other organizations had different ideas: T. Gilbert Pearson letter to George Shiras 3d, February 13, 1919, CUP-NMU.

To sort it all out: "Memorials to Roosevelt: A Book of Suggestions, Roosevelt Permanent Memorial National Committee," *Collier's Weekly,* 1919.

He sent out letters: Letters between George Shiras 3d and John Burnham, February–March, 1919, CUP-NMU.

Burnham and Nelson urged him to come north: John Burnham letter to George Shiras 3d, February 13, 1919, CUP-NMU.

Meanwhile, Burnham sent out press releases: "Argues for Wild Life Conservation: Project Would Have Roosevelt's Approval," press release from American Game Protective and Propagation Association, March 18, 1919, CUP-NMU.

For many members of the committee: "Adopt Memorials to Colonel Roosevelt," *New York Times,* March 25, 1919.

Burnham was disappointed: John Burnham letter to George Shiras 3d, March 26, 1919, CUP-NMU.

The memorial association also asked Shiras to write down: R. W. G. Vail letter to George Shiras 3d, March 7, 1923, CUP-NMU.

Later, Shiras served on its national committee: Gustavus Pope letter to George Shiras 3d, CUP-NMU.

He was on the Honorary Adviser Council: New York State College of Forestry at Syracuse University, 1920.

In his presidency alone: Theodore Roosevelt and Conservation, Theodore Roosevelt National Park, www.nps.gov/thro/index.htm.

For many years afterward, he and Fanny: Edith Roosevelt letter to George Shiras 3d, January 1, 1930, CUP-NMU.

In 1926 Shiras gave a speech in Marquette: "Roosevelt's Life Topic of Address," *Marquette Mining Journal,* October 26, 1926.

He recounted an evening spent as a guest at Oyster Bay: "Roosevelt's Life," *Marquette Mining Journal.*

CHAPTER 22

Elihu Root never believed the Migratory Bird Act could pass constitutional muster: De Sormo, *John Bird Burnham.*

Shiras didn't think the legal underpinnings were so weak: Shiras 3d, History of the First Migratory Bird Bill.

The hotbeds of resistance to the Migratory Bird Act: Shiras 3d, History of the First Migratory Bird Bill.

The judge declared the Weeks-McLean Act unconstitutional: "Protect Birds and Save Crops," *Washington Post.*

As laid out in Shiras's legal brief: Shiras 3d, History of the First Migratory Bird Bill.

In 1915 McReynolds argued the case in front of the US Supreme Court: David Currie, "The Constitution in the Supreme Court: 1921–1930," *Duke Law Journal,* 1986.

The AGPPA—mainly Burnham, Haskell, and Shiras: Haskell, *American Game Protective and Propagation Association.*

There was opposition: De Sormo, *John Bird Burnham.*

In 1916, E. W. Nelson became the new head of the Biological Survey: Protection of Migratory Birds hearing before the House Committee on Foreign Affairs, Sixty-Fourth Congress, February 3 and 7.

The enabling act did not pass until July 1918: De Sormo, *John Bird Burnham.*

The AGPPA members were considered zealots: De Sormo, *John Bird Burnham.*

It was a hard-knuckle fight to the end: George Shiras 3d letter to E. W. Nelson, January 29, 1919, Nelson and Goldman Collection.

When the enabling act became law: Ray Holland Papers on Enforcement of the Migratory Bird Treaty 1872–1974, Olin Library, Wesleyan University, Middletown, CT.

Senator Reed tried to nominate McAllister: George Bird Grinnell letter to US attorney general Clark McReynolds, GBGP.

Missouri appealed the arrest of McAllister: Musgrave and Flynn-O'Brien, "Federal Wildlife Law."

McAllister himself became the test case: Edward T. Swaine, "Putting Missouri v. Holland on the Map," *Missouri Law Review* 73, no. 4 (2008): 1007–1028, http://scholarship. law.missouri.edu/mlr/vol73/iss4/5.

Some thirty conservation organizations filed briefs with the court: "National Geographic Society Pays Tribute to Mr. Shiras," *Marquette Mining Journal,* July 9, 1942.

He claimed the state had a pecuniary interest as the owner of birds: David G. Lombardi, "The Migratory Bird Treaty Act: Steel Shot versus Lead Shot for Hunting Migratory Waterfowl," *Akron Law Review* 22, no. 3 (1989): 343–57.

Citing the Supremacy Clause: Lombardi, "Migratory Bird Treaty Act."

In his opinion, Holmes made reference: Max Lerner, *The Mind and Faith of Justice Holmes: His Speeches, Letters, and Judicial Opinions* (New York: Little, Brown, 1943).

Holland hung a picture: Ray Holland Papers.

The bird law first envisioned by George Shiras: "Get behind George Shiras," *Outer's Book* magazine, February 1918.

proved to be an exceptionally powerful and effective federal environmental statute: Burnham, 1917 National Parks Conference.

Forest and Stream editorialized the treaty: *Forest and Stream* magazine, May 1920.

In Bird-Lore, *T. Gilbert Pearson made sure:* *Bird-Lore,* National Audubon Society, May 1920.

Holland sent Shiras editorials: Editorials from *New York World,* the *New York Sun,* and the *New York Herald,* April 23, 1920.

ran a portrait of Shiras: "Conclusion of 15-Year Fight," *AGPPA Bulletin,* May 1920.

now that the law had been sustained: George Shiras 3d letter to George Bird Grinnell, May 1, 1920, GBGP.

He addressed Grinnell's praise: Shiras 3d to Grinnell, May 1, 1920.

Early the next year, Grinnell organized a tribute to Shiras: Marshall McLean letter to
George Grinnell, June 16, 1920, GBGP.

Grinnell bought a silver tea and coffee service: George Grinnell letter to George Shiras
3d, April 30, 1921, GBGP.

Shiras wrote a thank-you letter to all four clubs: George Shiras 3d letter to conservation
organizations, May 6, 1920, GBGP.

In a Forest and Stream editorial: "A Permanent Tribute to George Shiras 3d," *Forest and
Stream* magazine, December 1920.

CHAPTER 23

One clear legacy of Theodore Roosevelt: Theodore Roosevelt and Conservation, www.nps.
gov/thro/index.htm.

In 1918 Woodrow Wilson signed an executive order: www.nps.gov/articles/npshistory-
creation.htm.

Mather immediately encouraged the formation of the National Parks Association: www.npca.org.

a lobbying group to rally conservation organizations: George Shiras 3d letter to Robert
Sterling Yard, July 24, 1920, GBGP.

As agriculture proliferated: Michael Yochim, "Conservationists and the Battles to Keep
Dams out of Yellowstone Park: Hetch Hetchy Overturned," Yellowstone Lake,
6th Biennial Scientific Conference, 2002, http://www.georgewright.org/01yp_
yochim.pdf.

Agriculture interests in Idaho and Montana: Yochim, "Conservationists."

In 1916 the government allowed the flooding of Hetch Hetchy: Yochim, "Conservationists."

George Shiras had often been pragmatic: "Federal Control of Fish in the Great Lakes by
Treaty and by Direct Federal Action," *Marquette Mining Journal*, January 15, 1911.

He had witnessed the settlement of the Upper Peninsula: Shiras 3d, unpublished autobiography.

The trout, which had been so abundant: "Status of the Brook Trout in Lake Superior,"
US Fish and Wildlife Service.

But he had also watched the loggers throw up temporary dams: Fuller, *History of the Upper
Peninsula*.

The Yellowstone dam would enlarge the lake: Yochim, "Conservationists."

In this fight, he was clearly a preservationist: George Shiras 3d letter to Robert Sterling
Yard, July 24, 1920, GBGP.

no park would be safe if Yellowstone were violated: J. H. McFarland, "Exploiting the Yellowstone: Is It Necessary—or Merely Cheaper?" *The Outlook*, October 6, 1920.

He focused on the southeast bay: "The Proposed Yellowstone Dam: How It Would Affect
the Scenery, Wild Life, and Public Usefulness of Yellowstone Lake and the Surrounding Country," *Forest and Stream* magazine, 1921.

Shiras filed a legal brief against the dam: "Proposed Yellowstone Dam," *Forest and Stream*
magazine.

By early 1921, Walsh attempted to push a bill through Congress: Yochim, "Conservationists."

The Park Service had overcome the precedent of Hetch Hetchy: Yochim, "Conservationists."

CHAPTER 24

By 1921 George Shiras had summered in the Upper Peninsula: Camp of the Fiddling Cat logbook.

For the August issue of National Geographic magazine that year: Gilbert Grosvenor letter to George Shiras 3d, June 29, 1921, CUP-NMU.

George produced a paean to the Upper Peninsula: Shiras 3d, "Wild Life of Lake Superior."

The storytelling was anecdotal and the photographs intimate: Shiras 3d, "Wild Life of Lake Superior."

Not far from the wigwam was the mouth of the Dead River: Shiras 3d, "Wild Life of Lake Superior."

There were night images of deer raiding the camp gardens: Shiras 3d, "Wild Life of Lake Superior."

Back in 1900, the picture had run in the Detroit Journal: "Peter White Fighting Wolves," *Detroit Journal.*

there had been attempts to poison the wolves: "Peter White Fighting Wolves," *Detroit Journal.*

He admired their tenacity: Shiras 3d, "Wild Life of Lake Superior."

Gilbert Grosvenor was immensely pleased: Gilbert Grosvenor letter to George Shiras 3d, July 21, 1921, NGLA.

In 1923 the US Biological Survey asked him: Shiras 3d, *Hunting Wild Life*, vol. 2.

The situation had a profound impact on the science of game management: Christian C. Young, *In the Absence of Predators: Conservation and Controversy on the Kaibab Plateau* (Lincoln: University of Nebraska Press, 2002).

about maintaining a balance between predators and prey: Emergency Conservation Committee, *Compromised Conservation: Can the Audubon Society Explain* (pamphlet), May 1930, William T. Hornaday papers, Collections of the Manuscript Division, Library of Congress, Washington, DC (hereafter Hornaday papers).

The Kaibab, about sixty by forty miles in extent: "Timeless Heritage: A History of the Forest Service in the Southwest," Forest History Society, www.foresthistory.org.

The Kaibab Plateau was set aside as a forest preserve in 1893: Website of the Kaibab National Forest, http://www.fs.usda.gov/kaibab.

When the Kaibab National Forest was created in 1908: Michael Anderson, *Living at the Edge: Explorers, Exploiters, and Settlers of the Grand Canyon Region* (Grand Canyon Association, 1998).

Sheep, cattle, and horses had overgrazed the plateau: Chris Young, "Have We Forgotten What Happened at Kaibab?" *Field and Stream* magazine, January 2009.

Over the next thirty years, the Forest Service and Biological Survey killed: Barbara Morehouse, *A Place Called the Grand Canyon: Contested Geographies* (Tucson: University of Arizona Press, 1996).

By the early 1920s, however, deer were everywhere: Anderson, *Living at the Edge.*

E. W. Nelson, then head of the Biological Survey: Shiras 3d, *Hunting Wild Life*, vol. 2.

A private ranch with a lodge and cabins: "Timeless Heritage," www.foresthistory.org.

In the following days, he saw more evidence of overbrowsing: Shiras 3d, *Hunting Wild Life*, vol. 2.

It was a rare and delightful event to see the camera trap in action: Shiras 3d, *Hunting Wild Life*, vol. 2.

Although the Kaibab deer seemed tame: Shiras 3d, *Hunting Wild Life*, vol. 2.

From the VT Ranch, they made a day trip on a new road: Shiras 3d, *Hunting Wild Life*, vol. 2.

His solution was to allow hunting: Shiras 3d, *Hunting Wild Life*, vol. 2.

The committee went to the Kaibab in 1924: Young, *In the Absence of Predat*ors.

Nelson had been advocating more shooting: E. W. Nelson letter to Charles Sheldon, September 5, 1924, Nelson and Goldman Collection.

By the mid-1920s, the die-offs were dramatic: Young, *In the Absence of Predators*.

The deer problem on the Kaibab became a famous case study: Chris Young, "Defining the Range: Carrying Capacity in the History of Wildlife Biology and Ecology," *Journal of the History of Biology*, 1998.

Aldo Leopold, who had graduated from Yale: "Aldo Leopold's Southwest," Aldo Leopold Foundation, Baraboo, Wisconsin, http://www.aldoleopold.org.

Conservationists were learning the hard lessons of systems ecology: Young, *In the Absence of Predators*.

When he got back to Michigan and began working on his report: Shiras 3d, *Hunting Wild Life*, vol. 2.

Although George Junior was ninety years old that summer: Shiras 3d and Shiras, *Justice George Shiras Jr.*

he fell at Winfield's home and fractured his hip: "Death Follows Fall at Home, Former Member of US Supreme Court Called by Death," *Pittsburgh Press*, August 21, 1924.

In the biography he wrote of his father: Shiras 3d and Shiras, *Justice George Shiras Jr.*

In his obituary in the Marquette Mining Journal: "Obituary of George Shiras Jr.," *Marquette Mining Journal*.

CHAPTER 25

In the North American Review: De Sormo, *John Bird Burnham*.

Disputes in those years revolved around the politics: D. H. Madsen (Game and Fish Commissioner of Utah) letter to W. C. Henderson, acting chief of Biological Survey, April 1, 1926.

Hornaday, always distrustful of hunting interests, was aghast: William T. Hornaday, *Awake! America Object Lessons and Warnings* (New York: Moffat, Yard, 1918).

Others in the conservation community agreed: De Sormo, *John Bird Burnham*.

Hornaday, with access to wealthy donors: William T. Hornaday letter to Clarence Thompson (president of Stamford Trust Company), September 21, 1926, Hornaday papers.

Nelson was of the opinion that Hornaday was not getting anywhere: E. W. Nelson letter to Charles Sheldon, September 5, 1924, Nelson and Goldman Collection.

Shiras wrote to Hornaday: George Shiras 3d letter to William T. Hornaday, July 3, 1923, Hornaday papers.

Hornaday scoffed: William T. Hornaday letter to George Shiras 3d, July 10, 1923, Hornaday papers.

What exacerbated the situation was the introduction in Congress: J. Sanford Barnes (Currituck Shooting Club) letter to William T. Hornaday, February 10, 1925, Hornaday papers.

would create more sanctuaries but allow for public shooting: Ray Holland Papers.

Burnham and Nelson drafted the legislation: De Sormo, *John Bird Burnham.*

A compromise was suggested to strip hunting from the refuge bill: De Sormo, *John Bird Burnham.*

In his North American Review *essay:* De Sormo, *John Bird Burnham.*

As a director in AGPPA: "Get behind George Shiras," *Outer's Book*, February 1918.

He was named honorary vice president of the Quetico-Superior Council: Ernest Oberholtzer (president of Quetico-Superior Council) letter to George Shiras 3d, June 22, 1929, CUP-NMU.

urged Minnesota to purchase a million acres of cutover lands from bankrupt farmers: "Vast Hunting Grounds Proposed for Minnesota," Associated Press, May 19, 1929.

In 1924 Shiras also served on the executive committee: "The Case of Our Migratory Wild Fowl," *American Forests and Forest Life* magazine, American Forestry Association, July 1925.

The Game Refuge and Public Shooting Grounds Bill lost in the House: "A Good Bill Defeated," *Forest and Stream* magazine, April 1923.

To assuage Hornaday, Nelson agreed to survey game officials and wardens: E. W. Nelson letter to George Shiras 3d, March 3, 1924, Nelson and Goldman Collection.

Nelson had much invested in the Refuge Bill: Goldman, "Edward W. Nelson."

Hornaday wrote Nelson: William T. Hornaday letter to E. W. Nelson, June 3, 1924, Hornaday papers.

Nelson's feeling about Hornaday: E. W. Nelson letter to Charles Sheldon, June 27, 1924, Nelson and Goldman Collection.

Headlines in the New York Herald Tribune: "Gun Factories Back Bird Bill," *New York Herald Tribune*, June 4, 1926.

Hornaday and his allies raised a ruckus: Frank Chapman letter to George Shiras 3d, October 31, 1930, AMNH.

Hornaday's rhetoric became so shrill: Letters from Charles Sheldon to J. Sanford Barnes (of the Currituck Shooting Club) and E. W. Nelson, August 24, 1924, Nelson and Goldman Collection.

His cause was righteous: Emergency Conservation Committee, Compromised Conservation.

Through the years, Shiras had a ringside seat: George Shiras 3d letter to W. T. Hornaday, September 21, 1920, Hornaday papers.

Shiras wrote a long, angry letter to the committee: George Shiras 3d letter to Agricultural Committee of the United States Senate, January 24, 1927, Nelson and Goldman Collection.

The refuge bill never passed, and Hornaday did not get his bag limits: De Sormo, *John Bird Burnham.*

In 1931 Hornaday published a book: William T. Hornaday, *Thirty Years' War for Wildlife: Gains and Losses in the Thankless Task* (New York: Scribner's, 1931).

In 1934 the Federal Duck Stamp program: John F. Organ, Shane P. Mahoney, and Valerius
Geist, "Born in the Hands of Hunters: The North American Model of Wildlife
Conservation," *Wildlife Professional,* Fall 2010, https://www.wildlifedepartment.
com/aboutodwc/Born%20in%20the%20Hands%20of%20Hunters[6].pdf.

essentially AGPPA's idea of a federal waterfowl license: Ray Holland Papers.

wildlife management itself grew into a scientific discipline: Brulle and Benford, "From
Game Protection to Wildlife Management."

The American Game Protective and Propagation Association faded from the scene: History of
the Wildlife Management Institute, www.wildlifemanagementinstitute.org.

In 1927 Shiras published his final pamphlet: Shiras 3d, History of the First Migratory
Bird Bill.

CHAPTER 26

It was a task he could put off no longer: George Shiras 3d letter to E. W. Nelson, December 11, 1930, Nelson and Goldman Collection.

He gifted his photographic collection to the National Geographic Society: George Shiras 3d
letter to Gilbert Grosvenor, November 15, 1928, NGLA.

Two days later, Grosvenor accepted the gift: Gilbert Grosvenor letter to George Shiras 3d,
November 17, 1928, NGLA.

And there was his health: Shiras 3d and Shiras, *Justice George Shiras Jr.*

He hired E. W. Nelson to help him sort his negatives: Gilbert Grosvenor memo to Franklin
Fisher, February 12, 1930, NGLA.

By then Nelson had already written a foreword to the book: George Shiras 3d letter to Gilbert Grosvenor, June 25, 1929, NGLA.

Grosvenor approved: Gilbert Grosvenor letter to George Shiras 3d, July 3, 1929,
NGLA.

Several months later, Shiras and Nelson delivered 155 wooden boxes: Franklin Fisher memo
to Gilbert Grosvenor, February 11, 1930, NGLA.

Nelson sat down at the Cosmos Club: E. W. Nelson letter to Gilbert Grosvenor, February
10, 1930, NGLA.

They delivered volume 1 at the end of that year: George Shiras 3d letter to E. W. Nelson,
January 31, 1931, Nelson and Goldman Collection.

Concurrently, Shiras submitted for publication: George Shiras 3d letter to Ralph Graves,
December 13, 1930, NGLA.

Shiras was not in good shape: George Shiras 3d letter to E. W. Nelson, December 11,
1930, Nelson and Goldman Collection.

Grosvenor went to Wesley Heights the very next afternoon: George Shiras 3d letter to E. W.
Nelson, January 31, 1931, Nelson and Goldman Collection.

He was set to go to Johns Hopkins Hospital: George Shiras 3d letter to Gilbert Grosvenor, June 22, 1932, NGLA.

In a letter written to Nelson: George Shiras 3d letter to E. W. Nelson, January 1, 1931,
Nelson and Goldman Collection.

Take, for example, the two months spent in Marquette: Shiras 3d to Nelson, January 1,
1931.

The operation at Johns Hopkins was delayed: George Shiras 3d letter to Gilbert Grosvenor, January 7, 1931, NGLA.

Afterward, Shiras felt some remorse for his remarks to Grosvenor: Shiras 3d to Grosvenor, January 7, 1931.

While Shiras convalesced back home in Washington: E. W. Nelson letter to George Shiras 3d, January 1931, Nelson and Goldman Collection.

He had been sick himself and hospitalized: Nelson to Shiras 3d, January 1931.

Shiras responded with a few rejoinders: George Shiras 3d letter to E. W. Nelson, February 8, 1931, Nelson and Goldman Collection.

He sent a check for the unpaid balance: George Shiras 3d telegram to E. W. Nelson, February 9, 1931, CUP-NMU.

At the National Geographic, Grosvenor wrote a memo: Gilbert Grosvenor memo to Franklin Fisher, February 9, 1931, NGLA.

Fisher read the article: Franklin Fisher memo to Gilbert Grosvenor, May 8, 1931, NGLA.

Yet the article was salvageable: George Shiras 3d letter to Gilbert Grosvenor, March 13, 1934, NGLA.

shows how aware he was of the skimming habits of Geographic readers: George Shiras 3d letter to Franklin Fisher, April 14, 1931, NGLA.

Nelson did not rejoin Shiras until later in the spring: George Shiras 3d letter to Frank Chapman, April 8, 1932, AMNH.

He fashioned another contract: Memo between E. W. Nelson and George Shiras 3d, May 21, 1931, Nelson and Goldman Collection.

Shiras thought he might die before volume 2 was complete: George Shiras 3d letter to Gilbert Grosvenor, June 26, 1931, NGLA.

Grosvenor, however, was enthusiastic about the books: Gilbert Grosvenor letter to George Shiras 3d, July 1, 1931, NGLA.

Finally, he gives a warning regarding Nelson's editing: Grosvenor letter to Shiras 3d, July 1, 1931.

By 1932 Shiras was back in Washington: George Shiras 3d letter to Gilbert Grosvenor, June 23, 1932, NGLA.

Nelson, who had heart problems: Goldman, "Edward W. Nelson."

Grosvenor responded, "I have the highest respect for Dr. Nelson's scientific ability": Gilbert Grosvenor letter to George Shiras 3d, June 24, 1932, NGLA.

The manuscripts were complete: John Oliver La Gorce letter to George Shiras 3d, September 18, 1935, NGLA.

Then the galleys and proofs had to be prepared for shipment: Memos between Gilbert Grosvenor, Leo Borah, and John Oliver La Gorce, March to October 1935, NGLA.

Incredibly, Shiras's health improved: George Shiras 3d letter to Gilbert Grosvenor, May 9, 1933, NGLA.

He had a good summer in Marquette: Shiras 3d to Grosvenor, November 16, 1934.

That year, The Auk, the magazine of the American Ornithologists Union: The Auk, April 1934.

Shiras was still a member of the board of managers: George Shiras 3d letter to Gilbert Grosvenor, June 1 1933, NGLA.

Despite the economic stress: George Shiras 3d letter to Gilbert Grosvenor, November 16, 1934, NGLA.

Grosvenor and his staff winnowed down the material: George Shiras 3d letter to Gilbert Grosvenor, January 23, 1935, NGLA.

He theorized that winds in the middle of the lake never exceeded sixty miles per hour: George Shiras 3d letter to Gilbert Grosvenor, February 27, 1935, NGLA.

In the foreword of the book, Shiras and Nelson: Gilbert Grosvenor memo to staff regarding the foreword of *Hunting Wild Life with Camera and Flashlight*, NGLA.

It was a claim that the National Geographic Society took pains to research: Letters and memos between John Oliver La Gorce and E. John Long, August–October 1935, NGLA.

eventually letters were sent to Berlin: Verlag Ullstein letter to *National Geographic* magazine editors, August 3, 1935, NGLA.

Clearly, George Shiras 3d was a major pioneer in wildlife photography: Grosvenor memo to Borah, July 1, 1935.

At Whitefish Lake, he invented the camera trap: Sanderson and Trolle, "Monitoring Elusive Animals."

Shiras sometimes objected to the rewording and deletions: George Shiras 3d letter to Gilbert Grosvenor, January 7, 1931, NGLA.

The nature faker saga: Gilbert Grosvenor letter to George Shiras 3d, September 2, 1935, CUP-NMU.

ought to contain several paragraphs about his early political battles in Pittsburgh: George Shiras 3d letter to Gilbert Grosvenor, July 4, 1934, NGLA.

Grosvenor, however, was adamant that the volumes focus on Shiras's expeditions: Gilbert Grosvenor letter to George Shiras 3d, September 8, 1935, CUP-NMU.

When Shiras asked twice to keep the weather section: Grosvenor to Shiras 3d, September 8, 1935.

Shiras was an expert on mammals, but not on weather: W. R. Gregg (chief of the Weather Bureau, US Department of Agriculture) letter to Gilbert Grosvenor, June 11, 1935, NGLA.

He apologized in a letter: George Shiras 3d letter to Gilbert Grosvenor, September 24, 1935, CUP-NMU.

Shiras looked back at his life when he wrote the introduction: Original galley, Shiras 3d, *Hunting Wild Life with Camera and Flashlight.*

The magazine advertised the books in the October number: Advertising supplement to National Geographic magazine, October 1935.

The Pittsburgh Press ran a review: *Pittsburgh Press,* December 15, 1935.

The New York Times Book Review *called it a book of "incomparable beauty":* *New York Times,* January 26, 1936.

The journal Nature *called it:* *Nature,* January 1936.

Despite the efforts of the editors, there were mistakes and typographical errors: George Shiras 3d letter to John Oliver La Gorce, September 28, 1938, NGLA.

A third edition was considered but never executed: George Shiras 3d letter to Franklin Fisher, May 22, 1940, NGLA.

CHAPTER 27

a letter arrived at the society addressed to "Friend George": Shiras 3d, *Hunting Wild Life*, vol. 1.

He moved to the San Juan Islands around 1920: Shiras 3d, *Hunting Wild Life*, vol. 1.

In 1933, Shiras found himself referenced in a peculiar short story: Ernest Hemingway, "Homage to Switzerland," 1933.

the piece is remarkable for its complicated experimental structure: Jackson J. Benson, *New Critical Approaches to the Short Stories of Ernest Hemingway* (Durham, NC: Duke University Press, 1990).

In the third version, a gentleman approaches an American: Hemingway, "Homage to Switzerland."

One of his most famous short stories, "Big Two-Hearted River": Benson, *New Critical Approaches.*

Hemingway paints a literary portrait of the Upper Peninsula at the end of the logging period: Leopold, "Report on a Game Survey."

The cutover lands attracted dreamers and schemers: Olivia Ernst, "From Cutover to Clover: Rebranding the Upper Peninsula," CUP-NMU, http://www.hsmichigan.org/wp-content/uploads/2013/06/Cloverland.pdf.

Northern Michigan was mainly suited to grow trees: Fuller, *History of the Upper Peninsula.*

Shiras said so himself in the introduction to volume 1: Original galley, Shiras 3d, *Hunting Wild Life with Camera and Flashlight.*

Then came the Civilian Conservation Corps: "Drama of Michigan Forests," Forest History Society, www.foresthistory.org.

In the ten years between Roosevelt's inauguration: "Roosevelt's Tree Army," Michigan History Center, www.michigan.gov/mhc

His last magazine article appeared in the Michigan Sportsman: *Michigan Sportsman* magazine, July 1933.

Flash powder and chemical flashlights were still in use in 1933: "First Flash Bulb," Image.

There is no evidence that Shiras ever used a flashbulb: "First Flash Bulb," Image.

But a few paragraphs summed up his life's work: Michigan Sportsman magazine, July 1933.

In summer 1935, Shiras walked into the editorial offices: Original papers of George Shiras 3d handed to Gilbert Grosvenor, NGLA.

There were pristine copies of the influential pamphlets: Shiras 3d, Necessity for and Constitutionality of Protecting Migratory Birds.

batches of speeches given before the Marquette Rotary Club: "Shiras Urges Lake Superior Booster Move," *Marquette Mining Journal*, Michigan, June 12, 1936.

a legal brief on tariffs: George Shiras 3d, *The Illegality and the Impolicy of Tariff Treaties: Why the Protective Tariff System is Constitutional* (pamphlet), NGLA.

He left a book of scientific papers: Shiras-Michigan University Expedition to Whitefish Point, Museum of Zoology, University of Michigan, 1918.

which he financed: Shiras-Michigan University Expedition, Notes on the Birds of Alger

County, Norman A. Wood, University of Michigan, Museum of Zoology, April 8, 1918.

"These pamphlets are not to be taken away": Memo of Gilbert Grosvenor, NGLA.

not all of the wildlife negatives that he donated were preserved: Memos of *National Geographic* magazine, April 3 and 11, 1963, NGLA.

The two men baited the feeding station with seeds: Shiras 3d, *Hunting Wild Life*, vol. 2.

Both he and Fanny were thinking about posterity: "Shiras Urges Lake Superior Booster Move," *Marquette Mining Journal*, June 12, 1936.

rescued the stalled project of the one-hundred-room Northland Hotel: Obituary of Frances "Fanny" Shiras, *Marquette Mining Journal*.

Their most enduring legacy: "His Memory Flourishes," *Marquette Mining Journal*, February 5, 1953.

"benefit in the fields of beautification": "Peninsula City Given Big Gift," *Milwaukee Journal*, September 7, 1937.

On September 16, 1938, Fanny Shiras died: Certificate of death of Frances "Fanny" Shiras, Marquette County, Michigan Department of Health.

"When she failed to answer the usual morning summons": Obituary of Frances "Fanny" Shiras, *Marquette Mining Journal*.

He sent a china cabinet to John Oliver La Gorce: John Oliver La Gorce letter to George Shiras 3d, October 4 1938, NGLA.

In June, Shiras wrote to Grosvenor asking for help: George Shiras 3d letter to Gilbert Grosvenor, June 27, 1938, NGLA.

Ellie and Frank moved to Iron Mountain: "Frank J. Russell Died Yesterday in Florida," *Iron Mountain Daily News*, March 19, 1947.

Frank started an afternoon newspaper: "How Do You Do?" Editorial, *Iron Mountain Daily News*, September 1, 1925.

George began writing a biography of his father: "Justice George Shiras Interesting Subject," *Marquette Mining Journal*.

George also penned a political autobiography: Shiras 3d, unpublished autobiography.

It was only in these pages: Shiras 3d, *Pig Iron State*.

He occasionally exchanged letters with Gilbert Grosvenor: Letter to Gilbert Grosvenor from George Shiras 3d, July 4, 1934, NGLA.

candidates for a distinguished service Roosevelt Medal: Letter Gilbert Grosvenor from Hermann Hagedorn, president of the Theodore Roosevelt Association, February 18, 1940, NGLA.

Shiras died of pneumonia at home in Marquette: Certificate of death of George Shiras 3d, Marquette County, Michigan Department of Health.

He was buried in Park Cemetery: "Obituary of George Shiras 3d," *Marquette Mining Journal*.

hit the salient events of his life: "George Shiras, 83; Noted Naturalist, Pioneer in Taking Flashlight Photos of Wild Animals Is Dead in Marquette, Mich.," *New York Times*, March 24, 1942.

The Rotary Club of Marquette, of which Shiras was an honorary member: Rotary Club Pays Tribute to Shiras, *Marquette Mining Journal*, July 6, 1942

The Milwaukee Journal *captured his importance to sportsmen*: "Upper Peninsula

Fishermen Owe Lasting Thanks to Late George Shiras III," *Milwaukee Journal*, May 10, 1942.

he had faded to near obscurity: Voss and Bailly, *George Shiras*.

EPILOGUE

George Shiras died before finishing the biography of Junior: Shiras 3d and Shiras, *Justice George Shiras Jr.*

Winfield completed the manuscript using notes: "Justice George Shiras Interesting Subject," *Marquette Mining Journal*.

"At least once a year": Shiras 3d and Shiras, *Justice George Shiras Jr.*

John Hammer lived to be ninety-eight years old: Editorial in *Marquette Mining Journal*, 1957.

The State of Michigan named a picnic area: "Access Site Honors Memory of Hammer, Guide of Shiras," *Marquette Mining Journal*, 1953.

Ellen Shiras and Frank Russell never had children: "Frank J. Russell Died Yesterday in Florida," Iron Mountain Daily News, March 19, 1947.

Upon her death in 1963, Ellen donated: "Will of Mrs. Ellen K. Russell Leaves Nearly $1,000,000 to Charities in Upper Peninsula," *Iron Mountain News*, April 18, 1963.

The big clapboard homes in Ormond: Strickland, *Ormond's Historic Homes*.

It's impossible to imagine what the area was like in Shiras's day: Canaveral/Merritt's Island National Wildlife Refuge, brochure, map, descriptions, US Department of the Interior, https://www.fws.gov/refuge/merritt_island/.

Tomoka State Park to the north: Tomoka State Park, brochure, maps and description, Florida Division of Recreation and Parks, https://floridastateparks.org/.

In the West in the twentieth century, Alces americanus shirasi: Toweill and Vecellio, "Shiras Moose in Idaho."

The Yellowstone fires of 1988 removed much of the forest cover: Brimeyer and Thomas, "History of Moose Management in Wyoming."

In the Upper Peninsula, gray wolves were extirpated by the 1960s: Wolves in Michigan Management Plan, Michigan Department of Natural Resources, http://www.michigan.gov/dnr.

Agriculture never got much of a foothold in the Upper Peninsula: "Marquette Naturalist Recalls Early Adventures with Wild Life in U.P., Our Woods and Waters," *Saginaw Sunday News*, October 6, 1929.

There is little old growth left: Drama of Michigan Forests, www.foresthistory.org, Forest History Society, www.foresthistory.org.

Whitefish Lake remains a secluded, private lake: Laughing Whitefish Lake Preserve, map of George Shiras III Discovery Trail, www.nature.org/ourinitiatives/regions.

By the time of George's death: Sanderson and Mogens Trolle, "Monitoring Elusive Animals."

Biologists using trail cameras have discovered rare leopards in China, rhinos in Java: Hance, "Camera Traps Emerge."

What he would have to work with is a trail camera: Harris, Thompson, Childs, and Sanderson, "Automatic Storage and Analysis of Camera Trap Data."

INDEX

Page numbers in italic text indicate illustrations.

Abbott, Lawrence, 209, 212
Abbott, Lyman, 160–61
Advisory Board on Migratory Birds,
  232–33, 297
AGPPA (American Game Protective
  and Propagation Association),
  227–30, 234–35, 262–63, 271–77,
  297–99, 301–2, 304
Akeley, Carl, 323
Allegheny National Forest, 283
Allen, J. A., 199
Alpha Delta Phi fraternity, 58
American Field, 114
American Museum of Natural History,
  60, 126, 138, 161, 258
American Ornithologists' Union, 113,
  222
American Shooter, 299
American Society of Mammalogists,
  186
Anderson, Charlie, 190, 238, 242,
  247–49, 253, 286, 330
Anthony, Harold E., 248–53
Ascot view camera, 56
Atlantic Monthly, 100, 156–57
Audubon Society: and bird bill, 113,
  226; and *Bird-Lore*, 180; and bird
  treaty, 275–77; formation of, 221–
  22; and Louis Agassiz Fuertes, 144;
  and George Bird Grinnell, 60; and
  hunting controversy, 298, 301;

and William Long, 157; and Pelican
  Island, 113, 132; and Roosevelt
  memorial, 263, 265; and Weeks-
  McLean Act regulations, 233
Auk, The, 314
Autobiography of a Bird-Lover (Chapman
  1933), 139

Bacon, Robert, 211, 215
Ballinger, Richard, 199–200
Bancroft, Cecil F. P. "Banty," 35
Barro Colorado Tropical Research
  Institute, 253–54
Barton, Clara, 105
Bausch & Lomb lens, 59, *59*
Bawgum, Fred, *33*
Bayne, Thomas M., 70–71, 74, 315
Belden, James, 210, 217
Bell, Alexander Graham, 120–21, 236
Benson, Harry C., 183
Bierstadt, Edward, 61
Biological Survey, Bureau of: and
  bird bill, 226; and bird treaty, 271;
  and hunting controversy, 297–99,
  301–2; and Kaibab, 288–89; and
  Missouri v. Holland, 273, 275–76;
  and Shiras 3d, 148; and Shiras bear,
  245; and Shiras moose, 186–87; and
  Weeks-McLean Act regulations, 232
Bird-Lore, 180, 265, 276
Bison Society, 117

Blaine, James, 40

Blair, A. Z., 217

Blease, Coleman, 270

Blitz Pulver, 53–54, 249

Bly, Nellie, 100

Book of Birds, The (Henshaw 1912), 237

Boone and Crockett Club, 61, 113, 117–18, 126, 130, 190, 229, 243, 271, 277

Boundary Waters Canoe Area, 299

Boy Scouts, 154

Brassey, Henry, *33*

Brooks, Alfred H., 124

Brown, Jake, 25, *30*, *33*; and bear ruse, 27–28; and dog dispute, 26; and drinking, 93; and fishing, 29; and flashlight explosions, 53, 129; and gardening, 108, 333; as hunting guide, 90; and market hunting, 20; and *National Geographic*, 286; rediscovery of, 319–21; sense of humor, 88; and Shiras 3d, 21, 45–48, 51; and Whitefish Lake camp, 24, 31–32, 84–86

Brown, L. F., 152

Brown, Louisa, 306

Brown v. Board of Education, 116

Buffington, Joseph, 259

Bull Moose Party, 165, 201, 202, 204, 207–8. *See also* Progressive Party

Bureau of Reclamation, 280

Burnham, Henry, 231

Burnham, John Bird, 227–33, 262–65, 269, 271–73, 292, 296–99, 301–2, 304

Burroughs, John "Oom John," 154–59, 162, 185, 329

Burt, William, 12

Call of the Wild, The (London 1903), 151

Camp-Fire Club of America, 226, 229, 233, 277

Canadian Camp Club, 149

Canaveral National Seashore, 135, 331

Cannon, "Uncle Joe," 103, 110, 218

Carnegie, Andrew, 16, 64, 157, 270

Carnegie, Tom, 16

Carnegie Institution, 140, 262

Chapman, Frank: as autodidact, 126; in Bahamas, 140–43; and Cosmos Club, 117; and Explorers Club, 147; in Florida, 131–32, 137–39; and *Forest and Stream*, 60; *Handbook of Birds*, 222; and William T. Hornaday, 301; in Mexico, 144–46; and nature fakers, 157; in Panama, 246, 254; and Theodore Roosevelt, 115, 259; and Roosevelt Medal, 328; in Shiras 3d book, 304; on Shiras photos, 128–29; and surprise flashlight photos, 95; and wildlife photography, 180

Cheat Mountain Sportsmen Association, 44, 116

Childs, Helen P., 265

Citizen Bird (Wright 1897), 144, 222

Citizen's Party, 100–102, 116

Civilian Conservation Corps, 323

Clark, Billy, 227

Clark, Edward B., 158–59, 162–63

Cleveland, Grover, 40, 81

Cleveland Cliffs Iron Company, 173, 210, 237, 259, 333

Colliers Weekly, 120, 199, 321

Coolidge, Calvin, 283, 299

Cosgrave, John O'Hara, 162

Cosmopolitan, 100

Cosmos Club, 117–18, 119–20, 158, 187, 190, 232, 298, 306

Courtelyou, George, 103

Cowles, Anna Roosevelt, 220

Craig, R. H., 91

Custer, George, 60

Cutting, Heywood, 292

Daniels, Edwin F., 115

Debs, Eugene, 89, 208

Deer Family, The (Roosevelt 1902), 127

Denali National Park, 118, 190, 240

Department of Agriculture, 97, 112, 229, 232, 271, 292, 298

Detroit Journal, 42, 286

Detroit News, 201

Dickey, Charles C., 41

Dickey, James, 64

Dolliver, Jonathan, 199

Dugmore, A. Radclyffe, 151

Duquesne Club, 16, 64, 88, 103, 175

Dutcher, William, 222, 226, 296

Eastman, George, 45, 120

Eastman Kodak Company, 92

Edwards, William S., 37, 44

E. H. & T. Anthony, 56

Elkins, Stephen B., 44

Elk National Park, 110

Ely family, 18–24, 27–28, 32, 92

Emerson, Edwin, 211

Endangered Species Act, 275

Everybody's, 120, 158, 160, 162–63

Explorers Club, 147, 226

Fairchild, David, 236, 259

Feathers War, 222

Federal Duck Stamp program, 302

Field and Stream, 299

Fisher, Franklin, 310–11

Flagler, Henry, 133

Flannigan, Richard C., 212, 219

Flashlight Photographs of Wild Game (Shiras 1904), 121

Flinn, William, 65

Forest and Stream: and AGPPA, 299; and bird bill, 112; on bird treaty, 275; and George Bird Grinnell, 221; and Shiras 3d, 60–62, 103, 151, 175, 181–82, 184–85, 224–25, 235, 278; and Shiras collection, 324; and Yellowstone Dam fight, 281–82

Forest Organic Act, 111

Forest Reserve Act, 111

Forest Service, 109, 111, 173, 199, 265–66, 289, 292–93, 323, 333

Freeman, A. J., 86

Frick, Henry Clay, 16

Fuertes, Louis Agassiz, 10, 95, 137, 144–46, 237–38

Game Refuge and Public Shooting Grounds Bill, 298–300, 302

Garfield, James, 36

Garfield, James Jr., 199, 218

Goerz Dagor lens, 60

Goethals, George, 247

Gorgas, William, 247

Gorton, F. E., 185–86

Graflex, 148–49, 191–92

Graham, James L., 69–70

Graham, W. H., 101–3

Grand Canyon Game Preserve, 288

Grand Island Game Preserve, 129–30, 173–75, 181, 186, 236, 259, 293

Grand Teton National Park, 280

Grant, Madison, 117

Grant, Ulysses S., 16

Graves, Ralph, 307

Great Depression, 302, 322, 325

Great Peshtigo Fire, 77

Great War, 37, 148, 227, 235, 253, 260, 264, 271

Grinnell, George Bird: and AGPPA, 227; and Audubon Society, 113, 221; and Boone and Crockett Club, 61, 117, 274; and *Forest and Stream*, 60, 224–25, 281; and hunting controversy, 296; and nature fakers, 152; and Roosevelt Medal, 328; and Shiras 3d, 276–78; and Weeks-McLean Act regulations, 232–33

Grosvenor, Gilbert Hovey: in Florida, 259; and *National Geographic*, 119–21, 124, 186, 288; and Shiras 3d, 236–38, 257, 306–17; and Shiras collection, 303, 324, 327–28; son's death, 255

Hagedorn, Hermann, 263, 265, 328

Hammer, John, *58, 123, 150*; in
 Alaska, 192–94, 238–39, 241–42,
 245; and Jake Brown, 320; in
 Canada, 148–49, 170; death of,
 330; in Florida, 136–37, 324; at
 Grand Island, 129; at Henry's Lake,
 107–8; illness of, 190; at Kaibab,
 289–91; in Mexico, 144–46; and
 Shiras 3d, 62, 98, 123, 316; skills
 of, 54–56, 94–95, *96*; at Whitefish
 Lake, 85–91, 168, 284, 286; wife's
 death, 195; in Yellowstone, 177–79,
 182–86
Hancock, Winfield Scott, 36
*Handbook of Birds of Eastern North Amer-
 ica, The* (Chapman 1895), 222
Harding, Warren, 233
Harmony Society, 12, 15
Harrison, Benjamin, 64, 190, 288
Hasselborg, Allen, 239–45
Hayden, Jay, 201
Hearst, William Randolph, 156
Heller, Edward, 211
Hemingway, Ernest, 321–22
Herron, Elizabeth, 8
Hewitt, C. Gordon, 271
Hewitt, Ellen Sophia, 14
Hewitt, Morgan L., 14
Hiawatha National Forest, 229
Hindert, U. J., 115
*History of the First Migratory Bird Bill
 and Its Subsequent Enactment* (Shiras
 1927), 302
Hofer, Billy, 178, 182, 196
Holland, Ray, 273–76
Holmes, Oliver Wendell, 274–75, 276
Hood, John, 68
Hoover, Herbert, 314
Hornaday, William T.: on bird bill, 210,
 230; and bison, 174; and Boone
 and Crockett Club, 117; and John
 Burnham, 229, 272–73; and hunt-
 ing controversy, 296–302; and "Ma"
 Latham, 137; and nature fakers,

161–62; and Weeks-McLean Act
 regulations, 232–33
House, Edward M., 36–37
Howe, William, 31–32, 93, 108
Hubbard, Gardiner Greene, 120
Hudson's Bay Company, 320
*Hunting Wild Life with Camera and Flash-
 light* (Shiras 1935), 245, 303–6,
 308–10, 311–13, 314–15, 316–18
Huron Islands National Wildlife Ref-
 uge, 17

Impure Food and Drug Importation
 Act, 225
Izaak Walton, 9

Jones, B. F., 16
Jopling, A. O., 83, 87, 89, 91, 92, 95,
 176
Jungle Book, The (Kipling 1894), 151

Kaibab National Forest, 288–89
Kawbawgum, Charles, 285
Kearton, Cherry, 166
Kellogg, Frank, 264
Kennedy, Jean, 134
Kennedy, William M., 27, 44, 74
Kent Club, 40–41
Kipling, Rudyard, 151
Klondike Gold Rush, 228, 239
Knox, Philander, 103, 263
Kodak camera, 45

Lacey, John, 103–4, 117–18, 222,
 232–33
Ladies' Home Journal, 120
La Gorce, John Oliver, 119, 326
Lambert, Alexander, 211
La Pete, Jack, *33*; maple syrup of, 88;
 in *National Geographic* story, 285–86,
 320; return to Sioux by, 92–93; and
 Shiras 3d's childhood, 1–3, 18, 20;
 and Peter White, 14; and Whitefish
 Lake camp, 24, 31–32, 85

Latham, "Ma," 137
Laughing Whitefish Lake Preserve, 333
League of American Sportsmen, 226
League of Nations, 37, 264, 324
League of Wild Life Photographers, 180
Lee, Henry "Light Horse," 7
Lee, Robert E., 7
Leonard, Harry S., 227
Leopold, Aldo, 293
Lewis, Meriwether, 8
Lodge, Henry Cabot, 118, 263
Loeb, William Jr., 109, 112, 160, 162,
    166, 211
London, Jack, 147, 151, 157, 165
Long, William, 155, 157–65
Longworth, Nicholas, 178
Luther, Flavel S., 259–60, *261*

Magee, Christopher, 65
Marquette Chronicle, 206–7
Marquette Federation of Women's
    Clubs, 325
Marquette Mining Journal, 30, 41, 204–5,
    214, 295, 324
Marquette Rotary Club, 324
Marshall, Thomas, 262
Mather, Cotton, 14
Mather, Increase, 14
Mather, Stephen, 279–80, 293
Mather, William, 173–75, 210, 259–60
Mayer, Alfred G., 140–42
McAllister, Frank, 273–75
McClintock, Norman, 137–38
McCormick, Cyrus, Jr., 35–36
McDonald, William, 208
McKinley, William, 207, 213–14
McLean, Douglas "Ducker," *33*
McLean, George Payne, 229, 270, 272,
    283
McLean, Marshall, 233
McMillan, James, 31
McReynolds, James Clark, 271
Merriam, C. Hart, 117, 161, 166, 232,
    236, 239, 245, 328

Michigan Sportsman, 323
Midnight Series (Shiras 1896), 57, *63*,
    104, 267; compilation of, 62; and
    National Geographic, 172–73, 324;
    reception of, 95–97, 121; and Theo-
    dore Roosevelt, 103; and Edith Roo-
    sevelt, 266; and Ernest Thompson
    Seton, 154; and Shiras book, 306,
    317; and wildlife behavior, 128–29
Migratory Bird Conservation Act, 302
Migratory Bird Treaty, 38, 269–77, 297
Miller, James Martin, 218
Milwaukee Journal, 326, 328–29
Milwaukee Sentinel Journal, 42
Missouri v. Holland, 274
*Missouri v. Illinois & Sanitary District of
    Chicago*, 105–6
Mondell, Frank W., 108–9, 230–31,
    300
Monongahela National Forest, 44
Morris, Robert T., 152
Mount Olympus National Monument,
    110
Muir, John, 281
Muncie Morning News, 64
Murphy, John R., 72
My Tropical Air Castle (Chapman 1931),
    254

National Conference on Outdoor Rec-
    reation, 299–300
National Conservation Congress,
    229–30
National Elk Refuge, 109
National Farmers Union, 226
National Geographic magazine: and
    Louis Agassiz Fuertes, 144; influ-
    ence of, 237; and John Oliver La
    Gorce, 326; on Panama Canal, 246;
    Shiras 3d articles in, 17, *122*, 167,
    170, 194–95, 196, 284, 288
National Geographic Society: and
    Great Depression, 312; in Heming-
    way story, 321; history of, 119–21;

National Geographic Society
(*continued*)
and *Missouri v. Holland*, 274; and
Theodore Roosevelt, 258; and
Shiras 3d, 147, 236–37; and Shiras
3d book, 304, 312, 315; and Shiras
3d expeditions, 190, 246; and
Shiras 3d negatives, 303, 306; and
Shiras 3d papers, 235, 324
Nature Conservancy, 79, 333
Negro Citizen's Committee, 132
Nelson, E. W.: and bag limit dispute,
297–98, 300; and Biological Survey,
302; and bird treaty, 271, 276; and
Cosmos Club, 117; and Dall sheep,
190; and Kaibab, 289, 292–93; and
nature fakers, 161, 162; research in
Florida, 137; and Roosevelt memo-
rial, 262–65; and Shiras 3d, 304–6,
308–15; and Shiras book, 257; and
Shiras moose, 186–87
Nelson, Rasmus, 85, 87–88, 91
New Deal, 314, 323
Newett, George, 205–12, 214, 216–20
Newmyer, John, 68–69
New Nationalism, 196, 200, 204. *See
also* Progressive Party
New York Herald Tribune, 300–301
New York Independent, 51–52, 98, 324
New York Sun, 95, 161–62, 272, 276
New York Times Co. v. Sullivan, 208
New York Tribune, 36
New York World, 36, 211–12, 276
New York Zoological Park, 301
New York Zoological Society, 271
Noll, Samson, 19, 21, 24, 28, 32, *33*,
88, 93–94, 155
Norris, Frank, 100
North American Review, 100, 120, 157,
299
Norton Guide to Nature Writing, 165

Oakley, Annie, 136
Ojibwa people, 10, 17, 18, 22, 285

Oleomargarine Act of 1886, 225
Oliver, Henry, 16
Olmsted, Frederic Law, 153
Olympic Forest Reserve, 110
Olympic National Park, 110
Ormond Beach Property Owners Asso-
ciation, 259
Ormond-on-the-Halifax (Strickland
1980), 138
Osborne, Henry Fairfield, 117, 138,
259
Ottawa National Forest, 323
Our Vanishing Wildlife (Hornaday
1913), 210, 230
Outdoor Life, 97, 299
Outlook, The: and muckracking, 100;
and nature fakers, 157, 160–61;
and Theodore Roosevelt, 167, 200,
208–9, 212, 216, 220; and Shiras
3d, 195–97

Palmer, T. S., 271
Park Service, 107, 279–83, 289, 292–93
Pearson, T. Gilbert, 226, 233, 263, 276,
292, 298, 301
Permanent Wildlife Protection Fund,
297–98
Pictured Rocks National Lakeshore,
11, 24
Pierrepont, Edwards, 35
Pierrepont, Edwin, 35
Pig Iron pamphlet (Shiras 3d 1887),
65–66, 67, 327
Pinchot, Gifford: on deforestation, 229;
and Forest Service, 111; and William
Mather, 173; and Progressive poli-
tics, 200; and public lands, 280; and
Roosevelt libel suit, 211, 216; and
Roosevelt Medal, 328; and Roosevelt
memorial, 263–64; and Shiras 3d,
117; and William Howard Taft, 199
Pittsburg Club, 116
Pittsburg Commercial Gazette, 71, 73
Pittsburg Dispatch, 72, 101–2

Pittsburg Leader, 73
Pittsburg Press, 44, 189, 215
Plessy v. Ferguson, 116
Poco Folding cameras, 56, 59
Point State Park, 8
Pollock v. Farmers' Loan and Trust Company, 116
Porter, Stephen, 116
Pound, James, 209–10, 217, 219
Powell, John Wesley, 117, 120
Presque Isle Park, 153
Progressive Party, 165, 196, 201–8, 210, 226, 231, 314. *See also* Bull Moose Party; New Nationalism
Progressivism, 161, 225–26, 265–66, 296–97, 302, 323, 330–31
Pulitzer, Joseph, 156
Pullman Strike (1894), 116

Quay, Matthew S., 65–66, 100, 327

Ranch Life and the Hunting Trail (Roosevelt 1888), 127
Rapp, Johan George, 12
Recreation magazine, 96
Reed, James, 273
Republican National Committee, 248
Republican Party: and Ballinger-Pinchot controversy, 199–200; and Citizen's Party, 101; and conservation, 229; and corruption, 65, 69–74; Old Guard, 103, 165; and Progressivism, 198; and Theodore Roosevelt, 204, 205–6, 264; and Roosevelt libel suit, 209, 215; and Shiras 3d, 36, 42, 66–67, 115–16, 314; and Shiras Jr., 64; and William Howard Taft, 201; and tariffs, 40
Revel's Island Shooting Club, 79–82, 112, 116, 233, 299
Reynolds, Charles Bingham, 112, 224
Reynolds, Josiah G., 134
Rifle and Flashlight (Schillings 1906), 130, 315

Riis, Jacob, 211, 214–15, 267
Rixley, Presley, 215
Rochester Camera Manufacturing Company, 56
Rock, Dick, 108
Rockefeller, John D., 133, 138
Roosevelt, Alice, 178
Roosevelt, Edith, 167, 259, 263, 266
Roosevelt, Eleanor, 201
Roosevelt, Elliott, 201
Roosevelt, Emlen, 211
Roosevelt, Franklin, 302, 314, 323
Roosevelt, Kermit, 167
Roosevelt, Philip, 204, 211, 216
Roosevelt, Quentin, 260
Roosevelt, Robert, 10
Roosevelt, Theodore, *205, 261*; and AGPPA, 227; and Alpha Delta Phi fraternity, 37; and bird bill, 115, 229; and Boone and Crockett Club, 61; John Burnham on, 296; and John Burroughs, 154, 185; and conservation, 110–11, 113, 131–32, 222; death of, 262; and elk, 107; and Gilbert Grosvenor, 124; health of, 259; and hunting, 171; and Kaibab, 288–89; laws enacted by, 225; and libel suits, 203–5, 208–20, 256; memorials to, 265; and C. Hart Merriam, 239; modesty of, 267–68; and national parks, 279; and nature fakers, 152, 157–65; nickname of, 70; and outdoor recreation, 153; and *The Outlook*, 195; and personal tragedy, 257; and Progressive campaign, 199–202, 203–5; and public lands, 280; and Edith Roosevelt, 266; and Shiras 3d, 99, 103, 117–18, 130, 166–67, 189, 196–97, 262, 304; and Shiras 3d's book, 317; shooting of, 206–7; and William Howard Taft, 180; travels of, 258; and Trinity College, 41, 260; and Peter White, 175; writings of, 126–27

Roosevelt elk, 110

Roosevelt Medal, 328

Roosevelt Memorial Committee, 262–65

Roosevelt v. Newett, 205–20

Roosevelt Wild Life Forest Experimental Station, 265

Root, Elihu, 117, 161, 167, 263, 265, 328

Russell, Frank: civic activities of, 330–31; and Cloverland euphemism, 322; politics of, 202; and Roosevelt libel suit, 209, 210, 214; and Ellie Shiras, 327; George Shiras IV's obituary, 256; George Shiras Jr.'s obituary, 295. See also *Marquette Mining Journal*

Sargent, John, 263

Saturday Evening Post, 120, 281

Schillings, Charles, 130, 315

Schmid, William, 46

Schmid Detective Camera, 46, 51–52, 123, *123*

Schrank, John, 207

Science magazine, 157

Scott, Tom, 67

Scribner's magazine, 321

Second World War, 326

Secret Service, 211, 217

Seney National Wildlife Refuge, 323

Seton, Ernest Thompson, 151, 154–57, 165, 177

Seventeenth Amendment, 198

Shauver, Harvey C., 331

Sheldon, Charles, 118, 190, 191, 240, 262, 292, 298, 300, 304

Shelton, Daisy, 306

Sheridan, Phil, 16

Sherman, William Tecumseh, 16

Sherman Antitrust Act, 225

Shiras, Frances "Fanny" (White), *84*; children of, 83; civic activities of, 134; death of, 326; family of, 45, 86;

and flashlight signal, 62–63; Florida home of, 210, 306, 324; inheritance of, 176; loss of son, 256–57; philanthropy of, 325; and Theodore Roosevelt, 216; and Edith Roosevelt, 266; and Shiras 3d, 294, 309, 316; travels of, 190; and tribute to Shiras 3d, 277–78; wedding of, 41–42; Wesley Heights home of, 116

Shiras, Frank, 8, 12, 13, 14

Shiras, George IV, 68, *74*, 210, 238, 240–45, 256

Shiras, George Jr.: biography of, 297, 330; during Civil War, 14; death of, 30; and Duquesne Club, 16; family of, 13; and Marquette summers, 294; and Ormond Beach, 132, 134; and outdoor experiences, 28; residences of, 175; and Theodore Roosevelt, 103; and Supreme Court, 15, 64, 116, 138

Shiras, Lillie (Kennedy), 13, 64, 83, 132, 175

Shiras, Oliver P., 8, 12–13, 14, 103

Shiras, Winfield: birth of, 13; early outdoor experience, 17–18, 26–29; education of, 34–35, 238; first deer hunt, 1–5; law practice of, 41, 64, 116; parents of, 175; and Republican primary, 72; and Shiras 3d, 42

Shiras, Winfield Jr., 327, 330

Shiras bear, 296

Shiras moose, 177–88, 231, 245, 246

Shiras-Russell, Ellen Kennedy, 45, *84*, 86, 116, 202, 256, 257, 327, 330–31

Shive, John "Jack," 187

Silsbee, Thomas H., 144

Sloan, James, 211, 217

Smith, Edwin W., 88–90

Smith, Vic, 108

Smithsonian Institution, 211, 246, 253, 315

Soberania National Park, 253

Sporting Life magazine, 44

Sportsmen's Review, 299
Steffens, Lincoln, 65, 100
Stimson, Henry, 247
Stone, William A., 70–74, 100–102
Stowe, Harriett Beecher, 34
Strickland, Alice, 138
Stucker, J. M., 259
Superior National Forest, 331
Supreme Court (US): and Chicago
    Drainage Canal Case, 105–6; and
    migratory bird laws, 235, 269,
    271–74, 276; and *New York Times Co.
    v. Sullivan* (1964), 208; and Pro-
    gressive laws, 225–26; and George
    Shiras Jr., 15, 64, 74, 79, 103, 116,
    133, 190; and Howard Taft, 231
Swineford, A. P., 190

Taft, William Howard, 161, 167, 180,
    201, 221, 231, 263
Tarbell, Ida, 100
Tenth Amendment, 274
Teton Game Reserve, 109, 177
Theodore Roosevelt Association,
    264–65, 328
Thirty Years' War for Wildlife (Hornaday
    1931), 302
Thoreau, Henry David, 154
Through the Brazilian Wilderness (Roos-
    evelt 1920), 258
Tolletson Gun Club, 115
Tomoka State Park, 331
Tongass National Forest, 245
Towle, Tom, 191–94
Twain, Mark, 6
Tweed Organization, 65
Tyree, Frank H., 211

Uncle Tom's Cabin (Stowe), 34
Unicum shutter, 59, *59*

Verascope, 56
Virginia Coast Reserve, 79
Visart, E. V., 223

von Sternburg, Hermann Speck, 130

Wadsworth, James, 226
Walcott, Charles D., 106
Wallace, Henry, 292
Walsh, Tom, 280, 282
"Wayeeses the White Wolf" (Long
    1899), 158–60
Ways of the Wood Folk (Long 1899), 155
Weeks-McLean Act, 221, 229–34,
    270–72
Wells, Ida, 100
White, Ellen Sophia (Hewitt), 14, *84*,
    85–86, 173, 176
White, J. W., 69–70
White, Peter, *33*; and Jake Brown, 21;
    death of, 175–76; descendants of,
    333; and Sam P. Ely, 18; and John
    Hammer, 54, 55; journals of, 24,
    28–29; and Jack LaPete, 92; man-
    sion of, 212; and William Mather,
    173; and Frederic Law Olmsted,
    153; and Presque Isle Park, 285;
    as Shiras 3d's father-in-law, 41–42;
    success of, 12–15; and Whitefish
    Lake camp, 32, 83–88, 90–91; and
    wolves, 286
White Fang (London 1906), 151
Wild Animals I Have Known (Seton
    1898), 154
Wilderness Hunter, The (Roosevelt 1893),
    127
Wilderness Ways (Long 1900), 192
William Haskell, 271
Williams, G. Motts, 176
Wilmot, Thomas, 61
Wilson, Woodrow, 202, 208, 221, 232,
    260, 271, 279
Winchester Repeating Arms Company,
    227
Wister, Owen, 118
With Nature and a Camera (Kearton
    1897), 166
Wood, Leonard, 200, 263

World War II, 326
Wright, Mabel Osgood, 144, 157, 222
Wyman, James G., 72–74
Wyman, Walter, 106

Yellowstone National Park, 60, 79, 93,
    106–8, 177–88, 230–31, 279–83,
    331

Yosemite National Park, 280–81
Young, Olin H., 206–8, 215, 218
Young, S. B. M., 107, 180, 181, 183